KW-169-083

Contents

Introduction

The European Social Charter: a continually developing treaty

The Charter, thoroughly renovated and equipped with an effective and efficient system of supervision, is now a cornerstone of the European Human Rights model. It is experiencing an unprecedented wave of ratifications by member States of the Council of Europe, in accordance with the wish voiced by the Heads of State and Government at their meeting in Strasbourg in October 1997, on the occasion of the Council of Europe's Second Summit. By 18 October 2001, all member States had signed the Charter and 30 of them had ratified. Furthermore, since the entry into force of the Amsterdam Treaty, the Charter forms an integral part of the European Community structure.

The European Social Charter is the counterpart of the European Convention of Human Rights in the field of economic and social rights. It covers a broad range of rights related to housing, health, education, employment, social protection and non-discrimination.

The Charter has and will continue to evolve, not only through its case law but also by the addition of Protocols which have strengthened the rights it guarantees and improved the supervisory machinery: the Additional Protocol to the European Social Charter of 1988 added new rights. The system of supervision was reinforced on the one hand by the Amending Protocol of 1991 and on the other by the adoption of the Additional Protocol providing for a system of collective complaints in 1995. The revised European Social Charter, adopted in 1996, is a comprehensive treaty which brings together in a single instrument all the rights guaranteed by the Charter and the 1988 Additional Protocol, while amending certain of these rights and introducing new ones. It takes into account the changes in economic and social Human Rights that have occurred since the Charter was drafted and will progressively replace it.

The Charter's system of supervision is based on reports submitted by the Contracting Parties. The 1991 Amending Protocol to the Charter amends the supervisory procedure, and is already partially implemented since a decision by the Committee of Ministers asking the supervisory bodies to apply it in so far as the text of the Charter allows before its entry into force. The following bodies participate in the supervision procedure:

- the European Committee of Social Rights (committee of independent experts) composed of nine experts elected by the Committee of Ministers and assisted by an observer from the International Labour Organisation. The Committee examines the reports submitted by the Contracting Parties and makes a legal assessment of states observance of their obligations;

– the Governmental Committee, composed of representatives of the Contracting Parties to the Charter and assisted by observers from the European social partners. It prepares the decisions of the Committee of Ministers and in particular selects, on the basis of social, economic and other policy considerations, those situations which should be the subject of individual recommendations addressed to the Contracting Parties concerned;

– the Committee of Ministers, which adopts a resolution for the supervision cycle as a whole and issues recommendations to states, inviting them to change their legislation or practice.

The Parliamentary Assembly is also associated with the supervisory mechanism. Since 1992, it no longer participates directly, but may organise periodic social policy debates arising from the Conclusions of the European Committee of Social Rights.

The new edition

This third edition of the Collected Texts updates the previous edition (July 2000) up to 1 November 2001. Its aim is to provide clear and up-to-date information on the Social Charter's instruments and on how the various bodies participate in the control mechanism, and is available to all those interested.

The Collected Texts is a compilation of the following: the text of the European Social Charter and its three Protocols, the revised European Social Charter, and, for each instrument: the state of signature and ratification, the reservations and declarations, the texts of the explanatory reports to the Protocols and the revised Charter, as well as the European Committee of Social Rights' Rules of Procedure.

This text also contains documents issued by the monitoring bodies for each control cycle.

In addition to the instruments and basic texts which appear in the Collected Texts and also available in the Council of Europe publications series is a wide range of information on more specific human rights aspects. A list of these publications can be obtained by contacting the Human Rights Information Centre of the Directorate General of Human Rights at the Council of Europe.

For further information on the Council of Europe's Social Charter, please consult our web site: www.esc.coe.int

Régis Brillat
Executive Secretary of the European Social Charter
DG II, Human Rights

I. Basic texts

A. European Social Charter and Protocols

1. European Social Charter of 1961

Preamble

The governments signatory hereto, being members of the Council of Europe,

Considering that the aim of the Council of Europe is the achievement of greater unity between its members for the purpose of safeguarding and realising the ideals and principles which are their common heritage and of facilitating their economic and social progress, in particular by the maintenance and further realisation of human rights and fundamental freedoms;

Considering that in the European Convention for the Protection of Human Rights and Fundamental Freedoms signed at Rome on 4th November 1950, and the Protocol thereto signed at Paris on 20th March 1952, the member States of the Council of Europe agreed to secure to their populations the civil and political rights and freedoms therein specified;

Considering that the enjoyment of social rights should be secured without discrimination on grounds of race, colour, sex, religion, political opinion, national extraction or social origin;

Being resolved to make every effort in common to improve the standard of living and to promote the social well-being of both their urban and rural populations by means of appropriate institutions and action,

Have agreed as follows:

Part I

The Contracting Parties accept as the aim of their policy, to be pursued by all appropriate means, both national and international in character, the attainment of conditions in which the following rights and principles may be effectively realised:

1. Everyone shall have the opportunity to earn his living in an occupation freely entered upon.

2. All workers have the right to just conditions of work.

3. All workers have the right to safe and healthy working conditions.

4. All workers have the right to a fair remuneration sufficient for a decent standard of living for themselves and their families.

5. All workers and employers have the right to freedom of association in national or international organisations for the protection of their economic and social interests.

6. All workers and employers have the right to bargain collectively.

7. Children and young persons have the right to a special protection against the physical and moral hazards to which they are exposed.

8. Employed women, in case of maternity, and other employed women as appropriate, have the right to a special protection in their work.

9. Everyone has the right to appropriate facilities for vocational guidance with a view to helping him choose an occupation suited to his personal aptitude and interests.

10. Everyone has the right to appropriate facilities for vocational training.

11. Everyone has the right to benefit from any measures enabling him to enjoy the highest possible standard of health attainable.

12. All workers and their dependents have the right to social security.

13. Anyone without adequate resources has the right to social and medical assistance.

14. Everyone has the right to benefit from social welfare services.

15. Disabled persons have the right to vocational training, rehabilitation and resettlement, whatever the origin and nature of their disability.

16. The family as a fundamental unit of society has the right to appropriate social, legal and economic protection to ensure its full development.

17. Mothers and children, irrespective of marital status and family relations, have the right to appropriate social and economic protection.

18. The nationals of any one of the Contracting Parties have the right to engage in any gainful occupation in the territory of any one of the others on a footing of equality with the nationals of the latter, subject to restrictions based on cogent economic or social reasons.

19. Migrant workers who are nationals of a Contracting Party and their families have the right to protection and assistance in the territory of any other Contracting Party.

Part II

The Contracting Parties undertake, as provided for in Part III, to consider themselves bound by the obligations laid down in the following articles and paragraphs.

Article 1 – The right to work

With a view to ensuring the effective exercise of the right to work, the Contracting Parties undertake:

1. to accept as one of their primary aims and responsibilities the achievement and maintenance of as high and stable a level of employment as possible, with a view to the attainment of full employment;

2. to protect effectively the right of the worker to earn his living in an occupation freely entered upon;

3. to establish or maintain free employment services for all workers;

4. to provide or promote appropriate vocational guidance, training and rehabilitation.

Article 2 – The right to just conditions of work

With a view to ensuring the effective exercise of the right to just conditions of work, the Contracting Parties undertake:

1. to provide for reasonable daily and weekly working hours, the working week to be progressively reduced to the extent that the increase of productivity and other relevant factors permit;

2. to provide for public holidays with pay;

3. to provide for a minimum of two weeks annual holiday with pay;

4. to provide for additional paid holidays or reduced working hours for workers engaged in dangerous or unhealthy occupations as prescribed;

5. to ensure a weekly rest period which shall, as far as possible, coincide with the day recognised by tradition or custom in the country or region concerned as a day of rest.

Article 3 – The right to safe and healthy working conditions

With a view to ensuring the effective exercise of the right to safe and healthy working conditions, the Contracting Parties undertake:

1. to issue safety and health regulations;

2. to provide for the enforcement of such regulations by measures of supervision;

3. to consult, as appropriate, employers' and workers' organisations on measures intended to improve industrial safety and health.

Article 4 – The right to a fair remuneration

With a view to ensuring the effective exercise of the right to a fair remuneration, the Contracting Parties undertake:

1. to recognise the right of workers to a remuneration such as will give them and their families a decent standard of living;

2. to recognise the right of workers to an increased rate of remuneration for overtime work, subject to exceptions in particular cases;

3. to recognise the right of men and women workers to equal pay for work of equal value;

4. to recognise the right of all workers to a reasonable period of notice for termination of employment;

5. to permit deductions from wages only under conditions and to the extent prescribed by national laws or regulations or fixed by collective agreements or arbitration awards.

The exercise of these rights shall be achieved by freely concluded collective agreements, by statutory wage-fixing machinery, or by other means appropriate to national conditions.

Article 5 – The right to organise

With a view to ensuring or promoting the freedom of workers and employers to form local, national or international organisations for the protection of their economic and social interests and to join those organisations, the Contracting Parties undertake that national law shall not be such as to impair, nor shall it be so applied as to impair, this freedom. The extent to which the guarantees provided for in this Article shall apply to the police shall be determined by national laws or regulations. The principle governing the application to the members of the armed forces of these guarantees and the extent to which they shall apply to persons in this category shall equally be determined by national laws or regulations.

Article 6 – The right to bargain collectively

With a view to ensuring the effective exercise of the right to bargain collectively, the Contracting Parties undertake:

1. to promote joint consultation between workers and employers;

2. to promote, where necessary and appropriate, machinery for voluntary negotiations between employers or employers' organisations and workers' organisations, with a view to the regulation of terms and conditions of employment by means of collective agreements;

3. to promote the establishment and use of appropriate machinery for conciliation and voluntary arbitration for the settlement of labour disputes;

and recognise:

4. the right of workers and employers to collective action in cases of conflicts of interest, including the right to strike, subject to obligations that might arise out of collective agreements previously entered into.

Article 7 – The right of children and young persons to protection

With a view to ensuring the effective exercise of the right of children and young persons to protection, the Contracting Parties undertake:

1. to provide that the minimum age of admission to employment shall be fifteen years, subject to exceptions for children employed in prescribed light work without harm to their health, morals or education;

2. to provide that a higher minimum age of admission to employment shall be fixed with respect to prescribed occupations regarded as dangerous or unhealthy;

3. to provide that persons who are still subject to compulsory education shall not be employed in such work as would deprive them of the full benefit of their education;

4. to provide that the working hours of persons under sixteen years of age shall be limited in accordance with the needs of their development, and particularly with their need for vocational training;

5. to recognise the right of young workers and apprentices to a fair wage or other appropriate allowances;

6. to provide that the time spent by young persons in vocational training during the normal working hours with the consent of the employer shall be treated as forming part of the working day;

7. to provide that employed persons of under eighteen years of age shall be entitled to not less than three weeks' annual holiday with pay;

8. to provide that persons under eighteen years of age shall not be employed in night work with the exception of certain occupations provided for by national laws or regulations;

9. to provide that persons under eighteen years of age employed in occupations prescribed by national laws or regulations shall be subject to regular medical control;

10. to ensure special protection against physical and moral dangers to which children and young persons are exposed, and particularly against those resulting directly or indirectly from their work.

Article 8 – The right of employed women to protection

With a view to ensuring the effective exercise of the right of employed women to protection, the Contracting Parties undertake:

1. to provide either by paid leave, by adequate social security benefits or by benefits from public funds for women to take leave before and after childbirth up to a total of at least twelve weeks;

2. to consider it as unlawful for an employer to give a woman notice of dismissal during her absence on maternity leave or to give her notice of dismissal at such a time that the notice would expire during such absence;

3. to provide that mothers who are nursing their infants shall be entitled to sufficient time off for this purpose;

4. *a.* to regulate the employment of women workers on night work in industrial employment;

   b. to prohibit the employment of women workers in underground mining, and, as appropriate, on all other work which is unsuitable for them by reason of its dangerous, unhealthy, or arduous nature.

Article 9 – The right to vocational guidance

With a view to ensuring the effective exercise of the right to vocational guidance, the Contracting Parties undertake to provide or promote, as necessary, a service which will assist all persons, including the handicapped, to solve problems related to occupational choice and progress, with due regard to the individual's characteristics and their relation to occupational opportunity: this assistance should be available free of charge, both to young persons, including school children, and to adults.

Article 10 – The right to vocational training

With a view to ensuring the effective exercise of the right to vocational training, the Contracting Parties undertake:

1. to provide or promote, as necessary, the technical and vocational training of all persons, including the handicapped, in consultation with employers' and workers' organisations, and to grant facilities for access to higher technical and university education, based solely on individual aptitude;

2. to provide or promote a system of apprenticeship and other systematic arrangements for training young boys and girls in their various employments;

3. to provide or promote, as necessary:

   a. adequate and readily available training facilities for adult workers;

   b. special facilities for the re-training of adult workers needed as a result of technological development or new trends in employment;

4. to encourage the full utilisation of the facilities provided by appropriate measures such as:

   a. reducing or abolishing any fees or charges;

   b. granting financial assistance in appropriate cases;

   c. including in the normal working hours time spent on supplementary training taken by the worker, at the request of his employer, during employment;

   d. ensuring, through adequate supervision, in consultation with the employers' and workers' organisations, the efficiency of apprenticeship and other training arrangements for young workers, and the adequate protection of young workers generally.

Article 11 – The right to protection of health

With a view to ensuring the effective exercise of the right to protection of health, the Contracting Parties undertake, either directly or in co-operation with public or private organisations, to take appropriate measures designed *inter alia*:

1. to remove as far as possible the causes of ill-health;

2. to provide advisory and educational facilities for the promotion of health and the encouragement of individual responsibility in matters of health;

3. to prevent as far as possible epidemic, endemic and other diseases.

Article 12 – The right to social security

With a view to ensuring the effective exercise of the right to social security, the Contracting Parties undertake:

1. to establish or maintain a system of social security;

2. to maintain the social security system at a satisfactory level at least equal to that required for ratification of International Labour Convention (No. 102) Concerning Minimum Standards of Social Security;

3. to endeavour to raise progressively the system of social security to a higher level;

4. to take steps, by the conclusion of appropriate bilateral and multilateral agreements, or by other means, and subject to the conditions laid down in such agreements, in order to ensure:

   a. equal treatment with their own nationals of the nationals of other Contracting Parties in respect of social security rights, including the retention of benefits arising out of social security legislation, whatever movements the persons protected may undertake between the territories of the Contracting Parties;

   b. the granting, maintenance and resumption of social security rights by such means as the accumulation of insurance or employment periods completed under the legislation of each of the Contracting Parties.

Article 13 – The right to social and medical assistance

With a view to ensuring the effective exercise of the right to social and medical assistance, the Contracting Parties undertake:

1. to ensure that any person who is without adequate resources and who is unable to secure such resources either by his own efforts or from other sources, in particular by benefits under a social

security scheme, be granted adequate assistance, and, in case of sickness, the care necessitated by his condition;

2. to ensure that persons receiving such assistance shall not, for that reason, suffer from a diminution of their political or social rights;

3. to provide that everyone may receive by appropriate public or private services such advice and personal help as may be required to prevent, to remove, or to alleviate personal or family want;

4. to apply the provisions referred to in paragraphs 1, 2 and 3 of this article on an equal footing with their nationals to nationals of other Contracting Parties lawfully within their territories, in accordance with their obligations under the European Convention on Social and Medical Assistance, signed at Paris on 11th December 1953.

Article 14 – The right to benefit from social welfare services

With a view to ensuring the effective exercise of the right to benefit from social welfare services, the Contracting Parties undertake:

1. to promote or provide services which, by using methods of social work, would contribute to the welfare and development of both individuals and groups in the community, and to their adjustment to the social environment;

2. to encourage the participation of individuals and voluntary or other organisations in the establishment and maintenance of such services.

Article 15 – The right of physically or mentally disabled persons to vocational training, rehabilitation and social resettlement

With a view to ensuring the effective exercise of the right of the physically or mentally disabled to vocational training, rehabilitation and resettlement, the Contracting Parties undertake:

1. to take adequate measures for the provision of training facilities, including, where necessary, specialised institutions, public or private;

2. to take adequate measures for the placing of disabled persons in employment, such as specialised placing services, facilities for sheltered employment and measures to encourage employers to admit disabled persons to employment.

Article 16 – The right of the family to social, legal and economic protection

With a view to ensuring the necessary conditions for the full development of the family, which is a fundamental unit of society, the Contracting Parties undertake to promote the economic, legal and social protection of family life by such means as social and family benefits, fiscal arrangements, provision of family housing, benefits for the newly married, and other appropriate means.

Article 17 – The right of mothers and children to social and economic protection

With a view to ensuring the effective exercise of the right of mothers and children to social and economic protection, the Contracting Parties will take all appropriate and necessary measures to that end, including the establishment or maintenance of appropriate institutions or services.

Article 18 – The right to engage in a gainful occupation in the territory of other Contracting Parties

With a view to ensuring the effective exercise of the right to engage in a gainful occupation in the territory of any other Contracting Party, the Contracting Parties undertake:

1. to apply existing regulations in a spirit of liberality;
2. to simplify existing formalities and to reduce or abolish chancery dues and other charges payable by foreign workers or their employers;
3. to liberalise, individually or collectively, regulations governing the employment of foreign workers;

and recognise:

4. the right of their nationals to leave the country to engage in a gainful occupation in the territories of the other Contracting Parties.

Article 19 – The right of migrant workers and their families to protection and assistance

With a view to ensuring the effective exercise of the right of migrant workers and their families to protection and assistance in the territory of any other Contracting Party, the Contracting Parties undertake:

1. to maintain or to satisfy themselves that there are maintained adequate and free services to assist such workers, particularly in obtaining accurate information, and to take all appropriate steps, so far as national laws and regulations permit, against misleading propaganda relating to emigration and immigration;
2. to adopt appropriate measures within their own jurisdiction to facilitate the departure, journey and reception of such workers and their families, and to provide, within their own jurisdiction, appropriate services for health, medical attention and good hygienic conditions during the journey;
3. to promote co-operation, as appropriate, between social services, public and private, in emigration and immigration countries;
4. to secure for such workers lawfully within their territories, insofar as such matters are regulated by law or regulations or are subject to the control of administrative authorities, treatment not less

favourable than that of their own nationals in respect of the following matters:

    a. remuneration and other employment and working conditions;

    b. membership of trade unions and enjoyment of the benefits of collective bargaining;

    c. accommodation;

5. to secure for such workers lawfully within their territories treatment not less favourable than that of their own nationals with regard to employment taxes, dues or contributions payable in respect of employed persons;

6. to facilitate as far as possible the reunion of the family of a foreign worker permitted to establish himself in the territory;

7. to secure for such workers lawfully within their territories treatment not less favourable than that of their own nationals in respect of legal proceedings relating to matters referred to in this article;

8. to secure that such workers lawfully residing within their territories are not expelled unless they endanger national security or offend against public interest or morality;

9. to permit, within legal limits, the transfer of such parts of the earnings and savings of such workers as they may desire;

10. to extend the protection and assistance provided for in this article to self-employed migrants insofar as such measures apply.

Part III

Article 20 – Undertakings

1. Each of the Contracting Parties undertakes:

    a. to consider Part I of this Charter as a declaration of the aims which it will pursue by all appropriate means, as stated in the introductory paragraph of that part;

    b. to consider itself bound by at least five of the following articles of Part II of this Charter: Articles 1, 5, 6, 12, 13, 16 and 19;

    c. in addition to the articles selected by it in accordance with the preceding sub-paragraph, to consider itself bound by such a number of articles or numbered paragraphs of Part II of the Charter as it may select, provided that the total number of articles or numbered paragraphs by which it is bound is not less than 10 articles or 45 numbered paragraphs.

2. The articles or paragraphs selected in accordance with subparagraphs b and c of paragraph 1 of this article shall be notified to the Secretary General of the Council of Europe at the time when the instrument of ratification or approval of the Contracting Party concerned is deposited.

3. Any Contracting Party may, at a later date, declare by notification to the Secretary General that it considers itself bound by any articles or any numbered paragraphs of Part II of the Charter which it has not already accepted under the terms of paragraph 1 of this article. Such undertakings subsequently given shall be deemed to be an integral part of the ratification or approval, and shall have the same effect as from the thirtieth day after the date of the notification.

4. The Secretary General shall communicate to all the signatory governments and to the Director General of the International Labour Office any notification which he shall have received pursuant to this part of the Charter.

5. Each Contracting Party shall maintain a system of labour inspection appropriate to national conditions.

Part IV[1]

Article 21 – Reports concerning accepted provisions

The Contracting Parties shall send to the Secretary General of the Council of Europe a report at two-yearly intervals, in a form to be determined by the Committee of Ministers, concerning the application of such provisions of Part II of the Charter as they have accepted.

Article 22 – Reports concerning provisions which are not accepted

The Contracting Parties shall send to the Secretary General, at appropriate intervals as requested by the Committee of Ministers, reports relating to the provisions of Part II of the Charter which they did not accept at the time of their ratification or approval or in a subsequent notification. The Committee of Ministers shall determine from time to time in respect of which provisions such reports shall be requested and the form of the reports to be provided.

Article 23 – Communication of copies

1. Each Contracting Party shall communicate copies of its reports referred to in Articles 21 and 22 to such of its national organisations as are members of the international organisations of employers and trade unions to be invited under Article 27, paragraph 2, to be represented at meetings of the Sub-committee of the Governmental Social Committee.

2. The Contracting Parties shall forward to the Secretary General any comments on the said reports received from these national organisations, if so requested by them.

---

1. See Amending Protocol.

Article 24 – Examination of the reports

The reports sent to the Secretary General in accordance with Articles 21 and 22 shall be examined by a Committee of Experts, who shall have also before them any comments forwarded to the Secretary General in accordance with paragraph 2 of Article 23.

Article 25 – Committee of Experts[1]

1. The Committee of Experts shall consist of not more than seven members appointed by the Committee of Ministers from a list of independent experts of the highest integrity and of recognised competence in international social questions, nominated by the Contracting Parties.

2. The members of the committee shall be appointed for a period of six years. They may be reappointed. However, of the members first appointed, the terms of office of two members shall expire at the end of four years.

3. The members whose terms of office are to expire at the end of the initial period of four years shall be chosen by lot by the Committee of Ministers immediately after the first appointment has been made.

4. A member of the Committee of Experts appointed to replace a member whose term of office has not expired shall hold office for the remainder of his predecessor's term.

Article 26 – Participation of the International Labour Organisation

The International Labour Organisation shall be invited to nominate a representative to participate in a consultative capacity in the deliberations of the Committee of Experts.

Article 27 – Sub-committee of the Governmental Social Committee[2]

1. The reports of the Contracting Parties and the conclusions of the Committee of Experts shall be submitted for examination to a sub-committee of the Governmental Social Committee of the Council of Europe.

2. The sub-committee shall be composed of one representative of each of the Contracting Parties. It shall invite no more than two international organisations of employers and no more than two international trade union organisations as it may designate to be represented as observers in a consultative capacity at its meetings. Moreover, it may consult no more than two representatives of international non-governmental organisations having consultative

---

1. At the Deputies' 509th meeting in March 1994, the committee unanimously decided to increase the committee's membership from seven to nine. The committee is now called the European Committee of Social Rights.
2. The committee is now called the Governmental Committee.

status with the Council of Europe, in respect of questions with which the organisations are particularly qualified to deal, such as social welfare, and the economic and social protection of the family.

3. The sub-committee shall present to the Committee of Ministers a report containing its conclusions and append the report of the Committee of Experts.

Article 28 – Consultative Assembly[1]

The Secretary General of the Council of Europe shall transmit to the Consultative Assembly the conclusions of the Committee of Experts. The Consultative Assembly shall communicate its views on these conclusions to the Committee of Ministers.

Article 29 – Committee of Ministers[2]

By a majority of two-thirds of the members entitled to sit on the Committee, the Committee of Ministers may, on the basis of the report of the sub-committee, and after consultation with the Consultative Assembly, make to each Contracting Party any necessary recommendations.

Part V

Article 30 – Derogations in time of war or public emergency

1. In time of war or other public emergency threatening the life of the nation any Contracting Party may take measures derogating from its obligations under this Charter to the extent strictly required by the exigencies of the situation, provided that such measures are not inconsistent with its other obligations under international law.

2. Any Contracting Party which has availed itself of this right of derogation shall, within a reasonable lapse of time, keep the

---

1. In 1992, the Parliamentary Assembly decided to abstain from giving opinions on the conclusion of the Committee of Independent Experts and to use these conclusions as a basis for the periodical debates on social policy which it would be led to hold according to Article 6 of the Amending Protocol .
2. The Committee of Ministers decided that only the representatives of Contracting Parties to the Charter could vote in the Committee of Ministers when the latter acted as the "supervisory body" of the application of the Charter (April 1993, 492nd meeting of the Deputies). The latter was supplemented in June 1995 (541st meeting of the Deputies) by the following decision: "The Deputies specified that following their decision, adopted at the 492nd meeting [...] whereby "only the Representatives of those States which have ratified the Charter vote in the Committee of Ministers when the latter acts as a control organ of the application of the Charter", Recommendations under the European Social Charter are adopted by a majority of two-thirds of the Deputies casting a vote and a majority of the Contracting Parties to the Charter, (Article 9, paragraph 4, taken together with Article 10, paragraph 3, of the Rules of Procedure for the meetings of the Deputies)."

Secretary General of the Council of Europe fully informed of the measures taken and of the reasons therefor. It shall likewise inform the Secretary General when such measures have ceased to operate and the provisions of the Charter which it has accepted are again being fully executed.

3. The Secretary General shall in turn inform other Contracting Parties and the Director General of the International Labour Office of all communications received in accordance with paragraph 2 of this Article.

Article 31 – Restrictions

1. The rights and principles set forth in Part I when effectively realised, and their effective exercise as provided for in Part II, shall not be subject to any restrictions or limitations not specified in those parts, except such as are prescribed by law and are necessary in a democratic society for the protection of the rights and freedoms of others or for the protection of public interest, national security, public health, or morals.

2. The restrictions permitted under this Charter to the rights and obligations set forth herein shall not be applied for any purpose other than that for which they have been prescribed.

Article 32 – Relations between the Charter and domestic law or international agreements

The provisions of this Charter shall not prejudice the provisions of domestic law or of any bilateral or multilateral treaties, conventions or agreements which are already in force, or may come into force, under which more favourable treatment would be accorded to the persons protected.

Article 33 – Implementation by collective agreements

1. In member States where the provisions of paragraphs 1, 2, 3, 4 and 5 of Article 2, paragraphs 4, 6 and 7 of Article 7 and paragraphs 1, 2, 3 and 4 of Article 10 of Part II of this Charter are matters normally left to agreements between employers or employers' organisations and workers' organisations, or are normally carried out otherwise than by law, the undertakings of those paragraphs may be given and compliance with them shall be treated as effective if their provisions are applied through such agreements or other means to the great majority of the workers concerned.

2. In member States where these provisions are normally the subject of legislation, the undertakings concerned may likewise be given, and compliance with them shall be regarded as effective if the provisions are applied by law to the great majority of the workers concerned.

Article 34 – Territorial application

1. This Charter shall apply to the metropolitan territory of each Contracting Party. Each signatory government may, at the time of signature or of the deposit of its instrument of ratification or approval, specify, by declaration addressed to the Secretary General of the Council of Europe, the territory which shall be considered to be its metropolitan territory for this purpose.

2. Any Contracting Party may, at the time of ratification or approval of this Charter or at any time thereafter, declare by notification addressed to the Secretary General of the Council of Europe, that the Charter shall extend in whole or in part to a non-metropolitan territory or territories specified in the said declaration for whose international relations it is responsible or for which it assumes international responsibility. It shall specify in the declaration the articles or paragraphs of Part II of the Charter which it accepts as binding in respect of the territories named in the declaration.

3. The Charter shall extend to the territory or territories named in the aforesaid declaration as from the thirtieth day after the date on which the Secretary General shall have received notification of such declaration.

4. Any Contracting Party may declare at a later date, by notification addressed to the Secretary General of the Council of Europe, that, in respect of one or more of the territories to which the Charter has been extended in accordance with paragraph 2 of this Article, it accepts as binding any articles or any numbered paragraphs which it has not already accepted in respect of that territory or territories. Such undertakings subsequently given shall be deemed to be an integral part of the original declaration in respect of the territory concerned, and shall have the same effect as from the thirtieth day after the date of the notification.

5. The Secretary General shall communicate to the other signatory governments and to the Director General of the International Labour Office any notification transmitted to him in accordance with this Article.

Article 35 – Signature, ratification and entry into force

1. This Charter shall be open for signature by the members of the Council of Europe. It shall be ratified or approved. Instruments of ratification or approval shall be deposited with the Secretary General of the Council of Europe.

2. This Charter shall come into force as from the thirtieth day after the date of deposit of the fifth instrument of ratification or approval.

3. In respect of any signatory government ratifying subsequently, the Charter shall come into force as from the thirtieth day after the date of deposit of its instrument of ratification or approval.

4. The Secretary General shall notify all the members of the Council of Europe and the Director General of the International Labour Office of the entry into force of the Charter, the names of the Contracting Parties which have ratified or approved it and the subsequent deposit of any instruments of ratification or approval.

Article 36 – Amendments

Any member of the Council of Europe may propose amendments to this Charter in a communication addressed to the Secretary General of the Council of Europe. The Secretary General shall transmit to the other members of the Council of Europe any amendments so proposed, which shall then be considered by the Committee of Ministers and submitted to the Consultative Assembly for opinion. Any amendments approved by the Committee of Ministers shall enter into force as from the thirtieth day after all the Contracting Parties have informed the Secretary General of their acceptance. The Secretary General shall notify all the members of the Council of Europe and the Director General of the International Labour Office of the entry into force of such amendments.

Article 37 – Denunciation

1. Any Contracting Party may denounce this Charter only at the end of a period of five years from the date on which the Charter entered into force for it, or at the end of any successive period of two years, and, in each case, after giving six months notice to the Secretary General of the Council of Europe who shall inform the other Parties and the Director General of the International Labour Office accordingly. Such denunciation shall not affect the validity of the Charter in respect of the other Contracting Parties provided that at all times there are not less than five such Contracting Parties.

2. Any Contracting Party may, in accordance with the provisions set out in the preceding paragraph, denounce any article or paragraph of Part II of the Charter accepted by it provided that the number of articles or paragraphs by which this Contracting Party is bound shall never be less than 10 in the former case and 45 in the latter and that this number of articles or paragraphs shall continue to include the articles selected by the Contracting Party among those to which special reference is made in Article 20, paragraph 1, sub-paragraph b.

3. Any Contracting Party may denounce the present Charter or any of the articles or paragraphs of Part II of the Charter, under the conditions specified in paragraph 1 of this Article in respect of any territory to which the said Charter is applicable by virtue of a declaration made in accordance with paragraph 2 of Article 34.

Article 38 – Appendix

The appendix to this Charter shall form an integral part of it.

In witness whereof, the undersigned, being duly authorised thereto, have signed this Charter.

Done at Turin, this 18th day of October 1961, in English and French, both texts being equally authoritative, in a single copy which shall be deposited within the archives of the Council of Europe. The Secretary General shall transmit certified copies to each of the Signatories.

Appendix to the Social Charter

Scope of the Social Charter in terms of persons protected

1. Without prejudice to Article 12, paragraph 4, and Article 13, paragraph 4, the persons covered by Articles 1 to 17 include foreigners only insofar as they are nationals of other Contracting Parties lawfully resident or working regularly within the territory of the Contracting Party concerned, subject to the understanding that these Articles are to be interpreted in the light of the provisions of Articles 18 and 19.

   This interpretation would not prejudice the extension of similar facilities to other persons by any of the Contracting Parties.

2. Each Contracting Party will grant to refugees as defined in the Convention relating to the Status of Refugees, signed at Geneva on 28th July 1951, and lawfully staying in its territory, treatment as favourable as possible, and in any case not less favourable than under the obligations accepted by the Contracting Party under the said Convention and under any other existing international instruments applicable to those refugees.

Part I, paragraph 18, and Part II, Article 18, paragraph 1

It is understood that these provisions are not concerned with the question of entry into the territories of the Contracting Parties and do not prejudice the provisions of the European Convention on Establishment, signed at Paris on 13th December 1955.

Part II

Article 1, paragraph 2

This provision shall not be interpreted as prohibiting or authorising any union security clause or practice.

Article 4, paragraph 4

This provision shall be so understood as not to prohibit immediate dismissal for any serious offence.

Article 4, paragraph 5

It is understood that a Contracting Party may give the undertaking required in this paragraph if the great majority of workers are not permitted to suffer deductions from wages either by law or through collective agreements or arbitration awards, the exceptions being those persons not so covered.

Article 6, paragraph 4

It is understood that each Contracting Party may, insofar as it is concerned, regulate the exercise of the right to strike by law, provided that any further restriction that this might place on the right can be justified under the terms of Article 31.

Article 7, paragraph 8

It is understood that a Contracting Party may give the undertaking required in this paragraph if it fulfils the spirit of the undertaking by providing by law that the great majority of persons under eighteen years of age shall not be employed in night work.

Article 12, paragraph 4

The words "and subject to the conditions laid down in such agreements" in the introduction to this paragraph are taken to imply *inter alia* that with regard to benefits which are available independently of any insurance contribution a Contracting Party may require the completion of a prescribed period of residence before granting such benefits to nationals of other Contracting Parties.

Article 13, paragraph 4

Governments not Parties to the European Convention on Social and Medical Assistance may ratify the Social Charter in respect of this paragraph provided that they grant to nationals of other Contracting Parties a treatment which is in conformity with the provisions of the said Convention.

Article 19, paragraph 6

For the purpose of this provision, the term "family of a foreign worker" is understood to mean at least his wife and dependent children under the age of twenty-one years.

Part III

It is understood that the Charter contains legal obligations of an international character, the application of which is submitted solely to the supervision provided for in Part IV thereof.

Article 20, paragraph 1

It is understood that the "numbered paragraphs" may include articles consisting of only one paragraph.

Part V

Article 30

The term "in time of war or other public emergency" shall be so understood as to cover also the threat of war.

2. Additional Protocol of 1988

Preamble

The member States of the Council of Europe signatory hereto, resolved to take new measures to extend the protection of the social and economic rights guaranteed by the European Social Charter, opened for signature in Turin on 18 October 1961 (hereinafter referred to as "the Charter"),

Have agreed as follows:

Part I

The Parties accept as the aim of their policy to be pursued by all appropriate means, both national and international in character, the attainment of conditions in which the following rights and principles may be effectively realised:

1. All workers have the right to equal opportunities and equal treatment in matters of employment and occupation without discrimination on the grounds of sex.

2. Workers have the right to be informed and to be consulted within the undertaking.

3. Workers have the right to take part in the determination and improvement of the working conditions and working environment in the undertaking.

4. Every elderly person has the right to social protection.

Part II

The Parties undertake, as provided for in Part III, to consider themselves bound by the obligations laid down in the following articles:

Article 1 – Right to equal opportunities and equal treatment in matters of employment and occupation without discrimination on the grounds of sex

1. With a view to ensuring the effective exercise of the right to equal opportunities and equal treatment in matters of employment and occupation without discrimination on the grounds of sex, the Parties undertake to recognise that right and to take appropriate measures to ensure or promote its application in the following fields:

    – access to employment, protection against dismissal and occupational resettlement;

    – vocational guidance, training, retraining and rehabilitation;

    – terms of employment and working conditions including remuneration;

    – career development including promotion.

2. Provisions concerning the protection of women, particularly as regards pregnancy, confinement and the post-natal period, shall not be deemed to be discrimination as referred to in paragraph 1 of this Article.

3. Paragraph 1 of this Article shall not prevent the adoption of specific measures aimed at removing *de facto* inequalities.

4. Occupational activities which, by reason of their nature or the context in which they are carried out, can be entrusted only to persons of a particular sex may be excluded from the scope of this Article or some of its provisions.

Article 2 – Right to information and consultation

1. With a view to ensuring the effective exercise of the right of workers to be informed and consulted within the undertaking, the Parties undertake to adopt or encourage measures enabling workers or their representatives, in accordance with national legislation and practice:

    a. to be informed regularly or at the appropriate time and in a comprehensible way about the economic and financial situation of the undertaking employing them, on the understanding that the disclosure of certain information which could be prejudicial to the undertaking may be refused or subject to confidentiality; and

    b. to be consulted in good time on proposed decisions which could substantially affect the interests of workers, particularly on those decisions which could have an important impact on the employment situation in the undertaking.

2. The Parties may exclude from the field of application of paragraph 1 of this Article, those undertakings employing less than a

certain number of workers to be determined by national legislation or practice.

Article 3 – Right to take part in the determination and improvement of the working conditions and working environment

1. With a view to ensuring the effective exercise of the right of workers to take part in the determination and improvement of the working conditions and working environment in the undertaking, the Parties undertake to adopt or encourage measures enabling workers or their representatives, in accordance with national legislation and practice, to contribute:

    a. to the determination and the improvement of the working conditions, work organisation and working environment;

    b. to the protection of health and safety within the undertaking;

    c. to the organisation of social and socio-cultural services and facilities within the undertaking;

    d. to the supervision of the observance of regulations on these matters.

2. The Parties may exclude from the field of application of paragraph 1 of this Article, those undertakings employing less than a certain number of workers to be determined by national legislation or practice.

Article 4 – Right of elderly persons to social protection

With a view to ensuring the effective exercise of the right of elderly persons to social protection, the Parties undertake to adopt or encourage, either directly or in co-operation with public or private organisations, appropriate measures designed in particular:

1. to enable elderly persons to remain full members of society for as long as possible, by means of:

    a. adequate resources enabling them to lead a decent life and play an active part in public, social and cultural life;

    b. provision of information about services and facilities available for elderly persons and their opportunities to make use of them;

2. to enable elderly persons to choose their life-style freely and to lead independent lives in their familiar surroundings for as long as they wish and are able, by means of:

    a. provision of housing suited to their needs and their state of health or of adequate support for adapting their housing;

    b. the health care and the services necessitated by their state;

3. to guarantee elderly persons living in institutions appropriate support, while respecting their privacy, and participation in decisions concerning living conditions in the institution.

Part III

Article 5 – Undertakings

1. Each of the Parties undertakes:

   a. to consider Part I of this Protocol as a declaration of the aims which it will pursue by all appropriate means, as stated in the introductory paragraph of that Part;

   b. to consider itself bound by one or more articles of Part II of this Protocol.

2. The article or articles selected in accordance with sub-paragraph *b* of paragraph 1 of this Article, shall be notified to the Secretary General of the Council of Europe at the time when the instrument of ratification, acceptance or approval of the Contracting State concerned is deposited.

3. And Party may, at a later day, declare by notification to the Secretary General that it considers itself bound by any articles of Part II of this Protocol which it has not already accepted under the terms of paragraph 1 of this Article. Such undertakings subsequently given shall be deemed to be an integral part of the ratification, acceptance or approval, and shall have the same effect as from the thirtieth day after the date of the notification.

Part IV

Article 6 – Supervision of compliance with the undertakings given

The Parties shall submit reports on the application of those provisions of Part II of this Protocol which they have accepted in the reports submitted by virtue of Article 21 of the Charter.

Part V

Article 7 – Implementation of the undertakings given

1. The relevant provisions of Articles 1 to 4 of Part II of this Protocol may be implemented by:

   a. laws or regulations;

   b. agreements between employers or employers' organisations and workers' organisations;

   c. a combination of those two methods; or

   d. other appropriate means.

2. Compliance with the undertakings deriving from Articles 2 and 3 of Part II of this Protocol shall be regarded as effective if the provisions are applied, in accordance with paragraph 1 of this Article, to the great majority of the workers concerned.

Article 8 – Relations between the Charter and this Protocol

1. The provisions of this Protocol shall not prejudice the provisions of the Charter.

2. Articles 22 to 32 and Article 36 of the Charter shall apply, *mutatis mutandis*, to this Protocol.

Article 9 – Territorial application

1. This Protocol shall apply to the metropolitan territory of each Party. Any State may, at the time of signature or when depositing its instrument of ratification, acceptance or approval, specify by declaration addressed to the Secretary General of the Council of Europe, the territory which shall be considered to be its metropolitan territory for this purpose.

2. Any Contracting State may, at the time of ratification, acceptance or approval of this Protocol or at any time thereafter, declare by notification addressed to the Secretary General of the Council of Europe that the Protocol shall extend in whole or in part to a non-metropolitan territory or territories specified in the said declaration for whose international relations it is responsible or for which it assumes international responsibility. It shall specify in the declaration the article or articles of Part II of this Protocol which it accepts as binding in respect of the territories named in the declaration.

3. This Protocol shall enter into force in respect of the territory or territories named in the aforesaid declaration as from the thirtieth day after the date on which the Secretary General shall have notification of such declaration.

4. Any Party may declare at a later date by notification addressed to the Secretary General of the Council of Europe, that, in respect of one or more of the territories to which this Protocol has been extended in accordance with paragraph 2 of this Article, it accepts as binding any articles which it has not already accepted in respect of that territory or territories. Such undertakings subsequently given shall be deemed to be an integral part of the original declaration in respect of the territory concerned, and shall have the same effect as from the thirtieth day after the date on which the Secretary General shall have notification of such declaration.

Article 10 – Signature, ratification, acceptance, approval and entry into force

1. This Protocol shall be open for signature by member States of the Council of Europe who are signatories to the Charter. It is subject to ratification, acceptance or approval. No member State of the Council of Europe shall ratify, accept or approve this Protocol except at the same time as or after ratification of the Charter.

Instruments of ratification, acceptance of approval shall be deposited with the Secretary General of the Council of Europe.

2. This Protocol shall enter into force on the thirtieth day after the date of deposit of the third instrument of ratification, acceptance or approval.

3. In respect of any signatory State ratifying subsequently, this Protocol shall come into force as from the thirtieth day after the date of deposit of its instrument of ratification, acceptance or approval.

Article 11 – Denunciation

1. Any Party may denounce this Protocol only at the end of a period of five years from the date on which the Protocol entered into force for it, or at the end of any successive period of two years, and, in each case, after giving six months' notice to the Secretary General of the Council of Europe. Such denunciation shall not affect the validity of the Protocol in respect of the other Parties provided that at all times there are not less than three such Parties.

2. Any Party may, in accordance with the provisions set out in the preceding paragraph, denounce any article of Part II of this Protocol accepted by it, provided that the number of articles by which this Party is bound shall never be less than one.

3. Any Party may denounce this Protocol or any of the articles of Part II of the Protocol, under the conditions specified in paragraph 1 of this Article, in respect of any territory to which the Protocol is applicable by virtue of a declaration made in accordance with paragraphs 2 and 4 of Article 9.

4. Any Party bound by the Charter and this Protocol which denounces the Charter in accordance with the provisions of paragraph 1 of Article 37 thereof, will be considered to have denounced the Protocol likewise.

Article 12 – Notifications

The Secretary General of the Council of Europe shall notify the member States of the Council and the Director General of the International Labour Office of:

a. any signature;

b. the deposit of any instrument of ratification, acceptance or approval;

c. any date of entry into force of this Protocol in accordance with Articles 9 and 10;

d. any other act, notification or communication relating to this Protocol.

Article 13 – Appendix

The Appendix to this Protocol shall form an integral part of it.

In witness whereof the undersigned, being duly authorised thereto, have signed this Protocol.

Done at Strasbourg, this 5th day of May, 1988, in English and French, both texts being equally authentic, in a single copy which shall be deposited in the archives of the Council of Europe. The Secretary General of the Council in Europe shall transmit certified copies to each member State of the Council of Europe.

Appendix to the Protocol

Scope of the Protocol in terms of persons protected

1. The persons covered by Articles 1 to 4 include foreigners only insofar as they are nationals of other Parties lawfully resident or working regularly within the territory of the Party concerned subject to the understanding that these articles are to be interpreted in the light of the provisions of Articles 18 and 19 of the Charter. This interpretation would not prejudice the extension of similar facilities to other persons by any of the Parties.

2. Each Party will grant to refugees as defined in the Convention relating to the Status of Refugees, signed at Geneva on 28 July 1951 and in the Protocol of 31 January 1967, and lawfully staying in its territory, treatment as favourable as possible and in any case not less favourable than under the obligations accepted by the Party under the said instruments and under any other existing international instruments applicable to those refugees.

3. Each Party will grant to stateless persons as defined in the Convention on the Status of Stateless Persons done at New York on 28 September 1954 and lawfully staying in its territory, treatment as favourable as possible and in any case not less favourable than under the obligations accepted by the Party under the said instrument and under any other existing international instruments applicable to those stateless persons.

Article 1

It is understood that social security matters, as well as other provisions relating to unemployment benefit, old age benefit and survivor's benefit, may be excluded from the scope of this Article.

Article 1, paragraph 4

This provision is not to be interpreted as requiring the Parties to embody in laws or regulations a list of occupations which, by reason of their nature or the context in which they are carried out, may be reserved to persons of a particular sex.

35

Articles 2 and 3

1. For the purpose of the application of these articles, the term "workers' representatives" means persons who are recognised as such under national legislation or practice.

2. The term "national legislation and practice" embraces as the case may be, in addition to laws and regulations, collective agreements, other agreements between employers and workers' representatives, customs, as well as relevant case law.

3. For the purpose of the application of these articles, the term "undertaking" is understood as referring to a set of tangible and intangible components, with or without legal personality, formed to produce or provide services for financial gain and with power to determine its own market policy.

4. It is understood that religious communities and their institutions may be excluded from the application of these articles, even if these institutions are "undertakings" within the meaning of paragraph 3 Establishments pursuing activities which are inspired by certain ideals or guided by certain moral concepts, ideals and concepts which are protected by national legislation, may be excluded from the application of these articles to such an extent as is necessary to protect the orientation of the undertaking.

5. It is understood that where in a State the rights set out in Articles 2 and 3 are exercised in the various establishments of the undertaking, the Party concerned is to be considered as fulfilling the obligations deriving from these provisions.

Article 3

This provision affects neither the powers and obligations of States as regards the adoption of health and safety regulations for work-places, nor the powers and responsibilities of the bodies in charge of monitoring their application.

The terms social and socio-cultural services and facilities" are understood as referring to the social and/or cultural facilities for workers provided by some undertakings such as welfare assistance, sports fields, rooms for nursing mothers, libraries, children's holiday camps, etc.

Article 4, paragraph 1

For the purpose of the application of this paragraph, the term "for as long as possible" refers to the elderly person's physical, psychological and intellectual capacities.

Article 7

It is understood that workers excluded in accordance with paragraph 2 of Article 2 and paragraph 2 of Article 3 are not taken into account in establishing the number of workers concerned.

3. Amending Protocol of 1991

Preamble

The member States of the Council of Europe, signatory to this Protocol to the European Social Charter, opened for signature in Turin on 18 October 1961 (hereinafter referred to as "the Charter"),

Being resolved to take some measures to improve the effectiveness of the Charter, and particularly the functioning of its supervisory machinery;

Considering therefore that it is desirable to amend certain provisions of the Charter,

Have agreed as follows:

Article 1

Article 23 of the Charter shall read as follows:

"Article 23 – Communication of copies of reports and comments

1. When sending to the Secretary General a report pursuant to Articles 21 and 22, each Contracting Party shall forward a copy of that report to such of its national organisations as are members of the international organisations of employers and trade unions invited, under Article 27, paragraph 2, to be represented at meetings of the Governmental Committee. Those organisations shall send to the Secretary General any comments on the reports of the Contracting Parties. The Secretary General shall send a copy of those comments to the Contracting Parties concerned, who might wish to respond.

2. The Secretary General shall forward a copy of the reports of the Contracting Parties to the international non-governmental organisations which have consultative status with the Council of Europe and have particular competence in the matters governed by the present Charter.

3. The reports and comments referred to in Articles 21 and 22 and in the present article shall be made available to the public on request."

Article 2

Article 24 of the Charter shall read as follows:

"Article 24 – Examination of the reports

1. The reports sent to the Secretary General in accordance with Articles 21 and 22 shall be examined by a Committee of Independent Experts constituted pursuant to Article 25. The committee shall also have before it any comments forwarded to the Secretary General in accordance with paragraph 1 of Article 23.

On completion of its examination, the Committee of Independent Experts shall draw up a report containing its conclusions.

2. With regard to the reports referred to in Article 21, the Committee of Independent Experts shall assess from a legal standpoint the compliance of national law and practice with the obligations arising from the Charter for the Contracting Parties concerned.

3. The Committee of Independent Experts may address requests for additional information and clarification directly to Contracting Parties. In this connection the Committee of Independent Experts may also hold, if necessary, a meeting with the representatives of a Contracting Party, either on its own initiative or at the request of the Contracting Party concerned. The organisations referred to in paragraph 1 of Article 23 shall be kept informed.

4. The conclusions of the Committee of Independent Experts shall be made public and communicated by the Secretary General to the Governmental Committee, to the Parliamentary Assembly and to the organisations which are mentioned in paragraph 1 of Article 23 and paragraph 2 of Article 27."

Article 3

Article 25 of the Charter shall read as follows:

"Article 25 – Committee of Independent Experts

1. The Committee of Independent Experts shall consist of at least nine members elected by the Parliamentary Assembly by a majority of votes cast from a list of experts of the highest integrity and of recognised competence in national and international social questions, nominated by the Contracting Parties. The exact number of members shall be determined by the Committee of Ministers.

2. The members of the committee shall be elected for a period of six years. They may stand for re-election once.

3. A member of the Committee of Independent Experts elected to replace a member whose term of office has not expired shall hold office for the remainder of his predecessor's term.

4. The members of the committee shall sit in their individual capacity. Throughout their term of office, they may not perform any function incompatible with the requirements of independence, impartiality and availability inherent in their office."

Article 4

Article 27 of the Charter shall read as follows:

"Article 27 – Governmental Committee

1. The reports of the Contracting Parties, the comments and information communicated in accordance with paragraphs 1 of Article 23

and 3 of Article 24, and the reports of the Committee of Independent Experts shall be submitted to a Governmental Committee.

2. The committee shall be composed of one representative of each of the Contracting Parties. It shall invite no more than two international organisations of employers and no more than two international trade union organisations to send observers in a consultative capacity to its meetings. Moreover, it may consult representatives of international non-governmental organisations which have consultative status with the Council of Europe and have particular competence in the matters governed by the present Charter.

3. The Governmental Committee shall prepare the decisions of the Committee of Ministers. In particular, in the light of the reports of the Committee of Independent Experts and of the Contracting Parties, it shall select, giving reasons for its choice, on the basis of social, economic and other policy considerations the situations which should, in its view, be the subject of recommendations to each Contracting Party concerned, in accordance with Article 28 of the Charter. It shall present to the Committee of Ministers a report which shall be made public.

4. On the basis of its findings on the implementation of the Social Charter in general, the Governmental Committee may submit proposals to the Committee of Ministers aiming at studies to be carried out on social issues and on articles of the Charter which possibly might be updated."

Article 5

Article 28 of the Charter shall read as follows:

"Article 28 – Committee of Ministers

1. The Committee of Ministers shall adopt, by a majority of two-thirds of those voting, with entitlement to voting limited to the Contracting Parties, on the basis of the report of the Governmental Committee, a resolution covering the entire supervision cycle and containing individual recommendations to the Contracting Parties concerned.

2. Having regard to the proposals made by the Governmental Committee pursuant to paragraph 4 of Article 27, the Committee of Ministers shall take such decisions as it deems appropriate."

Article 6

Article 29 of the Charter shall read as follows:

"Article 29 – Parliamentary Assembly

The Secretary General of the Council of Europe shall transmit to the Parliamentary Assembly, with a view to the holding of periodical plenary debates, the reports of the Committee of Independent Experts and of the Governmental Committee, as well as the resolutions of the Committee of Ministers."

Article 7

1. This Protocol shall be open for signature by member States of the Council of Europe signatories to the Charter, which may express their consent to be bound by:

   a. signature without reservation as to ratification, acceptance or approval; or

   b. signature subject to ratification, acceptance or approval, followed by ratification, acceptance or approval.

2. Instruments of ratification, acceptance or approval shall be deposited with the Secretary General of the Council of Europe.

Article 8

This Protocol shall enter into force on the thirtieth day after the date on which all Contracting Parties to the Charter have expressed their consent to be bound by the Protocol in accordance with the provisions of Article 7.

Article 9

The Secretary General of the Council of Europe shall notify the member States of the Council of:

a. any signature;

b. the deposit of any instrument of ratification, acceptance or approval;

c. the date of entry into force of this Protocol in accordance with Article 8;

d. any other act, notification or communication relating to this Protocol.

In witness whereof the undersigned, being duly authorised thereto, have signed this Protocol.

Done at Turin, this 21st day of October 1991, in English and French, both texts being equally authentic, in a single copy which shall be deposited in the archives of the Council of Europe. The Secretary General of the Council of Europe shall transmit certified copies to each member State of the Council of Europe.

4. Additional Protocol of 1995 providing for a system of collective complaints

Preamble

The member States of the Council of Europe, signatories to this Protocol to the European Social Charter, opened for signature in Turin on 18 October 1961 (hereinafter referred to as "the Charter");

Resolved to take new measures to improve the effective enforcement of the social rights guaranteed by the Charter;

Considering that this aim could be achieved in particular by the establishment of a collective complaints procedure, which, *inter alia*, would strengthen the participation of management and labour and of non-governmental organisations,

Have agreed as follows:

Article 1

The Contracting Parties to this Protocol recognise the right of the following organisations to submit complaints alleging unsatisfactory application of the Charter:

a. international organisations of employers and trade unions referred to in paragraph 2 of Article 27 of the Charter;

b. other international non-governmental organisations which have consultative status with the Council of Europe and have been put on a list established for this purpose by the Governmental Committee;

c. representative national organisations of employers and trade unions within the jurisdiction of the Contracting Party against which they have lodged a complaint.

Article 2

1. Any Contracting State may also, when it expresses its consent to be bound by this Protocol, in accordance with the provisions of Article 13, or at any moment thereafter, declare that it recognises the right of any other representative national non-governmental organisation within its jurisdiction which has particular competence in the matters governed by the Charter, to lodge complaints against it.

2. Such declarations may be made for a specific period.

3. The declarations shall be deposited with the Secretary General of the Council of Europe who shall transmit copies thereof to the Contracting Parties and publish them.

Article 3

The international non-governmental organisations and the national non-governmental organisations referred to in Article 1.*b* and Article 2 respectively may submit complaints in accordance with the procedure prescribed by the aforesaid provisions only in respect of those matters regarding which they have been recognised as having particular competence.

Article 4

The complaint shall be lodged in writing, relate to a provision of the Charter accepted by the Contracting Party concerned and indicate in what respect the latter has not ensured the satisfactory application of this provision.

Article 5

Any complaint shall be addressed to the Secretary General who shall acknowledge receipt of it, notify it to the Contracting Party concerned and immediately transmit it to the Committee of Independent Experts.

Article 6

The Committee of Independent Experts may request the Contracting Party concerned and the organisation which lodged the complaint to submit written information and observations on the admissibility of the complaint within such time-limit as it shall prescribe.

Article 7

1. If it decides that a complaint is admissible, the Committee of Independent Experts shall notify the Contracting Parties to the Charter through the Secretary General. It shall request the Contracting Party concerned and the organisation which lodged the complaint to submit, within such time-limit as it shall prescribe, all relevant written explanations or information, and the other Contracting Parties to this Protocol, the comments they wish to submit, within the same time-limit.

2. If the complaint has been lodged by a national organisation of employers or a national trade union or by another national or international non-governmental organisation, the Committee of Independent Experts shall notify the international organisations of employers or trade unions referred to in paragraph 2 of Article 27 of the Charter, through the Secretary General, and invite them to submit observations within such time-limit as it shall prescribe.

3. On the basis of the explanations, information or observations submitted under paragraphs 1 and 2 above, the Contracting Party concerned and the organisation which lodged the complaint may submit any additional written information or observations within

such time-limit as the Committee of Independent Experts shall prescribe.

4. In the course of the examination of the complaint, the Committee of Independent Experts may organise a hearing with the representatives of the parties.

Article 8

1. The Committee of Independent Experts shall draw up a report in which it shall describe the steps taken by it to examine the complaint and present its conclusions as to whether or not the Contracting Party concerned has ensured the satisfactory application of the provision of the Charter referred to in the complaint.

2. The report shall be transmitted to the Committee of Ministers. It shall also be transmitted to the organisation that lodged the complaint and to the Contracting Parties to the Charter, which shall not be at liberty to publish it.

It shall be transmitted to the Parliamentary Assembly and made public at the same time as the resolution referred to in Article 9 or no later than four months after it has been transmitted to the Committee of Ministers.

Article 9

1. On the basis of the report of the Committee of Independent Experts, the Committee of Ministers shall adopt a resolution by a majority of those voting. If the Committee of Independent Experts finds that the Charter has not been applied in a satisfactory manner, the Committee of Ministers shall adopt, by a majority of two-thirds of those voting, a recommendation addressed to the Contracting Party concerned. In both cases, entitlement to voting shall be limited to the Contracting Parties to the Charter.

2. At the request of the Contracting Party concerned, the Committee of Ministers may decide, where the report of the Committee of Independent Experts raises new issues, by a two-thirds majority of the Contracting Parties to the Charter, to consult the Governmental Committee.

Article 10

The Contracting Party concerned shall provide information on the measures it has taken to give effect to the Committee of Ministers' recommendation, in the next report which it submits to the Secretary General under Article 21 of the Charter.

Article 11

Articles 1 to 10 of this Protocol shall apply also to the articles of Part II of the first Additional Protocol to the Charter in respect of the States

Parties to that Protocol, to the extent that these articles have been accepted.

Article 12

The States Parties to this Protocol consider that the first paragraph of the appendix to the Charter, relating to Part III, reads as follows:

"It is understood that the Charter contains legal obligations of an international character, the application of which is submitted solely to the supervision provided for in Part IV thereof and in the provisions of this Protocol."

Article 13

1. This Protocol shall be open for signature by member States of the Council of Europe signatories to the Charter, which may express their consent to be bound by:

   a. signature without reservation as to ratification, acceptance or approval; or

   b. signature subject to ratification, acceptance or approval, followed by ratification, acceptance or approval.

2. A member State of the Council of Europe may not express its consent to be bound by this Protocol without previously or simultaneously ratifying the Charter.

3. Instruments of ratification, acceptance or approval shall be deposited with the Secretary General of the Council of Europe.

Article 14

1. This Protocol shall enter into force on the first day of the month following the expiration of a period of one month after the date on which five member States of the Council of Europe have expressed their consent to be bound by the Protocol in accordance with the provisions of Article 13.

2. In respect of any member State which subsequently expresses its consent to be bound by it, the Protocol shall enter into force on the first day of the month following the expiration of a period of one month after the date of the deposit of the instrument of ratification, acceptance or approval.

Article 15

1. Any Party may at any time denounce this Protocol by means of a notification addressed to the Secretary General of the Council of Europe.

2. Such denunciation shall become effective on the first day of the month following the expiration of a period of twelve months after the date of receipt of such notification by the Secretary General.

Article 16

The Secretary General of the Council of Europe shall notify all the member States of the Council of:

a. any signature;

b. the deposit of any instrument of ratification, acceptance or approval;

c. the date of entry into force of this Protocol in accordance with Article 14;

d. any other act, notification or declaration relating to this Protocol.

In witness whereof the undersigned, being duly authorised thereto, have signed this Protocol.

Done at Strasbourg, this 9th day of November 1995, in English and French, both texts being equally authentic, in a single copy which shall be deposited in the archives of the Council of Europe. The Secretary General of the Council of Europe shall transmit certified copies to each member State of the Council of Europe.

B. Revised European Social Charter of 1996

Preamble

The governments signatory hereto, being members of the Council of Europe,

Considering that the aim of the Council of Europe is the achievement of greater unity between its members for the purpose of safeguarding and realising the ideals and principles which are their common heritage and of facilitating their economic and social progress, in particular by the maintenance and further realisation of human rights and fundamental freedoms;

Considering that in the European Convention for the Protection of Human Rights and Fundamental Freedoms signed at Rome on 4 November 1950, and the Protocols thereto, the member States of the Council of Europe agreed to secure to their populations the civil and political rights and freedoms therein specified;

Considering that in the European Social Charter opened for signature in Turin on 18 October 1961 and the Protocols thereto, the member States of the Council of Europe agreed to secure to their populations the social rights specified therein in order to improve their standard of living and their social well-being;

Recalling that the Ministerial Conference on Human Rights held in Rome on 5 November 1990 stressed the need, on the one hand, to preserve the indivisible nature of all human rights, be they civil, political, economic, social or cultural and, on the other hand, to give the European Social Charter fresh impetus;

Resolved, as was decided during the Ministerial Conference held in Turin on 21 and 22 October 1991, to update and adapt the substantive contents of the Charter in order to take account in particular of the fundamental social changes which have occurred since the text was adopted;

Recognising the advantage of embodying in a Revised Charter, designed progressively to take the place of the European Social Charter, the rights guaranteed by the Charter as amended, the rights guaranteed by the Additional Protocol of 1988 and to add new rights,

Have agreed as follows:

Part I

The Parties accept as the aim of their policy, to be pursued by all appropriate means both national and international in character, the attainment of conditions in which the following rights and principles may be effectively realised:

1. Everyone shall have the opportunity to earn his living in an occupation freely entered upon.

2. All workers have the right to just conditions of work.

3. All workers have the right to safe and healthy working conditions.

4. All workers have the right to a fair remuneration sufficient for a decent standard of living for themselves and their families.

5. All workers and employers have the right to freedom of association in national or international organisations for the protection of their economic and social interests.

6. All workers and employers have the right to bargain collectively.

7. Children and young persons have the right to a special protection against the physical and moral hazards to which they are exposed.

8. Employed women, in case of maternity, have the right to a special protection.

9. Everyone has the right to appropriate facilities for vocational guidance with a view to helping him choose an occupation suited to his personal aptitude and interests.

10. Everyone has the right to appropriate facilities for vocational training.

11. Everyone has the right to benefit from any measures enabling him to enjoy the highest possible standard of health attainable.

12. All workers and their dependents have the right to social security.

13. Anyone without adequate resources has the right to social and medical assistance.

14. Everyone has the right to benefit from social welfare services.

15. Disabled persons have the right to independence, social integration and participation in the life of the community.

16. The family as a fundamental unit of society has the right to appropriate social, legal and economic protection to ensure its full development.

17. Children and young persons have the right to appropriate social, legal and economic protection.

18. The nationals of any one of the Parties have the right to engage in any gainful occupation in the territory of any one of the others on a footing of equality with the nationals of the latter, subject to restrictions based on cogent economic or social reasons.

19. Migrant workers who are nationals of a Party and their families have the right to protection and assistance in the territory of any other Party.

20 All workers have the right to equal opportunities and equal treatment in matters of employment and occupation without discrimination on the grounds of sex.

21. Workers have the right to be informed and to be consulted within the undertaking.

22. Workers have the right to take part in the determination and improvement of the working conditions and working environment in the undertaking.

23. Every elderly person has the right to social protection.

24. All workers have the right to protection in cases of termination of employment.

25. All workers have the right to protection of their claims in the event of the insolvency of their employer.

26. All workers have the right to dignity at work.

27. All persons with family responsibilities and who are engaged or wish to engage in employment have a right to do so without being subject to discrimination and as far as possible without conflict between their employment and family responsibilities.

28. Workers' representatives in undertakings have the right to protection against acts prejudicial to them and should be afforded appropriate facilities to carry out their functions.

29. All workers have the right to be informed and consulted in collective redundancy procedures.

30 Everyone has the right to protection against poverty and social exclusion.

31. Everyone has the right to housing.

Part II

The Parties undertake, as provided for in Part III, to consider themselves bound by the obligations laid down in the following articles and paragraphs.

Article 1 – The right to work

With a view to ensuring the effective exercise of the right to work, the Parties undertake:

1. to accept as one of their primary aims and responsibilities the achievement and maintenance of as high and stable a level of employment as possible, with a view to the attainment of full employment;

2. to protect effectively the right of the worker to earn his living in an occupation freely entered upon;

3. to establish or maintain free employment services for all workers;

4. to provide or promote appropriate vocational guidance, training and rehabilitation.

Article 2 – The right to just conditions of work

With a view to ensuring the effective exercise of the right to just conditions of work, the Parties undertake:

1. to provide for reasonable daily and weekly working hours, the working week to be progressively reduced to the extent that the increase of productivity and other relevant factors permit;

2. to provide for public holidays with pay;

3. to provide for a minimum of four weeks' annual holiday with pay;

4. to eliminate risks in inherently dangerous or unhealthy occupations, and where it has not yet been possible to eliminate or reduce sufficiently these risks, to provide for either a reduction of working hours or additional paid holidays for workers engaged in such occupations;

5. to ensure a weekly rest period which shall, as far as possible, coincide with the day recognised by tradition or custom in the country or region concerned as a day of rest;

6. to ensure that workers are informed in written form, as soon as possible, and in any event not later than two months after the date of commencing their employment, of the essential aspects of the contract or employment relationship;

7. to ensure that workers performing night work benefit from measures which take account of the special nature of the work.

Article 3 – The right to safe and healthy working conditions

With a view to ensuring the effective exercise of the right to safe and healthy working conditions, the Parties undertake, in consultation with employers' and workers' organisations:

1. to formulate, implement and periodically review a coherent national policy on occupational safety, occupational health and the working environment. The primary aim of this policy shall be to improve occupational safety and health and to prevent accidents and injury to health arising out of, linked with or occurring in the course of work, particularly by minimising the causes of hazards inherent in the working environment;

2. to issue safety and health regulations;

3. to provide for the enforcement of such regulations by measures of supervision;

4. to promote the progressive development of occupational health services for all workers with essentially preventive and advisory functions.

Article 4 – The right to a fair remuneration

With a view to ensuring the effective exercise of the right to a fair remuneration, the Parties undertake:

1. to recognise the right of workers to a remuneration such as will give them and their families a decent standard of living;

2. to recognise the right of workers to an increased rate of remuneration for overtime work, subject to exceptions in particular cases;

3. to recognise the right of men and women workers to equal pay for work of equal value;

4. to recognise the right of all workers to a reasonable period of notice for termination of employment;

5. to permit deductions from wages only under conditions and to the extent prescribed by national laws or regulations or fixed by collective agreements or arbitration awards.

The exercise of these rights shall be achieved by freely concluded collective agreements, by statutory wage-fixing machinery, or by other means appropriate to national conditions.

Article 5 – The right to organise

With a view to ensuring or promoting the freedom of workers and employers to form local, national or international organisations for the protection of their economic and social interests and to join those organisations, the Parties undertake that national law shall not be such as to impair, nor shall it be so applied as to impair, this freedom. The extent to which the guarantees provided for in this article shall apply to the police shall be determined by national laws or regulations. The principle governing the application to the members of the armed forces of these guarantees and the extent to which they shall apply to persons in this category shall equally be determined by national laws or regulations.

Article 6 – The right to bargain collectively

With a view to ensuring the effective exercise of the right to bargain collectively, the Parties undertake:

1. to promote joint consultation between workers and employers;

2. to promote, where necessary and appropriate, machinery for voluntary negotiations between employers or employers' organisations and workers' organisations, with a view to the regulation of terms and conditions of employment by means of collective agreements;

3. to promote the establishment and use of appropriate machinery for conciliation and voluntary arbitration for the settlement of labour disputes;

and recognise:

4. the right of workers and employers to collective action in cases of conflicts of interest, including the right to strike, subject to obligations that might arise out of collective agreements previously entered into.

Article 7 – The right of children and young persons to protection

With a view to ensuring the effective exercise of the right of children and young persons to protection, the Parties undertake:

1. to provide that the minimum age of admission to employment shall be fifteen years, subject to exceptions for children employed in prescribed light work without harm to their health, morals or education;

2. to provide that the minimum age of admission to employment shall be eighteen years with respect to prescribed occupations regarded as dangerous or unhealthy;

3. to provide that persons who are still subject to compulsory education shall not be employed in such work as would deprive them of the full benefit of their education;

4. to provide that the working hours of persons under eighteen years of age shall be limited in accordance with the needs of their development, and particularly with their need for vocational training;

5. to recognise the right of young workers and apprentices to a fair wage or other appropriate allowances;

6. to provide that the time spent by young persons in vocational training during the normal working hours with the consent of the employer shall be treated as forming part of the working day;

7. to provide that employed persons of under eighteen years of age shall be entitled to a minimum of four weeks' annual holiday with pay;

8. to provide that persons under eighteen years of age shall not be employed in night work with the exception of certain occupations provided for by national laws or regulations;

9. to provide that persons under eighteen years of age employed in occupations prescribed by national laws or regulations shall be subject to regular medical control;

10. to ensure special protection against physical and moral dangers to which children and young persons are exposed, and particularly against those resulting directly or indirectly from their work.

Article 8 – The right of employed women to protection of maternity

With a view to ensuring the effective exercise of the right of employed women to the protection of maternity, the Parties undertake:

1. to provide either by paid leave, by adequate social security benefits or by benefits from public funds for employed women to take

leave before and after childbirth up to a total of at least fourteen weeks;

2. to consider it as unlawful for an employer to give a woman notice of dismissal during the period from the time she notifies her employer that she is pregnant until the end of her maternity leave, or to give her notice of dismissal at such a time that the notice would expire during such a period;

3. to provide that mothers who are nursing their infants shall be entitled to sufficient time off for this purpose;

4. to regulate the employment in night work of pregnant women, women who have recently given birth and women nursing their infants;

5. to prohibit the employment of pregnant women, women who have recently given birth or who are nursing their infants in underground mining and all other work which is unsuitable by reason of its dangerous, unhealthy or arduous nature and to take appropriate measures to protect the employment rights of these women.

Article 9 – The right to vocational guidance

With a view to ensuring the effective exercise of the right to vocational guidance, the Parties undertake to provide or promote, as necessary, a service which will assist all persons, including the handicapped, to solve problems related to occupational choice and progress, with due regard to the individual's characteristics and their relation to occupational opportunity: this assistance should be available free of charge, both to young persons, including schoolchildren, and to adults.

Article 10 – The right to vocational training

With a view to ensuring the effective exercise of the right to vocational training, the Parties undertake:

1. to provide or promote, as necessary, the technical and vocational training of all persons, including the handicapped, in consultation with employers' and workers' organisations, and to grant facilities for access to higher technical and university education, based solely on individual aptitude;

2. to provide or promote a system of apprenticeship and other systematic arrangements for training young boys and girls in their various employments;

3. to provide or promote, as necessary:

    a. adequate and readily available training facilities for adult workers;

    b. special facilities for the retraining of adult workers needed as a result of technological development or new trends in employment;

4. to provide or promote, as necessary, special measures for the retraining and reintegration of the long-term unemployed;

5. to encourage the full utilisation of the facilities provided by appropriate measures such as:

   a. reducing or abolishing any fees or charges;

   b. granting financial assistance in appropriate cases;

   c. including in the normal working hours time spent on supplementary training taken by the worker, at the request of his employer, during employment;

   d. ensuring, through adequate supervision, in consultation with the employers' and workers' organisations, the efficiency of apprenticeship and other training arrangements for young workers, and the adequate protection of young workers generally.

Article 11 – *The right to protection of health*

With a view to ensuring the effective exercise of the right to protection of health, the Parties undertake, either directly or in co-operation with public or private organisations, to take appropriate measures designed *inter alia*:

1. to remove as far as possible the causes of ill-health;

2. to provide advisory and educational facilities for the promotion of health and the encouragement of individual responsibility in matters of health;

3. to prevent as far as possible epidemic, endemic and other diseases, as well as accidents.

Article 12 – *The right to social security*

With a view to ensuring the effective exercise of the right to social security, the Parties undertake:

1. to establish or maintain a system of social security;

2. to maintain the social security system at a satisfactory level at least equal to that necessary for the ratification of the European Code of Social Security;

3. to endeavour to raise progressively the system of social security to a higher level;

4. to take steps, by the conclusion of appropriate bilateral and multilateral agreements or by other means, and subject to the conditions laid down in such agreements, in order to ensure:

   a. equal treatment with their own nationals of the nationals of other Parties in respect of social security rights, including the retention of benefits arising out of social security legislation, whatever movements the persons protected may undertake between the territories of the Parties;

   b. the granting, maintenance and resumption of social security rights by such means as the accumulation of insurance or employment periods completed under the legislation of each of the Parties.

Article 13 – *The right to social and medical assistance*

With a view to ensuring the effective exercise of the right to social and medical assistance, the Parties undertake:

1. to ensure that any person who is without adequate resources and who is unable to secure such resources either by his own efforts or from other sources, in particular by benefits under a social security scheme, be granted adequate assistance, and, in case of sickness, the care necessitated by his condition;

2. to ensure that persons receiving such assistance shall not, for that reason, suffer from a diminution of their political or social rights;

3. to provide that everyone may receive by appropriate public or private services such advice and personal help as may be required to prevent, to remove, or to alleviate personal or family want;

4. to apply the provisions referred to in paragraphs 1, 2 and 3 of this article on an equal footing with their nationals to nationals of other Parties lawfully within their territories, in accordance with their obligations under the European Convention on Social and Medical Assistance, signed at Paris on 11 December 1953.

Article 14 – *The right to benefit from social welfare services*

With a view to ensuring the effective exercise of the right to benefit from social welfare services, the Parties undertake:

1. to promote or provide services which, by using methods of social work, would contribute to the welfare and development of both individuals and groups in the community, and to their adjustment to the social environment;

2. to encourage the participation of individuals and voluntary or other organisations in the establishment and maintenance of such services.

Article 15 – *The right of persons with disabilities to independence, social integration and participation in the life of the community*

With a view to ensuring to persons with disabilities, irrespective of age and the nature and origin of their disabilities, the effective exercise of the right to independence, social integration and participation in the life of the community, the Parties undertake, in particular:

1. to take the necessary measures to provide persons with disabilities with guidance, education and vocational training in the framework of general schemes wherever possible or, where this is not possible, through specialised bodies, public or private;

2. to promote their access to employment through all measures tending to encourage employers to hire and keep in employment

persons with disabilities in the ordinary working environment and to adjust the working conditions to the needs of the disabled or, where this is not possible by reason of the disability, by arranging for or creating sheltered employment according to the level of disability. In certain cases, such measures may require recourse to specialised placement and support services;

3. to promote their full social integration and participation in the life of the community in particular through measures, including technical aids, aiming to overcome barriers to communication and mobility and enabling access to transport, housing, cultural activities and leisure.

Article 16 – The right of the family to social, legal and economic protection

With a view to ensuring the necessary conditions for the full development of the family, which is a fundamental unit of society, the Parties undertake to promote the economic, legal and social protection of family life by such means as social and family benefits, fiscal arrangements, provision of family housing, benefits for the newly married and other appropriate means.

Article 17 – The right of children and young persons to social, legal and economic protection

With a view to ensuring the effective exercise of the right of children and young persons to grow up in an environment which encourages the full development of their personality and of their physical and mental capacities, the Parties undertake, either directly or in co-operation with public and private organisations, to take all appropriate and necessary measures designed:

1. *a.* to ensure that children and young persons, taking account of the rights and duties of their parents, have the care, the assistance, the education and the training they need, in particular by providing for the establishment or maintenance of institutions and services sufficient and adequate for this purpose;

    b. to protect children and young persons against negligence, violence or exploitation;

    c. to provide protection and special aid from the state for children and young persons temporarily or definitively deprived of their family's support;

2. to provide to children and young persons a free primary and secondary education as well as to encourage regular attendance at schools.

Article 18 – The right to engage in a gainful occupation in the territory of other Parties

With a view to ensuring the effective exercise of the right to engage in a gainful occupation in the territory of any other Party, the Parties undertake:

1. to apply existing regulations in a spirit of liberality;

2. to simplify existing formalities and to reduce or abolish chancery dues and other charges payable by foreign workers or their employers;

3. to liberalise, individually or collectively, regulations governing the employment of foreign workers;

and recognise:

4. the right of their nationals to leave the country to engage in a gainful occupation in the territories of the other Parties.

Article 19 – The right of migrant workers and their families to protection and assistance

With a view to ensuring the effective exercise of the right of migrant workers and their families to protection and assistance in the territory of any other Party, the Parties undertake:

1. to maintain or to satisfy themselves that there are maintained adequate and free services to assist such workers, particularly in obtaining accurate information, and to take all appropriate steps, so far as national laws and regulations permit, against misleading propaganda relating to emigration and immigration;

2. to adopt appropriate measures within their own jurisdiction to facilitate the departure, journey and reception of such workers and their families, and to provide, within their own jurisdiction, appropriate services for health, medical attention and good hygienic conditions during the journey;

3. to promote co-operation, as appropriate, between social services, public and private, in emigration and immigration countries;

4. to secure for such workers lawfully within their territories, insofar as such matters are regulated by law or regulations or are subject to the control of administrative authorities, treatment not less favourable than that of their own nationals in respect of the following matters:

    a. remuneration and other employment and working conditions;

    b. membership of trade unions and enjoyment of the benefits of collective bargaining;

    c. accommodation;

5. to secure for such workers lawfully within their territories treatment not less favourable than that of their own nationals with

regard to employment taxes, dues or contributions payable in respect of employed persons;

6. to facilitate as far as possible the reunion of the family of a foreign worker permitted to establish himself in the territory;

7. to secure for such workers lawfully within their territories treatment not less favourable than that of their own nationals in respect of legal proceedings relating to matters referred to in this article;

8. to secure that such workers lawfully residing within their territories are not expelled unless they endanger national security or offend against public interest or morality;

9. to permit, within legal limits, the transfer of such parts of the earnings and savings of such workers as they may desire;

10. to extend the protection and assistance provided for in this article to self-employed migrants insofar as such measures apply;

11. to promote and facilitate the teaching of the national language of the receiving state or, if there are several, one of these languages, to migrant workers and members of their families;

12. to promote and facilitate, as far as practicable, the teaching of the migrant worker's mother tongue to the children of the migrant worker.

Article 20 – *The right to equal opportunities and equal treatment in matters of employment and occupation without discrimination on the grounds of sex*

With a view to ensuring the effective exercise of the right to equal opportunities and equal treatment in matters of employment and occupation without discrimination on the grounds of sex, the Parties undertake to recognise that right and to take appropriate measures to ensure or promote its application in the following fields:

a. access to employment, protection against dismissal and occupational reintegration;

b. vocational guidance, training, retraining and rehabilitation;

c. terms of employment and working conditions, including remuneration;

d. career development, including promotion.

Article 21 – *The right to information and consultation*

With a view to ensuring the effective exercise of the right of workers to be informed and consulted within the undertaking, the Parties undertake to adopt or encourage measures enabling workers or their representatives, in accordance with national legislation and practice:

a. to be informed regularly or at the appropriate time and in a comprehensible way about the economic and financial situation of the undertaking employing them, on the understanding that the disclosure of certain information which could be prejudicial to the undertaking may be refused or subject to confidentiality; and

b. to be consulted in good time on proposed decisions which could substantially affect the interests of workers, particularly on those decisions which could have an important impact on the employment situation in the undertaking.

Article 22 – The right to take part in the determination and improvement of the working conditions and working environment

With a view to ensuring the effective exercise of the right of workers to take part in the determination and improvement of the working conditions and working environment in the undertaking, the Parties undertake to adopt or encourage measures enabling workers or their representatives, in accordance with national legislation and practice, to contribute:

a. to the determination and the improvement of the working conditions, work organisation and working environment;

b. to the protection of health and safety within the undertaking;

c. to the organisation of social and socio-cultural services and facilities within the undertaking;

d. to the supervision of the observance of regulations on these matters.

Article 23 – The right of elderly persons to social protection

With a view to ensuring the effective exercise of the right of elderly persons to social protection, the Parties undertake to adopt or encourage, either directly or in co-operation with public or private organisations, appropriate measures designed in particular:

–   to enable elderly persons to remain full members of society for as long as possible, by means of:

   a. adequate resources enabling them to lead a decent life and play an active part in public, social and cultural life;

   b. provision of information about services and facilities available for elderly persons and their opportunities to make use of them;

–   to enable elderly persons to choose their life-style freely and to lead independent lives in their familiar surroundings for as long as they wish and are able, by means of:

   a. provision of housing suited to their needs and their state of health or of adequate support for adapting their housing;

   b. the health care and the services necessitated by their state;

–   to guarantee elderly persons living in institutions appropriate support, while respecting their privacy, and participation in decisions concerning living conditions in the institution.

Article 24 – The right to protection in cases of termination of employment

With a view to ensuring the effective exercise of the right of workers to protection in cases of termination of employment, the Parties undertake to recognise:

a. the right of all workers not to have their employment terminated without valid reasons for such termination connected with their capacity or conduct or based on the operational requirements of the undertaking, establishment or service;

b. the right of workers whose employment is terminated without a valid reason to adequate compensation or other appropriate relief.

To this end, the Parties undertake to ensure that a worker who considers that his employment has been terminated without a valid reason shall have the right to appeal to an impartial body.

Article 25 – The right of workers to the protection of their claims in the event of the insolvency of their employer

With a view to ensuring the effective exercise of the right of workers to the protection of their claims in the event of the insolvency of their employer, the Parties undertake to provide that workers' claims arising from contracts of employment or employment relationships be guaranteed by a guarantee institution or by any other effective form of protection.

Article 26 – The right to dignity at work

With a view to ensuring the effective exercise of the right of all workers to protection of their dignity at work, the Parties undertake, in consultation with employers' and workers' organisations:

1. to promote awareness, information and prevention of sexual harassment in the workplace or in relation to work and to take all appropriate measures to protect workers from such conduct;

2. to promote awareness, information and prevention of recurrent reprehensible or distinctly negative and offensive actions directed against individual workers in the workplace or in relation to work and to take all appropriate measures to protect workers from such conduct.

Article 27 – The right of workers with family responsibilities to equal opportunities and equal treatment

With a view to ensuring the exercise of the right to equality of opportunity and treatment for men and women workers with family responsibilities and between such workers and other workers, the Parties undertake:

1. to take appropriate measures:

    a. to enable workers with family responsibilities to enter and remain in employment, as well as to re-enter employment after an absence due to those responsibilities, including measures in the field of vocational guidance and training;

b. to take account of their needs in terms of conditions of employment and social security;

c. to develop or promote services, public or private, in particular child daycare services and other childcare arrangements;

2. to provide a possibility for either parent to obtain, during a period after maternity leave, parental leave to take care of a child, the duration and conditions of which should be determined by national legislation, collective agreements or practice;

3. to ensure that family responsibilities shall not, as such, constitute a valid reason for termination of employment.

Article 28 – The right of workers' representatives to protection in the undertaking and facilities to be accorded to them

With a view to ensuring the effective exercise of the right of workers' representatives to carry out their functions, the Parties undertake to ensure that in the undertaking:

a. they enjoy effective protection against acts prejudicial to them, including dismissal, based on their status or activities as workers' representatives within the undertaking;

b. they are afforded such facilities as may be appropriate in order to enable them to carry out their functions promptly and efficiently, account being taken of the industrial relations system of the country and the needs, size and capabilities of the undertaking concerned.

Article 29 – The right to information and consultation in collective redundancy procedures

With a view to ensuring the effective exercise of the right of workers to be informed and consulted in situations of collective redundancies, the Parties undertake to ensure that employers shall inform and consult workers' representatives, in good time prior to such collective redundancies, on ways and means of avoiding collective redundancies or limiting their occurrence and mitigating their consequences, for example by recourse to accompanying social measures aimed, in particular, at aid for the redeployment or retraining of the workers concerned.

Article 30 – The right to protection against poverty and social exclusion

With a view to ensuring the effective exercise of the right to protection against poverty and social exclusion, the Parties undertake:

a. to take measures within the framework of an overall and co-ordinated approach to promote the effective access of persons who live or risk living in a situation of social exclusion or poverty, as well as their families, to, in particular, employment, housing, training, education, culture and social and medical assistance;

b. to review these measures with a view to their adaptation if necessary.

Article 31 – *The right to housing*

With a view to ensuring the effective exercise of the right to housing, the Parties undertake to take measures designed:

1. to promote access to housing of an adequate standard;
2. to prevent and reduce homelessness with a view to its gradual elimination;
3. to make the price of housing accessible to those without adequate resources.

Part III

Article A – *Undertakings*

1. Subject to the provisions of Article B below, each of the Parties undertakes:

    a. to consider Part I of this Charter as a declaration of the aims which it will pursue by all appropriate means, as stated in the introductory paragraph of that part;

    b. to consider itself bound by at least six of the following nine articles of Part II of this Charter: Articles 1, 5, 6, 7, 12, 13, 16, 19 and 20;

    c. to consider itself bound by an additional number of articles or numbered paragraphs of Part II of the Charter which it may select, provided that the total number of articles or numbered paragraphs by which it is bound is not less than sixteen articles or sixty-three numbered paragraphs.

2. The articles or paragraphs selected in accordance with sub-paragraphs *b* and *c* of paragraph 1 of this article shall be notified to the Secretary General of the Council of Europe at the time when the instrument of ratification, acceptance or approval is deposited.

3. Any Party may, at a later date, declare by notification addressed to the Secretary General that it considers itself bound by any articles or any numbered paragraphs of Part II of the Charter which it has not already accepted under the terms of paragraph 1 of this article. Such undertakings subsequently given shall be deemed to be an integral part of the ratification, acceptance or approval and shall have the same effect as from the first day of the month following the expiration of a period of one month after the date of the notification.

4. Each Party shall maintain a system of labour inspection appropriate to national conditions.

Article B – Links with the European Social Charter and the 1988 Additional Protocol

1. No Contracting Party to the European Social Charter or Party to the Additional Protocol of 5 May 1988 may ratify, accept or approve this Charter without considering itself bound by at least the provisions corresponding to the provisions of the European Social Charter and, where appropriate, of the Additional Protocol, to which it was bound.

2. Acceptance of the obligations of any provision of this Charter shall, from the date of entry into force of those obligations for the Party concerned, result in the corresponding provision of the European Social Charter and, where appropriate, of its Additional Protocol of 1988 ceasing to apply to the Party concerned in the event of that Party being bound by the first of those instruments or by both instruments.

Part IV

Article C – Supervision of the implementation of the undertakings contained in this Charter

The implementation of the legal obligations contained in this Charter shall be submitted to the same supervision as the European Social Charter.

Article D – Collective complaints

1. The provisions of the Additional Protocol to the European Social Charter providing for a system of collective complaints shall apply to the undertakings given in this Charter for the States which have ratified the said Protocol.

2. Any State which is not bound by the Additional Protocol to the European Social Charter providing for a system of collective complaints may when depositing its instrument of ratification, acceptance or approval of this Charter or at any time thereafter, declare by notification addressed to the Secretary General of the Council of Europe, that it accepts the supervision of its obligations under this Charter following the procedure provided for in the said Protocol.

Part V

Article E – Non-discrimination

The enjoyment of the rights set forth in this Charter shall be secured without discrimination on any ground such as race, colour, sex, language, religion, political or other opinion, national extraction or social origin, health, association with a national minority, birth or other status.

Article F – Derogations in time of war or public emergency

1. In time of war or other public emergency threatening the life of the nation any Party may take measures derogating from its obligations under this Charter to the extent strictly required by the exigencies of the situation, provided that such measures are not inconsistent with its other obligations under international law.

2. Any Party which has availed itself of this right of derogation shall, within a reasonable lapse of time, keep the Secretary General of the Council of Europe fully informed of the measures taken and of the reasons therefor. It shall likewise inform the Secretary General when such measures have ceased to operate and the provisions of the Charter which it has accepted are again being fully executed.

Article G – Restrictions

1. The rights and principles set forth in Part I when effectively realised, and their effective exercise as provided for in Part II, shall not be subject to any restrictions or limitations not specified in those parts, except such as are prescribed by law and are necessary in a democratic society for the protection of the rights and freedoms of others or for the protection of public interest, national security, public health, or morals.

2. The restrictions permitted under this Charter to the rights and obligations set forth herein shall not be applied for any purpose other than that for which they have been prescribed.

Article H – Relations between the Charter and domestic law or international agreements

The provisions of this Charter shall not prejudice the provisions of domestic law or of any bilateral or multilateral treaties, conventions or agreements which are already in force, or may come into force, under which more favourable treatment would be accorded to the persons protected.

Article I – Implementation of the undertakings given

1. Without prejudice to the methods of implementation foreseen in these articles the relevant provisions of Articles 1 to 31 of Part II of this Charter shall be implemented by:

    a. laws or regulations;

    b. agreements between employers or employers' organisations and workers' organisations;

    c. a combination of those two methods;

    d. other appropriate means.

2. Compliance with the undertakings deriving from the provisions of paragraphs 1, 2, 3, 4, 5 and 7 of Article 2, paragraphs 4, 6 and 7 of

Article 7, paragraphs 1, 2, 3 and 5 of Article 10 and Articles 21 and 22 of Part II of this Charter shall be regarded as effective if the provisions are applied, in accordance with paragraph 1 of this article, to the great majority of the workers concerned.

Article J – Amendments

1. Any amendment to Parts I and II of this Charter with the purpose of extending the rights guaranteed in this Charter as well as any amendment to Parts III to VI, proposed by a Party or by the Governmental Committee, shall be communicated to the Secretary General of the Council of Europe and forwarded by the Secretary General to the Parties to this Charter.

2. Any amendment proposed in accordance with the provisions of the preceding paragraph shall be examined by the Governmental Committee which shall submit the text adopted to the Committee of Ministers for approval after consultation with the Parliamentary Assembly. After its approval by the Committee of Ministers this text shall be forwarded to the Parties for acceptance.

3. Any amendment to Part I and to Part II of this Charter shall enter into force, in respect of those Parties which have accepted it, on the first day of the month following the expiration of a period of one month after the date on which three Parties have informed the Secretary General that they have accepted it.

In respect of any Party which subsequently accepts it, the amendment shall enter into force on the first day of the month following the expiration of a period of one month after the date on which that Party has informed the Secretary General of its acceptance.

4. Any amendment to Parts III to VI of this Charter shall enter into force on the first day of the month following the expiration of a period of one month after the date on which all Parties have informed the Secretary General that they have accepted it.

Part VI

Article K – Signature, ratification and entry into force

1. This Charter shall be open for signature by the member States of the Council of Europe. It shall be subject to ratification, acceptance or approval. Instruments of ratification, acceptance or approval shall be deposited with the Secretary General of the Council of Europe.

2. This Charter shall enter into force on the first day of the month following the expiration of a period of one month after the date on which three member States of the Council of Europe have expressed their consent to be bound by this Charter in accordance with the preceding paragraph.

3. In respect of any member State which subsequently expresses its consent to be bound by this Charter, it shall enter into force on the first day of the month following the expiration of a period of one month after the date of the deposit of the instrument of ratification, acceptance or approval.

Article L – Territorial application

1. This Charter shall apply to the metropolitan territory of each Party. Each signatory may, at the time of signature or of the deposit of its instrument of ratification, acceptance or approval, specify, by declaration addressed to the Secretary General of the Council of Europe, the territory which shall be considered to be its metropolitan territory for this purpose.

2. Any signatory may, at the time of signature or of the deposit of its instrument of ratification, acceptance or approval, or at any time thereafter, declare by notification addressed to the Secretary General of the Council of Europe, that the Charter shall extend in whole or in part to a non-metropolitan territory or territories specified in the said declaration for whose international relations it is responsible or for which it assumes international responsibility. It shall specify in the declaration the articles or paragraphs of Part II of the Charter which it accepts as binding in respect of the territories named in the declaration.

3. The Charter shall extend its application to the territory or territories named in the aforesaid declaration as from the first day of the month following the expiration of a period of one month after the date of receipt of the notification of such declaration by the Secretary General.

4. Any Party may declare at a later date by notification addressed to the Secretary General of the Council of Europe that, in respect of one or more of the territories to which the Charter has been applied in accordance with paragraph 2 of this article, it accepts as binding any articles or any numbered paragraphs which it has not already accepted in respect of that territory or territories. Such undertakings subsequently given shall be deemed to be an integral part of the original declaration in respect of the territory concerned, and shall have the same effect as from the first day of the month following the expiration of a period of one month after the date of receipt of such notification by the Secretary General.

Article M – Denunciation

1. Any Party may denounce this Charter only at the end of a period of five years from the date on which the Charter entered into force for it, or at the end of any subsequent period of two years, and in either case after giving six months' notice to the Secretary General of the Council of Europe who shall inform the other Parties accordingly.

2.   Any Party may, in accordance with the provisions set out in the preceding paragraph, denounce any article or paragraph of Part II of the Charter accepted by it provided that the number of articles or paragraphs by which this Party is bound shall never be less than sixteen in the former case and sixty-three in the latter and that this number of articles or paragraphs shall continue to include the articles selected by the Party among those to which special reference is made in Article A, paragraph 1, sub-paragraph b.

3.   Any Party may denounce the present Charter or any of the articles or paragraphs of Part II of the Charter under the conditions specified in paragraph 1 of this article in respect of any territory to which the said Charter is applicable, by virtue of a declaration made in accordance with paragraph 2 of Article L.

Article N – Appendix

The appendix to this Charter shall form an integral part of it.

Article O – Notifications

The Secretary General of the Council of Europe shall notify the member States of the Council and the Director General of the International Labour Office of:

a.   any signature;

b.   the deposit of any instrument of ratification, acceptance or approval;

c.   any date of entry into force of this Charter in accordance with Article K;

d.   any declaration made in application of Articles A, paragraphs 2 and 3, D, paragraphs 1 and 2, F, paragraph 2, L, paragraphs 1, 2, 3 and 4;

e.   any amendment in accordance with Article J;

f.   any denunciation in accordance with Article M;

g.   any other act, notification or communication relating to this Charter.

In witness whereof, the undersigned, being duly authorised thereto, have signed this revised Charter.

Done at Strasbourg, this 3rd day of May 1996, in English and French, both texts being equally authentic, in a single copy which shall be deposited in the archives of the Council of Europe. The Secretary General of the Council of Europe shall transmit certified copies to each member State of the Council of Europe and to the Director General of the International Labour Office.

Appendix to the revised European Social Charter

Scope of the revised European Social Charter in terms of persons protected

1. Without prejudice to Article 12, paragraph 4, and Article 13, paragraph 4, the persons covered by Articles 1 to 17 and 20 to 31 include foreigners only in so far as they are nationals of other Parties lawfully resident or working regularly within the territory of the Party concerned, subject to the understanding that these articles are to be interpreted in the light of the provisions of Articles 18 and 19.

This interpretation would not prejudice the extension of similar facilities to other persons by any of the Parties.

2. Each Party will grant to refugees as defined in the Convention relating to the Status of Refugees, signed in Geneva on 28 July 1951 and in the Protocol of 31 January 1967, and lawfully staying in its territory, treatment as favourable as possible, and in any case not less favourable than under the obligations accepted by the Party under the said convention and under any other existing international instruments applicable to those refugees.

3. Each Party will grant to stateless persons as defined in the Convention on the Status of Stateless Persons done in New York on 28 September 1954 and lawfully staying in its territory, treatment as favourable as possible and in any case not less favourable than under the obligations accepted by the Party under the said instrument and under any other existing international instruments applicable to those stateless persons.

Part I, paragraph 18, and Part II, Article 18, paragraph 1

It is understood that these provisions are not concerned with the question of entry into the territories of the Parties and do not prejudice the provisions of the European Convention on Establishment, signed in Paris on 13 December 1955.

Part II

Article 1, paragraph 2

This provision shall not be interpreted as prohibiting or authorising any union security clause or practice.

Article 2, paragraph 6

Parties may provide that this provision shall not apply:

a. to workers having a contract or employment relationship with a total duration not exceeding one month and/or with a working week not exceeding eight hours;

b. where the contract or employment relationship is of a casual and/or specific nature, provided, in these cases, that its non-application is justified by objective considerations.

Article 3, paragraph 4

It is understood that for the purposes of this provision the functions, organisation and conditions of operation of these services shall be determined by national laws or regulations, collective agreements or other means appropriate to national conditions.

Article 4, paragraph 4

This provision shall be so understood as not to prohibit immediate dismissal for any serious offence.

Article 4, paragraph 5

It is understood that a Party may give the undertaking required in this paragraph if the great majority of workers are not permitted to suffer deductions from wages either by law or through collective agreements or arbitration awards, the exceptions being those persons not so covered.

Article 6, paragraph 4

It is understood that each Party may, insofar as it is concerned, regulate the exercise of the right to strike by law, provided that any further restriction that this might place on the right can be justified under the terms of Article G.

Article 7, paragraph 2

This provision does not prevent Parties from providing in their legislation that young persons not having reached the minimum age laid down may perform work in so far as it is absolutely necessary for their vocational training where such work is carried out in accordance with conditions prescribed by the competent authority and measures are taken to protect the health and safety of these young persons.

Article 7, paragraph 8

It is understood that a Party may give the undertaking required in this paragraph if it fulfils the spirit of the undertaking by providing by law that the great majority of persons under eighteen years of age shall not be employed in night work.

Article 8, paragraph 2

This provision shall not be interpreted as laying down an absolute prohibition. Exceptions could be made, for instance, in the following cases:

a. if an employed woman has been guilty of misconduct which justifies breaking off the employment relationship;

b. if the undertaking concerned ceases to operate;

c. if the period prescribed in the employment contract has expired.

Article 12, paragraph 4

The words "and subject to the conditions laid down in such agreements" in the introduction to this paragraph are taken to imply *inter alia* that with regard to benefits which are available independently of any insurance contribution, a Party may require the completion of a prescribed period of residence before granting such benefits to nationals of other Parties.

Article 13, paragraph 4

Governments not Parties to the European Convention on Social and Medical Assistance may ratify the Charter in respect of this paragraph provided that they grant to nationals of other Parties a treatment which is in conformity with the provisions of the said convention.

Article 16

It is understood that the protection afforded in this provision covers single-parent families.

Article 17

It is understood that this provision covers all persons below the age of eighteen years, unless under the law applicable to the child majority is attained earlier, without prejudice to the other specific provisions provided by the Charter, particularly Article 7.

This does not imply an obligation to provide compulsory education up to the above-mentioned age.

Article 19, paragraph 6

For the purpose of applying this provision, the term "family of a foreign worker" is understood to mean at least the worker's spouse and unmarried children, as long as the latter are considered to be minors by the receiving State and are dependent on the migrant worker.

Article 20

1. It is understood that social security matters, as well as other provisions relating to unemployment benefit, old age benefit and survivor's benefit, may be excluded from the scope of this article.

2. Provisions concerning the protection of women, particularly as regards pregnancy, confinement and the post-natal period, shall not be deemed to be discrimination as referred to in this article.

3. This article shall not prevent the adoption of specific measures aimed at removing *de facto* inequalities.

4. Occupational activities which, by reason of their nature or the context in which they are carried out, can be entrusted only to persons of a particular sex may be excluded from the scope of this article or some of its provisions. This provision is not to be interpreted as requiring the Parties to embody in laws or regulations a list of occupations which, by reason of their nature or the context in which they are carried out, may be reserved to persons of a particular sex.

Articles 21 and 22

1. For the purpose of the application of these articles, the term "workers' representatives" means persons who are recognised as such under national legislation or practice.

2 The terms 'national legislation and practice" embrace as the case may be, in addition to laws and regulations, collective agreements, other agreements between employers and workers' representatives, customs as well as relevant case law.

3 For the purpose of the application of these articles, the term "undertaking" is understood as referring to a set of tangible and intangible components, with or without legal personality, formed to produce goods or provide services for financial gain and with power to determine its own market policy.

4 It is understood that religious communities and their institutions may be excluded from the application of these articles, even if these institutions are "undertakings" within the meaning of paragraph 3. Establishments pursuing activities which are inspired by certain ideals or guided by certain moral concepts, ideals and concepts which are protected by national legislation, may be excluded from the application of these articles to such an extent as is necessary to protect the orientation of the undertaking.

5 It is understood that where in a state the rights set out in these articles are exercised in the various establishments of the undertaking, the Party concerned is to be considered as fulfilling the obligations deriving from these provisions.

6. The Parties may exclude from the field of application of these articles, those undertakings employing less than a certain number of workers, to be determined by national legislation or practice.

Article 22

1. This provision affects neither the powers and obligations of states as regards the adoption of health and safety regulations for workplaces, nor the powers and responsibilities of the bodies in charge of monitoring their application.

2. The terms "social and socio-cultural services and facilities" are understood as referring to the social and/or cultural facilities for

71

workers provided by some undertakings such as welfare assistance, sports fields, rooms for nursing mothers, libraries, children's holiday camps, etc.

Article 23, paragraph 1

For the purpose of the application of this paragraph, the term "for as long as possible" refers to the elderly person's physical, psychological and intellectual capacities.

Article 24

1. It is understood that for the purposes of this article the terms "termination of employment" and "terminated" mean termination of employment at the initiative of the employer.

2. It is understood that this article covers all workers but that a Party may exclude from some or all of its protection the following categories of employed persons:

    a. workers engaged under a contract of employment for a specified period of time or a specified task;

    b. workers undergoing a period of probation or a qualifying period of employment, provided that this is determined in advance and is of a reasonable duration;

    c. workers engaged on a casual basis for a short period.

3. For the purpose of this article the following, in particular, shall not constitute valid reasons for termination of employment:

    a. trade union membership or participation in union activities outside working hours, or, with the consent of the employer, within working hours;

    b. seeking office as, acting or having acted in the capacity of a workers' representative;

    c. the filing of a complaint or the participation in proceedings against an employer involving alleged violation of laws or regulations or recourse to competent administrative authorities;

    d. race, colour, sex, marital status, family responsibilities, pregnancy, religion, political opinion, national extraction or social origin;

    e. maternity or parental leave;

    f. temporary absence from work due to illness or injury.

4. It is understood that compensation or other appropriate relief in case of termination of employment without valid reasons shall be determined by national laws or regulations, collective agreements or other means appropriate to national conditions.

Article 25

1. It is understood that the competent national authority may, by way of exemption and after consulting organisations of employers and workers, exclude certain categories of workers from the protection provided in this provision by reason of the special nature of their employment relationship.

2. It is understood that the definition of the term "insolvency" must be determined by national law and practice.

3. The workers' claims covered by this provision shall include at least:

    a the workers' claims for wages relating to a prescribed period, which shall not be less than three months under a privilege system and eight weeks under a guarantee system, prior to the insolvency or to the termination of employment;

    b the workers' claims for holiday pay due as a result of work performed during the year in which the insolvency or the termination of employment occurred;

    c the workers' claims for amounts due in respect of other types of paid absence relating to a prescribed period, which shall not be less than three months under a privilege system and eight weeks under a guarantee system, prior to the insolvency or the termination of the employment.

4. National laws or regulations may limit the protection of workers' claims to a prescribed amount, which shall be of a socially acceptable level.

Article 26

It is understood that this article does not require that legislation be enacted by the Parties.

It is understood that paragraph 2 does not cover sexual harassment.

Article 27

It is understood that this article applies to men and women workers with family responsibilities in relation to their dependent children as well as in relation to other members of their immediate family who clearly need their care or support where such responsibilities restrict their possibilities of preparing for, entering, participating in or advancing in economic activity. The terms "dependent children" and "other members of their immediate family who clearly need their care and support" mean persons defined as such by the national legislation of the Party concerned.

Articles 28 and 29

For the purpose of the application of this article, the term "workers' representatives" means persons who are recognised as such under national legislation or practice.

Part III

It is understood that the Charter contains legal obligations of an international character, the application of which is submitted solely to the supervision provided for in Part IV thereof.

Article A, paragraph 1

It is understood that the numbered paragraphs may include articles consisting of only one paragraph.

Article B, paragraph 2

For the purpose of paragraph 2 of Article B, the provisions of the revised Charter correspond to the provisions of the Charter with the same article or paragraph number with the exception of:

a. Article 3, paragraph 2, of the revised Charter which corresponds to Article 3, paragraphs 1 and 3, of the Charter;

b. Article 3, paragraph 3, of the revised Charter which corresponds to Article 3, paragraphs 2 and 3, of the Charter;

c. Article 10, paragraph 5, of the revised Charter which corresponds to Article 10, paragraph 4, of the Charter;

d. Article 17, paragraph 1, of the revised Charter which corresponds to Article 17 of the Charter.

Part V

Article E

A differential treatment based on an objective and reasonable justification shall not be deemed discriminatory.

Article F

The terms "in time of war or other public emergency" shall be so understood as to cover also the threat of war.

Article I

It is understood that workers excluded in accordance with the appendix to Articles 21 and 22 are not taken into account in establishing the number of workers concerned.

Article J

The term "amendment" shall be extended so as to cover also the addition of new articles to the Charter.

II. Signatures, ratifications, declarations and reservations

A. Signatures and ratifications of the European Social Charter, its Protocols and the revised European Social Charter

Situation at 12 November 2001

Member States	European Social Charter 1961		Additional Protocol 1988		Amending Protocol 1991		Collective Complaints Protocol 1995		Revised European Social Charter 1996	
	Signature	Ratification	Signature	Ratification	Signature	Ratification	Signature	Ratification	Signature	Ratification
Albania	(1)	–	(1)	–	(1)	–	(1)	–	21/09/98	–
Andorra	(1)	–	(1)	–	(1)	–	(1)	–	04/11/00	–
Armenia	–	–	–	–	–	–	–	–	18/10/01	–
Austria	22/07/63	29/10/69	04/12/90	–	07/05/92	13/07/95	07/05/99	–	07/05/99	–
Azerbaijan	–	–	–	–	–	–	–	–	18/10/01	–
Belgium	18/10/61	16/10/90	20/05/92	–	22/10/91	21/09/00	14/05/96	–	03/05/96	–
Bulgaria	(2)	(2)	(3)	(3)	(2)	(2)	(4)	(4)	21/09/98	07/06/00
Croatia	08/03/99	–	08/03/99	–	08/03/99	–	08/03/99	–	–	–
Cyprus	22/05/67	07/03/68	05/05/88	(3)	21/10/91	01/06/93	09/11/95	06/08/96	03/05/96	27/09/00
Czech Republic	27/05/92*	3/11/99	27/05/92*	17/11/99	27/05/92*	17/11/99	–	–	04/11/00	–
Denmark	18/10/61	03/03/65	27/08/96	27/08/96	–	**	09/11/95	–	03/05/96	–
Estonia	(2)	(2)	(3)	(3)	(2)	(2)	(2)	–	04/05/98	11/09/00
Finland	09/02/90	29/04/91	09/02/90	29/04/91	16/03/92	18/08/94	09/11/95	17/07/98	03/05/96	–
France	18/10/61	09/03/73	22/06/89	(2)	21/10/91	24/05/95	09/11/95	07/05/99	03/05/96	07/05/99
Georgia	(1)	–	(1)	–	(1)	–	(1)	–	30/06/00	–

* date of signature by the Czech and Slovak Federal Republic.

** State whose ratification is necesary for the entry into force of the Protocol.

(1) State having signed the Revised Social Charter.

(2) State having ratified the Revised Social Charter.

(3) State having accepted the rights (or certain of the rights) guaranteed by the Protocol by ratifying the Revised Charter.

(4) State having accepted the collective complaints procedure by a declaration made in application of Article D para. 2 of Part IV of the Revised Social Charter.

Member States	European Social Charter 1961		Additional Protocol 1988		Amending Protocol 1991		Collective Complaints Protocol 1995		Revised European Scoial Charter 1996	
	Signature	Ratification	Signature	Ratification	Signature	Ratification	Signature	Ratification	Signature	Ratification
Germany	18/10/61	27/01/65	05/05/88	–	–	**	–	–	–	–
Greece	18/10/61	06/06/84	05/05/88	18/06/98	29/11/91	12/09/96	18/06/98	18/06/98	03/05/96	–
Hungary	13/12/91	08/07/99	–	–	13/12/91	**	–	–	–	–
Iceland	15/01/76	15/01/76	05/05/88	–	–	**	–	–	04/11/98	–
Ireland	18/10/61	07/10/64	(3)	(3)	14/05/97	14/05/97	04/11/00	04/11/00	04/11/00	04/11/00
Italy	18/10/61	22/10/65	05/05/88	26/05/94	21/10/91	27/01/95	09/11/95	03/11/97	03/05/96	05/07/99
Latvia	29/05/97	–	29/05/97	–	29/05/97	–	–	–	–	–
Liechtenstein	09/10/91	–	–	–	–	–	–	–	–	–
Lithuania	(2)	(2)	(3)	(3)	(2)	(2)	(2)	–	08/09/97	29/06/01
Luxembourg	18/10/61	10/10/91	05/05/88	–	21/10/91	**	–	–	11/02/98	–
Malta	26/05/88	04/10/88	–	–	21/10/91	16/02/94	–	–	–	–
Moldova	(1)	–	(1)	–	(1)	–	(1)	–	03/11/98	08/11/01
Netherlands	18/10/61	22/04/80	14/06/90	05/08/92	21/10/91	01/06/93	–	–	–	–
Norway	18/10/61	26/10/62	10/12/93	10/12/93	21/10/91	21/10/91	20/03/97	20/03/97	07/05/01	07/05/01
Poland	26/11/91	25/06/97	–	–	18/04/97	25/06/97	–	–	–	–
Portugal	01/06/82	30/09/91	(1)	–	24/02/92	08/03/93	09/11/95	20/03/98	03/05/96	(5)

Member States	European Social Charter 1961		Additional Protocol 1988		Amending Protocol 1991		Collective Complaints Protocol 1995		Revised European Scoial Charter 1996	
	Signature	Ratification	Signature	Ratification	Signature	Ratification	Signature	Ratification	Signature	Ratification
Romania	04/10/94	(2)	(3)	(3)	(2)	(2)	(2)	–	14/05/97	07/05/99
Russia	(1)	–	(1)	–	(1)	–	(1)	–	14/09/00	–
San Marino	–	–	–	–	–	–	–	–	18/10/01	–
Slovakia	27/05/92*	22/06/98	27/05/92*	22/06/98	27/05/92*	22/06/98	18/11/99	–	18/11/99	–
Slovenia	11/10/97	(2)	11/10/97	(3)	11/10/97	(2)	11/10/97	(4)	11/10/97	07/05/99
Spain	27/04/78	06/05/80	05/05/88	24/01/00	21/10/91	24/01/00	–	–	23/10/00	–
Sweden	18/10/61	17/12/62	05/05/88	05/05/89	21/10/91	18/03/92	09/11/95	29/05/98	03/05/96	29/05/98
Switzerland	06/05/76	–	–		–		–	–	–	–
"The former Yugoslav Republic of Macedonia"	05/05/98	–	05/05/98	–	–	–	–	–	–	–
Turkey	18/10/61	24/11/89	05/05/98	–	–	**	–	–	–	–
Ukraine	02/05/96	–	(1)	–	(1)	–	(1)	–	07/05/99	–
United Kingdom	18/10/61	11/07/62	–	–	21/10/91	**	–	–	07/11/97	–

* date of signature by the Czech and Slovak Federal Republic.

** State whose ratification is necesary for the entry into force of the Protocol.

(1) State having signed the Revised Social Charter.

(2) State having ratified the Revised Social Charter.

(3) State having accepted the rights (or certain of the rights) guaranteed by the Protocol by ratifying the Revised Charter.

(4) State having accepted the collective complaints procedure by a declaration made in application of Article D para. 2 of Part IV of the Revised Social Charter.

(5) Instrument of ratification announced but not yet deposited.

B. Tables of accepted provisions

**Table showing details of acceptance of the provisions
of the European Social Charter (1961)**

Provision of the Charter	Austria	Belgium	Czech Republic	Denmark	Finland	Germany
Article 1 (1)	■	■	■	■	■	■
Article 1 (2)	■	■	■	■	■	■
Article 1 (3)	■	■	■	■	■	■
Article 1 (4)	■	■	□	■	■	■
Article 2 (1)	□	■	■	□	■	■
Article 2 (2)	■	■	■	■	■	■
Article 2 (3)	■	■	■	■	■	■
Article 2 (4)	■	■	■	□	■	■
Article 2 (5)	■	■	■	■	■	■
Article 3 (1)	■	■	■	■	□	■
Article 3 (2)	■	■	■	■	□	■
Article 3 (3)	■	■	■	■	■	■
Article 4 (1)	■	■	□	■	□	■
Article 4 (2)	■	■	■	■	■	■
Article 4 (3)	■	■	■	■	■	■
Article 4 (4)	□	■	■	□	□	□
Article 4 (5)	■	■	■	□	■	■
Article 5	■	■	■	■	■	■
Article 6 (1)	■	■	■	■	■	■
Article 6 (2)	■	■	■	■	■	■

■ accepted   □ not accepted

	Greece	Hungary	Iceland	Luxembourg	Malta	Netherlands*	Poland	Slovakia	Spain	Turkey	United Kingdom
1	■	■	■	■	■	■	■	■	■	■	■
2	■	■	■	■	■	■	■	■	■	■	■
3	■	■	■	■	■	■	■	■	■	■	■
4	■	■	■	■	■	■	■	■	■	■	■
5	■	■	■	■	■	■	■	■	■	□	□
6	■	■	□	■	■	■	□	■	■	□	□
7	■	■	■	■	■	■	■	■	■	□	□
8	■	■	□	■	□	■	■	■	■	□	■
9	■	■	■	■	■	■	■	■	■	□	■
10	■	■	■	■	■	■	■	■	■	□	■
11	■	■	■	■	■	■	■	■	■	□	■
12	■	■	■	■	■	■	■	■	■	■	■
13	■	□	■	■	■	■	□	■	■	■	■
14	■	□	■	■	■	■	■	■	■	■	■
15	■	□	■	■	■	■	■	■	■	■	□
16	■	□	■	□	■	■	■	■	■	□	■
17	■	□	■	■	■	■	■	■	■	■	■
18	□	■	■	■	■	■	■	■	■	□	■
19	□	■	■	■	■	■	■	■	■	□	■
20	□	■	■	■	■	■	■	■	■	□	■

---

* As regards the Netherlands Antilles and Aruba, the Kingdom of the Netherlands has accepted Articles 1, 5, 6 and 16 and Article 1 of the Additional Protocol.

Provision of the Charter	Austria	Belgium	Czech Republic	Denmark	Finland	Germany
Article 6 (3)	■	■	■	■	■	■
Article 6 (4)		■	■	■	■	■
Article 7 (1)		■	■		■	■
Article 7 (2)	■	■	■		■	■
Article 7 (3)	■	■	■		■	■
Article 7 (4)	■	■	■	■	■	■
Article 7 (5)	■	■	■		■	■
Article 7 (6)		■	■			■
Article 7 (7)	■	■	■		■	■
Article 7 (8)	■	■	■		■	■
Article 7 (9)	■	■	■			■
Article 7 (10)	■	■	■	■	■	■
Article 8 (1)	■	■	■	■		■
Article 8 (2)	■	■	■	■		■
Article 8 (3)	■	■	■			■
Article 8 (4)	■	■	■			
Article 9	■	■		■	■	■
Article 10 (1)	■	■		■	■	■
Article 10 (2)	■	■		■	■	■
Article 10 (3)	■	■		■	■	■
Article 10 (4)	■	■		■	■	

	Greece	Hungary	Iceland	Luxembourg	Malta	Netherlands*	Poland	Slovakia	Spain	Turkey	United Kingdom
									1		
				2							

---

* As regards the Netherlands Antilles and Aruba, the Kingdom of the Netherlands has accepted Articles 1, 5, 6 and 16 and Article 1 of the Additional Protocol.
1. Spain has denounced sub-paragraph *b* with effect on 5 June 1991.
2. Only the provisions of paragraph 4 *a* and *d* have been accepted.

Provision of the Charter	Austria	Belgium	Czech Republic	Denmark	Finland	Germany
Article 11 (1)	■	■	■	■	■	■
Article 11 (2)	■	■	■	■	■	■
Article 11 (3)	■	■	■	■	■	■
Article 12 (1)	■	■	■	■	■	■
Article 12 (2)	■	■	■	■	■	■
Article 12 (3)	■	■	■	■	■	■
Article 12 (4)	■	■	■	■	■	■
Article 13 (1)	■	■	■	■	■	■
Article 13 (2)	■	■	■	■	■	■
Article 13 (3)	■	■	■	■	■	■
Article 13 (4)	■	■	■	■	■	■
Article 14 (1)	■	■	■	■	■	■
Article 14 (2)	■	■	■	■	■	■
Article 15 (1)	■	■		■	■	■
Article 15 (2)	■	■	■	■	■	■
Article 16	■	■	■	■	■	■
Article 17	■	■	■	■	■	■
Article 18 (1)	■	■		■	■	■
Article 18 (2)	■	■		■	■	■
Article 18 (3)		■		■	■	■
Article 18 (4)	■	■	■	■	■	■

Greece	Hungary	Iceland	Luxembourg	Malta	Netherlands*	Poland	Slovakia	Spain	Turkey	United Kingdom

---

*   As regards the Netherlands Antilles and Aruba, the Kingdom of the Netherlands
    has accepted Articles 1, 5, 6 and 16 and Article 1 of the Additional Protocol.

Provision of the Charter	Austria	Belgium	Czech Republic	Denmark	Finland	Germany
Article 19 (1)	■	■			■	■
Article 19 (2)	■	■			■	■
Article 19 (3)	■	■			■	■
Article 19 (4)		■			■	■
Article 19 (5)	■	■			■	■
Article 19 (6)	■	■			■	■
Article 19 (7)		■			■	■
Article 19 (8)		■			■	■
Article 19 (9)	■	■	■		■	■
Article 19 (10)		■				■

Table showing details of acceptance of the 1988 Additional Protocol

Provision of the Charter	Austria	Belgium	Czech Republic	Denmark	Finland	Germany
Article 1			■	■	■	
Article 2			■	■	■	
Article 3			■	■	■	
Article 4			■	■	■	

Greece	Hungary	Iceland	Luxembourg	Malta	Netherlands*	Poland	Slovakia	Spain	Turkey	United Kingdom

Greece	Hungary	Iceland	Luxembourg	Malta	Netherlands*	Poland	Slovakia	Spain	Turkey	United Kingdom

---

*   As regards the Netherlands Antilles and Aruba, the Kingdom of the Netherlands has accepted Articles 1, 5, 6 and 16 and Article 1 of the Additional Protocol.

Table showing details of acceptance of the provisions of the revised European Social Charter (1996)

■ accepted   □ not accepted

(● = accepted, ○ = not accepted)

Provision of the revised Charter	Bulgaria	Cyprus	Estonia	France	Ireland	Italy	Lithuania	Moldova	Norway	Portugal	Romania	Slovenia	Sweden
Article 1 (1)	●	●	●	●	●	●	●	●	●	●	●	●	●
Article 1 (2)	●	●	●	●	●	●	●	●	●	●	●	●	●
Article 1 (3)	●	●	●	●	●	●	●	●	●	●	●	●	●
Article 1 (4)	●	●	●	●	●	●	●	●	●	●	●	●	●
Article 2 (1)	○	●	●	●	●	●	●	●	●	●	●	●	●
Article 2 (2)	●	●	●	●	●	●	●	●	●	●	●	●	●
Article 2 (3)	○	●	○	●	●	●	●	●	●	●	○	●	●
Article 2 (4)	●	○	○	○	●	●	●	●	●	●	●	●	●
Article 2 (5)	●	●	●	●	●	●	●	●	●	●	●	●	●
Article 2 (6)	●	○	●	●	●	●	●	●	●	●	●	●	●
Article 2 (7)	●	●	●	●	●	●	●	●	○	●	●	●	●
Article 3 (1)	●	●	●	●	●	●	●	●	○	●	●	●	●
Article 3 (2)	●	●	●	●	●	●	●	●	●	●	●	●	●
Article 3 (3)	●	●	●	●	●	●	●	●	●	●	●	●	●
Article 3 (4)	●	○	○	●	●	●	●	●	○	○	○	●	●
Article 4 (1)	●	○	○	●	●	●	●	●	○	●	●	●	●
Article 4 (2)	●	●	●	●	●	●	●	●	○	●	●	●	●
Article 4 (3)	●	●	●	●	●	●	●	●	●	●	●	●	●
Article 4 (4)	●	●	●	●	●	●	●	●	●	●	●	●	●
Article 4 (5)	●	○	●	●	●	●	●	●	●	●	●	●	●
Article 5	●	●	●	●	●	●	●	●	●	●	●	●	●

Provision of the revised Charter	Bulgaria	Cyprus	Estonia	France	Ireland	Italy	Lithuania	Moldova	Norway	Portugal	Romania	Slovenia	Sweden
Article 6 (1)	■	■	■	■	■	■	■	■	■	■	■	■	■
Article 6 (2)	■	■	■	■	■	■	■	■	■	■	■	■	■
Article 6 (3)	■	■	■	■	■	■	■	■	■	■	■	■	■
Article 6 (4)	■	■	■	■	■	■	■	■	■	■	■	■	■
Article 7 (1)	■	■	■	■	■	■	■	■	■	■	■	■	■
Article 7 (2)	■	■	■	■	■	■	■	■	■	■	■	■	■
Article 7 (3)	■	■	■	■	■	■	■	■	■	■	■	■	■
Article 7 (4)	■	■	■	■	■	■	■	■		■	■	■	■
Article 7 (5)	■			■	■	■	■		■	■	■	■	
Article 7 (6)	■			■	■	■	■		■	■	■	■	
Article 7 (7)	■		■	■	■	■	■	■	■	■	■	■	■
Article 7 (8)	■	■	■	■	■	■	■	■	■	■	■	■	■
Article 7 (9)	■		■	■	■	■	■	■		■	■	■	■
Article 7 (10)	■	■	■	■	■	■	■	■	■	■	■	■	■
Article 8 (1)	■	■	■	■	■	■	■	■	■	■	■	■	■
Article 8 (2)	■	■	■	■	■	■	■	■		■	■	■	
Article 8 (3)	■	■	■	■		■	■	■	■	■	■	■	■
Article 8 (4)	■		■	■	■	■	■	■	■	■	■	■	■
Article 8 (5)	■		■	■	■	■	■	■		■	■	■	
Article 9		■	■	■	■	■	■	■	■	■	■	■	■
Article 10 (1)		■	■	■	■	■	■		■	■		■	■
Article 10 (2)		■		■	■	■	■	■	■	■		■	■
Article 10 (3)		■		■	■	■	■		■	■	■	■	■
Article 10 (4)		■	■	■	■	■	■		■	■		■	■

Provision of the revised Charter	Bulgaria	Cyprus	Estonia	France	Ireland	Italy	Lithuania	Moldova	Norway	Portugal	Romania	Slovenia	Sweden
Article 10 (5)		X		X			X	X	X	X		X	X
Article 11 (1)	X	X	X	X	X	X	X	X	X	X	X	X	X
Article 11 (2)	X	X	X	X	X	X	X	X	X	X	X	X	X
Article 11 (3)	X	X	X	X	X	X	X	X	X	X	X	X	X
Article 12 (1)	X	X	X	X	X	X	X	X	X	X	X	X	X
Article 12 (2)	X	X	X	X	X	X		X	X	X	X	X	X
Article 12 (3)	X	X	X	X	X	X	X	X	X	X	X	X	X
Article 12 (4)		X	X	X	X	X	X	X	X	X	X	X	
Article 13 (1)	X	X		X	X	X	X	X	X	X	X		X
Article 13 (2)	X	X	X	X	X	X	X	X	X	X	X	X	X
Article 13 (3)	X	X	X	X	X	X	X	X	X	X	X	X	X
Article 13 (4)		X	X		X	X		X	X	X			X
Article 14 (1)	X	X	X	X	X	X	X		X	X		X	X
Article 14 (2)	X	X	X	X	X	X	X		X	X	X	X	X
Article 15 (1)		X	X	X	X	X	X	X	X	X	X	X	X
Article 15 (2)		X	X	X	X	X	X	X	X	X	X	X	X
Article 15 (3)		X	X	X	X	X	X	X		X		X	X
Article 16	X		X	X	X	X	X	X	X	X	X	X	X
Article 17 (1)			X	X	X	X	X	X	X	X	X	X	X
Article 17 (2)	X		X	X	X	X	X	X	X	X	X	X	X
Article 18 (1)					X	X	X	X		X		X	X
Article 18 (2)	X	X	X	X	X	X				X			X
Article 18 (3)		X	X	X	X	X				X	X	X	X
Article 18 (4)	X	X		X	X	X	X		X	X	X	X	X

Provision of the revised Charter	Bulgaria	Cyprus	Estonia	France	Ireland	Italy	Lithuania	Moldova	Norway	Portugal	Romania	Slovenia	Sweden
Article 19 (1)		■	■	■	■	■	■		■	■		■	■
Article 19 (2)		■	■	■	■	■			■	■		■	■
Article 19 (3)		■	■	■	■	■	■		■	■		■	■
Article 19 (4)		■	■	■	■	■			■	■		■	■
Article 19 (5)		■	■	■	■	■	■		■	■		■	■
Article 19 (6)		■	■	■	■	■	■		■	■		■	■
Article 19 (7)		■	■	■	■	■	■	■	■	■		■	■
Article 19 (8)		■	■	■	■	■		■		■	■	■	■
Article 19 (9)		■	■	■	■	■	■	■	■	■	■	■	■
Article 19 (10)		■	■	■	■	■	■	■	■	■	■	■	■
Article 19 (11)		■	■	■	■	■	■	■	■	■	■	■	■
Article 19 (12)		■	■	■	■	■		■	■	■	■	■	■
Article 20	■	■	■	■	■	■	■	■	■	■	■	■	■
Article 21	■		■	■		■	■	■	■	■	■	■	■
Article 22	■		■	■	■	■	■		■		■	■	■
Article 23		■	■	■	■	■		■	■	■	■	■	■
Article 24	■	■	■	■	■	■	■	■	■	■	■	■	
Article 25	■		■	■	■		■	■		■	■	■	■
Article 26 (1)	■		■		■	■	■		■		■	■	■
Article 26 (2)	■		■		■	■	■		■				
Article 27 (1)			■		[1]	■	■	■	[1]	■		■	■
Article 27 (2)	■		■	■	■	■	■	■	■	■	■	■	■
Article 27 (3)	■	■	■	■	■	■	■			■		■	■

___
Sub-paragraph c./Alinéa c.

Provision of the revised Charter	Bulgaria	Cyprus	Estonia	France	Ireland	Italy	Lithuania	Moldova	Norway	Portugal	Romania	Slovenia	Sweden
Article 28	■	■	■	■	■	■	■	■		■	■	■	
Article 29	■		■	■	■	■	■	■		■	■	■	■
Article 30				■	■		■		■	■		■	■
Article 31 (1)				■		■		■		■			■
Article 31 (2)				■		■		■		■			
Article 31 (3)				■		■	■			■	■		■

94

C. Reservations and declarations

1. Reservations and declarations relating to the European Social Charter

Austria

Declaration made at the time of signature, on 22 July 1963 (Or. Fr.)

The Austrian Government desires that this signature be interpreted as a gesture of European solidarity. In signing the Charter Austria joins the great majority of the member countries of the Council of Europe who by their signatures have acknowledged the Charter's principles. The question of ratification will be examined carefully by Austria; the fact cannot be concealed, however, that in view of the present legal position of Austria considerable difficulties arise, which for the present prevent ratification of several of the essential Articles of the Charter.

Declaration contained in the instrument of ratification, deposited on 29 October 1969 (Or. Germ.)

The Republic of Austria declares, in accordance with Article 20, paragraph 2, that it considers itself bound by the following Articles and paragraphs of the European Social Charter:

- Article 1,
- Article 5,
- Article 12,
- Article 13,
- Article 16; furthermore

- Article 2, paragraphs 2, 3, 4, 5 ;
- Article 3, paragraphs 1, 2, 3 ;
- Article 4, paragraphs 1, 2, 3, 5 ;
- Article 6, paragraphs 1, 2, 3 ;
- Article 7, paragraphs 2, 3, 4, 5, 7, 8, 9, 10 ;
- Article 8, paragraphs 1, 2, 3, 4 ;
- Article 9,
- Article 10, paragraphs 1, 2, 3, 4 ;
- Article 11, paragraphs 1, 2, 3 ;
- Article 14, paragraphs 1, 2 ;
- Article 15, paragraphs 1, 2 ;
- Article 17,
- Article 18, paragraphs 1, 2, 4 ;
- Article 19, paragraphs 1, 2, 3, 5, 6, 9.

Belgium

> *Declaration made at the time of deposit of the instrument of ratification on 16 October 1990* (Or. Fr.)

The Permanent Representative declared that his Government accepts in their entirety the undertakings arising out of the Charter.

Cyprus

> *Declaration made at the time of signature, on 22 May 1967, and contained in the instrument of ratification, deposited on 7 March 1968* (Or. Engl.)

The Republic of Cyprus undertakes to pursue and carry out faithfully the stipulations contained in Part I of the Charter and also, in accordance with the provisions of paragraph 1 (b) and (c) of Article 20, the stipulations contained in the following articles of Part II of the Charter:

a. in accordance with the provisions of paragraph 1 (b) of Article 20:

  – Articles 1, 5, 6, 12 and 19;

b. in accordance with the provisions of paragraph 1 (c) of Article 20:

  – Articles 3, 9, 11, 14 and 15.

> *Declaration contained in a Note Verbale from the Permanent Representation of Cyprus, dated 20 October 1988, registered at the Secretariat General on 25 October 1988* (Or. Engl.)

According to Article 20 paragraph 3 of the European Social Charter, the Government of the Republic of Cyprus considers itself bound by the following numbered paragraphs of Part II of the Charter:

  – paragraph 3 of Article 2: annual holiday with pay
  – paragraph 5 of Article 2: weekly rest period
  – paragraph 7 of Article 7: annual holiday with pay to employed persons under 18 years of age
  – paragraph 8 of Article 7: night work of persons under 18 years of age
  – paragraph 2 of Article 8: unlawful notice of dismissal given to a woman during her absence on maternity leave.

> *Declaration contained in a Note Verbale from the Permanent Representation of Cyprus, dated 10 February 1992, registered at the Secretariat General on 12 February 1992* (Or. Engl.)

According to Article 20 paragraph 3 of the European Social Charter, the Government of the Republic of Cyprus considers itself bound by the following numbered paragraphs of Part II of the Charter:

  – paragraph 1 of Article 2: reasonable daily and weekly working hours

- paragraph 1 of Article 7: minimum age for admission to employment
- paragraph 3 of Article 7: safeguarding the full benefit of compulsory education
- paragraph 1 of Article 8: maternity leave.

Czech Republic

Declaration contained in the instrument of ratification, deposited on 3 November 1999 (Or. Engl.)

In accordance with Article 20 of the European Social Charter:

1. the Czech Republic undertakes to pursue the aims stated in Part I of the Charter;
2. the Czech Republic considers itself bound by the following provisions:
   - Article 1, paragraphs 1, 2 and 3
   - Articles 2 and 3
   - Article 4, paragraphs 2, 3, 4 and 5
   - Articles 5, 6, 7, 8, 11, 12, 13 and 14
   - Article 15, paragraph 2
   - Articles 16 and 17
   - Article 18, paragraph 4
   - Article 19, paragraph 9

Denmark

Declaration contained in a letter from the Permanent Representative of Denmark, dated 23 February 1965, handed to the Secretary General at the time of deposit of the instrument of ratification, on 3 March 1965 (Or. Engl.)

The Kingdom of Denmark considers herself bound by the following articles and paragraphs:

a. in accordance with Article 20, paragraph 1 (b):
   - Articles 1, 5, 6, 12, 13 and 16;

b. in accordance with Article 20, paragraph 1 (c):
   - Article 2, paragraphs 2, 3 and 5,
   - Article 3,
   - Article 4, paragraphs 1, 2, and 3,[1]
   - Article 8, paragraph 1,
   - Article 9,
   - Article 10,
   - Article 11,

---

1. The additional underlined paragraph was notified by letter from the Ministry of Foreign Affairs of Denmark, dated 24 July 1979, registered at the Secretariat General on 10 August 1979 (Or. Engl.).

- Article 14,
- Article 15,
- Article 17,
- Article 18.

In conformity with Article 34 of the Charter, the metropolitan territory of Denmark to which the provisions of the Charter shall apply is declared to be the territory of the Kingdom of Denmark with the exception of the Faroe Islands and Greenland.

Finland

Declaration contained in a letter from the Permanent Representative, dated 29 April 1991, handed to the Secretary General at the time of deposit of the instrument of acceptance, on 29 April 1991 (Or. Engl.)

The Government of Finland considers itself bound by the following Articles and numbered paragraphs of Part II of the Charter:

- Articles 1, 2 ;
- paragraph 3 of Article 3 ;
- paragraphs 2, 3 and 5 of Article 4 ;
- Articles 5 and 6 ;
- paragraphs 1, 2, 3, 4, 5, 7, 8 and 10 of Article 7 ;
- paragraph 2 of Article 8 ;
- Articles 9 to 18; and
- paragraphs 1, 2, 3, 4, 5, 6, 7, 8 and 9 of Article 19.

France

Declarations and Reservations contained in a letter from the Permanent Representative of France, dated 5 March 1973, handed to the Secretary General at the time of deposit of the instrument of approbation, on 9 March 1973 (Or. Fr.)

I. In accordance with the provisions of paragraph 1 (b) and (c) of Article 20

List of Articles which France is able to accept in respect of all the obligations specified in each of the numbered paragraphs:

- the right to work (Article 1);
- the right to safe and healthy working conditions (Article 3);
- the right to a fair remuneration (Article 4);
- the right to organise (Article 5);
- the right to bargain collectively (Article 6);
- the right of children and young persons to protection (Article 7);
- the right of employed women to protection (Article 8);
- the right to vocational guidance (Article 9);

- the right to vocational training (Article 10);
- the right to protection of health (Article 11);
- the right to social security (Article 12);
- the right to benefit from social welfare services (Article 14);
- the right of physically or mentally disabled persons to vocational training, rehabilitation and social resettlement (Article 15);
- the right of the family to social, legal and economic protection (Article 16);
- the right of mothers and children to social and economic protection (Article 17);
- the right to engage in a gainful occupation in the territory of other Contracting Parties (Article 18);
- the right of migrant workers and their families to protection and assistance (Article 19).

List of Articles which France accepts in respect of the obligations specified in the numbered paragraphs:

- Article 2, paragraphs 1, 2, 3 and 5;
- Article 13, paragraphs 1, 3 and 4.

II. Reservations by the French Government[1]

- Article 2, paragraph 4

According to paragraph 4 of Article 2 concerning "the right to just conditions of work", member States must "provide for additional paid holidays or reduced working hours for workers engaged in dangerous or unhealthy occupations as prescribed". However, in France, efforts to protect workers against the risks to which they are exposed are directed towards improving working conditions in order to eliminate dangerous or unhealthy situations. Consequently, the French Government cannot undertake to comply with the provisions of paragraph 4 of Article 2.

- Article 13, paragraph 2

Paragraph 2 of Article 13 on "the right to social and medical assistance", requires each member State to "ensure that persons receiving such assistance shall not, for that reason, suffer from a diminution of their political or social rights". However, Article L 230-3 of the French Electoral Code provides that persons exempt from payment of local rates and persons receiving assistance from social welfare offices cannot be elected to municipal councils. This provision, originating in the Local Government Act of 1884, was originally intended to apply to assistance to paupers, which was then still provided at the discretion

---

1. Reservations withdrawn by a letter from the Minister for External Affairs, dated 29 March 1984, registered at the Secretariat General on 27 April 1984 (Or. Fr.).

of the municipal authorities; it has since largely lost its point, as tax arrangements and social welfare are now usually governed by general texts, and current court practice is to regard the Electoral Code's provisions concerning ineligibility as not applicable to persons receiving assistance under statutory schemes. While the Government would be in favour of rescinding Article L 230-3 in order to allow for this development, it is bound to state that, as domestic legislation stands at present, Article 13, paragraph 2 of the Charter is incompatible with the above-mentioned provision.

III. Declaration of interpretation regarding Article 12, paragraph 4 (a)

Article 12, paragraph 4 (a) concerns equality of social security treatment between nationals of each of the Contracting Parties and those of the other Parties.

The maternity allowance payable under Article L 519 of the French Social Security Code is of such a nature as not to be covered by Article 12, paragraph 4 (a).

The allowance is not intended, as are family allowances, for the maintenance of children. It was introduced for essentially demographic reasons, for the specific purpose of encouraging the birth of French children in France, and hence has a specifically national and territorial character.

However, the national character of this allowance has been criticised in international bodies, which believe that it should be extended to all insured persons resident in French territory. The French Government has accordingly decided recently to investigate the possibility of complying with their wishes.

The French Government asks that formal note now be taken of its intention, pointing out that it will require some considerable time to complete the relevant investigations because of the procedure involved, which entails consulting not only the various ministerial departments concerned, but also family associations, employers' organisations and trade unions.

Germany

> *Declaration contained in a letter from the Permanent Representative of the Federal Republic of Germany, dated 28 September 1961* (Or. Germ.)

In the Federal Republic of Germany, pensionable civil servants (*Beamte*), judges and soldiers are subject to special terms of service and loyalty under public law, based in each case on an act of sovereign power. Under the national legal system of the Federal Republic of Germany they are debarred, on grounds of public policy and State security, from striking or taking other collective action in cases of conflicts of interest. Nor do they have the right to bargain collectively since the regulation of their rights and obligations in relation to their employers is a function of the freely elected legislative bodies.

Hence, with reference to the provisions of items 2 and 4 of Article 6 of Part II of the Social Charter the Permanent Representative of the Federal Republic of Germany to the Council of Europe feels obliged to point out that in the view of the Government of the Federal Republic of Germany those provisions do not relate to the above-mentioned categories of persons.

The above declaration does not relate to the legal status of non-pensionable civil servants (*Angestellte*) and workmen in the public service.

Declaration contained in a letter from the Permanent Representative of the Federal Republic of Germany, dated 22 January 1965, handed to the Secretary General at the time of deposit of the instrument of ratification, on 27 January 1965 (Or. Fr.)

The Federal Republic of Germany considers itself bound by the following Articles and paragraphs:

a. in accordance with Article 20, paragraph 1 (b):

- Articles 1, 5, 6, 12, 13, 16 and 19,

b. in accordance with Article 20, paragraph 1 (c),

- Article 1,
- Article 2,
- Article 3,
- Article 4, paragraphs 1, 2, 3 and 5,
- Article 7, paragraphs 2, 3, 4, 5, 6, 7, 8, 9 and 10,
- Article 8, paragraphs 1 and 3,
- Article 9,
- Article 10, paragraphs 1, 2 and 3,
- Article 11,
- Article 14,
- Article 15,
- Article 17,
- Article 18.

Declaration contained in a letter from the Permanent Representative of the Federal Republic of Germany, dated 22 January 1965, handed to the Secretary General at the time of deposit of the instrument of ratification, on 27 January 1965 (Or. Fr.)

The European Social Charter of 18 October 1961 will also apply to Land Berlin with effect from the date on which it enters into force for the Federal Republic of Germany.

Greece

> *Declaration made at the time of deposit of the instrument of ratification, on 4 June 1984* (Or. Fr.)

Greece does not consider itself bound by Articles 5 and 6 of Part II of the Charter (Article 20, paragraph 1, sub-paragraph b.).

Hungary

> *Declaration made at the time of deposit of the instrument of ratification on 8 July 1999* (Or. Fr.)

The Republic of Hungary undertakes to consider itself bound, in accordance with Article 20, paragraph 1, sub-paragraphs b and c, by Articles 1, 2, 3, 5, 6, 8, 9, 11, 13, 14, 16 and 17 of the European Social Charter

Iceland

> *Declaration contained in the instrument of approval, deposited on 15 January 1976* (Or. Engl.)

In accordance with Article 20, paragraph 2, Iceland considers itself bound by the following Articles and paragraphs of the Charter:

- Articles 1, 3, 4, 5, 6, 11, 12, 13, 14, 15, 16, 17, and 18; also Article 2, paragraphs 1, 3 and 5.

Ireland

> *Declaration contained in the instrument of ratification, deposited on 7 October 1964* (Or. Engl.)

The Government of Ireland do hereby confirm and ratify the Charter and undertake faithfully to perform and carry out the stipulations contained in Parts I, III, IV and V of the Charter, and, in accordance with the provisions of paragraph 1 (b) and 1 (c) of Article 20, the stipulations contained in the following Articles and paragraphs of Part II of the Charter:

Under paragraph 1 (b) of Article 20:

- Articles 1, 5, 6, 13, 16 and 19.

Under Paragraph 1 (c) of Article 20:

- Article 2
- Article 3
- Paragraphs 1, 2, 4 and 5 of Article 4
- Paragraphs 2, 3, 4, 5, 6, 8 and 10 of Article 7
- Paragraphs 1 and 4 of Article 8
- Article 9

- Article 10
- Paragraph 3 of Article 11
- Paragraphs 1, 3 and 4 of Article 12
- Articles 14, 15, 17 and 18.

Italy

Declaration made at the time of deposit of the instrument of ratification, on 22 October 1965 (Or. Fr.)

The Italian Government accepts in their entirety the undertakings arising out of the Charter.

Luxembourg

Declaration made at the time of deposit of the instrument of ratification, on 10 October 1991 (Or. Fr.)

In accordance with Article 20 of the Charter, the Grand-Duchy of Luxembourg considers itself bound by the following provisions of the said Charter:

- Articles 1, 2, 3, 4 paragraphs 1, 2, 3 and 5
- Articles 5 and 6 paragraphs 1, 2 and 3
- Articles 7 and 8 paragraphs 1, 2 and 3
- Articles 9, 10, 11, 12, 13, 14, 15, 16, 17, 18 and 19.

Malta

Declaration contained in the instrument of ratification, deposited on 4 October 1988 (Or. Engl.)

The Government of the Republic of Malta undertakes

I.   in accordance with Article 20, paragraph 1(a) to consider Part I of the said Charter as a declaration of the aims which it will pursue by all appropriate means, as stated in the introductory paragraph thereof, and,

II. in accordance with Article 20, paragraph 1(b) of the Charter, to consider itself bound by Articles 1, 5, 6, 13 and 16 of Part II of the Charter; and in accordance with Article 20 paragraph 1(c), by the following Articles and Paragraphs of the same Part:

Articles: 3, 4, 7, 9, 11, 14 15, 17;

Paragraphs: 1, 2, 3 and 5 of Article 2;
1, 2, and 4 of Article 8;
1, 2, 3, and 4(a) and (d) of Article 10;
1 and 3 of Article 12, and,
4 of Article 18

Netherlands

> *Declaration made at the time of signature, on 18 October 1961* (Or. Engl.)

Having regard to the equality, from the point of view of public law, between the Netherlands, Surinam and the Dutch West Indies, the terms "metropolitan" and "non-metropolitan" appearing in the European Social Charter lose their original meaning as far as the Kingdom of the Netherlands is concerned, and will therefore be considered, in the case of the Kingdom, as meaning, respectively, "European" and "non-European".

> *Declaration contained in a letter from the Ministry of Foreign Affairs of the Netherlands, dated 31 March 1980, handed to the Secretary General at the time of deposit of the instrument of ratification, on 22 April 1980* (Or. Fr.)

As regards the Kingdom in Europe, the Kingdom of the Netherlands considers herself bound by Articles 1, 2, 3, 4 and 5; Article 6, paragraphs 1, 2 and 3; Article 6, paragraph 4 (except for civil servants); Articles 7, 8, 9, 10, 11, 12, 13, 14, 15, 16, 17, 18 and Article 19, paragraphs 1, 2, 3, 4, 5, 6, 7 and 9;

As regards the Netherlands Antilles, the Kingdom of the Netherlands considers herself bound by Articles 1 and 5, Article 6 (except for civil servants) and Article 16.

> *Declaration contained in a letter from the Minister for Foreign Affairs of the Netherlands, dated 21 January 1983, registered at the Secretariat General on 8 February 1983* (Or. Fr.)

As regards the Kingdom in Europe, the Kingdom of the Netherlands will consider itself bound by paragraphs 8 and 10 of Article 19 of the Charter as from the date of entry into force – for the Kingdom (the Kingdom in Europe) – of the European Convention on the Legal Status of Migrant Workers, which was concluded at Strasbourg on 24 November 1977.

> *Declaration contained in a letter from the Permanent Representative of the Netherlands, dated 24 December 1985, registered at the Secretariat General on 3 January 1986* (Or. Engl.)

The island of Aruba, which is at present still part of the Netherlands Antilles, will obtain internal autonomy as a country within the Kingdom of the Netherlands as of 1 January 1986. Consequently the Kingdom will from then on no longer consist of two countries, namely the Netherlands (the Kingdom in Europe) and the Netherlands Antilles (situated in the Caribbean region), but will consist of three countries, namely the said two countries and the country Aruba.

As the changes being made on 1 January 1986 concern a shift only in the internal constitutional relations within the Kingdom of the

Netherlands, and as the Kingdom as such will remain the subject under international law with which treaties are concluded, the said changes will have no consequences in international law regarding treaties concluded by the Kingdom which already apply to the Netherlands Antilles, including Aruba. These treaties will remain in force for Aruba in its new capacity of country within the Kingdom. Therefore these treaties will as of 1 January 1986, as concerns the Kingdom of the Netherlands, apply to the Netherlands Antilles (without Aruba) and Aruba.

Consequently the treaties referred to in the annex, to which the Kingdom of the Netherlands is a Party and which apply to the Netherlands Antilles, will as of 1 January 1986 as concerns the Kingdom of the Netherlands apply to the Netherlands Antilles and Aruba.

List of Conventions referred to by the Declaration

...

35. European Social Charter (1961)

...

Norway

> *Declaration contained in the instrument of ratification, deposited on 26 October 1962* (Or. Engl.)

Having seen and examined the European Social Charter, signed at Turin on the 18th October 1961, we hereby approve, ratify and confirm the said Social Charter, and undertake to carry out the stipulations contained in Parts I, III, IV and V of the Charter, and also, in accordance with the provisions of paragraph 1 (b) and (c) of Article 20, the stipulations contained in the following Articles and paragraphs of Part II of the Charter:

In accordance with the provisions of paragraph 1 (b) of Article 20:
- Articles 1, 5, 6, 12, 13 and 16.

As regards Article 12, the undertaking is subject to the reservation that Norway, under paragraph 4 of this article, will be permitted in the bilateral and multilateral agreements therein mentioned to stipulate, as a condition for granting equal treatment, that foreign seamen should be domiciled in the country to which the vessel belongs.

In accordance with the provisions of paragraph 1 (c) of Article 20
- Article 2
- Article 3
- Article 4
- Paragraphs 2, 3, 5, 6, 7, 8 and 10 of Article 7
- Article 9
- Article 10

- Article 11
- Article 14
- Article 15
- Article 17
- Paragraphs 1, 2, 3, 4, 5, 6, 7, 9 and 10 of Article 19.

In conformity with Article 34 of the Charter, We further do declare that the metropolitan territory of Norway to which the provisions of the Charter shall apply, shall be the territory of the Kingdom of Norway with the exception of Svalbard (Spitzbergen) and Jan Mayen. The Charter shall not apply to the Norwegian dependencies.

Poland

Declaration contained in the instrument of ratification, deposited on 25 June 1997 (Or. Engl./Pol.)

According to Article 20 of the Charter, the Republic of Poland considers itself bound by provisions of the Charter as the following:

- Article 1   The right to work (paragraphs 1-4, all)
- Article 2   The right to just conditions of work (paragraphs 1, 3-5)
- Article 3   The right to safe and healthy working conditions (paragraphs 1-3, all)
- Article 4   The right to a fair remuneration (paragraphs 2-5)
- Article 5   The right to organise
- Article 6   The right to bargain collectively (paragraphs 1-3)
- Article 7   The right of children and young persons to protection (paragraphs 2, 4, 6-10)
- Article 8   The right of employed women to protection (paragraphs 1-4, all)
- Article 9   The right to vocational guidance
- Article 10   The right to vocational training (paragraphs 1-2)
- Article 11   The right to protection of health (paragraphs 1-3, all)
- Article 12   The right to social security (paragraphs 1-4, all)
- Article 13   The right to social and medical assistance (paragraphs 2 and 3)
- Article 14   The right to benefit from social welfare services (paragraph 1)
- Article 15   The right of physically or mentally disabled persons to vocational training, rehabilitation and social resettlement (paragraphs 1-2, all)
- Article 16   The right of the family to social, legal and economic protection

- Article 17   The right of mothers and children to social and economic protection
- Article 18   The right to engage in a gainful occupation in the territory of other Contracting Parties (paragraph 4)
- Article 19   The right of migrant workers and their families to protection and assistance (paragraphs 1-10, all)

Portugal

Declarations and Reservation contained in the instrument of ratification, deposited on 30 September 1991 (Or. Port./Fr.)

In accordance with paragraph 1 (a) of Article 20, Portugal undertakes to consider Part I of this Charter as a declaration setting out the aims which it will pursue by all appropriate means, as stated in the introductory paragraph of that Part;

In accordance with paragraph 1 (b) of Article 20, Portugal considers itself bound by Articles 1, 5, 6, 12, 13, 16 and 19 of Part II;

In accordance with paragraph 1 (c) of Article 20, Portugal considers itself bound by the remaining articles of Part II;

The obligations entered into under paragraph 4 of Article 6 shall in no way invalidate the prohibition of lockouts, as specified in paragraph 3 of Article 57 of the Constitution of the Portuguese Republic.

Slovakia

Declaration contained in the instrument of ratification, deposited on 22 June 1998 (Or. Engl.)

In accordance with Article 20, paragraph 2, of the European Social Charter, the Slovak Republic considers itself bound by the following provisions of the European Social Charter:

- Article 1   The right to work (paragraphs 1-4)
- Article 2   The right to just conditions of work (paragraphs 1-5)
- Article 3   The right to safe and healthy working conditions (paragraphs 1-3)
- Article 4   The right to a fair remuneration (paragraphs 1-5)
- Article 5   The right to organise
- Article 6   The right to bargain collectively (paragraphs 1-4)
- Article 7   The right of children and young persons to protection (paragraphs 1-10)
- Article 8   The right of employed women to protection (paragraphs 1-4)
- Article 9   The right to vocational guidance
- Article 10   The right to vocational training (paragraphs 1-4)

- Article 11   The right to protection of health (paragraphs 1-3)
- Article 12   The right to social security (paragraphs 1-4)
- Article 13   The right to social and medical assistance (paragraphs 1-3)
- Article 14   The right to benefit from social welfare services (paragraphs 1-2)
- Article 15   The right of physically or mentally disabled persons to vocational training, rehabilitation and social resettlement (paragraphs 1-2)
- Article 16   The right of the family to social, legal and economic protection
- Article 17   The right of mothers and children to social and economic protection
- Article 18   The right to engage in a gainful occupation in the territory of other Contracting Parties (paragraphs 1, 2, 4)

Spain

Declaration contained in the instrument of ratification, deposited on 6 May 1980 (Or. Sp.)

Spain declares that it will interpret and apply Articles 5 and 6 of the European Social Charter, read with Article 31 and the Appendix to the Charter, in such a way that their provisions will be compatible with those of Articles 28, 37, 103.3 and 127 of the Spanish Constitution.

Declaration contained in a letter from the Permanent Representative dated 4 December 1990, registered at the Secretary General on 4 December 1990 (Or. Engl.)

Denunciation of acceptance of Article 8 (4) (b).

Sweden

Declaration contained in a letter from the Ministry of Foreign Affairs of Sweden, dated 23 November 1962, handed to the Secretary General at the time of deposit of the instrument of ratification, on 17 December 1962 (Or. Fr.)

With reference to Article 20, paragraph 2 of the European Social Charter, signed in Turin on 18 October 1961, I have the honour to inform you that the Swedish Government considers itself bound by the Articles and paragraphs of the Charter mentioned below:

In accordance with the provisions of Article 20, paragraph 1, sub-paragraph (b)

- Articles 1, 5, 6, 13 and 16

In accordance with the provisions of Article 20, paragraph 1, sub-paragraph (c), the following additional Articles and paragraphs:

- Article 2, paragraphs 3 and 5
- Article 3
- Article 4, paragraphs 1, 3 and 4[1]
- Article 7, paragraphs 1, 2, 3, 4, 7, 8, 9 and 10[1]
- Article 8, paragraphs 1 and 3
- Article 9
- Article 10
- Article 11
- Article 12, paragraphs 1, 2 and 3
- Article 14
- Article 15
- Article 17
- Article 18
- Article 19, paragraphs 1, 2, 3, 4, 5, 6, 7, 8, 9 and 10.[1]

Turkey

Declaration contained in the instrument of ratification, deposited on 24 November 1989 (Or. Engl.)

The Republic of Turkey declares, in accordance with Article 20, paragraph 2, that it considers itself bound by the following Articles and paragraphs of the European Social Charter:

a. In accordance with Article 20, paragraph 1 (b):

- Articles 1, 12, 13, 16 and 19.

b. In accordance with Article 20, paragraph 1 (c):

- Articles 9, 10, 11, 14, 17 and 18 with all their paragraphs.
- Article 4, paragraphs 3 and 5.
- Article 7, paragraphs 3, 4, 5, 6, 8 and 9.

United Kingdom

Declaration contained in the instrument of ratification, deposited on 11 July 1962 (Or. Engl.)

The Government of the United Kingdom of Great Britain and Northern Ireland, having considered the Charter aforesaid, hereby confirm, ratify and undertake faithfully to perform and carry out the stipulations contained in Parts I, III, IV and V of the Charter, and, in accordance with the provisions of paragraph 1 (b) and (c) of Article 20, the stipulations contained in the following Articles and paragraphs of Part II of the Charter:

---

1. The additional underlined paragraphs were notified by letter from the Minister of Foreign Affairs of Sweden, dated 25 June 1979, registered at the Secretariat General on 2 July 1979 (Or. Fr.).

In accordance with the provisions of paragraph 1 (b) of Article 20:

- Articles 1, 5, 6, 13, 16 and 19.

In accordance with the provisions of paragraph 1 (c) of Article 20[1]:

- Paragraphs 2, 3, 4 and 5 of Article 2;
- Article 3;
- Paragraphs 1, 2, 4 and 5 of Article 4;
- Paragraphs 2, 3, 5, 6, 8, 9 and 10 of Article 7;
- Paragraphs 1 and 4 of Article 8;
- Articles 9, 10 and 11;
- Paragraph 1 of Article 12;
- Articles 14, 15, 17 and 18.

Declaration contained in a letter from the Permanent Representative of the United Kingdom, dated 16 September 1963 (Or. Engl.)

In accordance with Article 34 (2) of the Charter, Her Majesty's Government in the United Kingdom declare that the Charter shall extend to the Isle of Man.

The Articles and paragraphs of Part II of the Charter accepted as binding in respect of the Isle of Man are the same as those which have been accepted as binding in the United Kingdom.

2. Reservations and declarations relating to the 1988 Additional Protocol

Czech Republic

Declaration contained in the instrument of ratification, deposited on 17 November 1999 (Or. Engl.)

In accordance with Article 5 of the Additional Protocol to the European Social Charter:

1. the Czech Republic undertakes to pursue the aims stated in Part I of the Additional Protocol to the European Charter;

2. the Czech Republic considers itself bound by the following provisions of the Additional Protocol to the European Social Charter:

    - Article 1
    - Article 2

---

1. The United Kingdom has denounced acceptance of Articles:
- 8 para. 4 a) as from 26 February 1988 (letter from the Permanent Representative of the United Kingdom, dated 26 June 1987, registered at the Secretariat General on 30 June 1987 (Or. Engl.))..
- 7 para. 8 and 8 para. 4 b) as from 26 February 1990 (letter from the Permanent Representative of the United Kingdom, dated 21 August 1989, registered at the Secretariat General on 23 August 1989 (Or. Engl.)).

- Article 3
- Article 4

Denmark

Declaration contained in the instrument of ratification, deposited on 27 August 1996 (Or. Fr.).

Denmark declares that, until further notice, the Protocol shall not apply to the Faroe Islands and to Greenland.

Finland

Declaration contained in a letter from the Permanent Representative, dated 29 April 1991, handed to the Secretary General at the time of deposit of the instrument of acceptance, on 29 April 1991 (Or. Engl.)

The Government of Finland considers itself bound by the following Articles of the Protocol:

- Articles 1 to 4.

France

Reservation and Declaration made at the time of signature, on 22 June 1989 (Or. Fr.)

Reservation:

Non-contributory benefits provided for by French law subject to a condition of nationality shall only be awarded to nationals of the member States of the European Community and of those States which have concluded a convention on reciprocity with France on the award of equivalent non-contributory benefits to French nationals residing in those States.

Declaration:

This Protocol shall apply not only to the French metropolitan territory (Article 9, paragraph 1), but also to the French overseas departments.

Italy

Declaration contained in a letter from the Permanent Representative of Italy, dated 26 May 1994, handed to the Secretary General at the time of deposit of the instrument of ratification, on 26 May 1994 (Or. Fr.)

The Government of Italy declares that the provisions of Article 4, paragraph 2, letter a, are to be understood as having a programmatic character.

111

Netherlands

> *Declaration made at the time of signature, on 14 June 1990* (Or. Fr.)

Having regard to the equality, from the point of view of public law, between the Netherlands, the Dutch West Indies and Aruba, the terms "metropolitan" and "non-metropolitan" appearing in the Additional Protocol lose their original meaning as far as the Kingdom of the Netherlands is concerned, and will therefore be considered, in the case of the Kingdom, as meaning, respectively, "European" and "non-European".

> *Declarations contained in the instrument of acceptance deposited on 5 August 1992* (Or. Engl.)

The Netherlands accepts the Additional Protocol for the Kingdom in Europe and Aruba.

In accordance with Article 5, paragraph 1, sub-paragraph b of the Additional Protocol, the Kingdom of the Netherlands considers itself bound by Articles 1, 2 and 3 of Part II of the Additional Protocol with regard to the Kingdom in Europe and bound by Article 1 of Part II with regard to Aruba.

> *Declaration from the Minister for Foreign Affairs dated 28 September 1992, registered at the Secretariat General on 12 October 1992* (Or. Engl.)

The Kingdom of the Netherlands accepts the Additional Protocol for the Netherlands Antilles.

In accordance with Article 5, paragraph 1, sub b, of the Additional Protocol, the Kingdom of the Netherlands considers itself bound by Article 1 of Part II with regard to the Netherlands Antilles.

Norway

> *Declaration contained in the instrument of approval, deposited on 10 December 1993* (Or. Engl.)

The Protocol shall not apply to Svalbard, Jan Mayen and the Norwegian Antarctic Dependencies.

3. Reservations and declarations relating to the 1991 Amending Protocol

Austria

> *Declaration contained in the instrument of ratification, deposited on 13 July 1995* (Or. Engl./Ger.)

The Republic of Austria declares that with regard to Article 4 she considers herself bound only by the English text.

Netherlands

> *Declaration contained in the instrument of acceptance, deposited on 1 June 1993* (Or. Engl.)

The Kingdom of the Netherlands accepts the said Protocol for the Kingdom in Europe, for the Netherlands Antilles and for Aruba.

4. Reservations and declarations relating to the 1995 Additional Protocol providing for a system of collective complaints

Finland

> *Declaration contained in a letter from the President of Finland, dated 21 August 1998, registered at the Secretariat General on 26 August 1998* (Or. Engl.)

The Government of Finland declares, in accordance with Article 2 of the Additional Protocol to the European Social Charter providing for a system of collective complaints, that Finland recognizes the right of any representative national non-governmental organisation within its jurisdiction which has particular competence in the matters governed by the Charter, to lodge complaints against it.

5. Reservations and declarations relating to the revised Social Charter

Bulgaria

> *Declaration contained in the instrument of ratification deposited on 7 June 200* (Or. Engl.)

In accordance with Part III, Article A, paragraph 1, of the Charter, the Republic of Bulgaria declares the following:

1. The Republic of Bulgaria considers Part I of this Charter as a declaration of the aims which it will pursue by all appropriate means both national and international in character, as stated in the introductory paragraph of that Part.

2. The Republic of Bulgaria considers itself bound by the following Articles of Part II of the Charter:
    - Article 1
    - Article 2, paragraphs 2, 4-7
    - Article 3
    - Article 4, paragraphs 2-5
    - Articles 5, 6, 7, 8, 11
    - Article 12, paragraphs 1 and 3
    - Article 13, paragraphs 1-3

113

- Articles 14, 16
- Article 17, paragraph 2
- Article 18, paragraph 4,
- Articles 20, 21, 22, 24, 25, 26
- Article 27, paragraphs 2 and 3
- Articles 28 and 29.

3. In accordance with Part IV, Article D, paragraph 2, of the Charter, the Republic of Bulgaria accepts the supervision of its obligations under this Charter following the procedure provided in the Additional Protocol to the European Social Charter providing for a system of collective complaints of 9 November 1995.

Denmark

Declaration/Reservation contained in a Note Verbale from the Permanent Representative, dated 2 May 1996, handed to the Secretary General at the time of signature, on 3 May 1996 (Or. Engl.)

The Danish Government makes reservations with regard to the following provisions of the Social Charter (Revised): Article 2, paragraph 7, Article 24, Article 27, Article 28, Article 29 and Part V, Article E.

Estonia

Declaration contained in a Note Verbale from the Ministry of Foreign Affairs of Estonia, handed at the time of deposit of the instrument of ratification on 11 September 2000 (Or. Fr.)

In accordance with Part III, Article A, paragraph 2, of the Charter, the Republic of Estonia notifies that it considers itself bound by the following articles of Part II of the Charter:

- Article 1   The right to work (paragraphs 1-4, in full);
- Article 2   The right to just conditions of work (paragraphs 1-3, 5-7);
- Article 3   The right to safe and healthy working conditions (paragraphs 1-3);
- Article 4   The right to a fair remuneration (paragraphs 2, 3, 4, 5);
- Article 5   The right to organise (in full);
- Article 6   The right to bargain collectively (paragraphs 1-4, in full);
- Article 7   The right of children and young persons to protection (paragraphs 1-4, 7-10);
- Article 8   The right of employed women to protection of maternity (paragraphs 1-5, in full);
- Article 9   The right to vocational guidance (in full);

- Article 10   The right to vocational training (paragraphs 1, 3, 4);

- Article 11   The right to protection of health (paragraphs 1-3, in full);

- Article 12   The right to social security (paragraphs 1-4, in full);

- Article 13   The right to social and medical assistance (paragraphs 1-3);

- Article 14   The right to benefit from social welfare services (paragraphs 1,2, in full);

- Article 15   The right of persons with disabilities to independence, social integration and participation in the life of the community (paragraphs 1-3, in full);

- Article 16   The right of the family to social, legal and economic protection (in full);

- Article 17   the right of children and young persons to social, legal and economic protection (paragraphs 1, 2, in full);

- Article 19   The right of migrant workers and their families to protection and assistance (paragraphs 1-12, in full);

- Article 20   The right to equal opportunities and equal treatment in matters of employment and occupation without discrimination on the grounds of sex (in full);

- Article 21   the right to information and consultation (in full);

- Article 22   The right to take part in the determination and improvement of the working conditions and working environment (in full);

- Article 24   The right to protection in cases of termination of employment (in full);

- Article 25   The right of workers to the protection of their claims in the event of the insolvency of their employer (in full);

- Article 27   The right of workers with family responsibilities to equal opportunities and treatment (1-3, in full);

- Article 28   the right of workers representatives to protection in the undertaking and facilities to be accorded to them (in full);

- Article 29   The right to information and consultation in collective redundancy procedures (in full).

Period covered: 01/11/00 -
The preceding statement concerns Article(s): A

Ireland

> *Declaration contained in the instrument of ratification and in a letter from the Permanent Representative of Ireland, dated 4 November 2000, deposited on 4 November 2000 (Or. Engl.)*

In accordance with Part III, Article A, of the Charter, Ireland considers itself bound by all the provisions of the Charter, except :
- Article 8, paragraph 3;
- Article 21, paragraphs a and b;
- Article 27, paragraph 1, sub-paragraph c;
- Article 31.

Period covered: 01/01/01 -
The preceding statement concerns Article(s): A

> *Declaration contained in the instrument of ratification and in a letter from the Permanent Representative of Ireland, dated 4 November 2000, deposited on 4 November 2000 (Or. Engl.)*

In view of the general wording of Article 31 of the Charter, Ireland is not in a position to accept the provisions of this article at this time. However, Ireland will follow closely the interpretation to be given to the provisions of Article 31 by the Council of Europe with a view to their acceptance by Ireland at a later date.

Period covered: 01/01/01 -
The preceding statement concerns Article(s): 31

Italy

> *Declaration contained in a Note Verbale from the Permanent Representation, handed to the Secretary General at the time of deposit of the instrument of ratification, on 5 July 1999 (Or. Engl.)*

Italy does not consider itself bound by Article 25 (the right of workers to the protection of their claims in the event of the insolvency of their employer) of the Charter.

Lithuania

> *Declaration contained in the instrument of ratification deposited on 29 June 2001 (Or. Engl.)*

The Republic of Lithuania declares that it considers itself bound by the provisions of the following Articles of the Charter: Articles 1-11 of Part II, sub-paragraphs 1, 3 and 4 of Article 12, sub-paragraphs 1-3 of Article 13, Articles 14-17, sub-paragraphs 1 and 4 of Article 18, sub-paragraphs 1, 3, 5, 7, 9-11 of Article 19, Articles 20-22, Articles 24-29 and sub-paragraphs 1 and 2 of Article 31.

Period covered: 01/08/01 -
The preceding statement concerns Article(s): A

Norway

Declaration contained in the instrument of ratification deposited on 7 May 2001 (Or. Engl.)

The Kingdom of Norway declares that it considers itself bound by Articles 1, 4-6, 9-17, 20-25, 30 and 31, as well as, moreover, by the provisions of Article 2, paragraphs 1-6, Article 3, paragraphs 2-3, Article 7, paragraphs 1-3, 5-8 and 10, Article 8, paragraphs 1 and 3, Article 19, paragraphs 1-7 and 9-12 and Article 27, paragraphs 1c and 2, of the Charter.

Period covered: 01/07/01 -
The preceding statement concerns Article(s): A

Declaration contained in the instrument of ratification deposited on 7 May 2001 (Or. Engl.)

In conformity with Part VI, Article L, of the revised European Social Charter, the Norwegian Government declares that the metropolitan territory of Norway to which the provisions of the revised European Social Charter shall apply, shall be the territory of the Kingdom of Norway with the exception of Svalbard (Spitzbergen) and Jan Mayen. The revised European Social Charter shall not apply to the Norwegian dependencies.

Period covered: 01/07/01 -
The preceding statement concerns Article(s): L

Romania

Declarations contained in the instrument of ratification deposited on 7 May 1999 (Or. Fr.)

1. In accordance with the provisions of Article A, paragraph 1, of Part III of the Charter, Romania accepts Part I of the Charter as a declaration of the aims which it will pursue by all appropriate means and considers itself bound by the provisions of Article 1; Articles 4-9; Articles 11, 12, 16, 17, 20, 21, 24, 26, 28 and 29, as well as, moreover, by the provisions of Article 2, paragraphs 1, 2, 4-7; Article 3, paragraphs 1-3; Article 13, paragraphs 1-3; Article 15, paragraphs 1 and 2; Article 18, paragraphs 3 and 4; Article 19, paragraphs 7 and 8, and Article 27, paragraph 2.

2. Romania declares that it accepts that the application of the legal commitments contained in the European Social Charter (revised) is subject to the control mechanism provided for in Part IV of the European Social Charter adopted in Turin, on 18 October 1961.

Slovenia

Declarations contained in a Note Verbale handed to the Secretary General at the time of deposit of the instrument of ratification, on 7 May 1999 (Or. Engl.)

In according with Part III, Article A, paragraph 2, of the Charter, the Republic of Slovenia notifies that it considers itself bound by the following Articles of Part II of this Charter: 1, 2, 3, 4, 5, 6, 7, 8, 9, 10, 11, 12, 13 (paragraphs 2 and 3), 14, 15, 16, 17, 18 (paragraphs 1, 3 and 4), 19, 20, 21, 22, 23, 24, 25, 26, 27, 28, 29, 30 and 31.

In accordance with Part IV, Article D, paragraph 2, of the Charter, the Republic of Slovenia declares that it accepts the supervision of its obligations under this Charter following the procedure provided for in the Additional Protocol to the European Social Charter providing for a system of collective complaints, done at Strasbourg, on 9 November 1995.

Sweden

Declarations contained in the instrument of ratification deposited on 29 May 1998 (Or. Engl.)

In accordance with Part III, Article A, paragraph 2, of the Charter, Sweden considers itself bound by the following Articles in Part II.

- Article 1   The right to work (paragraphs 1-4, all)
- Article 2   The right to just conditions of work (paragraphs 3, 5-6)
- Article 3   The right to safe and healthy working conditions (paragraphs 1- 3)
- Article 4   The right to a fair remuneration (paragraphs 1, 3-4)
- Article 5   The right to organise
- Article 6   The right to bargain collectively (paragraphs 1-4, all)
- Article 7   The right of children and young persons to protection (paragraphs 1-4, 7-10)
- Article 8   The right of employed women to protection of maternity (paragraphs 1 and 3)
- Article 9   The right to vocational guidance
- Article 10   The right to vocational training (paragraphs 1-5, all)
- Article 11   The right to protection of health (paragraphs 1-3, all)
- Article 12   The right to social security (paragraphs 1-3)
- Article 13   The right to social and medical assistance (paragraphs 1-4, all)

- Article 14   The right to benefit from social welfare services (paragraphs 1-2, all)

- Article 15   The right of persons with disabilities to independence, social integration and participation in the life of the community (paragraphs 1-3, all)

- Article 16   The right of the family to social, legal and economic protection

- Article 17   The right of children and young persons to social, legal and economic protection (paragraphs 1-2, all)

- Article 18   The right to engage in a gainful occupation in the territory of other Parties (paragraphs 1-4, all)

- Article 19   The right of migrant workers and their families to protection and assistance (paragraphs 1-12, all)

- Article 20   The right to equal opportunities and equal treatment in matters of employment and occupation without discrimination on the grounds of sex

- Article 21   The right to information and consultation

- Article 22   The right to take part in the determination and improvement of the working conditions and working environment

- Article 23   The right of elderly persons to social protection

- Article 25   The right of workers to the protection of their claims in the event of the insolvency of their employer

- Article 26   The right to dignity at work (paragraphs 1-2, all)

- Article 27   The right of workers with family responsibilities to equal opportunities and equal treatment (paragraphs 1-3, all)

- Article 29   The right to information and consultation in collective redundancy procedures

- Article 30   The right to protection against poverty and social exclusion

- Article 31   The right to housing (paragraphs 1-3, all)

Sweden considers that preferential treatment shall not be considered as incompatible with Article E of the Charter.

III. Explanatory reports

A. Explanatory report to the 1988 Additional Protocol

Introduction

1. In the Declaration on Human Rights of 27 April 1978, the Member States of the Council of Europe decided "to give priority to the work undertaken in the Council of Europe of exploring the possibility of extending the lists of rights of the individual, notably rights in the social, economic and cultural field, which should be protected by European conventions or any other appropriate means".

2. Further to this declaration, the Committee of Ministers of the Council of Europe initiated extensive consultations with a number of steering committees which were invited to draw up opinions on the possibility of including new economic and social rights in instruments such as the European Convention on Human Rights and the European Social Charter (hereafter "the Charter").

3. The Steering Committee for Social Affairs (CDSO) was instructed to take the lead in this process with regard to the Charter.

4. Having been instructed in 1980, in its initial terms of reference (Decision No. CM/174/240180), to "undertake a review of the rights incorporated in the European Social Charter to determine whether they should be updated or supplemented" and "to consider whether there are any rights which might be suitable for inclusion in the European Convention on Human Rights", the CDSO was instructed in 1981 (Decision No. CM/252/250981) "to undertake the drafting of a preliminary working paper presenting in standard-setting form the various proposals for the rights to be incorporated in an additional Protocol to the European Social Charter".

5. Subsequently, on the basis of this working paper drafted by the CDSO, the Committee of Ministers adopted a third set of terms of reference (Decision No. CM/219/190183) asking the CDSO to "prepare a preliminary draft for a Protocol to the European Social Charter".

6. The CDSO carried out this task at meetings which it held in March, July and October 1983 and again in April, July and October 1984 and adopted the text of a preliminary draft additional protocol including an appendix forming an integral part of it.

7. At their 378th meeting, the Ministers' Deputies (November-December 1984) considered it necessary to consult management and labour and instructed (386th meeting, June 1985) the CDSO to re-examine the preliminary draft additional protocol in the light of the views expressed by the European Trade Union Confederation (ETUC) and the Union of Industries of the European Community (UNICE) on the occasion of the annual meeting of the Liaison Committee between the Council of Europe and management and labour (LCML) held on 18 and 19 February 1985.

8. Furthermore, in response to the wish expressed by the Assembly in its Recommendation 1022 (1986) on the European Social Charter for "a political appraisal", the Ministers' Deputies (394th meeting, March 1986) decided to consult the Assembly on the text of the preliminary draft additional protocol before finalising the position of the Committee of Ministers on the matter.

On 26 January 1987, the Assembly adopted Opinion No. 131 (1987) proposing some amendments to the preliminary draft both as regards the wording of the rights proposed and also the conditions for ratification of the future protocol and the scope of its application to persons *ratione personae*.

9. The Committee of Ministers adopted the Additional Protocol to the Charter on 26 November 1987 during its 81st session; this Protocol was opened for signature on 5 May 1988.

General remarks

10. The Protocol is to be regarded as an instrument which, although in some respects is an "extension" of the Charter, is nonetheless legally independent of it.

11. Its structure has deliberately been modelled on that of the Charter; thus there is the same sub-division into a Part I, containing a general statement of rights and principles having the force of "aims", and a Part II presenting the same rights in the form of detailed rules and stating explicitly the Parties' undertakings. Equally, the articles which follow have been grouped into Parts III, IV and V, corresponding to those parts of the Charter with the same numbering.

12. For the same reasons of harmony, the introductory sentences to Parts I and II of the Protocol are identical to those appearing in the Charter.

13. The Protocol, however, takes into account developments in labour legislation, the definition of social policies and, to some extent, terminology, since the Charter was drawn up. For this reason, new expressions have sometimes been used, the exact meaning of which has been indicated where necessary; on the

other hand, when the same concepts are used, they should as a rule be interpreted in association with the corresponding provision of the Charter.

Part I

14. As stated above, this part enunciates the right and principles guaranteed in accordance with the corresponding articles of Part II.

15. The wording of Part I and of Article 5, paragraph 1.a, of Part III of the Protocol reproduces that of Part I and Article 20 of the Charter respectively. Thanks to the flexible drafting of these texts, they have been accepted by a number of states, not all of which have the same concept of economic and social rights and, in particular, of the way in which they are exercised.

16. In the introductory paragraph to Part I, it will be noted that the Parties acknowledge the aim of their policy to be "the attainment of conditions in which the following rights and principles may be effectively realised". In other words, a state may choose not to intervene directly if, according to its legal and institutional system, this is the best way of attaining the "conditions in which the [...] rights" in question "may be effectively realised", without the need to express any reservations whatsoever to this end.

17. Whilst right No. 1 opens with the words "All workers", rights Nos. 2 and 3 begin "Workers". The latter wording was chosen because Articles 2 and 3 provide for the possible exclusion from their scope undertakings employing less than a certain number of workers and further allow the rights in question to be exercised by delegation. It was therefore deemed preferable to avoid any inconsistency between the enunciation of the rights in Part I and the conditions of their exercise stipulated in the corresponding articles in Part II.

18. The term "workers" in right No. 1 in Part I shall be taken to include unemployed persons, persons seeking employment, those undergoing vocational training and all other potential workers.

19. Rights Nos. 2 and 3 refer to the concept of "undertaking", which is defined in the appendix (see paragraphs 68 and 69 below).

Part II

Article 1, paragraph 1

20. The obligation on the Parties under paragraph 1 is, *inter alia*, to "ensure" or to "promote" the application of the right to equal treatment; this is to allow for the fact that the obligation in question may be met as much by government action (legislation, regulations, etc.) as by action by employers and labour (collective agreements) or individuals (bilateral agreements and contracts). The

obligation to ensure equal treatment may further be met both by judicial processes and by such other appropriate means as exist or may be instituted by each Party.

21. The list of fields in which the provision is applicable reflects developments since the Charter's adoption. Reference is made, for instance, to occupational resettlement, a concept which does not appear as such in the Charter. The expression "occupational resettlement" covers several situations: the resumption of employment after a voluntary or involuntary break, moving from one job to another without a break, possibly after retraining. The term "retraining" covers any supplementary training to enable workers to adapt their knowledge and skills to industrial, technological and scientific progress.

22. The expression "terms of employment and working conditions" refers to all rights and situations associated with the specific position of the worker in his or her occupational relations and working environment. As stated, however, in the appendix, social security matters "may be excluded" (see paragraph 67 below).

23. It was understood that by the expression "terms of employment [...] including remuneration;" in the third sub-paragraph of paragraph 1, the equal treatment intended by this provision is wider in scope than the principle of "equal pay for work of equal value" in Article 4, paragraph 3, of the Charter. "Remuneration" shall, moreover, be understood to mean basic or minimum wages or salary plus all other benefits paid directly or indirectly in cash or kind by the employer to the worker by reason of the latter's employment.

Article 1, paragraph 2

24. Within the meaning of this paragraph, the protection afforded women is that guaranteed by current provisions in matters of pregnancy, confinement and post-natal care. The word "particularly" means, however, that other kinds of protection, essential in other situations, are admissible.

25. The protective provisions referred to are not only those of domestic legislation but also those resulting from international law. Articles 8 and 17 of the Charter are therefore not affected as such by this article of the Protocol (see also Article 8 of the Protocol – "Relations between the Charter and this Protocol"). It is understood that where several texts coexist, the provision most favourable to the persons concerned shall prevail. It is, however, acknowledged that in this particular context (equality between the sexes) it will sometimes be difficult to establish which measure is the most favourable to women, as opinions may differ. Account will need to be taken of changing attitudes in this regard.

Article 1, paragraph 3

26. This provision takes into account the need to expedite the elimination of continuing *de facto* inequalities generally affecting women. The specific measures permissible but not obligatory under this provision shall be transitional and repealed gradually once equality has been achieved.

Article 1, paragraph 4

27. As stated in the appendix, this paragraph allows Parties to exclude occupations without requiring them to embody a list thereof in laws or regulations. The Parties would, however, need to take care to state in the reports that they will submit under Article 6, whether any activities – and if so, which ones – are reserved to persons of a particular sex and the reasons for and criteria governing such reservation. The Parties will bear in mind that the intention is to gradually reduce the number of excluded activities to a strict minimum.

28. This paragraph also refers to the "context in which [certain occupations] are carried out" as a factor which may warrant their being reserved to workers of a particular sex. Such circumstances should ordinarily be quite exceptional. The accessibility of an occupational activity to persons of either sex or its restriction to persons of a particular sex is to be determined by the "nature" of the work. The words "context in which [certain occupations] are carried out" are accordingly to be construed restrictively.

Articles 2 and 3

29. The conjunction "or" used in the expression "workers or their representatives" is not exclusive. It simply means that the rights afforded by these two provisions may be exercised by workers, or by their representatives, or by both, and the fact that they are conferred upon one group does not mean that they cannot be conferred upon the other, as stipulated in the articles themselves.

30. The expression "in accordance with national legislation and practice" in the introductory sentence of each of these two articles covers:

    i. the adoption or encouragement of the "measures" envisaged to ensure the exercise of the rights mentioned in the two articles;

    ii. the designation of such workers' representatives as may be associated with the exercise of those rights.

31. A definition of "workers' representatives" is given in the appendix. It is drawn from Article 3 of the International Labour Organisation (ILO) Convention No. 135 concerning protection and facilities to be afforded to workers' representatives in the undertaking, so as

127

to harmonise the definitions contained in the various international instruments.

32. With regard to point 30.i above, the Parties may naturally proceed by means of legislation or regulations but may also leave workers' representatives and employers to arrange the implementation of the provision by means of collective agreements, other agreements or any other form of voluntary negotiation. Implementation must, however, be effective and adequate.

33. In particular the Parties may leave management and labour to decide the level at which workers or their representatives are normally informed and consulted and take part (Articles 2 and 3): undertaking, production unit, sector or branch, or even local regional or national level, etc.

34. With regard to point 30.ii above, it shall likewise be permissible for Parties, in the above-mentioned conditions, to leave workers and their organisations to prescribe procedures and rules for the designation of representatives having access to information, consultation and participation in the determining of working conditions in the undertaking and for deciding at which level (local, regional, national, undertaking, branch, etc.) these rights are to be exercised.

35. The "national practice" mentioned earlier – which includes collective agreements and other contracts or agreements between employers and workers' representatives – also covers all customary practices between management and labour as well as existing or future judicial decisions in the matters referred to in the two articles.

36. The expression "certain number of workers to be determined by national legislation or practice" in Article 2, paragraph 2, and Article 3, paragraph 2, implies that the number in question may by determined in legislation or regulations, result from agreements between the Parties or be the result of long-standing custom, etc., although these methods are not necessarily mutually exclusive.

Article 2, paragraph 1

37. The term "undertaking" is defined in the appendix. It should be noted that, although the undertaking should have the power to make decisions regarding its market policy, it is not essential for workers to be informed at the place at which the undertaking's management makes such decisions. On the contrary, this provision allows the Parties complete discretion to fix, or to leave management and labour to determine freely, the various levels of information and consultation, which need not coincide with the decision-making level. In the case of, for instance, decentralised undertakings, information and consultation should in any event,

to be effective, occur in the various production units if they are also practised at the decision-making centres. See also the comment in the appendix about the "establishments of the undertaking".

38. With regard to multinational undertakings, the definition of the term "undertaking" shall be understood to apply to each production unit enjoying decision-making powers and located in the territory of a Party.

39. Sub-paragraph a of this paragraph stipulates that only information about the economic and financial situation of the undertaking must be communicated (subject to the proviso about secrecy and confidentiality). Other information, for example about industrial property or manufacturing or trade secrets, need not be disclosed.

40. This restriction supplements the general restriction which may be applied to the exercise of the rights set forth in this Protocol pursuant to Article 31 of the Charter, to which Article 8 of the Protocol refers.

41. It goes without saying that under this provision the possibility of refusing to disclose certain information or of requiring confidentiality may naturally be included not only in legislation or regulations but also in collective agreements or other agreements between employers and workers' representatives.

42. The expression "and in a comprehensible way" in sub-paragraph a has been inserted following a proposal by the Assembly in Opinion No. 131, which considered it useful to describe more precisely the kind of information to be disclosed.

43. In order to be effective, "consultation" in the relevant fields should be preceded by the furnishing of appropriate "information": the scope of consultation is thus coterminous with that of the information provision, the only restrictions being those provided in sub-paragraph b, emphasised by the use of the co-ordinating conjunction "and" at the end of sub-paragraph a.

Article 2, paragraph 2

44. This paragraph makes it possible for the Parties to apply the provisions on information and consultation of workers only to undertakings employing more than a certain number of workers. This option was included because it appeared that for reasons of efficiency and having regard also to the special circumstances associated with the size of certain undertakings, the establishment of specific information and consultation structures was, in many countries, envisaged or required only when the number of employees exceeded a certain minimum. The establishment of such structures is generally not obligatory in undertakings employing

fewer workers than the number stipulated in legislation, regulations or agreements in force between the Parties. Moreover, in small undertakings, information and consultation processes often exist in fact and operate readily, making the introduction of rigid and sometimes complex procedures unnecessary.

45. The Parties have accordingly been given the option of providing for the creation of information and consultation structures or systems only when the number of employees exceeds a certain level. If this option is exercised, the threshold (or thresholds) will need to be indicated in the reports to be submitted under Article 6. In the case of undertakings with fewer employees than the thresholds(s), the Parties will not, on the other hand, be required to explain information and consultation procedures but may communicate such information thereon as is in their possession.

46. It should further be noted that only the criterion of the undertaking's size (number of employees) is mentioned in this article, as other criteria relating to the undertaking's nature or activities may be covered by the appendix to the Protocol (Articles 2 and 3, paragraph 4), and/or by Article 31 of the Charter, to which Article 8 of the Protocol refers. The possibility that undertakings may also be excluded because collective agreements or other agreements applying to them contain no provisions relating to information or consultation is, on the other hand, covered by Article 7 of the Protocol. In this case, however, the workers not afforded this right must be a minority or, more exactly, those enjoying the right to be informed and consulted must constitute the great majority of the workers concerned in the country in question.

Article 3, paragraph 1

47. The matters listed in this article are frequently covered by collective agreements or other agreements between employers and workers' representatives.

48. Sub-paragraph c comes from a proposal of the Assembly (see Opinion No. 131) and, for a better understanding of the text, a certain number of the services and facilities thus referred to have been listed in the appendix.

49. This article in no way prejudices the right to bargain collectively provided for in Article 6 of the Charter, as is clear from Article 8 of the Protocol.

50. The expression "to take part in" covers all situations in which workers or their representatives are in any way whatsoever associated with the procedures for making decisions or taking certain measures, without, however, enjoying a right of joint decision-making or of veto over decisions still the responsibility of the head of the undertaking.

51. The contribution to the "supervision of the observance" of health and safety regulations is to be effected pursuant to the rules in force in each country and without prejudice to the jurisdiction and responsibilities of the bodies and authorities vested with the necessary powers. The role of workers or their representatives is not to replace the bodies responsible for this supervision but rather to ensure that supervision is as effective as possible.

Article 3, paragraph 2

52. The earlier comments on the analogous provision in Article 2 also apply here.

Article 4

53. The use in this article of the expression "in particular" indicates that the provisions enumerated are not exhaustive. The means indicated are therefore intended simply for guidance. The Parties are free to adopt any other measures appropriate to the full achievement of the aim referred to in paragraph 4 of Part I and repeated in the introductory sentence of this article.

Article 4, paragraph 1

54. The expression "full members" means that elderly persons must suffer no ostracism on account of their age, since the right to take part in society's various fields of activity is not granted or refused depending on whether an elderly person has retired or is still vocationally active or whether such a person is still of full legal capacity or is subject to some restrictions in this respect *(diminutio capitis)*.

55. The concept of "adequate resources" is to be interpreted in the light of Article 13 and, if necessary, Article 12 of the Charter. It is moreover understood that there is no inconsistency between the concept of "social assistance" used in Article 13 of the Charter and the concept of "social protection" embodied in Article 4 of the Protocol.

Article 4, paragraph 2

56. The ability of elderly people to remain in their familiar surroundings should be assessed in relation to their psychological and physical state, their living conditions, the standard of their accommodation, etc.

57. The "services" referred to in sub-paragraph 2.b include, where appropriate, admission to specialised institutions for elderly persons. This provision therefore assumes the existence of an adequate number of institutions and should be interpreted in the

light of the introduction to the article, whereby each Party undertakes to adopt or promote appropriate measures either on its own
or in co-operation with relevant public or private organisations.

Article 4, paragraph 3

58. This paragraph specifically concerned with elderly persons living
in institutions should be read in conjunction with the other paragraphs of Article 4. It follows that the measures advocated in paragraphs 1 and 2 are also applicable to persons living in institutions,
but only in so far as this mode of life does not render their implementation impossible or manifestly irrelevant.

59. Respect for privacy is mentioned only in relation to elderly persons living in institutions, a situation warranting special mention.
Everyone in all circumstances is naturally entitled to respect for
his or her private life as guaranteed by the European Convention
on Human Rights.

Other provisions of the Protocol

60. In addition to the "substantive" articles, the Protocol contains a
number of supplementary provisions whose purpose is:

    a. to stipulate the extent of the undertakings subscribed to by the
    Parties (Article 5);

    b. to recall the supervision procedure (Article 6);

    c. to stipulate the means of implementing the Protocol (Article 7);

    d. to explain the relationship between the Protocol and the
    Charter (Article 8);

    e. to lay down the conditions for the signature, ratification, entry
    into force and denunciation of the Protocol, its territorial appli-
    cation and the notifications relating to these matters (Articles 9
    to 12);

    f. to stipulate that the appendix forms an integral part of the
    Protocol (Article 13).

61. These provisions call for no special comment; their wording is
clear. Furthermore, they follow the model final clauses for conventions and agreements concluded within the Council of
Europe.

62. It should, however, be pointed out that Article 7, which enunciates
in its paragraph 2 the exclusions Parties may avail themselves of,
pursuant to paragraph 2 of Articles 2 and 3, is largely based on
Article 33 of the Charter but nevertheless departs from it to clarify
the various modes of implementation envisaged.

63. In practice, however, the enjoyment of the rights set forth in
Articles 2 and 3 may be guaranteed only to the great majority of

workers concerned and therefore need not necessarily be afforded to all workers.

64. On the other hand, all the persons mentioned in Articles 1 and 4 must be guaranteed the rights set out there. There is no possibility of leaving a minority of workers or elderly persons outside the scope of the laws, regulations, collective agreements, etc., by means of which the implementation of the undertakings given in these articles is fulfilled.

Appendix to the Protocol

65. The appendix, which forms an integral part of the Protocol, includes a number of definitions, comments and interpretations of and on the "substantive" articles of the Protocol.

66. As regards "persons protected", it is pointed out that in its Opinion No. 131 the Assembly proposed not to restrict the protection of the four new rights to nationals of the Parties. Since the Protocol is a legal instrument distinct from the Charter, there was no obligation from a legal point of view to make the scope of its application to persons identical to that laid down in the Charter. It was considered, nevertheless, that the close relationship created between the two instruments militated in favour of a degree of harmonisation and the need to have an identical field of application to persons won the day. It was stressed that the extension of the application of the Protocol to any persons of whatever nationality was not legally excluded and that in practice most of the rights falling within the social or labour field by their very nature benefit in principle and without distinction all persons lawfully residing or working regularly in the territory of a Party.

67. The provision of the appendix relating to Article 1 allow the exclusion of, from "terms of employment and working conditions", social security matters within the meaning of ILO Convention No. 102 concerning minimum standards of social security, that is to say its nine traditional branches. It was agreed that this text is to be construed as also allowing the exclusion, from the field of application of Article 1, of conditions of employment genuinely linked to social security matters and other benefits mentioned.

68. Under the heading "Articles 2 and 3", paragraph 4 of the appendix has been inserted, *inter alia*, to meet the situation in the Federal Republic of Germany where certain categories of undertakings with an "orientation" *(Tendenzbetriebe)* are excluded from the scope of the 1972 Act on the Organisation of Undertakings or from certain of its provisions. These are "companies and establishments that directly and predominantly:

1. pursue political, coalition, religious, charitable, educational, scientific or artistic objects; or

    2. serve purposes of publishing or expressing opinions covered by the second sentence of section 5 (1) of the Basic Law (Constitution)."

69. Under the heading "Articles 2 and 3", paragraph 5 of the appendix refers to "establishments of the undertaking". In fact an undertaking may consist of one or more production units economically and legally bound to a single management centre. Such production units then constitute as many component establishments of the undertaking, and it is understood that where within a state rights Nos. 2 and 3 are effectively exercised within the various establishments of the undertaking in question, the Party concerned shall be deemed to fulfil its obligations under these provisions.

B. Explanatory report to the 1991 Amending Protocol

Background

1. On 5 November 1990 an informal ministerial conference on human rights was held in Rome. One of the topics discussed was the European Social Charter, with the result that the Committee of Ministers of the Council of Europe was invited to take the necessary measures so that a detailed study of the role, contents and operation of the European Social Charter might be undertaken as soon as possible.

2. At their 449th meeting (November-December 1990), the Ministers' Deputies decided to authorise the convening of an *ad hoc* committee, the Committee on the European Social Charter (Charte-Rel), which would have the task of making proposals for improving the effectiveness of the European Social Charter and more particularly the functioning of its supervisory machinery.

3. The Committee was composed of experts designated by each member state. In addition, representatives of the Parliamentary Assembly, ILO, ETUC and UNICE took part in its meetings, but without the right to vote. The Committee of Independent Experts and the Governmental Committee as well as several other Council of Europe committees also participated in this work.

4. At its first meeting (February 1991), the Committee decided to concentrate, in the first instance, on the improvement of the supervisory machinery before addressing the reform of the substance of the Charter. As concerns the improvement of the supervisory machinery, its efforts resulted in three reforms which together make up a coherent whole: the present Protocol; the draft Additional Protocol laying down a system of collective complaints; the change in the reporting procedure, which the Committee of Ministers decided in September 1992 to introduce for a trial period of four years.

5. The Charte-Rel Committee adopted the draft Protocol at its third meeting (September 1991) and decided to communicate the text to the Committee of Ministers.

6. The Committee of Ministers, to which Parliamentary Assembly Recommendation 1168 (1991) had also been referred, adopted the text of the Protocol on 16 October 1991 and agreed that it should be opened for signature on 21 October 1991 in Turin, at a ministerial conference commemorating the 30th anniversary of the signature of the European Social Charter.

General structure of the Protocol

7. At the very outset of its work, the Charte-Rel Committee was unanimous on two preconditions for any significant improvement in
   the functioning of the Charter:

   a. a political will should be clearly expressed in the supervisory
   process. The main weakness of the present functioning of the
   system of supervision lay in the absence of any political sanc-
   tion. The Committee of Ministers ought to adopt individual
   recommendations on the basis of Article 29 of the Charter – a
   step which it had so far never taken;

   b. a substantial and rapid increase in the resources available for
   implementing the Charter, particularly the resources of the
   Secretariat, was required.

8. A consensus also emerged on various other points:

   a. the Governmental Committee ought to be retained;

   b. it was essential to clarify the functions and competences of the
   various supervisory organs, particularly those of the
   Committee of Independent Experts and of the Governmental
   Committee;

   c. according to its own representatives, the role of the
   Parliamentary Assembly ought to be revised: it should cease to
   be a supervisory organ in the strict sense of the term and
   become a political body for stimulation and discussion;

   d. the length of the supervisory procedure ought in any event to
   be reduced;

   e. it was necessary to improve the participation of the social partners within the national framework;

   f. efforts should be made to promote the Charter and make it
   better known, especially at national level.

9. The discussion was devoted for the most part to the clarification
   of the respective powers of the Committee of Independent Experts
   and the Governmental Committee. The text finally adopted is
   based on the idea that, of these two bodies, the Committee of
   Independent Experts alone would be competent to make a legal
   assessment of whether the national legislation, regulations and
   practices of a Contracting Party complied with its undertakings
   under the Charter. The role of the Governmental Committee
   would be to examine national situations and provide a specific
   viewpoint based on social, economic and other policy considerations. It could select the most problematical situations for consideration by the Committee of Ministers, suggesting, where
   appropriate, that the Ministers adopt one or more recommendations for the attention of this or that state. In this context, the
   Governmental Committee would not be a political organ *per se*, but
   rather a guide assisting the Committee of Ministers in reaching its

decisions. Through its role as a forum of governmental experts examining the reasons for the various states' main difficulties in the implementation of the provisions of the Charter, the Governmental Committee could play an important part in instigating measures to ensure social progress in Europe.

10. These considerations[1] had several consequences, the main ones being as follows:

   a. for the Committee of Independent Experts: increase in the number of members; modified procedure for election of members;

   b. for the Governmental Committee: to consider the more frequent use of paragraph 2 of Article 27 of the Charter, under the terms of which the Governmental Committee may consult international non-governmental organisations having consultative status with the Council of Europe in respect of questions with which such organisations are particularly qualified to deal;

   c. for the Committee of Ministers: adoption of individual recommendations; modification of the majority provided for under Article 29;

   d. for the Parliamentary Assembly: new role (see paragraph 8.c above);

   e. changes necessary prior to the conclusions of the Committee of Independent Experts, above all, gathering information as full and as balanced as possible. In this connection, special mention may be made of the possibility for the Committee of Independent Experts to refer directly to the Contracting Parties to request additional or more detailed information and to hold meetings with governmental representatives.

11. Not all these proposals required amendments to the Charter in order to be implemented. Nevertheless, in the light of past experience, the Charte-Rel Committee felt that several of the proposals should be incorporated into the text of the Charter.

Comments

Article 1

12. This article amends Article 23. Apart from purely technical changes, it introduces a new system for communicating copies of governmental reports and observations on these reports.

---

1. To which must be added the taking into account of the recent increase in the number of Contracting Parties (see below, paragraph 26).

Paragraph 1

13. Compared with the original text, the amended text states that when submitting their reports to the Secretary General governments shall send a copy to national organisations of employers and workers; the copy may of course be sent in the national language before being translated into one of the official languages of the Council of Europe.

14. The last two sentences replace the existing paragraph 2. Henceforth, both sides of industry can send their observations on the governmental reports directly to the Secretary General of the Council of Europe, while governments will also have the chance to submit their comments.

Paragraph 2

15. This paragraph is new. It provides that certain international non-governmental organisations (INGOs) shall be informed. This provision, which is mainly inspired by the important role which INGOs may play in developing the Charter and giving it fresh impetus, should be read in conjunction with Article 27, paragraph 2, and with the draft Additional Protocol introducing a system of collective complaints. There is merely a duty to inform: in contrast to the national social partners mentioned in paragraph 1, these INGOs will not have an opportunity to pass comments on governments' reports.

Paragraph 3

16. This paragraph is also new. With the aim of helping to promote the Charter and improve knowledge about it, provision is made for reports and comments to be communicated on request, without this implying a duty for the national authorities or the Council of Europe to make these documents the subject of an actual publication.

Article 2

17. This article amends Article 24 pertaining to the examination of governmental reports by the Committee of Independent Experts, whose powers and functions it defines.

Paragraph 1

18. This paragraph reproduces the text of the existing Article 24 with some technical changes.

Paragraph 2

19. Like the two following paragraphs, this paragraph is new and represents one of the essential provisions of the Protocol. In conjunction with paragraphs 3 and 4 of the new Article 27, it is intended to express in the text of the Charter the new allocation

of powers between the Committee of Independent Experts and the Governmental Committee (see paragraph 9 above). It therefore clearly states that the task of the Committee of Independent Experts is to assess national law and practice in relation to provisions under the Charter from a legal standpoint.

Paragraph 3

20. In this paragraph, provision is made for practical measures to introduce greater flexibility into the procedure, especially by helping to avoid misunderstandings – which cause tension and delays – between the Committee of Independent Experts and governments.

21. Accordingly, when examining a particular report, the Committee may get in touch directly with the government concerned in order to obtain information or clarifications without having to wait for the government's next report.

22. Similarly, the Committee may also hold a meeting with representatives of a Contracting Party. It was nevertheless considered that such meetings should remain the exception and that they should not be of a compulsory character.

23. Informing employers and workers (on a national and international level) in accordance with the last sentence may be done in various ways. Their organisations should at least be informed by the government concerned of the holding and outcome of the meeting.[1] Moreover, it would be possible for a government to invite representatives of the organisations in its country, which satisfy the criteria of paragraph 1 of Article 23, to attend the meeting of the Committee of Independent Experts together with its own representatives.

Paragraph 4

24. Like paragraph 3 of Article 23 as amended, this paragraph is designed to promote the Charter and encourage better participation by the various bodies concerned, by providing for the widest possible publicity of the relevant work.

Article 3

25. As indicated above (paragraph 10), certain provisions in the Protocol are the direct result of the new distribution of powers between the Committee of Independent Experts and the Governmental Committee. The amendments to Article 25 are an illustration of this change. This article refers to the membership of

---

1. See the new Article 27, paragraph 1, which speaks of "information communicated in accordance with paragraphs 1 of Article 23 and 3 of Article 24".

the Committee of Independent Experts whose title is given official status here.

Paragraph 1

26. Between October 1988 and October 1991, six new states ratified the Charter, which represents a remarkable increase compared with past events.[1] During the preparation of the Protocol it also became increasingly likely that the Additional Protocol of 1988 would enter into force in the near future, as in fact happened on 4 September 1992. As a result, many voices were raised to recommend, as did the Committee itself, an increase in the membership of the Committee of Independent Experts. This would enable it to have a more representative composition and to enjoy more satisfactory working conditions for coping with its workload.

27. Currently, the Committee of Independent Experts consists of "not more than seven members". Under the terms of this paragraph 1, the number is increased to nine, which is moreover regarded as a minimum ("at least nine members"). Thus, in order to meet new needs in the future without having to amend the text of the Charter each time, it is provided that the Committee of Ministers will fix the exact number of members of the Committee of Independent Experts.

28. In order to strengthen the independence of the Experts it is provided that they will no longer be appointed by the Committee of Ministers but elected by the Parliamentary Assembly from a list drawn up by the Contracting Parties.

Paragraph 2

29. The term of office of members of the Committee remains at six years but, in the future, it can be renewed only once.

30. The second sentence of this paragraph and the whole of paragraph 3 of the present text of Article 25 have been deleted because they have become superfluous, since the Committee of Independent Experts is already functioning and the system of partial renewal of membership is already operative.

Paragraph 3

31. This paragraph repeats the text of the existing paragraph 4, apart from a few technical changes.

Paragraph 4

32. This paragraph draws on the provisions recently incorporated into the European Convention on Human Rights by Protocol No. 8

---

1. The seven ratifications necessary for the Charter to enter into force were made in less than three-and-a-half years, but nineteen years were needed for seven additional ratifications.

(new Article 23 and Article 40, paragraph 7; see also Article 4, paragraph 7, of the European Convention for the Prevention of Torture and Inhuman or Degrading Treatment or Punishment). The provisions it contains are of course intended for each member of the Committee, but also for governments of Contracting Parties when they submit candidates for election.

Article 4

33. This article amends Article 27[1] which deals with the membership and duties of the Governmental Committee, whose title is also given official status here.

Paragraph 1

34. This paragraph supplements the present paragraph 1 by mentioning further documents to be communicated to the Governmental Committee, namely: the comments by national organisations of employers and workers on governmental reports; the government's comments in reply (Article 23, paragraph 1) and any further information provided on the occasion of a meeting of the Committee of Independent Experts with the representatives of a Contracting Party (Article 24, paragraph 3).

Paragraph 2

35. Compared with the present text, it should be noted that the number of representatives of international non-governmental organisations who may be consulted by the Governmental Committee is no longer limited to two.[2] In addition, the qualifications of these INGOs are defined in more general terms, and examples have been omitted.

Paragraph 3

36. Like paragraph 2 of the new Article 24, this paragraph is another essential provision of the Protocol. It defines the powers of the Governmental Committee as described above in paragraph 9. Basically, the idea is to make a clear distinction between its powers and those of the Committee of Independent Experts, which is achieved above all in the words "on the basis of social, economic and other policy considerations"[3] which contrasts with the expression "from a legal standpoint", contained in paragraph 2 of the new Article 24.

---

1. Article 26 concerning participation of the International Labour Organisation is unchanged.
2. As indicated above in paragraph 10.b, the hope was expressed that the Governmental Committee would make more frequent use of this possibility provided under the Charter.
3. For purely linguistic reasons the French and English versions are not strictly identical, but their meaning is the same.

37. In the same spirit as the remarks made in paragraph 7.b above, the accent is placed here on the individual recommendations which should be adopted by the Committee of Ministers.

38. The last sentence corresponds to the existing paragraph 3, but some changes have been introduced. In view of the new powers assigned to each of the two committees, the report by the Committee of Independent Experts acquires a new status of its own and is no longer an appendix to the Governmental Committee's report. Again with a view to promoting the Charter and making it more familiar to all those concerned (see paragraphs 16 and 24 above), the Governmental Committee's reports will be made public.

Paragraph 4

39. This paragraph supplements the foregoing one by extending the functions of the Governmental Committee beyond those of a mere monitoring body. Accordingly, it will be able to submit proposals to the Committee of Ministers for the preparation of studies on social issues or on articles of the Charter in need of revision.

Article 5

40. This article in fact amends the original Article 29 of the Charter because, with a view to highlighting the fact that the Parliamentary Assembly will no longer intervene directly in the supervisory procedure, the order of Articles 28 and 29 has been inverted.

Paragraph 1

41. This paragraph is based on the text of Article 29 but introduces major amendments, all of which are designed to make it possible for the Committee of Ministers to adopt individual recommendations.

42. The present majority (two-thirds of the Council of Europe member states, whether or not they are Parties to the Charter), was found to constitute an obstacle, since a few abstentions might prevent the required majority from being achieved. States not party to the Charter have indeed tended to abstain. For this reason, the new rule provides that only Contracting Parties may take part in the voting and that the two-thirds majority will be based on those voting (no account being taken of abstentions).

43. In order to highlight the need for the Committee of Minister to adopt individual recommendations taking account of the proposals by the Governmental Committee, the wording has been made more binding: "shall adopt ... individual recommendations", instead of "may ... make ... any necessary recommendations".

44. It is specified that the resolution adopted by the Committee of Ministers shall cover "the entire supervision cycle"[1] as the recommendations will concern only some of the provisions that have been monitored.

45. In accordance with what was stated above in paragraph 40 and which has been made explicit in the new Article 29, the obligation on the Committee of Ministers to consult the Parliamentary Assembly has been discarded.

Paragraph 2

46. With regard to the functions to be performed by the Committee of Ministers, this paragraph corresponds to paragraph 4 of the new Article 27.

Article 6

47. From the very outset of the work on the Protocol, the representatives of the Parliamentary Assembly on the Charte-Rel Committee[2] expressed the wish that the Assembly's role should be changed: it should no longer be a supervisory body as such, systematically verifying the application of all the provisions of the Charter for all Contracting Parties; rather, it should organise periodic debates on selected topics of social policy. This change should allow the Assembly to express its point of view on the action resulting from the Charter in the light of major debates on social policy, without necessarily being tied by the timetable of the control procedure. The said procedure would thereby be simplified and speeded up.

48. This new conception of the Assembly's role is spelt out in Article 6 of the Protocol, which in effect amends the present Article 28 of the Charter. As already pointed out (paragraph 40 above), the order of Articles 28 and 29 has been inverted to bring out more clearly that the Assembly, although still associated with the implementation of the Charter, is no longer implicated in the supervisory procedure as such.

Articles 7 to 9

49. These articles, which contain the final clauses of the Protocol, correspond to the models adopted by the Committee of Ministers of the Council of Europe.

---

1. The notion of "supervision cycle" may vary according to the modifications made to the reporting procedure (see above, paragraph 4).
2. See also Resolution 967 (1991) and Recommendation 1168 (1991) of the Parliamentary Assembly.

C. Explanatory report to the 1995 Protocol

Background

1. The idea of setting up a system of collective complaints for the European Social Charter along the lines of the existing International Labour Organisation (ILO) arrangements is not new (see, for example, Recommendation 839 (1978) of the Parliamentary Assembly). It has been revived as part of the efforts initiated in 1991 to give a new impetus to the Charter.

2. The introduction of a system of this type is designed to increase the efficiency of supervisory machinery based solely on the submission of governmental reports. In particular, this system should increase participation by management and labour and non-governmental organisations (already improved by the Protocol amending the Social Charter of 21 October 1991). The way in which the machinery as a whole functions can only be enhanced by the greater interest that these bodies may be expected to show in the Charter. The procedure provided for in the Protocol will also be shorter than that for examining reports. The system of collective complaints is to be seen as a complement to the examination of governmental reports, which naturally constitutes the basic mechanism for the supervision of the application of the Charter.

3. The committee set up by the Committee of Ministers in December 1990 to draw up proposals for reforming the Charter (Committee on the European Social Charter, Charte-Rel) examined this matter from the outset. At its second meeting (22-24 May 1991), it decided to set up a working party to draw up proposals on ways of establishing a collective complaints system under the Charter, and on the operation of such a system. The working party, which met on 3 and 4 July 1991, submitted most of its proposals in the form of draft articles for incorporation in a protocol to the Charter. It was agreed that all other procedural details could be laid down in rules of procedure drawn up by the body responsible for ruling on the admissibility of complaints (in this case the Committee of Independent Experts).

4. In the light of the comments submitted in particular by the Committee of Independent Experts and international organisations of employers and trade unions (UNICE and ETUC), the Charte-Rel Committee examined the report of the working party at its third meeting (3-6 September 1991) and adopted draft articles

for an additional protocol to the Charter. This draft was transmitted to the Committee of Ministers.

5. Bearing in mind the decision to hold a ministerial conference in Turin on 21 and 22 October 1991 to mark the thirtieth anniversary of the signing of the European Social Charter, the Ministers' Deputies agreed that the examination of this draft "should be pursued both by the Experts, who would meet in Turin on 21 October 1991 in the morning, and by the Ministers' meeting in Turin". In the Final Resolution of the conference the Ministers – after stressing the importance, for the purposes of the effectiveness and development of the Charter, of the widest possible participation by management and labour, and stating that a majority of them considered that such participation would be strengthened by the introduction of a system of collective complaints – recommended that the Committee of Ministers "examine at their earliest opportunity a draft protocol providing for a system of collective complaints, with a view to its adoption and opening for signature".

6. In the meantime the Parliamentary Assembly had adopted Recommendation 1168 (1991). The appendix to this recommendation contained a new article 25bis on the collective complaints procedure (see also Resolution 967 (1991)).

7. The Charte-Rel Committee resumed examination of the draft protocol at its fourth meeting (3-6 February 1992), following which it decided to set up another working party, which met on 30 and 31 March 1992. The Committee finalised the text of the draft protocol at its fifth meeting (18-20 May 1992) and decided to transmit it to the Committee of Ministers for adoption.

8. After consulting the Committee of Independent Experts and the Parliamentary Assembly, the Committee of Ministers adopted the text of the Protocol on 22 June 1995 and opened it for signature on 9 November 1995.

General structure of the Additional Protocol

9. The structure of the Protocol is simple. It basically answers two questions: who? how? Who can submit complaints and who examines them? Following which procedure?

10. The following organisations can submit complaints, sometimes subject to certain conditions: international and national organisations of employers and trade unions and other international and national non-governmental organisations (in the case of national NGOs, a declaration by the state concerned recognising this right is required).

11. The complaint is initially examined by the Committee of Independent Experts which, after determining admissibility, reviews both sides' explanations and information as well as any observations submitted by other Contracting Parties to the Protocol or by international organisations of employers or trade unions referred to in paragraph 2 of Article 27 of the Charter. The Committee then draws up a report containing, in particular, conclusions as to whether or not the state concerned has complied with the Charter. This report is transmitted *inter alia* to the Committee of Ministers and made public no more than four months later. On the basis of this report the Committee of Ministers adopts a resolution and, if the conclusions of the Committee of Independent Experts are negative, addresses a recommendation to the state concerned. The latter should provide information on the measures taken to comply with the recommendation of the Committee of Ministers in its next report to the Secretary General under Article 21 of the Charter.

Comments

Preamble

12. The preamble gives the main reasons why the member states of the Council of Europe decided to adopt the Protocol and the aim pursued.

13. In the second paragraph, the term "new measures" highlights the fact that improvements have already been made in the form of the first Additional Protocol (5 May 1988), the Protocol amending the Social Charter (21 October 1991) and changes to the system of governmental reports (decision of the Ministers' Deputies of September 1992, 479th meeting, item 25).

14. The last paragraph of the preamble refers implicitly to the Final Resolution of the Turin Conference (see paragraph 5 above) and also expressly mentions non-governmental organisations other than those of management and labour.

Article 1

15. The main purpose of this article is to indicate the organisations that are entitled to submit complaints solely by virtue of the fact that the Protocol is in force *vis-à-vis* the state concerned. In the introductory sentence it establishes the principle of recognition of this right by the Contracting Parties and briefly describes the scope of complaints.

16. The organisations concerned are mentioned in three separate paragraphs.

a. international organisations of employers and trade unions

17. This refers to organisations that can take part in the work of the Governmental Committee as laid down in paragraph 2 of Article 27 of the Charter;

b. other international non-governmental organisations (INGOs)

18. By virtue of the aforementioned paragraph 2 of Article 27 of the Charter, these other organisations are also entitled to take part in the work of the Governmental Committee. The fact that they are mentioned in the Protocol highlights the originality of the European Social Charter as compared to other equivalent international systems. In fact several provisions of the Charter are not exclusively concerned with the world of work and do not fall within the direct competence of management and labour. In this connection, it should be noted that in the Amending Protocol the new paragraph 2 of Article 23 lays down special arrangements for notifying these organisations.

19. However, in contrast to the arrangements for international organisations of employers and trade unions, a mere reference to paragraph 2 of Article 27 was not deemed sufficient in the case of INGOs. Therefore, in order to be entitled to submit a complaint, an INGO must not only have consultative status with the Council of Europe, but must also appear on a special list.

20. This list is drawn up by the Governmental Committee using the following procedure, laid down by the Committee of Ministers (decision of 22 June 1995):

    – INGOs which hold consultative status with the Council of Europe and consider themselves particularly competent in any of the matters governed by the Charter are invited to express their wish to be included on a special list of INGOs entitled to submit complaints;

    – each application must be supported by detailed and accurate documentation aiming to show in particular that the INGO has access to authoritative sources of information and is able to carry out the necessary verifications, to obtain appropriate legal opinions, etc., in order to draw up complaint files that meet basic requirements of reliability;

    – all applications are transmitted to the Governmental Committee, accompanied by an opinion of the Secretary General which reflects the degree of interest and participation shown by the INGO in its normal dealings with the Council of Europe;

    – an application is considered accepted by the Governmental Committee unless it is rejected in a ballot by a simple majority of votes cast;

    – inclusion on the special list is valid for a period of four years, after which it lapses unless the organisation applies for renewal in the six-month period preceding the expiry date. The procedure described above applies to renewal applications.

21. The inclusion of an INGO on this list does not relieve the Committee of Independent Experts, when examining admissibility, from the obligation to ascertain that the complaint actually falls within a field in which the INGO concerned has been recognised as being particularly competent (see paragraph 29 below).

c. national organisations of employers and trade unions

22. As laid down in paragraph 1 of Article 23 of the Charter, each Contracting Party must forward a copy of its report to certain of its national organisations of employers and trade unions. It is only normal that organisations of this type should be entitled to submit complaints, because they are very well informed of the situation in their country. For this reason those who drafted the Protocol considered that it would be wrong to restrict this right to the national organisations mentioned in Article 23 (that is those which are members of the international organisations referred to in paragraph 2 of Article 27).

23. To ensure the efficient functioning of the procedure established by the Protocol and in view of the very large number of trade unions operating in some states, it was deemed necessary to stipulate that the organisation must be "representative". The Committee of Independent Experts will judge whether the organisation meets this criterion when examining whether the complaint is admissible, in the light of information and observations submitted by the state and the organisation concerned (see Article 6). In the absence of any criteria on a national level, factors such as the number of members and the organisation's actual role in national negotiations should be taken into account.

24. It is also stipulated that, in order to be admissible, a complaint must be submitted by a national organisation within the jurisdiction of the Contracting Party concerned.

Article 2

25. The Charter does not refer specifically to national non-governmental organisations (NGOs) other than organisations of employers and trade unions. Nevertheless, for the same reasons as those invoked in respect of international non-governmental organisations (paragraph 18) and national organisations of employers and trade unions (paragraph 22), it was thought that these national NGOs should also be entitled to submit complaints. However, recognition of this right is not mandatory for parties to the Protocol, but optional: NGOs may only submit a complaint against a state if the state in question has previously issued a declaration recognising that NGOs are entitled to do so. In addition,

according to paragraph 2, such declarations may be made for a specific period.

26. With the same aim of preserving the efficiency of the machinery for examining collective complaints, NGOs are subject to the same conditions as laid down for international non-governmental organisations and national organisations of employers and trade unions: they must be "representative" and particularly "qualified" in issues covered by the Charter. The Committee of Independent Experts will judge whether these criteria are met when examining whether the complaint is admissible in the light of information submitted by both parties (see Article 6 and paragraph 23 above). As in respect of INGOs (see, paragraph 21 above and paragraph 29 below), the Committee should ascertain that the complaint actually falls within a field in which the NGO concerned is particularly competent.

27. As is the case for national organisations of employers and trade unions, NGOs must come within the jurisdiction of the state against which their complaint is made.

28. Subject to the considerations set out in the previous two paragraphs, when a state makes a declaration on the basis of this article, it recognises the right of all NGOs within its jurisdiction to submit complaints without, for example, drawing up a national list. In similar vein, it may not restrict this right to certain articles or paragraphs of the Charter.

Article 3

29. This article specifies that international and national non-governmental organisations may only submit complaints in respect of those matters regarding which they have been recognised as having particular competence.

Article 4

30. This article lays down three admissibility conditions which were deemed sufficiently important to be specifically mentioned in a separate article of the Protocol. These conditions complement those laid down in Articles 1 and 2, which specify the organisations entitled to submit complaints.

31. As indicated in paragraph 3 above, the Committee of Independent Experts may stipulate the conditions governing the admissibility of complaints in its rules of procedure. It must take account of the fact that the following was agreed in the course of negotiations within the Charte-Rel Committee:

   – a complaint may be declared admissible even if a similar case has already been submitted to another national or international body;

- the fact that the substance of a complaint has been examined as part of the "normal" government reports procedure does not in itself constitute an impediment to the complaint's admissibility. It has been agreed to give the Committee of Independent Experts a sufficient margin of appreciation in this area;
- because of their "collective" nature, complaints may only raise questions concerning non-compliance of a state's law or practice with one of the provisions of the Charter. Individual situations may not be submitted.

Article 5

32. This article does not invite any specific comments, but two general remarks can be made.

33. The adverb "immediately" underlines that one of the advantages of the new procedure is its rapidity. This comment also applies to Articles 6 and 7, which invite the Committee of Independent Experts in several instances to prescribe time-limits for the submission of information and explanations.

34. It has been agreed that when the Committee of Independent Experts takes action under the Protocol, its membership shall be that laid down in Articles 25 and 26 of the Charter, namely with the participation of an ILO representative.

Article 6

35. This article concerns the assessment of the admissibility of complaints. The submissions of both parties must be examined: the state concerned and the organisation that lodged the complaint are invited by the Committee of Independent Experts to submit information and observations, and a complaint can only be declared admissible if the state concerned has had the opportunity to state its case. However, the article does not create an obligation for the Committee of Independent Experts to request such information, in order to permit it to reject a complaint that is manifestly inadmissible of its own volition.

Article 7

36. This article lays down the main stages in the examination of the merits of complaints. Again, heavy emphasis is placed on the fact that submissions from both parties must be examined and on its corollary, namely the need to work within reasonable time limits.

37. Paragraph 1 establishes a distinction between information and the possibility of submitting comments. All Contracting Parties to the Charter are notified that a complaint is admissible (first sentence). However (second sentence), only Contracting Parties to the Protocol may submit comments. These provisions reflect the fact

that the follow-up to a complaint may be of interest to states other than the one directly concerned, while providing that those states that have not agreed to be bound by the Protocol are not entitled to submit comments.

38. Paragraph 2 takes account of the key role played by international organisations of employers and trade unions in the supervisory machinery provided for by the Charter in giving them the possibility of submitting observations on complaints lodged by other organisations.

39. Paragraph 3 makes provision for each party concerned to react to the other party's comments.

40. Paragraph 4 authorises the Committee of Independent Experts to organise hearings with representatives of the state concerned and the organisation that lodged the complaint. In view of the fact that the previous paragraphs of this article make ample provision for both parties to make submissions, hearings of this type need not be organised systematically. It is simply an option available to the Committee of Independent Experts, which is responsible for determining on the basis of the available information whether a meeting with the representatives of the parties is necessary. Meetings of this type can also be arranged at the request of one of the parties.

Article 8

41. Paragraph 1 corresponds to the final stage of the consideration of the merits of the complaint by the Committee of Independent Experts. The Committee draws up a report featuring in particular its legal assessment of the complaint. This provision must be read in the light of the new paragraph 2 of Article 24 of the Charter (Article 2 of the Protocol amending the Charter).

42. Paragraph 2 specifies to which bodies the report of the Committee of Independent Experts is to be sent and lays down rules on its publication.

43. Initially (first sub-paragraph) the report, which is transmitted to the Committee of Ministers, the organisation that lodged the complaint and the Contracting Parties to the Charter, remains confidential (see, *mutatis mutandis*, paragraph 2 of Article 31 of the European Convention on Human Rights).

It should be borne in mind here that the whole of the procedure for considering complaints is confidential. It was not thought necessary to specify this in the Protocol because the rules of procedure of the Committee of Independent Experts already stated that its sessions "shall be held in private. All working documents shall be confidential". Nevertheless, this does not imply a total lack of information. In line with the procedure used within the framework of the European Convention on Human Rights, the following may be made public: the fact that a given organisation has lodged a complaint against a given state, the basis of the complaint and the decision on its admissibility.

44. Subsequently (second sub-paragraph) the report is transmitted to the Parliamentary Assembly and made public. This may take place at two different times:

    – either four months after the report has been transmitted to the Committee of Ministers;

    – or when the resolution referred to in Article 9 is adopted by the Committee of Ministers, if this occurs before four months have elapsed.

Article 9

45. This article deals with the role of the Committee of Ministers, which intervenes immediately after the Committee of Independent Experts.

46. The duties of the Committee of Ministers are similar to those it carries out as supervisory body in the procedure instituted by the Charter.

    On the basis of the report of the Committee of Independent Experts, the Committee of Ministers adopts a resolution, by a majority of those voting. However, if the conclusions of the Committee of Independent Experts are negative, the Committee of Ministers must adopt a recommendation addressed to the state concerned. In view of the importance of this decision and in accordance with the new rule introduced by the Amending Protocol (Article 5), a two-thirds majority of those voting is required.

    The Committee of Ministers cannot reverse the legal assessment made by the Committee of Independent Experts. However, its decision (resolution or recommendation) may be based on social and economic policy considerations.

47. In respect of the resolution as well as the recommendation, only the Contracting Parties to the Charter are entitled to take part in the vote.

48. The Charte-Rel Committee had foreseen that the Governmental Committee would not be involved in the procedure for examining complaints, but the Committee of Ministers decided before adopting the Protocol to add a second paragraph to this article, according to which the Committee of Ministers may decide, where the report of the Committee of Independent Experts raises new issues, by a two-thirds majority of the Contracting Parties to the Charter, to consult the Governmental Committee.

Article 10

49. Once the Committee of Ministers has adopted a recommendation, appropriate follow-up must be ensured. In line with the practice adopted for other international supervisory machinery (European Convention on Human Rights, ILO, Human Rights Committee, etc.), Article 10 requires the state concerned to provide information on the measures it has taken to give effect to the Committee of Ministers' recommendation.

50. This information will be contained in the "next report" that the state concerned submits to the Secretary General under Article 21 of the Charter. In other words, the state may not wait until the time when it would normally submit a report on the provision(s) concerned by the complaint; it must provide the information required in the report immediately following the decision of the Committee of Ministers.

Article 11

51. Throughout the Protocol, only the Charter itself is mentioned. This article specifies that if a state is also bound by the first Additional Protocol (5 May 1988), complaints may be submitted on the basis of the articles it has accepted.

52. If further protocols to the Charter are adopted in future, they must contain a provision specifying that this Protocol applies to the articles of these other protocols that have been accepted.

Article 12

53. In the course of the negotiations, the question arose as to whether the adoption of a system of collective complaints would be fully compatible with the wording of the appendix to the Charter concerning Part III, which states that "It is understood that the Charter contains legal obligations of an international character, the application of which is submitted solely to the supervision provided for in Part IV thereof."

54. To avoid any ambiguity, it was decided to include the present Article 12.

Articles 13 to 15

55. These articles, which contain the final clauses of the Protocol, conform to the model adopted by the Committee of Ministers of the Council of Europe.

D. Explanatory report to the revised European Social Charter

Introduction

1. On 5 November 1990 an Informal Ministerial Conference on human rights was held in Rome. One of the topics discussed was the European Social Charter, with the result that the Council of Europe's Committee of Ministers was invited to take the necessary steps so that a detailed study of the role, contents and operation of the European Social Charter might be undertaken as soon as possible.

2. At their 449th meeting (November-December 1990), the Ministers' Deputies decided to authorise the convening of an *ad hoc* committee, the Committee on the European Social Charter (Charte-Rel). Under its terms of reference, the Committee was instructed to make proposals for improving the effectiveness of the European Social Charter, and particularly the functioning of its supervisory machinery.

3. The Committee was composed of experts appointed by each member state. Its meetings were attended in a non-voting capacity by representatives of the Parliamentary Assembly, the International Labour Organisation, the European Trade Union Confederation and the Union of Industrial and Employers' Confederations of Europe. The Committee of Independent Experts and the Governmental Committee of the European Social Charter were also involved in the work along with several other Council of Europe committees.

4. At its twelfth meeting (10-14 October 1994), the Charte-Rel Committee adopted a draft revised European Social Charter and decided to submit it to the Committee of Ministers for adoption.

5. After consulting the Committee of Independent Experts and the Parliamentary Assembly, the Committee of Ministers adopted the text entitled the revised European Social Charter on 3 April 1996 and opened it for signature on 3 May 1996.

6. According to the practice of the Council of Europe, this explanatory report has no binding value and was drafted only with a view to explaining the content of the revised Charter. The Committee of Ministers authorised its publication when adopting the revised European Social Charter.

7. From the outset, the aim has been that amendments to the text of the Charter should not represent a lowering of the level of

protection provided for therein. It was also agreed that the reform would involve taking account both of developments in social and economic rights as reflected in other international instruments and in the legislation of member states and also of social problems not covered by the other international instruments in force. Furthermore, all amendments were to be made bearing in mind the need to ensure equal treatment of men and women.

8. The revised European Social Charter takes account of developments in labour law and social policies since the Charter was drawn up in 1961. The revised Charter is a comprehensive international treaty which brings together in a single instrument all the rights guaranteed in the Charter and the 1988 Additional Protocol, along with the amendments to these rights and the new rights adopted by the Charte-Rel Committee.

   The instrument has been drafted in such a way as to be autonomous, but with the same supervisory machinery as the Charter. It does not conflict with the Charter but is intended to eventually replace it.

9. The revised Charter presents Parts I and II in the same way as they are presented in the Charter and the 1988 Additional Protocol, adding the new rights at the end of each part. This presentation was deemed preferable since it had the advantage of being familiar, of avoiding confusion with the original texts and the existing case law and of facilitating the presentation of national reports. This will also allow new rights to be added in the future without changing the structure of the text.

10. The revised European Social Charter does not provide for denunciation of the former Charter. However, if a Contracting State accepts the provisions of the revised Charter, the corresponding provisions of the initial Charter and its Protocol cease to apply to that state. In this way, states are not simultaneously bound by undertakings at different levels.

11. The terminology used in the revised Charter is in conformity with the model final clauses adopted by the Committee of Ministers in 1981, in particular the term "Contracting Party" in the Charter has been replaced by "Party".

Part I

12. This part corresponds to Part I of the Charter. Similarly to this Part I, it contains a general statement of rights and principles setting out the aim for the policy of the Parties and each point of Part I corresponds to the Article of Part II with the same number.

13. As in the case of the Charter, Part I contains a declaration of a political nature which has to be accepted as a whole, irrespective

of whether the corresponding provisions of Part II are accepted or not.

14. The wording of points 8, 15 and 17 has been brought into line with the revised Articles 8, 15 and 17. The amendments made to Articles 2, 3, 7, 10, 11, 12 and 19 have not required that any changes be made to Part I.

15. Points 20 to 23 have been taken from the 1988 Additional Protocol to the Charter and have not been amended.

16. Points 24 to 31 correspond to the new Articles contained in the revised Charter.

Part II

17. Part II contains the economic and social rights provided for by the revised European Social Charter. As in the case of the Charter, those rights may be accepted selectively, subject to a minimum number of acceptances (see Article A below).

18. As there is no explanatory report to the Charter, it was considered preferable not to explain the rights contained in Part II of the revised Charter. Only the differences with the Charter will therefore be mentioned, as well as the new provisions set out.

19. Articles 1 to 19 reproduce the text of the corresponding Articles of the Charter with the following differences:

Article 1 – The right to work

20. No amendment.

Article 2 – The right to just conditions of work

21. Two paragraphs have been amended (paragraphs 3 and 4), the others remain unchanged:

Paragraph 3

22. This provision provides for an increase in annual holidays, from the two weeks provided by the Charter to four weeks.

Paragraph 4

23. This provision, which in the Charter provides for additional paid holidays or reduced working hours for workers engaged in dangerous or unhealthy occupations, has been amended so as to reflect present-day policies which aim to eliminate the risks to which workers are exposed. The idea is that additional paid holidays or reduced working hours should only be provided where it has not been possible to eliminate or reduce sufficiently the risks inherent in dangerous or unhealthy occupations. This provision

should be seen as a complement to the revised Article 3, which emphasises the prevention of occupational accidents.

24. Two new paragraphs have been added:

Paragraph 6

25. The obligation on the Parties under this paragraph is to ensure that workers are informed about the essential aspects of their contract or employment relationship.

26. The "essential aspects" of the contract or employment relationship of which workers shall be informed have not been specified in the provision. However, reference as to the minimum requirements in this respect may be found in European Community Directive (91/533) on an employer's obligation to inform employees of the conditions applicable to the contract or employment relationship (Article 2). In principle the provision covers all workers, but the appendix stipulates that two exceptions can be made, namely Parties may provide that the provisions shall not apply to workers whose contract of employment covers a very short period of time or whose contract or employment relationship is of a casual or of a specific nature provided it is justified by objective considerations.

Paragraph 7

27. The general recognition of the fact that night work places special constraints on workers, both men and women led to the inclusion of this paragraph in the revised Charter. Furthermore, whereas Article 8, paragraph 4.a of the Charter provided that the employment of women workers in general for night work in industrial employment should be regulated, the corresponding provision in the revised Charter protects women only in the case of maternity. The other women previously protected by Article 8, paragraph 4.a of the Charter are therefore now covered by Article 2, paragraph 7 of the revised Charter on the same conditions as men, in conformity with the principle of equality. It should however be pointed out that the new provision does not require the existence of regulations.

28. The provision contains no definition of night work, which is to be provided by national legislation or practice.

Article 3 – The right to safe and healthy working conditions

29. This Article contains two new paragraphs (paragraphs 1 and 4) and two paragraphs (paragraphs 2 and 3) which, together with the new preamble of the Article correspond, respectively, to Article 3, paragraphs 1 and 3 of the Charter and to Article 3, paragraph 2 and 3 of the Charter.

30. The requirement for consultation with employers' and workers' organisations which is contained in Article 3, paragraph 3 of the Charter has been included in the preamble of Article 3 of the revised Charter and consequently applies to the four paragraphs contained in Article 3 of this instrument.

Paragraph 1

31. This paragraph obliges the Parties to formulate, implement and periodically review a coherent national policy on occupational safety, occupational health and the working environment. It emphasises that the aim of this policy shall be to improve occupational safety and health and to prevent accidents and injury to health, *inter alia*, by minimising risks.

Paragraph 2

32. This paragraph corresponds to Article 3, paragraphs 1 and 3 of the Charter.

Paragraph 3

33. This paragraph corresponds to Article 3, paragraphs 2 and 3 of the Charter.

Paragraph 4

34. This provision provides that the Parties shall promote the progressive development of occupational health services for all workers with essentially preventive and advisory functions.

35. The terms "occupational health services" shall include the French concept of *médecine du travail.*

36. In the appendix it is provided that for the purposes of this provision the function, organisation and conditions of operation of occupational health services shall be determined by national laws or regulations, collective agreements or other means appropriate to national conditions.

Article 4 – The right to a fair remuneration

37. No amendment.

Article 5 – The right to organise

38. No amendment.

Article 6 – The right to bargain collectively

39. No amendment.

Article 7 – The right of children and young persons to protection

40. Three paragraphs have been amended (paragraphs 2, 4 and 7), the others remain unchanged:

Paragraph 2

41. The minimum age required by this provision for admission to employment in prescribed occupations regarded as dangerous or unhealthy, which was not specified by the Charter, has been fixed at 18 years in the revised Charter. This provision has been inspired by the Council of the European Communities Directive 94/33 on the protection of young people at work.

Paragraph 4

42. The minimum age-limit provided for by this provision for regulation of the working hours has been raised to 18 years as compared to the 16 years provided for in the Charter.

Paragraph 7

43. The length of annual holidays with pay for young workers has been increased, from the three weeks provided in the Charter to four weeks.

Article 8 – The right of employed women to protection of maternity

44. In order to take into account the principle of equality, this Article, which corresponds to Article 8 of the Charter, has been modified so as to protect women exclusively in the case of maternity. This is a result, *inter alia*, of the changes made to the heading and to the introductory sentence. As stated in the heading of the provision it applies only to employed women.

45. Three paragraphs have been amended (1, 2 and 4), paragraph 3 remains unchanged:

Paragraph 1

46. As compared to the Charter, the length of maternity leave has been increased from twelve to fourteen weeks.

Paragraph 2

47. This provision of the revised Charter extends the minimum period of protection against dismissal for pregnant women as compared to the corresponding provision of the Charter. The period runs from the time a woman notifies her employer that she is pregnant until the end of her maternity leave.

48. There are some exceptions to the protection against dismissal during this period. These exceptions have been included in an appendix to the provision. They cover, *inter alia*, cases of serious

misconduct, cases in which the enterprise ceases to operate and cases in which the period prescribed in the employment contract has expired. These exceptions correspond to the case law of the Committee of Independent Experts.

Paragraph 4

49. This paragraph amends Article 8, paragraph 4.a of the Charter. The basic idea behind it, which has been taken from ILO Convention No. 171 (Night Work) of 1990 and from European Community Directive 92/85 on the introduction of measures to encourage improvements in the safety and health at work of pregnant workers and workers who have recently given birth or are breastfeeding, is that regulations on the employment of women for night work are needed only in the case of maternity. It is thus more restrictive than Article 8, paragraph 4.a of the Charter, which concerns the regulation of night work for women in general, but at the same time it is wider in its scope as it is not limited to regulating night work for women in industrial employment. Article 2, paragraph 7 offers protection for both men and women performing night work.

50. The definition of the women workers covered by the provision has been inspired by European Community Directive 92/85. "Pregnant women" in this context shall mean pregnant workers who inform their employer of their condition, in accordance with national legislation and/or practice. By "women who have recently given birth" is meant workers who have recently given birth within the meaning of national legislation and/or national practice and who inform their employer of their condition in accordance with that legislation and/or practice. Finally, "women who are nursing their infants" refers to workers who are breastfeeding within the meaning of national legislation and/or national practice and who inform their employer of their condition in accordance with that legislation and/or practice.

Paragraph 5

51. This paragraph, which amends Article 8, paragraph 4.b of the Charter, limits the prohibition of employment of women in underground mining and in all other work which is unsuitable by reason of its dangerous, unhealthy or arduous nature to the case of maternity as defined in the preceding paragraph. It requires Parties to take appropriate measures to protect the employment rights of the women concerned. By this it has been understood that such workers should be given the possibility to transfer to suitable work, or to be granted leave from work if a transfer is not feasible, with the payment of salary or other adequate allowance and without loss of status, seniority or access to promotion.

Article 9 – The right to vocational guidance

52. No amendment.

Article 10 – The right to vocational training

53. One paragraph has been added (paragraph 4); the others remain unchanged, therefore paragraph 4 of the Charter has become paragraph 5 of the revised Charter.

Paragraph 4

54. The idea behind this new paragraph, which has been added to Article 10, is that it is necessary to adopt "special" measures for the retraining and reintegration of the long-term unemployed, as their possibilities of re-entering the labour market are particularly few.

Article 11 – The right to protection of health

55. One paragraph has been amended (paragraph 3); the others remain unchanged:

Paragraph 3

56. This paragraph corresponds to Article 11, paragraph 3 of the Charter, with the addition of the word "and accidents". What is required from the Parties is to follow a policy of accident prevention, but each state will be able to decide on its own measures to that end.

Article 12 – The right to social security

57. One paragraph has been amended (paragraph 2); the others remain unchanged:

Paragraph 2

58. Reference is made in this paragraph to the European Code of Social Security. The difference between ILO Convention No. 102 and the European Code of Social Security relates to the minimum requirements as to how many parts must be accepted for the ratification of these instruments (three for the Convention; six for the Code). The ratification of the revised Code requires a higher standard of social security than is required for the ratification of ILO Convention No. 102.

59. The authors of the text considered that the European Code of Social Security (Revised) could be taken into account in relation to Article 12, paragraph 3.

Article 13 – The right to social and medical assistance

60. No amendment.

Article 14 – The right to benefit from social welfare services

61. No amendment.

Article 15 – The right of persons with disabilities to independence, social integration and participation in the life of the community

62. Article 15 has been amended.

63. The protection of the disabled afforded by this Article has been extended as compared to that afforded by Article 15 of the Charter, as it no longer applies only to vocational rehabilitation but to the right of persons with disabilities to independent social integration, personal autonomy and participation in the life of the community in general. The words "effective exercise of the right to independence" contained in the introductory sentence to the provision imply, *inter alia*, that disabled persons should have the right to an independent life.

64. Under this provision Parties must aim to develop a coherent policy for people with disabilities. The provision takes a modern approach to how the protection of the disabled shall be carried out, for example by providing that guidance, education and vocational training be provided whenever possible in the framework of general schemes rather than in specialised institutions, an approach which corresponds to that of Recommendation No. R (92) 6 of the Committee of Ministers of the Council of Europe. It not only provides the possibility, but to a large extent obliges Parties to adopt positive measures for the disabled.

65. It is understood that the term "sheltered employment" in paragraph 2 also covers working co-operatives.

Article 16 – The right of the family to social, legal and economic protection

66. The text of the Article itself has not been amended, although as the protection offered to "mothers" by Article 17 of the Charter has not been maintained in the new version of Article 17 contained in the revised Charter, Article 16 of the latter instrument will now cover this group. It must be pointed out that the "mothers" in question may be single parents, but they may also be living in a couple. The protection particularly concerns women who are not covered by Article 8 and/or who are not covered by any social security scheme providing the necessary financial assistance during a reasonable period before and after confinement, as well as adequate medical care during confinement.

67. The revised Charter contains a statement in the appendix to this provision, to the effect that the protection afforded by it also covers single-parent families.

Article 17 – The right of children and young persons to social, legal and economic protection

68. Article 17 has been amended.

69. Whereas the general protection of children in the Charter is contained in Article 7, which refers almost exclusively to the protection of children at work, this Article of the revised Charter offers protection for children and young persons outside the context of work and addresses the special needs arising from their vulnerability.

70. This provision protects children, irrespective of such factors as their birth status and the marital status of their parents. In confirmation of the case law of the Committee of Independent Experts, according to which certain rights such as the right of children to inheritance are covered by Article 17 of the Charter, the word "legal" has been added to its title.

71. The appendix to Article 17 defines the scope of the provision in that it covers all persons below the age of 18 years, unless under the law applicable to the child majority is attained earlier. The provision covers these children without prejudice to the other specific provisions provided by the Charter, particularly Article 7.

Paragraph 1

72. The word "parents" in paragraph 1.a should be understood as also including legal guardians or other individuals legally responsible for the child.

Paragraph 2

73. Under this paragraph, children and young persons have the right to access to free primary and secondary education, which does not imply that they have a right to exercise this right for example in a private school.

74. It follows from the appendix that this paragraph does not imply an obligation to provide compulsory education up to the age of 18 years. The reason that there is no mention of compulsory education in the paragraph itself is that in some states only primary education is compulsory, whereas in others secondary education is also compulsory.

Article 18 – The right to engage in a gainful occupation in the territory of other Parties

75. No amendment.

Article 19 – The right of migrant workers and their families to protection and assistance

76. Paragraphs 1 to 10 have not been amended.

Paragraph 6

77. Only the appendix to paragraph 6, which gives the definition of the term "family of a foreign worker", has been amended as compared to the appendix to the corresponding provision of the Charter. Instead of covering the migrant worker's wife, it now covers the spouse of the migrant worker, whether a wife or a husband. Furthermore, the appendix now provides that unmarried children of migrant workers are covered as long as they are considered to be minors by the receiving state and are dependent on the migrant worker. This amendment has been added as the age of majority is 18 years in most Contracting Parties, whereas the Charter provides for an age-limit of 21 years for the entry of children of migrant workers. The words "at least" have been maintained to indicate that states may decide to extend the notion of the family of the migrant worker.

78. Two new paragraphs have been added:

Paragraph 11

79. This paragraph has been considered important for the protection of migrant workers' health and safety at work and for the guarantee of their rights in other respects relating to work, as well as in facilitating their integration and that of their families.

Paragraph 12

80. The underlying reason for this paragraph is the importance for the children of migrant workers of maintaining their cultural and linguistic heritage, *inter alia*, in order to provide them with a possibility of reintegration if and when the migrant worker returns home.

81. Articles 20 to 23 correspond to the provisions of Articles 1 to 4 of the Additional Protocol of 1988. Paragraphs 2, 3 and 4 of Article 1, paragraph 2 of Article 2 and paragraph 2 of Article 3 have been moved to the appendix for the purposes of harmonisation. This change does not affect the nature and scope of the legal obligations accepted under these provisions.

82. The explanatory report to the Additional Protocol of 1988 remains relevant.

83. Articles 24 to 31 are new provisions which guarantee the following rights:

Article 24 – The right to protection in cases of termination of employment

84. This provision, which must be accepted in its entirety, sets out two general principles:

   a. the right not to be dismissed unless there are valid grounds;

b. the right to adequate compensation or other relief in cases of unfair dismissal.

85. It further establishes the right for a worker who considers that his rights under paragraph a have been interfered with to an appeal to obtain, if appropriate, his rights under paragraph b.

86. The provision has been inspired by ILO Convention No. 158 (Termination of Employment) of 1982. As to the nature of the impartial body mentioned in the last paragraph of the Article, reference is made to Article 8 of the ILO Convention.

87. The appendix clarifies the terms "termination of employment" and "terminated" which shall mean termination of employment at the initiative of the employer.

88. The second paragraph of the appendix deals with the scope *ratione personae* of the provision. It makes it possible for the Parties to exclude some categories of employed persons from its scope.

89. The third paragraph of the appendix contains a non-exhaustive list of non-valid grounds for termination of employment.

90. The fourth paragraph of the appendix clarifies that compensation or other appropriate relief in case of termination of employment without valid reasons shall be determined by national laws or regulations, collective agreements or other means appropriate to national conditions.

Article 25 – The right of workers to the protection of their claims in the event of the insolvency of their employer

91. This provision has been inspired by ILO Convention No. 173 (Protection of Workers' Claims (Employers' insolvency)) of 1992 and of European Community Directive 80/987 on the approximation of the laws of the member states relating to the protection of employees in the event of the insolvency of their employer. It lays down the general principle of the right of workers to protection of their claims in the event of the insolvency of their employer.

92. It provides not only for the possibility of a guarantee institution, but also for any other form of protection. The possibility of a combination of the existence of privileges and of an organisation to guarantee the payment of salaries is not excluded by this provision. In fact, a guarantee institution alone ensures the protection of workers as it secures the payment of salaries owed provided that they are superior to the assets of the enterprise. The establishment of such an institution, which will take over the rights of the workers to whom it has paid an advance, is perfectly compatible with a system of privileges.

93. The first paragraph of the appendix prescribes that certain categories of workers may be excluded by reason of the special nature of their employment relationship. The workers concerned are particularly public employees and managerial staff in small undertakings.

94. The second paragraph of the appendix states that the term "insolvency" must be determined by national law and practice. It is understood that this term shall include situations in which proceedings have been opened relating to an employer's assets with a view to the collective reimbursement of his creditors, but may also apply to other situations in which workers' claims cannot be paid by reason of the financial situation of the employer, for example, where the amount of the employer's assets is recognised as being insufficient to justify the opening of insolvency proceedings.

95. The third paragraph of the appendix sets out the minimum requirement according to which claims shall be protected. The "other types of paid absence" referred to in sub-paragraph c have the same sense as in the ILO Convention.

96. Finally, the fourth paragraph of the appendix provides that national laws or regulations may limit the protection of workers' claims to a prescribed amount, which must nevertheless be of a socially acceptable level.

Article 26 – The right to dignity at work

97. The purpose of this Article is to guarantee workers the right to dignity at work and in connection with work. It emphasises the promotion of awareness and prevention of sexual harassment and victimisation, but does not require that Parties ensure protection against such conduct. In addition, it follows from the appendix that Parties do not need to enact legislation. However, they are required to take "all appropriate measures" to protect workers.

98. The two paragraphs contained in the Article may be accepted separately.

Paragraph 1

99. This paragraph deals exclusively with sexual harassment, which may be defined as unwanted conduct of a sexual nature, or other conduct based on sex affecting the dignity of workers, including the conduct of superiors and colleagues.

Paragraph 2

100. This paragraph aims at forms of victimising conduct affecting the right to dignity at work (victimisation, defined as bullying) other than sexual harassment and has been defined in the text of the provision itself. The definition has been taken from existing national

regulations dealing with this problem and comprises recurrent reprehensible or distinctly negative and offensive acts by superiors and colleagues affecting the dignity of a worker in the workplace or in relation with work. An example illustrating this would be that of a worker who for reasons of hostility on the part of the employer and/or his colleagues, is systematically excluded from discussions relating to the organisation of work to which his colleagues are invited to take part. Another example could be not giving a worker an office or duties corresponding to his grade and functions for similar reasons.

101. The appendix specifies that this paragraph does not cover sexual harassment.

Article 27 – The right of workers with family responsibilities to equal opportunities and equal treatment

102. This provision provides for equality of opportunity and treatment for workers with family responsibilities. It has been inspired by ILO Convention No. 156 (Workers with Family Responsibilities) of 1981 as well as Recommendation No. 165 (Workers with Family Responsibilities) of 1981.

103. The appendix to this Article gives a definition of men and women workers with family responsibilities. It refers to national legislation for a definition of the terms "dependent children" and "other members of their immediate family who clearly need their care and support".

Paragraph 1

104. The term "appropriate" in this paragraph shall mean suitable to national conditions and possibilities.

105. Sub-paragraph b corresponds to Article 4, paragraph b of the ILO Convention.

Article 28 – The right of workers' representatives to protection in undertaking and facilities to be accorded to them

106. This provision of the revised Charter aims to protect workers' representatives in the enterprise, a group which is not covered by Article 5 unless the representative is also a trade union representative. The provision has been inspired by ILO Convention No. 135 (Workers' Representatives) of 1971.

107. A definition of the term "workers' representatives" is given in the appendix to the Article which describes it as meaning persons who are recognised as such under national legislation or practice. This definition is based on that of the appendix to Articles 21 and 22. It is understood that national legislation or practice may provide

that workers' representatives are elected representatives or trade union delegates.

108. Sub-section b of the Article, which corresponds to Article 2 of the ILO Convention, provides that workers' representatives shall be afforded such facilities as will enable them to carry out their functions. The only limitation in the context of the revised Charter is that account shall be taken of the industrial relations system of the country and the needs, size and capabilities of the undertaking concerned. Examples of facilities to be granted to workers' representatives may be found in ILO Recommendation No. 143 (Workers' Representatives) of 1971.

Article 29 – The right to information and consultation in collective redundancy procedures

109. Under this Article the Parties undertake to ensure that employers inform and consult workers' representatives prior to collective redundancies. When drafting this Article the Committee examined European Community Directive 92/56 of 1992 amending Directive 75/129 on the approximation of the laws of the member states relating to collective redundancies as well as ILO Convention No. 158 (Termination of Employment) of 1982. The information and consultation shall concern the possibilities of avoiding collective redundancies, limiting their number or mitigating their consequences. Recourse to social measures providing aid for redeploying or retraining the workers concerned is mentioned as an example of ways of mitigating the consequences of collective redundancies.

110. It is understood that recourse to social measures in this context is not solely the responsibility of the employer.

111. A definition of the term "workers' representatives" is given in the appendix to the Article as meaning persons recognised as such under national legislation or practice. This definition is based on that of the appendix to Articles 21 and 22.

Article 30 – The right to protection against poverty and social exclusion

112. This Article provides for a comprehensive and co-ordinated approach, with relief of poverty and social exclusion as the essential and explicit aim. It also provides that measures corresponding to this approach are reviewed and adapted to new situations.

113. The purpose of the Article is not to repeat the juridical aspects of the protection covered by other Articles of the revised Charter although Parties may naturally refer to information given in respect of other provisions when reporting under this provision.

114. The term "poverty" in this context covers persons who find themselves in various situations ranging from severe poverty, which may have been perpetuated for several generations, to temporary situations entailing a risk of poverty. The term "social exclusion" refers to persons who find themselves in a position of extreme poverty through an accumulation of disadvantages, who suffer from degrading situations or events or from exclusion, whose rights to benefit may have expired a long time ago or for reasons of concurring circumstances. Social exclusion also strikes or risks to strike persons who without being poor are denied access to certain rights or services as a result of long periods of illness, the breakdown of their families, violence, release from prison or marginal behaviour as a result for example of alcoholism or drug addiction.

115. It must be noted that the Article does not expressly mention the guarantee of minimum resources. The reason is that such protection is already provided for by Article 13 of the revised Charter and covered by this Article where reference is made in paragraph a to "effective access to [....] social assistance".

116. Among the obligations subscribed to under Article 30, a series of measures is included, which may or may not imply financial benefits, and which concern both persons in a situation of exclusion and those who risk finding themselves in such a situation. States subscribing to this provision are encouraged to restrict financial benefits to those who cannot help themselves by their own means.

117. The review of mechanisms under paragraph b of the Article is of a general character and each Party shall decide how it should be organised, depending on national conditions. This review may, in order for the measures mentioned in the provision to be effective, include consultations with the social partners and various other organisations, including organisations representing persons who find themselves in a situation of poverty or social exclusion.

Article 31 – The right to housing

118. In order to ensure a right to housing, this provision obliges Parties to take measures in so far as possible aiming to progressively eliminate homelessness, to promote access to housing of an adequate standard and to make the price of housing accessible to those without adequate resources. By housing of an "adequate standard" is meant housing which is of an acceptable standard with regard to health requirements. For a definition of the terms "without adequate resources" reference is made to Article 13.

119. It will be for the competent authorities of each state to decide, at national level, on appropriate housing standards.

Part III

Article A – Undertakings

120. Article A, concerning undertakings, follows the same pattern as the corresponding provision, that is Article 20 of the Charter.

121. As is the case in the Charter, paragraph 1.a obliges states to consider themselves bound by all the aims put forward in Part I.

122. Paragraph 1.b determines the extent of the hard core of the revised Charter which comprises Articles 1, 5, 6, 7, 12, 13, 16, 19 and 20. In relation to the Charter, two new Articles, 7 and 20, have been added in view of their particular importance.

123. Consequently, the number of hard core Articles which have to be accepted by Parties has been increased to six.

124. Following a proposal from the organisations representing management and labour, the Committee had originally planned to make Articles 5 and 6 of the revised Charter compulsory. This would have meant that no state could have ratified the revised Charter without agreeing to be bound by these two provisions. This was motivated by the particular and fundamental importance which these two provisions have always had for the protection of economic and social rights. However, the Committee finally decided not to make acceptance of Articles 5 and 6 compulsory, in order not to detract from the existing flexibility of this legal instrument, which is entirely constructed on an à la carte basis. The Committee also considered that making acceptance of Articles 5 and 6 compulsory might slow down the ratification of the revised Charter. It therefore decided against doing so, with a view to enabling more states to accept the new and amended provisions in the revised Charter. However, states which ratify the revised Charter must take all possible steps to accept Articles 5 and 6 as rapidly as possible.

125. Paragraph 1.c relates to the corresponding provision in Article 20 of the Charter. It establishes the minimum number of Articles or paragraphs which a state must accept on ratification of the revised Charter. The Committee thought it preferable to keep the same proportion between the minimum number of provisions which must be accepted and the total number of provisions contained in the revised Charter. Accordingly, it decided that states must accept not less than sixteen Articles, instead of ten as previously, or sixty-three paragraphs, instead of forty-five as previously.

126. Paragraphs 2, 3 and 4 of Article A reiterate, *mutatis mutandis*, the corresponding provisions of the Social Charter.

Article B – Links with the European Social Charter and the Additional Protocol of 1988

127. The purpose of paragraph 1 of Article B is to ensure that the undertakings entered into by states under the Charter are replaced by those which they have accepted under the revised Charter, upon ratification of the latter. In practice this means that, for states which have ratified the revised Charter, Parts I and II of the latter will replace Parts I and II of the Charter. For reasons of clarity and legal certainty, it is essential that states should not be bound by two sets of substantive provisions, some of which may be at variance as a result of the revision of the Charter itself.

128. Paragraph 2 has another specific purpose, namely to ensure that when states ratify the revised Charter they do not implicitly denounce certain provisions of the Charter. States which accepted more than the minimum number of provisions established by Article 20 of the Charter might be tempted, when ratifying the revised Charter, not to be bound by certain provisions of the revised Charter corresponding to provisions of the Charter which they had previously accepted. This might apply, for example, to provisions with which in the opinion of the supervisory bodies the states in question do not comply. Of course, it will always be possible for states to denounce certain provisions of the Charter, in accordance with the relevant provisions thereof, before ratifying the revised Charter. However, the denunciation must be explicit, not implicit.

129. For this purpose, the appendix to Article B, paragraph 2 specifies which provisions of the revised Charter correspond to the provisions of the Charter. The term "correspond" is used here in the sense of "to replace". Generally speaking, each Article of the revised Charter corresponds to the Article with the same number in the Charter. However, there are some exceptions, which are listed in the appendix. The appendix specifies which undertakings in the new Charter must be accepted in order to respect the principle of correspondence laid down in paragraph 2. As regards the Protocol, Articles 20, 21, 22 and 23 of the revised Charter correspond to Articles 1, 2, 3 and 4 of the Protocol.

Part IV

Article C – Supervision of compliance with the undertakings contained in this Charter

130. Given that the two Charters are to co-exist, at least during a transitional period, the drafters of the revised Charter thought it essential that the two legal instruments be supervised in the same manner. Consequently, they did not wish to create separate supervision machinery for the revised Charter and instead simply specified in Article C that undertakings entered into under the

revised Charter would be subject to the same supervision procedure as that provided for in the Charter.

131. Furthermore, this provision is of an open-ended nature and the supervisory procedure will therefore be the same as that which applies to the Charter at any given time. In so doing, the drafters of the revised Charter wished to adopt a neutral attitude with regard to the Turin Protocol amending the Charter's supervision machinery. In view of some states' reservations and difficulties in accepting the new supervision procedure set out in this Protocol, they decided that the revised Charter should not interfere with this issue. Consequently, before the Turin Protocol comes into force, the revised Charter will use the supervisory machinery applicable to the Charter, and after it comes into force, it will use the new supervision procedure. In addition, since states which ratify the revised Charter are still Parties to the Charter, the Turin Protocol will only come into force when it has been ratified by all twenty states which are currently Parties to the Charter. The revised Charter therefore has no influence on the number of ratifications necessary for the entry into force of the Turin Protocol.

Article D – Collective complaints

132. The Committee considered it necessary to include a provision in the revised Charter providing that a state which had ratified the Additional Protocol providing for a system of collective complaints, before ratifying the revised Charter, should be obliged to accept the supervision of its obligations under the revised Charter in accordance with the procedure set out in the Protocol. It is important that ratification of the revised Charter should not in practice result in denunciation of the Protocol on collective complaints. In addition, given that the Parties' undertakings in Parts I and II of the Charter are replaced by the undertakings in the revised Charter, it would be logical for a state which has ratified the Protocol on collective complaints to accept that such complaints should cover the undertakings entered into under the revised Charter.

133. Paragraph 2 is intended to allow states which ratify the revised Charter before ratifying the Protocol on collective complaints to agree to be bound by the latter by declaration. The main purpose of this provision is to prevent states from having to submit too many legal instruments to their national parliaments for ratification. With a view to simplification, a state may therefore declare itself bound by the Protocol on collective complaints when it ratifies the revised Charter.

134. It is obvious, however, that the provisions of paragraph 2 can only apply once the Protocol on collective complaints has come into force.

Part V

Article E – Non-discrimination

135. This new Article of the revised Charter confirms the case law of the Committee of Independent Experts in respect of the Charter, that is that the non-discrimination clause in the preamble to the Charter applies to all the provisions of the Charter. Accordingly, the revised Charter does not allow discrimination on any of the grounds listed in this Article in respect of any of the rights contained in the instrument.

136. The Article has been based on Article 14 of the European Convention on Human Rights which contains a more extensive enumeration of grounds than the preamble to the Charter. The grounds enumerated in the Article are the same as those contained in the preamble to the Charter, with the addition of some grounds mentioned in the Convention. However, with respect to some of these latter grounds, the Committee of Independent Experts has already indicated in its case law that they apply to the rights guaranteed under the Charter. The words "such as" contained in the provision indicate that the list of grounds on which discrimination is not permitted is not exhaustive. It is understood that this provision prohibits, *inter alia*, the refusal to employ women on grounds of pregnancy. It also provides for non-discrimination in access to health care. These are merely two examples. The appendix to the new Article provides that differential treatment based on an objective and reasonable justification shall not be deemed to be discriminatory. An objective and reasonable justification may be such as the requirement of a certain age or a certain capacity for access to some forms of education. Whereas national extraction is not an acceptable ground for discrimination, the requirement of a specific citizenship might be acceptable under certain circumstances, for example for the right to employment in the defence forces or in the civil service.

137. In addition, it is understood that this provision must not be interpreted so as to extend the scope ratione personae of the revised Charter which is defined in the appendix to the instrument and which includes foreigners only in so far as they are nationals of other parties lawfully resident or working regularly within the territory of the Party concerned.

Articles F – Derogations in time of war or public emergency

Article G – Restrictions

Article H – Relations between the Charter and domestic law or international agreements

138. These three Articles correspond, *mutatis mutandis*, to the provisions of Articles 30, 31 and 32 of Part V of the Charter.

Article I – Implementation of the undertakings given

139. The model for this provision has been Article 7 of the Additional Protocol to the Charter of 1988. The first paragraph provides that without prejudice to the methods of implementation foreseen in Articles 1 to 31 of Part II of the revised Charter, this provision may be implemented by any of the means enumerated in the paragraph. This composition has been chosen so as not to interfere with the case law of the Committee of Independent Experts according to which a certain form of implementation, such as legislation, is sometimes required. The word "shall" indicates that the method chosen must be efficient.

140. The second paragraph provides that in respect of the provisions enumerated therein, the undertakings deriving from these provisions are considered as being fulfilled as long as they are applied to the great majority of the workers concerned. This paragraph contains all the provisions included in Article 33 of the Charter and Article 7, paragraph 2 of the Additional Protocol to the Charter, with the addition of Article 2, paragraph 7 of the revised Charter.

Article J – Amendments

141. Having noted that Article 36 of the Charter had never been used, *inter alia*, because it was very restrictive, the Committee wanted to introduce an amendment clause into the revised Charter which would allow for the subsequent development of the treaty. This provision is based on texts already used by the Council of Europe for other European treaties.

142. According to paragraph 2, all amendments shall be examined by the Governmental Committee, before being submitted for approval to the Committee of Ministers after consultation with the Parliamentary Assembly. The Committee of Ministers shall take its decision by a two-thirds majority; after approval by the Committee of Ministers, the text shall be communicated to the Parties for acceptance.

143. If the amendment relates to Parts I and II of the revised Charter it shall enter into force when three states have informed the Secretary General that they accept it. In this connection, it should be noted that such amendments must be intended to extend the rights guaranteed by the Charter. In addition, the appendix to this provision stipulates that the term "amendment" also covers the

addition of new Articles containing new rights; this issue had been raised at a Charte-Rel Committee meeting.

144. On the other hand, amendments to Parts III to VI shall not enter into force until they have been accepted by all the parties to the revised Charter.

145. It was also agreed that member states of the Council of Europe which are parties neither to the Charter nor to the revised Charter should be able to participate in work on amending the revised Charter, but that this would be for the Committee of Ministers to decide once an amendment procedure had commenced.

Part VI

146. Part VI contains the text of the final clauses of the revised Charter. It is modelled on the final clauses adopted by the Committee of Ministers of the Council of Europe for treaties drawn up within the Organisation, although it does also reproduce some of the provisions appearing in Part VI of the Charter.

Appendix

Scope of the revised European Social Charter in terms of persons protected

147. The scope *ratione personae* of the Charter has been defined in the appendix according to which the Charter includes foreigners "only in so far as they are nationals of other Contracting Parties lawfully resident or working regularly within the territory of the Contracting Party concerned".

IV. European Committee of Social Rights[1]

---

1. During the 158th session (16-20 November 1998), the Committee of
   Independent Experts of the European Social Charter decided to henceforth
   adopt the name of the European Committee of Social Rights (see
   Conclusions XIV-2, p. 22).

A. Composition (18 October 2001)

List of members[1] .... *Term of office*

Mr Stein EVJU, President
Professor of Labour Law and Commercial Law
Norwegian School of Management
Sandvika (Norway) 31/12/2002

Mr Nikitas ALIPRANTIS, Vice-President
Professor, Democritos University of Thrace
Komotini (Greece) 31/12/2002

Mr Konrad GRILLBERGER, Vice-President
Professor
Director of the Institute of Labour Law and Social Legislation
University of Salzburg (Austria) 31/12/2004

Mr Matti MIKKOLA, General rapporteur
Professor of Labour Law
Department of Private Law
University of Helsinki (Finland)
Professor of Social Policy
University of Tartu (Estonia) 31/12/2006

Mr Rolf BIRK, Professor of Labour Law
Director of the Institute of Labour Law and
Industrial Relations in the European Community
University of Trier (Germany) 31/12/2006

Mr Alfredo BRUTO DA COSTA, Assistant Professor
Portuguese Catholic University
Lisbon (Portugal) 31/12/2002

Mrs Micheline JAMOULLE, Professor
Law Faculty
University of Liège (Belgium) 31/12/2002

Mr Tekin AKILLIOĞLU, Professor of Public Law
Director of the Human Rights Centre
University of Ankara (Turkey) 31/12/2002

---

1. In order of precedence, in conformity with Article 5 of the Rules of Procedure.

Mr Jean-Michel BELORGEY, *Conseiller d'Etat*
Head of the International Co-operation Unit
Reports and Studies' Section
Conseil d'Etat, Paris (France) 31/12/2006

Mrs Csilla KOLLONAY LEHOCZKY, Professor
Legal Studies Department
Central European University
Budapest (Hungary) 31/12/2006

Ms Polonca KONČAR, Professor
Law Faculty
University of Ljubljana (Slovenia) 31/12/2004

Mr Gerard QUINN, Professor
Law Faculty
National University of Ireland at Galway (Ireland) 31/12/2004

B. Election of members of the Committee

1. Increase in the number of members from seven to nine

Decision adopted by the Committee of Ministers in March 1994 at the 509th meeting of the Ministers' Deputies

1. The Representatives to the Committee of Ministers, representing the Contracting Parties to the Charter, agreed unanimously to increase from seven to nine the number of members of the Committee of Independent Experts, it being understood that no further increase will be envisaged outside the context of a modification of Article 25 of the Charter.

2. Increase in the number of members from nine to fifteen

Decision 4.2 adopted by the Committee of Ministers during the 751st meeting of the Ministers' Deputies (2 and 7 May 2001)

A. The Deputies, in their composition limited to the representatives of the Contracting Parties to the European Social Charter or to the revised Charter[1], agreed unanimously to increase from nine to fifteen the number of members of the European Committee of Social Rights in the following manner:

  a. creation of three seats for a term of office starting on 1 August 2001 and ending on 31 December 2004;

  b. subsequent creation of three seats on a date to be determined by the Deputies taking into account the criteria appearing in Document GR-H(2001)9, point 12.[2]

---

1. Austria, Belgium, Bulgaria, Cyprus, Czech Republic, Denmark, Estonia, Finland, France, Germany, Greece, Hungary, Iceland, Ireland, Italy, Luxembourg, Malta, the Netherlands, Norway, Poland, Portugal, Romania, Slovakia, Slovenia, Spain, Sweden, Turkey and the United Kingdom

2. If no unanimous agreement is found on the immediate increase of six seats, the creation of three new seats may be deferred. The decision to increase from 9 to 15 seats could be taken, but only the creation of 3 new seats would be implemented immediately. It would be up to the Deputies to decide, from amongst the six new seats, which ones to create first and which to create later. In this case, the Secretariat suggests the following solution: the immediate creation of three seats:
    – 1 in Group I;
    – 1 in Group III;
    – 1 in Group V.
    Later on, 1 seat can be created in Group IV and 2 seats in Group V.
    The date or dates of creation are to be decided by the Deputies depending on the criteria agreed by the Deputies, for example: the increase in the number of states linked to the Charter or the revised Charter (currently 28), the increase in the number of ratifications of the revised Charter (currently 9) and the development in the number of collective complaints (10 cases registered so far).

3. Election Procedure

Decision 4.2 adopted by the Committee of Ministers during the 751st meeting of the Ministers' Deputies (2 and 7 May 2001)

...

B.   The Deputies

1.   adopted the following procedure for filling the three seats created on the European Committee of Social Rights, with terms of office starting on 1 August 2001 and ending on 31 December 2004;

   a. each Contracting Party to the European Social Charter or the revised European Social Charter will be entitled to communicate to the Secretary General of the Council of Europe, by 15 June 2001 at the latest, the name of a candidate whom it considers suitable for the vacant seats, bearing in mind that the vacancies concern groups I (one seat), III (one seat) and V (one seat) and having regard to Article 25 of the Charter as it appears in Article 3 of the Protocol amending the European Social Charter as well as to the agreed rules concerning nationality[1], and also taking into account Recommendation No. R (81) 6 of the Committee of Ministers adopted on 30 April 1981[2];

   b. the Secretary General will then communicate the list of names submitted to the Committee of Ministers, which will carry out an election by secret ballot at the Deputies' 759th meeting on 4 July 2001;

   c. the candidate or candidates having obtained an absolute majority of the votes cast and the highest number of votes will be declared elected;

   d. if one or all the seats remain vacant after the first ballot, there will be a second round of voting and the candidate or candidates having obtained the highest number of votes will be declared elected.

2.   agreed, for the purposes of this election, to allocate the 43 member states as follows[3]:

   First group (three seats) (one seat vacant)

   Armenia, **Austria, Czech Republic, Germany, Hungary,** Liechtenstein, **Slovakia** and Switzerland.

---

1. The Committee can only have one member of a certain nationality.
2. The Recommendation concerns the participation of women and men in an equitable proportion in committees and other bodies set up in the Council of Europe. The Committee is currently composed of 7 men and 2 women.
3. The countries that have ratified the Charter or the revised Charter appear in bold in the text.

Second group (three seats) (no seat vacant)

Azerbaijan, **Belgium, Bulgaria,** France, **Luxembourg,** Moldova, **Netherlands, Romania and Turkey.**

Third group (three seats) (one seat vacant)

Denmark, Finland, Iceland, Ireland, Norway, Sweden and the United Kingdom.

Fourth group (two seats) (no seat vacant)

Albania, Andorra, **Cyprus,** Georgia, **Greece,** Italy, **Malta, Portugal,** San Marino and **Spain.**

Fifth group (one seat) (one seat vacant)

Croatia, **Estonia,** "The former Yugoslav Republic of Macedonia", Latvia, Lithuania, **Poland,** Russian Federation, Ukraine and **Slovenia.**

C. Rules of Procedure

The European Committee of Social Rights, committee of independent experts established pursuant to the European Social Charter;

> – whereas it is a body entrusted, on the basis of Articles 24 and 25 of the Charter as modified in the Amending Protocol (1991), with the independent assessment of the conformity of the situation in each Contracting Party with the obligations arising under the Charter, the 1988 Additional Protocol to the Charter and the 1996 revised European Social Charter and with examining collective complaints as provided for in the 1995 Additional Protocol providing for a system of collective complaints;

> – considering that to carry out its work it is desirable to formally set down its Rules of Procedure;

Hereby, on 9 September 1999, adopts the following Rules of Procedure which enter into force on this same date and replace the Rules of Procedure adopted on 4 July 1983 and the Rules of Procedure for the collective complaints adopted on 21 March 1997:

Part I: Members of the Committee

Rule 1: Duties of Committee members

Members shall perform their duties with the requirements of independence, impartiality and availability inherent in their office and shall keep secret the Committee's deliberations.

Rule 2: Incompatibility

Members of the Committee shall not during their term of office perform any function which is incompatible with the requirements of independence, impartiality or availability inherent in their office.

Rule 3: Solemn declaration

Before taking up duties, each member of the Committee shall, at the first meeting of the Committee at which the member is present after election, take the following declaration:

"I solemnly declare that I will exercise my functions as a member of this Committee with the requirements of independence, impartiality and availability inherent in my office and that I will keep secret the Committee's deliberations."

Rule 4: Terms of Office – Resignation

1. The duration of the term of office of members of the Committee shall be calculated as from the date fixed by the Committee of Ministers.

2. A member's resignation shall be notified in writing to the President of the Committee who shall transmit it to the Secretary General of the Council of Europe.

Rule 5: Order of precedence

1. Members of the Committee shall take precedence after the President, the Vice-President(s) and General Rapporteur according to the length of time they have been in office.

2. Members having the same length in office shall take precedence according to age.

3. Re-elected members shall take precedence having regard to the duration of their previous term of office.

Part II: President and Bureau of the Committee

Rule 6: Elections

1. The Committee shall elect the President, one or more Vice-Presidents and a General Rapporteur, who shall together constitute the Bureau of the Committee. The members of the Bureau shall be elected for a period of two years. Until such time as the President is elected, the meeting shall be chaired by the oldest member of the Committee present.

    The members of the Bureau are eligible for re-election.

2. If a member of the Bureau withdraws from office before his term of office in the Bureau has expired, the Committee shall elect a successor for the remainder of that term.

3. Elections shall be held for each position by secret ballot, unless the Committee unanimously agrees otherwise in a particular case. Only the members present shall take part. The member who has obtained an absolute majority of the votes cast shall be elected. If no member receives such majority, a second ballot shall take place. The member receiving the most votes shall then be elected. In the event of a tie, the longest serving member shall be elected. If the members concerned have the same length of time in office, the oldest of them shall be elected.

Rule 7: President and Vice-Presidents

1. The President shall direct the work and chair the sessions of the Committee. He or she retains all his voting and other rights as a

member of the Committee. He or she fulfils all other functions bestowed on him by these Rules and by the Committee.

2. In these Rules, the term "President" shall refer to any member fulfilling the office of President.

3. The Vice-President shall take the place of the President if the latter is unable to carry out his duties or if the office of President is vacant. If the Committee has elected another or several other Vice-Presidents, each of them shall replace the other Vice-Presidents if they are unable to carry out their duties or if their offices are vacant according to the order of precedence laid down in Rule 5. If the President and Vice-President(s) are at the same time unable to carry out their duties or if their offices are at the same time vacant, the duties of President shall be carried out by another member of the Committee according to the order of precedence laid down in Rule 5.

4. The President may delegate certain of his duties to the Vice-President(s).

Rule 8: Role of the General Rapporteur

The General Rapporteur co-ordinates the work of the Rapporteurs. In particular he or she supervises the coherence of the conclusions on the various articles and states the case law before the Committee if necessary.

Rule 9: Role of the Bureau

1. The Bureau shall direct the work of the Committee and shall perform all other functions conferred upon it by these Rules of Procedure and by the Committee.

2. If one or more members of the Bureau are unable to carry out their duties, they shall be replaced by other members of the Committee in accordance with the rules of precedence laid down in Rule 5.

Part III: Representative of the International Labour Organisation

Rule 10: Participation

1. With a view to enabling the representative of the International Labour Organisation to participate in the deliberations of the Committee, as provided for in Article 26 of the European Social Charter, the working documents of the Committee shall be communicated to the International Labour Office.

2. The representative from the International Labour Organisation is invited to participate in the plenary sessions of the Committee as well as in the meetings of the working groups.

Part IV: Secretariat

Rule 11: Staff

The Secretary General shall provide the Committee with the necessary staff, including the Secretary to the Committee, as well as with the administrative and other services required for the fulfilment of its duties.

Part V: Working of the Committee

Rule 12: Sessions

1. The Committee shall fix the numbers and dates of its sessions, taking into account existing budgetary allocations. The sessions shall be convened in accordance with the President's instructions.

2. The draft agenda is prepared in agreement with the President.

3. The notice of each session shall indicate its place, date and starting time and its probable duration, and be accompanied by the draft agenda and the provisional list of working papers and related documents. Except in cases of emergency, the notice shall be sent to the members at least one month before the starting date.

4. Members who are unable to attend a meeting shall give notice thereof, as soon as possible, to the Secretary to the Committee, who shall inform the President.

5. Sessions and deliberations of the Committee shall be held in private. All working documents shall be confidential.

Rule 13: Quorum and voting

1. A majority of members entitled to sit shall constitute a quorum for holding a session of the Committee. Each member shall have one vote. The decisions of the Committee shall be taken by a majority of those present.

2. When a decision has been taken by the Committee on a particular question, consideration of that question shall be resumed only if a member of the Committee so requests and if that request is approved by a two-thirds majority of votes cast.

Rule 14: Minutes and Conclusions

1. After each meeting, the Secretary to the Committee shall prepare draft minutes for submission to the members of the Committee, which shall approve the final text.

2. The Committee's conclusions shall also contain any dissenting opinions on particular questions of substance at the request of their authors.

Rule 15: Working languages

The working languages of the Committee shall be English and French.

Part VI: Procedure for examination of reports

Rule 16: Rapporteurs

The Committee shall designate a Rapporteur for each provision of the Charter, the 1988 Additional Protocol to the Charter and the revised Charter.

Rule 17: Working groups

1. The Committee may form working groups, composed of four or five members of the Committee, with a view to preparing its decisions.

2. The meetings of the working groups are chaired by a member of the Bureau or by default by another member chosen by the group.

3. A group will function when at least three members of the Committee are present.

Rule 18: Meetings with States

1. The Committee may decide to organise meetings with representatives of a State, as provided for in Article 24 paragraph 3 of the Charter as amended by the 1991 Amending Protocol, either on its own initiative or at the request of the State concerned. The Committee shall decide whether or not to act upon a request made by a State.

2. The international organisations of employers and trade unions referred to in Article 27 paragraph 2 of the Charter shall be invited to participate in these meetings. These organisations shall inform their national member organisations.

3. The meetings shall be public unless the President decides otherwise.

Part VII: Collective complaints procedure

Rule 19: Lodging of complaints

Collective complaints submitted under the 1995 Additional Protocol providing for a system of collective complaints shall be addressed to the Secretary to the Committee acting on behalf of the Secretary General of the Council of Europe.

Rule 20: Signature

Complaints shall be signed by the person(s) with the competence to represent the complainant organisation. The Committee decides on any questions concerning this matter.

Rule 21: Languages

1. Complaints made by the organisations listed in Article 1 paragraphs a and b of the Protocol shall be submitted in one of the official languages of the Council of Europe.

2. Complaints made by organisations listed in Article 1 paragraph c and Article 2 paragraph 1 of the Protocol may be submitted in a language other than one of the official languages of the Council of Europe. For these complaints, the Secretary to the Committee is authorised in his correspondence with the complainants to use a language other than one of the official languages of the Council of Europe.

Rule 22: Representatives of the States and of the complainant organisation

1. The States shall be represented before the Committee by the agents they appoint. These may have the assistance of advisers.

2. The organisations referred to in paragraphs 2 and 3 of the Protocol shall be represented by a person appointed by the organisation to this end. They may have the assistance of advisers.

3. The names and titles of the representatives and of any advisers shall be notified to the Committee.

Rule 23: Order in which to handle a complaint

Complaints shall be registered with the Secretariat of the Committee in chronological order. The Committee shall deal with complaints in the order in which they become ready for examination. It may, however, decide to give precedence to a particular complaint.

Rule 24: Rapporteurs

1. For each complaint a member of the Committee shall be appointed by the President to act as Rapporteur.

2. The Rapporteur shall follow the proceedings. He or she shall inform the Committee at each of its sessions of the progress of the proceedings and of the procedural decisions taken by the President since the previous session.

3. The Rapporteur shall elaborate a draft decision on admissibility of the complaint for adoption by the Committee, followed by, as the case may be, a draft report for the Committee of Ministers as provided for in Article 8 of the Protocol.

Rule 25: Role of the President

1. The President shall take the decisions provided for in Rules 26 to 29.

2. The President shall set the time limits mentioned under Article 6 and under Article 7 paragraphs 1, 2 and 3 of the Protocol. He or she may grant, in exceptional cases and following a well-founded request, an extension of these time limits.

3. The President may, in the name of the Committee, take any necessary measures in order that the procedure may be correctly carried out.

4. The President may especially, in order to respect a reasonable time limit for dealing with complaints, decide to convene additional sessions of the Committee.

Rule 26: Observations on the admissibility

1. Before the Committee decides on admissibility, the President of the Committee may ask the State concerned for written information and observations, within a time limit that he or she decides, on the admissibility of the complaint.

2. The President may also ask the organisation that lodged the complaint to respond, on the same conditions, to the observations made by the State concerned.

Rule 27: Admissibility assessment

1. The Rapporteur shall within the shortest possible time limit elaborate a draft decision on admissibility. It shall contain:

    a. a statement of the relevant facts;

    b. an indication of the issues arising under the Charter in the complaint;

    c. a proposal on the admissibility of the complaint.

2. The Committee's decision on admissibility of the complaint shall be accompanied by reasons and be signed by the President, the Rapporteur and the Secretary to the Committee.

3. The Committee's decision on admissibility of the complaint shall be made public.

4. The States party to the Charter or the revised Charter shall be notified about the decision.

5. If the complaint is declared admissible, copies of the complaint and the observations of the parties shall be transmitted, upon request, to States party to the Protocol and to the international organisations of employers and trade unions referred to in paragraph 2 of Article 27 of the Charter. They shall also have the

possibility to consult the appendices to the complaint at the Secretariat.

Rule 28: Assessment of the merits of the complaint – written procedure

1. If a complaint has been declared admissible, the Committee asks the State concerned to make its observations on the merits of the complaint within a time limit that it decides.

2. The President then invites the organisation that lodged the complaint to respond, on the same conditions, to these observations and to submit all relevant written explanations or information to the Committee.

3. The States party to the Protocol as well as the States having ratified the revised Social Charter and having made a declaration under Article D paragraph 2 shall be invited to make comments within the same time limit as that decided above under paragraph 1.

4. The international organisations of employers and trade unions referred to in Article 27 paragraph 2 of the Charter shall be invited to make observations on complaints lodged by national organisations of employers and trade unions and by non-governmental organisations.

5. The observations submitted in application of paragraphs 3 and 4 shall be transmitted to the organisation that lodged the complaint and to the State concerned.

6. Any information received the by the Committee in application of Article 7 paragraphs 1, 2 and 3 of the Protocol shall be transmitted to the State concerned and to the complainant organisation.

Rule 29: Hearing

1. The hearing provided for under Article 7 paragraph 4 of the Protocol may be held at the request of one of the parties or on the Committee's initiative. The Committee shall decide whether or not to act upon a request made by one of the parties.

2. The State concerned and the complainant organisation as well as the States and organisations referred to under Article 7 of the Protocol that have submitted written observations during the proceedings shall be invited to the hearing.

3. The hearing shall be public unless the President decides otherwise.

Rule 30: The Committee's decision on the merits

1. The Committee's decision on the merits of the complaint contained in the report provided for in Article 8 of the Protocol shall

be accompanied by reasons and be signed by the President, the Rapporteur and the Secretary to the Committee. Any dissenting opinions shall be appended to the Committee's decision at the request of their authors.

2. The report containing the decision in question shall be transmitted to the Committee of Ministers and to the Parliamentary Assembly.

3. The Committee's decision on the merits of the complaint shall be made public at the moment of the adoption of a resolution by the Committee of Ministers in conformity with Article 9 of the Protocol or at the latest four months after the report was transmitted to the Committee of Ministers.

4. When the Committee's decision has become public, all documents registered with the Secretariat shall be accessible to the public unless the Committee decides otherwise following a proposal by the Rapporteur.

Part VIII: Amendment to the Rules of Procedure

Rule 31: Amendments

Any rule may be amended upon motion made after notice by one of its members when such motion is carried, at a session of the Committee, by a majority of all its members. Notice of such a motion shall be delivered in writing at least two months before the session at which it is to be discussed. Such notice of motion shall be communicated to all members of the Committee at the earliest possible moment.

V. Governmental Committee

A. Composition

European Social Charter

Article 27 – Sub-committee of the Governmental Social Committee[1]

1. The reports of the Contracting Parties and the conclusions of the Committee of Experts shall be submitted for examination to a sub-committee of the Governmental Social Committee of the Council of Europe.

2. The sub-committee shall be composed of one representative of each of the Contracting Parties. It shall invite no more than two international organisations of employers and no more than two international trade union organisations as it may designate to be represented as observers in a consultative capacity at its meetings. Moreover, it may consult no more than two representatives of international non-governmental organisations having consultative status with the Council of Europe, in respect of questions with which the organisations are particularly qualified to deal, such as social welfare, and the economic and social protection of the family.

Decision on the participation of member states from central and eastern European signatories to the Social Charter in meetings of the Governmental Committee

Adopted by the Committee of Ministers on 22 October 1992 at the 482nd meeting of the Ministers' Deputies

The Deputies

1. agreed that observers from member states from central and eastern Europe, having signed the European Social Charter, can be invited to attend meetings of the Governmental Committee, for the purpose of preparing the ratification of this instrument;[...]

Decision to invite signatory states to participate as observers in meetings of the Governmental Committee

Adopted by the Committee of Ministers on 17 December 1998 at the 653rd meeting of the Ministers' Deputies

The Deputies

Decided to invite signatory States of the European Social Charter or the revised European Social Charter to take part as observers in the meetings of the Governmental Committee of the European Social Charter.

---

1. The Committee is now called the "Governmental Committee".

B. Rules of Procedure[1]

Article 1: Convocation

1. Sessions of the Committee shall be convened by letter addressed by the Secretary General to the Government of each Contracting Party.

2. A copy of the letter of convocation shall be sent

   a. to the representative of each Contracting Party who attended the previous session of the Committee

   b. to the Permanent Representative to the Council of Europe of the government of each Contracting Party.

3. Letters of convocation shall, in general, be sent at least six weeks before the date fixed for the opening of the session.

Article 2: Appointment of Representatives

1. Each Contracting Party shall communicate to the Secretary General of the Council of Europe, whenever possible at least one month before the date fixed for the opening of the session, the name and address of the representative whom it appoints.

2. A representative may be accompanied by one or more advisers.

Article 3: Sessions

1. The Committee shall fix the date of its sessions in consultation with the Secretary General.

2. When a meeting has been convened, any request for postponement must reach the Secretary General not less than three weeks before the date originally fixed for the opening of the meeting. A decision in favour of postponement shall be considered as having been taken when a majority of the governments shall have notified the Secretary General of their agreement ten days before the date previously fixed.

3. Sessions shall be held at the seat of the Council of Europe at Strasbourg, unless the Committee decides otherwise.

---

1. Adopted by the Committee on 4 October 1968 and amended on 19 September 1986.

Article 4: Chairman and Vice-Chairman

1. The Chairman and the first and second Vice-Chairmen shall be elected by a majority of the votes cast for the duration of a supervision cycle[1] at the session preceding the beginning of the cycle. They shall be eligible for re-election.

2. Independently of his function as representative, the Chairman shall direct the work and preside at session of the Committee; he shall participate in votes as representative.

3. Whenever the Chairman is unable to act, he shall be replaced by the first Vice-Chairman; if the latter is unable to act, he shall be replaced by the second Vice-Chairman in the same way.

Article 5: Secretariat

1. The Secretary General or his representative may at any time make an oral or written statement on any matter under consideration.

2. The Secretary General shall provide the Committee with the necessary staff and facilities.

3. The Secretariat shall be responsible for the preparation and distribution of all documents to be examined by the Committee.

Article 6: Agenda

The agenda shall be adopted at the beginning of each session on the basis of a draft prepared by the Secretariat.

Article 7: Languages

1. The official languages of the Committee shall be those of the Council of Europe.

2. Any representative or other participant may, however, use a language other than an official language, provided that he shall himself provide for interpretation into one of the official languages.

3. Working documents submitted to the Committee in a language other than one of the official languages should be translated by the issuing government if the Committee finds it essential. If, in that event, a translation in writing is required by the Committee, the minimum essential parts of the document should be translated.

Article 8: Privacy of sessions

Sessions shall be held in private.

---

1. "Supervision cycle" means the period during which the Governmental Committee examines the national reports of all the States Parties to the European Social Charter.

Article 9: Quorum

The Committee shall be validly constituted only when two-thirds of the representatives are present.

Article 10: Voting

1. Without prejudice to the provisions of Article 11, the Committee shall take decisions by a two-thirds majority of the votes cast.

2. Procedural questions shall be decided by a majority of the votes cast. If any question arises as to whether a matter is procedural or not, it shall not be treated as procedural unless the Committee so decides by a two-thirds majority of the votes cast.

3. "Votes cast" means the votes of representatives voting for or against; representatives abstaining on a vote are considered as not having cast a vote.

Article 11: Reports of the Committee

1. The Committee's report referred to at paragraph 3, Article 27, of the European Social Charter shall not be adopted by means of a vote.

2. The text of the part(s) covering the Committee's work and discussions shall indicate the opinions expressed in the Committee on any question raised and shall indicate whether all the members, or only a majority, held these opinions. The opinions of the minority may also be indicated in the report at the latter's request.

3. Concerning the Committee's conclusion, the report shall indicate the number of representatives participating in the vote, the number of votes in favour and against, and the number of abstentions. Any minority opinion may be indicated in the report at the request of the representatives concerned.

4. At the request of the organisations referred to in Article 13, paragraph 1, of the present Rules, their observations made orally at the various sessions shall be appended to the Committee's report.

Article 12: Minutes

At the end of each session the Committee shall adopt the minutes of its deliberations on the basis of a draft submitted by the Secretariat.

Article 13: International organisations of employers and of trade unions

1. The invitation issued in accordance with the terms of paragraph 2 of Article 27 of the European Social Charter to international organisations of employers and to trade unions shall be valid for a supervision cycle, it shall be considered as renewed without further agreement.

2. These organisations shall participate in a consultative capacity, at the debates of the Committee: they shall receive all the documents referred to at paragraph 3 of Article 5 of these Rules of procedure.

Article 14: Consultation of certain non-governmental organisations

1. The Secretariat shall communicate to the Committee at the beginning of each supervision cycle, the list of international non-governmental organisations having consultative status with the Council of Europe, which are referred to at paragraph 2 of Article 27 of the European Social Charter.

2. If the Committee decides to consult one or more of these organisations, in accordance with Article 27 paragraph 2 of the European Social Charter, it shall fix the date and manner of such consultation.

Article 15: Amendment of the Rules of Procedure

1. These rules may be amended at any time.

2. Amendments shall be adopted by a two-thirds majority of the votes cast.

C. Working methods[1]

I. *Mandate of the Committee*

The Committee, following the request made in the final resolution of the Ministerial Conference in Turin and in the decision of the Committee of Ministers of 11 December 1991 that the supervisory bodies apply the Amending Protocol as far as possible before its entry into force, refrains from the formulation of legal interpretations of the provisions of the Charter and assumes the responsibilities foreseen in Article 4 of the Amending Protocol.[2] The provision in question reads as follows:

> "*Article 4*
>
> 3. *The Governmental Committee shall prepare the decisions of the Committee of Ministers. In particular, in the light of the reports of the Committee of Independent Experts and of the Contracting Parties, it shall select, giving reasons for its choice, on the basis of social, economic and other policy considerations the situations which should, in its view, be the subject of recommendations to each Contracting Party concerned, in accordance with Article 28 of the Charter. It shall present to the Committee of Ministers a report which shall be made public.*
>
> 4. *On the basis of its findings on the implementation of the Social Charter in general, the Governmental Committee may submit proposals to the Committee of Ministers aiming at studies to be carried out on social issues and on articles of the Charter which possibly might be updated.*"

II. *General observations on the national reports and on the conclusions of the Committee of Independent Experts*

The Committee comments on the national reports and on the conclusions of the Committee of Independent Experts in particular on the General Introduction to the Conclusions. The Committee drafts an introduction in which it indicates the developments since the previous cycle of supervision and, if need be, its suggestions on the application of Article 4 para. 4 of the Amending Protocol.

---

1. Adopted by the Committee during the 87th meeting (24-26 March 1998).
2. The delegations of Denmark, Germany and Iceland are still not in favour of the immediate application of the new role of the Governmental Committee (Article 4 of the Protocol amending the European Social Charter) and wish to wait for formal ratification of that instrument.

III. *Examination of negative conclusions:*

A. *Procedure*

The Committee:

- considers the conclusions provision by provision;

- takes a vote in respect of each negative conclusion of the Committee of Independent Experts, unless there is a consensus not to take a vote; the first vote will be on whether to suggest that a recommendation be addressed to the state concerned. Regarding recommendations, the Committee decides to respect the same voting rules as those of the Committee of Ministers (two-thirds majority of votes cast and simple majority of Contracting Parties);

- where there is no majority in favour of a recommendation, it will then also take a vote on whether to address a warning to the state concerned (two-thirds majority of votes cast). If a warning follows a negative conclusion, it serves as an indication to the state that, unless it takes measures to comply with its obligations under the Charter, a recommendation will be proposed in the next part of a cycle where this provision is under examination;

- where neither a recommendation nor a warning is proposed, the Committee may find that it necessary to express an opinion on the national situation or on the conclusion of the Committee of Independent Experts in its report to the Committee of Ministers.

- the Committee's vote on a national situation will be final unless a delegate expressly requests a further vote at the end of the part of the cycle.

- in so far as the examination concerns a Contracting Party submitting its first report, the subject of the first set of conclusions of the Committee of Independent Experts, the Committee issues a warning rather than a recommendation in the case of negative conclusions. The Committee considers this approach necessary in order to give the countries concerned some time to consider and respond to the findings of the Committee of Independent Experts.

B. *Selection criteria*

a. does the provision in question belong to the hard core of the Charter or of the revised Charter?

b. is the provision among those which have been updated by the revised Social Charter?

c. since which cycle has the situation been criticised?

d. is there a significant number of persons not protected and what are the consequences of non-compliance for those involved?

e. how serious does the Committee of Independent Experts consider the situation to be?

f. has the Parliamentary Assembly expressed an opinion during its periodical debates on the Charter as to the importance of the protection guaranteed by the provision in question?

g. have the social partners expressed an opinion on the seriousness of this type of breach?

h. what was the Governmental Committee's position in response to the previous conclusion of the Committee of Independent Experts on this point? Was a recommendation adopted by the Committee of Ministers?

i. is the country taking or planning to take measures to modify the criticised situation?

j. does the criticised situation also concern another provision of the Charter?

k. what was the decision of the Committee in similar situations?

IV. *Examination of adjournments for lack of information*

A. *Procedure*

The Committee:

- no longer examines during sessions the national situations having been the object of an adjourned conclusion following a question asked by the Committee of Independent Experts for the first time except if a delegation calls for such an examination; these situations will nevertheless be referred to in the working document and in the report to the Committee of Ministers, as a reminder. The delegates concerned can, however, transmit written information to the Secretariat which they would like to be included in the Committee's reports.

- takes a vote on each situation in which the Committee of Independent Experts has repeatedly had to defer a conclusion for lack of information; a warning is adopted with a two-thirds majority of votes cast; a warning in respect of an adjourned conclusion will be made in cases of repeated lack of information, as an encouragement to submit all the relevant information in the report. Here again, the state will be informed that if the information is not submitted, a proposal for a recommendation will follow in the next cycle.

B. *Selection criteria*

a. cycle since which the Committee of Independent Experts has found it impossible to take a conclusion because of lack of information;

205

    b. whether the Governmental Committee has issued a warning or proposed a recommendation and whether a recommendation was adopted;

    c. practical reasons given by the state concerned to explain its failure to respond;

    d. failure to submit reports and information requested within the time limit;

    e. failure to submit reports to the social partners and comments made by social partners.

V. *Report to the Committee of Ministers*

The report indicates developments since the previous supervision cycle, showing positive and negative changes in the national situations.

It contains, *inter alia,* general observations on the measures taken by the different states to comply with recommendations made by the Committee of Ministers, as well as the proposals for individual recommendations to be addressed to the states by the Committee of Ministers.

Only the proposals for first recommendations are appended to the draft resolution; the renewal of recommendations still to be acted upon is mentioned only in the draft resolution ending the supervision cycle.

VI. *Follow-up of individual recommendations*

Contracting Parties shall report on the measures taken to comply with the recommendations made by the Committee of Ministers.

VI. Committee of Ministers

A. Composition

Statute of the Council of Europe

Article 14

Each member shall be entitled to one representative on the Committee of Ministers and each representative shall be entitled to one vote. Representatives on the Committee shall be the Ministers for Foreign Affairs. When a Minister for Foreign Affairs is unable to be present or in other circumstances where it may be desirable, an alternate may be nominated to act for him, who shall, whenever possible, be a member of his government.

Rules of Procedure for the meetings of the Ministers' Deputies

Article 1 – Appointment of the Ministers' Deputies

In accordance with Article 14 of the Rules of Procedure of the Committee of Ministers, each Minister for Foreign Affairs shall appoint a Deputy to act on his behalf outside the meetings held at the level of the Ministers for Foreign Affairs.

Article 2 – Powers of the Committee of Ministers meeting at the Deputy level

1. The Committee of Ministers meeting at the Deputy level – hereinafter referred to as "the Deputies" – is empowered to deal with all matters within the competence of the Committee of Ministers and to take decisions on its behalf.

2. Decisions taken by the Deputies shall have the same force and effect as decisions taken by the Committee of Ministers meeting at the level of the Ministers for Foreign Affairs.

3. The Deputies shall, however, not take decisions on any matter which, in the view of one or more of them, should by reason of its political importance be dealt with by the Committee of Ministers meeting at ministerial level.

B. Council of Europe Ministerial Conference on the European Social Charter (Turin, 21-22 October 1991)

1. Final resolution

The Ministers participating in the Ministerial Conference meeting in Turin on 21 and 22 October 1991 on the occasion of the 30th anniversary of the European Social Charter,

1. Considering that the aim of the Council of Europe is the achievement of greater unity between its Members for the purpose of safeguarding and realising the ideals and principles which are their common heritage and of facilitating their economic and social progress, in particular by the maintenance and further realisation of human rights and fundamental freedoms;

2. Recalling to mind that the Ministerial Conference on Human Rights held in Rome on 5 November 1990 stressed the need, on the one hand, to preserve the indivisible nature of all human rights, be they civil or political, economic, social or cultural and, on the other hand, to give the European Social Charter fresh impetus;

3. Stressing the importance of the European Social Charter as an instrument for safeguarding and promoting basic social rights in Europe;

4. Welcoming the ratification of the Charter by twenty member States of the Council of Europe to date, and noting with satisfaction the work undertaken in other States with a view to ratifying the Charter as soon as possible;

5. Expressing the hope that the first additional Protocol to the Charter, opened for signature on 5 May 1988, may enter into force in the near future;

6. Welcoming the follow-up action taken on the results of the Ministerial Conference on Human Rights by the Committee of Ministers in setting up the Committee on the European Social Charter with the task of making proposals for improving the effectiveness of the Charter and the functioning of its supervisory machinery;

7. Thanking the Italian Government for taking the initiative of convening, on the occasion of the 30th anniversary of the Charter, a ministerial conference which provides an opportunity to examine the results achieved by this Committee;

8. Noting that this Committee's work has resulted in the adoption, by the Committee of Ministers, of an Amending Protocol to be opened for signature at the present conference, and in the preparation of an optional draft additional protocol providing for a system of collective complaints;

9. Convinced that the entry into force of the Amending Protocol will contribute decisively towards improving the supervisory machinery of the Charter;

10. Stressing the important improvement for the effectiveness and development of the Charter which would result from the fullest possible participation by the social partners, and noting that a majority of Ministers consider that such participation would be strengthened by the establishment of a system of collective complaints;

11. Considering that, in order to give full effect to the efforts being made, it would be timely to update and adapt the substantive contents of the Charter in order to take account in particular of the fundamental social changes which have occurred since the text was adopted;

12. Taking note of Resolution 967 and Recommendation 1168 on the future of the Social Charter of the Council of Europe, unanimously adopted by the Parliamentary Assembly respectively on 28 June and 24 September 1991;

Express the firm hope that the political will, which made it possible for the first time to adopt an Amending Protocol to the European Social Charter, can be maintained for the implementation and further development of this reform;

Urge the member States of the Council of Europe to become Parties at the earliest possible opportunity to the Amending Protocol to the European Social Charter;

Request both the States party to the Charter and the supervisory bodies to envisage the application of certain of the measures provided for in this Protocol before its entry into force, in so far as the text of the Charter will allow;

Draw the attention of the Committee of Ministers of the Council of Europe to the fact that an appreciable and rapid strengthening of the resources available to the Charter is a precondition of any significant improvement in the functioning of this instrument;

Call on the organs concerned to reflect on the revision of the reporting procedure, particularly as regards its frequency;

Recommend that the Committee of Ministers of the Council of Europe:

a. examine at their earliest opportunity a draft protocol providing for a system of collective complaints, with a view to its adoption and opening for signature;

b. take the necessary steps for the immediate implementation of measures for improving the Charter which do not require any amendment to its text;

c. extend in 1992 the terms of reference originally assigned to the Committee on the European Social Charter to allow the task of giving fresh impetus to the Charter to be completed.

2. Decision relating to the application of the 1991 Amending Protocol

Adopted by the Committee of Ministers on 11 December 1991 at the 467th meeting the Ministers' Deputies

The Deputies

4. requested the States party to the Charter and the supervisory bodies to envisage the application of certain of the measures provided for in this Protocol before its entry into force, in so far as the text of the Charter will allow.

C. Decision on voting in the Committee of Ministers

Adopted by the Committee of Ministers in April 1993 at the 492nd meeting of the Ministers' Deputies

The Deputies

1. agreed unanimously to the introduction of the rule whereby only the Representatives of those States which have ratified the Charter vote in the Committee of Ministers when the latter acts as a control organ of the application of the Charter.

D. Decision on the adoption of recommendations under the European Social Charter

Adopted by the Committee of Ministers on 22 June 1995 at the 541st meeting of the Ministers' Deputies

The Deputies specified that following their decision, adopted at the 492nd meeting (April 1993, item 15) whereby "only the Representatives of those States which have ratified the Charter vote in the Committee of Ministers when the latter acts as a control organ of the application of the Charter," Recommendations under the European Social Charter are adopted by a majority of two-thirds of the Deputies casting a vote and a majority of the Contracting Parties to the Charter, (Article 9, paragraph 4 taken together with Article 10, paragraph 3 of the Rules of Procedure for the meetings of the Deputies).

E. Rules of Procedure for the adoption of recommendations under the European Social Charter

Adopted by the Committee of Ministers on 17 December 1998 at the 653rd meeting of Ministers' Deputies

1. If the chairmanship of the Committee of Ministers is held by the representative of a State concerned by a draft recommendation, that representative shall step down from the Chair during the discussion on the draft recommendation.

2. When the Committee of Ministers acts as a control organ of the application of the Charter, only the representatives of those States which have ratified it shall vote.

3. A recommendation pursuant to the European Social Charter shall be adopted by a two-thirds majority of the Deputies voting and a majority of the Charter Contracting Parties (Article 9, paragraph 4 combined with Article 10, paragraph 3 of the Ministers' Deputies' Rules of Procedure).

4. A proposal for a recommendation shall only be put to the vote at the express request of the Contracting Party concerned. Where no vote has been requested, the recommendation shall be regarded as adopted.

5. A Contracting Party may request a debate within the Committee of Ministers on the subject of a proposed recommendation by the Governmental Committee. Prior to the debate, the Contracting Party is invited to submit its written observations.

VII. Parliamentary Assembly

Letter from the President of the Assembly to the Chairman of the Ministers' Deputies

Strasbourg, 3 September 1992

Dear Mr Chairman,

Further to the decision taken by the Ministers' Deputies at their 203rd meeting, I have received the 11th report of the Governmental Committee for the Social Charter on the 2nd group of States for the period 1987-1988.

As you know, the Assembly has taken the view, in Resolution 967 and Recommendation 1168 (1991) on renewal of the Social Charter, that reports of the Governmental Committee and the Committee of Independent Experts should henceforth be made available to it as a basis *inter alia* for preparing periodical social policy debates, not for communication of its views on a particular set of conclusions of the Independent Experts' Committee as currently provided for under Article 28 of the Charter.

This view reflects the position agreed by governments and expressed in Article 6 of the Amending Protocol opened for signature at the Ministerial Conference in Turin, 21-22 October 1991. In the Final Resolution of the Conference, Ministers took note of Resolution 967 and Recommendation 1168 and of their unanimous adoption by the Parliamentary Assembly. Moreover, they requested the supervisory bodies to envisage the application of certain of the measures provided for in the Amending Protocol, before its entry into force, in so far as the text of the Charter would allow.

Accordingly, I am transmitting the 11th report of the Governmental Committee (2nd Group of States) for the period 1987-1988, together with the corresponding conclusions of the Committee of Independent Experts, to the Social, Health and Family Affairs Committee of the Assembly for information. This information will form a basis for the preparation of the next major social policy debate of the Assembly. The conclusions of this debate may accordingly be regarded as incorporating the views of the Assembly on the 11th control cycle (2nd group of States) for the period 1987-1988.

Miguel Angel MARTINEZ

VIII. Reporting system

A. Decisions on the submission of national reports under the European Social Charter in accordance with Article 21 (1961)

1. Decision to provisionally divide the states into two groups

Adopted by the Committee of Ministers on 27 January 1984 at the 336th meeting of the Ministers' Deputies

The Deputies

i. decided that, for the presentation of reports as provided for in Article 21 of the European Social Charter, the Contracting Parties of the Charter would be divided into two groups, with:

    a. the Governments of Denmark, Iceland, Ireland, Norway, the Netherlands, Sweden and the United Kingdom being asked to submit a report in the even years, beginning in 1984;

    b. the Governments of Austria, Cyprus, France, the Federal Republic of Germany, Italy and Spain reporting in the odd years, beginning in 1985;

    on the understanding that this procedure would be introduced on a trial basis for a period of 6 years;

2. Renewal of the decision to divide the Contracting States into two groups

Adopted by the Committee of Ministers in October 1989 at the 429th meeting of the Ministers' Deputies

The Deputies agreed to renew definitively the decision to divide the Contracting States into two approximately equal groups for the submission of the reports provided for in Article 21 of the European Social Charter

3. Decision on the adoption of a system for the presentation of reports for a trial period of four years

Adopted by the Committee of Ministers on 17 September 1992 at the 479th meeting of the Ministers' Deputies

The Deputies

1. approved, for a trial period of four years, the new system for submission of the reports of the European Social Charter, as set out in the following table.

Proposal of the Charte-Rel Committee concerning the reporting system

Year X	Year X + 1	Year X + 2	Year X + 3	Year X + 4
3 hard-core (1.5.6)	3 hard-core (12, 13, 16, 19)	3 hard-core (1.5.6)	3 hard-core (1.5.6)	3 hard-core (1.5.6)
3 other Articles (2, 3, 4)	3 other Articles (7, 17, 18)	3 other Articles (9, 10, 15)	3 other Articles (2, 3, 4)	3 other Articles (2, 3, 4)
+	+	+	+	+
negative conclusions adjournments and additional information referring to Articles 9, 10 and 15	negative conclusions adjournments and additional information referring to Articles 8, 11 and 14	negative conclusions adjournments and additional information referring to Articles 2, 3 and 4	negative conclusions adjournments and additional information referring to Articles 7, 17 and 18	negative conclusions adjournments and additional information referring to Articles 9, 10 and 15

2. agreed that certain States Parties to the Charter could continue to submit their reports in accordance with the current procedure (reports every two years on all the accepted provisions);

3. invited all the States Parties to the Charter, with the exception of those countries wishing to continue with the current procedure, to report in accordance with the following conditions on the provisions indicated for year x:

   – in 1992

   - all the States would report on the articles set for the year x.

   - States in the first group would also report on provisions which had given rise to negative conclusions, adjournments or requests for additional information by the Committee of Independent Experts during cycle XII-1.

   – in 1993

   all States would report on the articles selected for year X + 1.

   States in the second group would also report on provisions which had given rise to negative conclusions, adjournments or requests for additional information by the Committee of Independent Experts during cycle XII-2.

   – in 1994

   the new system would apply fully.

   In the case of States belonging to the second group, the deadline for the submission of reports could if necessary be extended to 30 November 1992;

4. Agreed that States which have ratified the Charter recently will submit full reports twice, on a biennial basis, in accordance with the timetable set out in the following calendar:

Belgium:	1st report in 1993; 2nd in 1995
Finland:	1st report in 1994; 2nd in 1996
Luxembourg:	1st report in 1994; 2nd in 1996
Malta:	[1st report in 1991]; 2nd in 1993
Portugal:	1st report in 1994; 2nd in 1996
Turkey:	1st report in 1992; 2nd in 1994

4. Decision reached after the four-year period

Adopted by the Committee of Ministers on 19 October 1995 at the 547th meeting of the Ministers' Deputies

The Deputies

1. agreed to consider at a later meeting, after consulting the members of the Governmental Committee of the European Social Charter, the proposals relating to Article 21 of the European Social Charter, put forward in particular by the United Kingdom and Finland, with the aim of reaching a unanimous agreement between the Contracting Parties;

2. decided, in application of Article 21 of the European Social Charter, that in the meantime, if a contrary decision is not reached, the Contracting Parties to the Charter would submit their reports on the application of those provisions of the Charter which they had accepted in accordance with the following rules:

   – 30 June 1996 (cycle XIII-5): full reports from Finland, Luxembourg and Portugal and reports on the application of the Additional Protocol (first reports: Italy, Norway; second reports: Finland, the Netherlands and Sweden);

   – 30 June 1997 (cycle XIV-1), then every two years: full reports from the first group of States (Austria, Belgium, Cyprus, Denmark, France, Germany, Greece, Iceland, Malta, Spain);

   – 30 June 1998 (cycle XIV-2), then every two years: full reports from the second group of States (Finland, Ireland, Italy, Luxembourg, the Netherlands, Norway, Portugal, Sweden, Turkey, the United Kingdom).

5. Decision on the new system for the presentation of reports

Adopted by the Committee of Ministers in September 1996 at the 573rd meeting of the Ministers' Deputies

The Deputies, having observed that there is a unanimous agreement of the Contracting Parties to the European Social Charter,

1. approved the new system of presentation of reports under the European Social Charter as it appears in the table below;

2. agreed that this system will apply from the XIVth cycle of supervision (30 June 1997);

3. agreed that the new Contracting Parties to the Charter and to the Additional Protocol of 1988 will submit complete reports twice, on a two year basis, before applying the new system.

6. Table showing future supervision cycles (in application of the European Social Charter (1961)).

Table showing the system for the presentation of reports on the application of the European Social Charter (1961)

Reference Period	Date of submission of reports	Provisions	Conclusions of the European Committee of Social Rights	Governmental Committee Report	Committee of Ministers Decision
XVI-1 1999-2000	30 June 2001	Hard Core	28 February 2002	October 2002	December 2002
XVI-2 1997-2000	either 30 June 2001, or 31 March 2002	Second part of other provisions	31 December 2002	October 2003	December 2003
XVII-1 2001-2002	30 June 2003	Hard Core	28 February 2004	October 2004	December 2004
XVII-2 1999-2002	either 30 June 2003, or 31 March 2004	First part of other provisions	31 December 2004	October 2005	December 2005

B. System for the presentation of reports on the application of the revised European Social Charter (1996)

Adopted by the Committee of Ministers at the 689th meeting of the Ministers' Deputies on 24-25 November 1999

The Committee of Ministers adopted the system for the presentation of reports on the revised European Social Charter, as explained in the document CM(99)157 [below]

1. During their informal meeting in May 1999, the European Committee of Social Rights, (committee of independent experts) and the Governmental Committee of the Social Charter discussed the matter of the presentation of reports on the application of the revised European Social Charter, with a view to making a proposal to the Committee of Ministers on the subject.

2. At its 92nd meeting in September 1999, the Governmental Committee adopted the proposal below and decided to transmit it to the Committee of Ministers with a view to its adoption.

3. It should be recalled that the revised Charter entered into force on 1 July 1999.

4. The system for the presentation of reports accepted by the two Committees is as follows:

   – report every two years on the hard core provisions (30 June of odd years)

   – report every four years on the other provisions (31 March of even years, alternatively report on half the provisions concerned)

5. The hard core provisions are articles 1, 5, 6, 7, 12, 13, 16, 19 and 20.

6. The other provisions are divided into two groups:

   – 2, 3, 4, 9, 10, 15, 21, 22, 24, 26, 28, 29 (12 articles and 31 paragraphs)

   – 8, 11, 14, 17, 18, 23, 25, 27, 30, 31 (10 articles and 26 paragraphs)

7. The first reports will be submitted:

   – 30 June 2001 for the hard core

   – 31 March 2002 for the first part of the other provisions

   – 30 June 2003 for the hard core

   – 31 March 2004 for the second part of the other provisions

8. In order to simplify states' work as well as that of the supervisory bodies, that states are not required to submit two full reports, as was the case under the 1961 Social Charter, before submitting the partial reports described in point 4 above.

9. In order to avoid too long a delay between the entry into force of the Charter for a state and the date when the supervisory bodies will have been in a position to examine all provisions accepted by it, it has been agreed that the first report concerning non hard core provisions should exceptionally cover all of these provisions. These reports are featured in bold in the table below.

10. The system is shown in the table below.

Table showing the system for the presentation of reports on the application of the revised European Social Charter (1996)

Publication of Conclusions	Date for the submission of reports	Provisions	Reference period[1]	France, Italy, Romania, Slovenia and Sweden	Bulgaria	Cyprus, Estonia, Ireland, Lithuania and Norway	States having ratified between 01/7/2001 and 31/3/2002
2002	30 June 2001	Hard core	1999-2000	1st report			
2003	31 March 2002	First part of other provisions	1999-2000	**2nd report**[2]	**1st report**[2]		
2004	30 June 2003	Hard core	2001-2002	3rd report	2nd report	1st report	
2005	31 March 2004	Second part of other provisions	2001-2002	4th report	3rd report	**2nd report**[2]	**1st report**[2]
2006	30 June 2005	Hard core	2003-2004	5th report	4th report	3rd report	2nd report
2007	31 March 2006	First part of other provisions	2001-2004	6th report	5th report	4th report	3rd report
2008	30 June 2007	Hard core	2005-2006	7th report	6th report	5th report	4th report
2009	31 March 2008	Second part of other provisions	2003-2006	8th report	7th report	6th report	5th report

1. To be adapted according to the date of entry into force of the revised European Social Charter in respect of each State.
2. The reports featured in bold indicate the first report covering exceptionally all non-hard core provisions (item 9 of the document CM(99)157).

C. Form for the reports submitted in pursuance of the European Social Charter[1]

(To be completed in English or French)

For the period .... to ....

made by the Government of.............................in accordance with Article 21 of the European Social Charter, on the measures taken to give effect to the accepted provisions of the European Social Charter, the instrument of ratification or approval of which was deposited on ....

This report also covers the application of such provisions in the following non-metropolitan territories to which, in conformity with Article 34, they have been declared applicable: ....

In accordance with Article 23 of the Charter, copies of this report have been communicated to..
....[2]

The reports drawn up on the basis of this Form should give, for each accepted provision of the European Social Charter, any useful information on measures adopted to ensure its application, mentioning in particular:

1. any laws or regulations, collective agreements or other provisions that contribute to such application;

2. any judicial decisions on questions of principle relating to these provisions;

3. any factual information enabling an evaluation of the extent to which these provisions are applied; this concerns particularly questions specified in this Form.

The Contracting Parties' reports should be accompanied by the principal laws and regulations on which the application of the accepted provisions of the Charter is based. These may be sent in their original language and translation in one of the official languages of the Council of Europe may be asked for in exceptional circumstances.

---

1. Adopted by the Committee of Ministers on 24 November 1999 at the 689th meeting of the Ministers' Deputies and modified by the Committee of Ministers on 17 January 2001 at the 737th meeting of the Ministers' Deputies.
2. Please state whether you have received any observations from these national organisations of employers and workers, and supply those they have asked you to transmit. The information provided would be usefully supplemented by your communicating a summary of all other observations, to which you might add any comments that you consider useful.

The replies of the governments should, wherever appropriate, specify explicitly:

a. whether they are only concerned with the situation of nationals or whether they apply equally to the nationals of the other Contracting Parties (see Appendix to the Charter, points 1 and 2);

b. whether they are valid for the national territory in its entirety, including the non-metropolitan territories if any to which the Charter applies by virtue of Article 34;

c. whether they apply to all categories of persons included in the scope of the provision.

The Form indicates for each Article and paragraph those cases in which a state bound by obligations under certain International Labour Conventions may find it sufficient to supply a copy of the relevant reports submitted to the ILO on the application of these conventions in so far as the latter cover the same field of application as the relevant provision of the Charter.

The information required, especially statistics, should, unless otherwise stated, be supplied for the period covered by the report.

Where statistics are requested for any provision, it is understood that, if complete statistics are lacking, governments may supply data or estimates based on ad hoc studies, specialised or sample surveys, or other scientifically valid methods, whenever they consider the information so collected to be useful.

The report should as far as possible be submitted by E-mail to the address social.charter@coe.int and a diskette in Word format should be appended. If this is not possible, the Contracting Parties are requested to submit their reports in five copies and the appendices in two copies.

Contracting parties are requested:

– as far as first reports are concerned: to reply to all questions appearing in this Form;

– as far as subsequent reports are concerned: to update the information given in the previous report.

Article 1: The right to work

Article 1 para. 1

"With a view to ensuring the effective exercise of the right to work, the Contracting Parties undertake:

to accept as one of their primary aims and responsibilities the achievement and maintenance of as high and stable a level of employment as possible, with a view to the attainment of full employment;"

Question A

Please indicate the policy followed by your government in attempting to reach and maintain full employment. Please supplement with details of the measures and programmes implemented to achieve as high and stable a level of employment as possible.

Please indicate, if possible, the trend in total employment policy expenditure over the past five years, including the relative shares of "active" (job creation, training, etc.) and "passive" (financial compensation, etc.) measures.

Please indicate the active policy measures taken in order to favour access to employment of groups most exposed to or affected by unemployment (eg. women, the young,[1] older workers, the long-term unemployed,[2] the disabled, immigrants and/or ethnic minorities). Please give indications on the number of beneficiaries from these measures and information, if possible, on their impact on employment.

Question B

Please indicate the trends in employment[3] covering all sectors of the economy. In connection with this, indicate as far as possible, the activity rate,[4] the employment rate[5] and the breakdown of employment by region, by sex, by age, by employment status (employed, self-employed), by type of employment (full time and part time, permanent and fixed term, temporary), and by sector of activity.

Please give the trend of the figures and percentages of unemployed in your country, including the proportion of unemployed to the total labour force. Please give a break-down of the unemployed by region, category, sex, age and by length of unemployment.

Question C

Please indicate the trend in the number and the nature of vacant jobs in your country.

Article 1 para. 2

"With a view to ensuring the effective exercise of the right to work, the Contracting Parties undertake:

---

1. Aged between fifteen and twenty-four.
2. Persons without employment for over one year and seeking employment.
3. Reference is made to the definition of employment adopted by the Thirteenth International Conference of Labour Statisticians (Geneva, 1982) or any further versions.
4. The activity rate represents the total labour force as a percentage of the population aged 15 years and over and living in private households. The labour force is defined as the sum of persons in employment plus the unemployed.
5. The employment rate represents persons in employment as a percentage of the population aged 15-64 years and living in private households.

> *to protect effectively the right of the worker to earn his living in an occupation freely entered upon;"*

[The Appendix to the Charter stipulates that this provision shall not be interpreted as prohibiting or authorising any union security clause or practice.]

Elimination of all forms of discrimination in employment

Question A

Please give information concerning legislative or other measures taken to ensure the elimination of all discrimination in employment which might be based on sex, social or national origin, political opinion, religion, race, colour or age and to promote effectively equal opportunities in seeking employment and in taking up an occupation.[1]

Please give information in this respect on existing sanctions and remedies in cases of discrimination in employment.

Question B

Please indicate any methods adopted:

to seek the co-operation of employers' and workers' organisations and other appropriate bodies in promoting the acceptance and observance of the above policy of non-discrimination;

b. to ensure the acceptance and observance of the above policy through educational efforts.

Question C

Please indicate the guarantees, including applicable sanctions and remedies, which prevent any discrimination in regard to members of workers' organisations at the time of engagement, promotion or dismissal.

Prohibition of forced labour

Question D

Please indicate whether any form of forced or compulsory labour is authorised or tolerated.[2]

Question E

If so, please describe the nature and scope of any such labour and indicate the extent to which recourse has been had thereto during the reference period.

---

1. The term "discrimination" in this Form is to be understood in terms of ILO Convention No. 111 (Discrimination, Employment, Occupations), Article 1.
2. The term "forced or compulsory labour" in this Form is to be understood in terms of ILO Convention No. 29 (Forced Labour), Article 2..

Question F

Please indicate what measures are being taken to secure the complete abolition of forced or compulsory labour and the date by which these measures will be fully implemented.

Question G

Please give information concerning the conditions under which work is carried out in prison establishments.

Article 1 para. 3

"With a view to ensuring the effective exercise of the right to work, the Contracting Parties undertake:

to establish or maintain free employment services for all workers;"

Question A

Please describe the operation of free employment services available in your country, indicating the age, sex and nature of occupation of persons placed by them in employment and persons seeking employment.

Please indicate as far as possible the number of vacancies, the placement rate and the duration of unemployment of persons placed.

Question B

Please describe the organisation of public employment services in your country indicating the accompanying measures for the unemployed, and where appropriate, the steps taken to revise the geographical distribution of local and regional employment centres and to redeploy resources when the changing patterns of economic activity and of population so warrant.

Question C

If both public and private free employment services exist in your country, please describe the steps taken to co-ordinate such services, and to determine the conditions governing the operation of private employment agencies.

Question D

Please indicate whether and how the participation of representatives of employers and workers in the organisation and operation of the employment services and in the development of employment services policy is provided for.

Question E

Please indicate what legislation or administrative guarantees are provided to ensure that these services are available to all.

Article 1 para. 4

> "With a view to ensuring the effective exercise of the right to work, the Contracting Parties undertake:
>
> to provide or promote appropriate vocational guidance, training and rehabilitation."

Please indicate, illustrating with relevant data as far as possible, what measures have been taken to provide or promote:

a. vocational guidance;[1]

b. vocational training;[2]

c. vocational rehabilitation;[3]

with the aim of giving everyone the possibility of earning his living in an occupation freely entered upon.

Please indicate whether equal access is ensured for all those interested, including nationals of the other Contracting Parties to the Charter lawfully resident or working regularly in your territory, and disabled people.

Article 2: The right to just conditions of work

Article 2 para. 1

> "With a view to ensuring the effective exercise of the right to just conditions of work, the Contracting Parties undertake:
>
> to provide for reasonable daily and weekly working hours, the working week to be progressively reduced to the extent that the increase of productivity and other relevant factors permit;"

Question A

Please indicate what statutory provisions apply in respect of the number of working hours, daily and weekly and the duration of the daily rest period.

Question B

Please indicate what rules concerning normal working hours and overtime are usual in collective agreements, and what is the scope of these rules.

---

1. If your country has accepted Article 9, it is not necessary to describe the vocational guidance services here.
2. If your country has accepted the four paragraphs of Article 10, it is not necessary to describe the vocational training services here.
3. If your country has accepted the two paragraphs of Article 15, it is not necessary to describe the rehabilitation services for physically or mentally handicapped persons.

Question C

Please indicate the average working hours in practice for each major professional category.

Question D

Please indicate to what extent working hours have been reduced by legislation, by collective agreements, or in practice during the reference period and, in particular, as a result of increased productivity.

Question E

Please describe, where appropriate, any measures permitting derogations from legislation in your country regarding daily and weekly working hours and the duration of the daily rest period (see also Article 2 paras. 2, 3 and 5).

Please indicate the reference period to which such measures may be applied.

Please indicate whether any such measures are implemented by legislation or by collective agreement and in the latter case, at what level these agreements are concluded and whether only representative trade unions are entitled to conduct negotiations in this respect.

Question F

If some workers are not covered by provisions of this nature, whether contained in legislation, collective agreements or other measures, please state what proportion of all workers is not so covered (see Article 33 of the Charter).

Article 2 para. 2

"With a view to ensuring the effective exercise of the right to just conditions of work, the Contracting Parties undertake:

to provide for public holidays with pay;"

Question A

Please indicate the number of public holidays with pay laid down by legislation, stipulated by collective agreement or established by practice during the last calendar year.

Question B

Please indicate what rules apply to public holidays with pay according to legislation, collective agreements or practice.

Please describe, where appropriate, whether measures permitting derogation from legislation in your country regarding daily and weekly working hours have an impact on rules pertaining to public holidays with pay.

Question C

If some workers are not covered by provisions of this nature, whether contained in legislation, collective agreements, or other measures, please state what proportion of all workers is not so covered (see Article 33 of the Charter).

Article 2 para. 3

"With a view to ensuring the effective exercise of the right to just conditions of work, the Contracting Parties undertake:

to provide for a minimum of two weeks annual holiday with pay;"

Question A

Please indicate the length of annual holidays under legislative provisions or collective agreements; please also indicate the minimum period of employment entitling workers to annual holidays.

Please describe, where appropriate, whether measures permitting derogation from statutory rules in your country regarding daily and weekly working hours have an impact on rules pertaining to the duration of annual holidays.

Question B

Please indicate the effect of incapacity for work through illness or injury during all or part of annual holiday on the entitlement to annual holidays.

Question C

Please indicate if it is possible for workers to renounce their annual holiday.

Question D

Please indicate the customary practice where legislation or collective agreements do not apply.

Question E

If some workers are not covered by provisions of this nature, whether contained in legislation, collective agreements or other measures, please state what proportion of all workers is not covered (see Article 33 of the Charter).

Article 2 para. 4

"With a view to ensuring the effective exercise of the right to just conditions of work, the Contracting Parties undertake:

to provide for additional paid holidays or reduced working hours for workers engaged in dangerous or unhealthy occupations as prescribed;"

Question A

Please state the occupations regarded as dangerous or unhealthy. If a list exists of these occupations, please supply it.

Question B

Please state what provisions apply under legislation or collective agreements or otherwise in practice as regards reduced working hours or additional paid holidays in relation to this provision.

Question C

If some workers are not covered by provisions of this nature, whether contained in legislation, collective agreements or other measures, please state what proportion of all workers concerned is not covered (see Article 33 of the Charter).

Article 2 para. 5

"With a view to ensuring the effective exercise of the right to just conditions of work, the Contracting Parties undertake:

to ensure a weekly rest period which shall, as far as possible, coincide with the day recognised by tradition or custom in the country or region concerned as a day of rest."

Question A

Please indicate what provisions apply according to legislation, collective agreements or otherwise in practice as regards weekly rest periods.

Please indicate whether postponement of the weekly rest period is provided for these provisions and, if so, please indicate under what circumstances and over what period of reference.

Please indicate, where appropriate, whether measures derogating from statutory rules in your country regarding daily and weekly working time have an impact on rules relating to the weekly rest period.

Question B

Please indicate what measures have been taken to ensure that workers obtain their weekly rest period in accordance with this paragraph.

Question C

If some workers are not covered by provisions of this nature, whether contained in legislation, collective agreements or other measures, please state what proportion of all workers is not covered (see Article 33 of the Charter).

Please indicate, for Article 2 as a whole, the rules applying to workers in atypical employment relationships (fixed-term contracts, part-time, replacements, temporaries, etc.).

245

Article 3: The right to safe and healthy working conditions

Article 3 para. 1

"With a view to ensuring the effective exercise of the right to safe and healthy working conditions, the Contracting Parties undertake:

to issue safety and health regulations;"

Question A

Please list the principal legislative or administrative provisions issued in order to protect the physical and mental health and the safety of workers, indicating clearly:

a. their material scope of application (risks covered and the preventive and protective measures provided for), and

b. their personal scope of application (whatever their legal status – employees or not – and whatever their sector of activity, including home workers and domestic staff).

Please specify the rules adopted to ensure that workers under atypical employment contracts enjoy the same level of protection as other workers in an enterprise.

Question B

Please indicate the special measures taken to protect the health and safety of workers engaged in dangerous or unhealthy work.

Article 3 para. 2

"With a view to ensuring the effective exercise of the right to safe and healthy working conditions, the Contracting Parties undertake:

to provide for the enforcement of such regulations by measures of supervision;"

Question A

Please indicate the methods applied by the Labour Inspection to enforce health and safety regulations and please also give information, inter alia, statistical, on:

a. the places of work, including the home, subjected to the control of the Labour Inspection, indicating the categories of enterprises exempted from this control;

b. the number of control visits carried out;

c. the proportion of workers covered by these visits.

Question B

Please describe the system of civil and penal sanctions guaranteeing the application of health and safety regulations and also provide information on violations committed:

a. the number of violations;

b. the sectors in which they have been identified;

c. the action, including judicial, taken in this respect.

Question C

Please provide statistical information on occupational accidents, including fatal accidents, and on occupational diseases by sectors of activity specifying what proportion of the labour force is covered by the statistics. Please describe also the preventive measures taken in each sector.

Article 3 para. 3

> "With a view to ensuring the effective exercise of the right to safe and healthy working conditions, the Contracting Parties undertake:
>
> to consult, as appropriate, employers' and workers' organisations on measures intended to improve industrial safety and health."

Please indicate if consultations with workers' and employers' organisations are provided for in this connection by law, if they take place in practice and at what level (national, regional, at the sectoral or enterprise level).

Article 4: The right to a fair remuneration

Article 4 para. 1

> "With a view to ensuring the effective exercise of the right to a fair remuneration, the Contracting Parties undertake:
>
> to recognise the right of workers to a remuneration such as will give them and their families a decent standard of living."
>
> "...The exercise of this right shall be achieved by freely concluded collective agreements, by statutory wage-fixing machinery, or by other means appropriate to national conditions;"

Question A

Please state what methods are provided and what measures are taken to provide workers with a fair wage, having regard to national living standards and particularly to the changes in the cost of living index and in national income.[1]

Question B

Please specify if these include methods for fixing minimum wage standards by law or collective agreements.

---

1. If your country has accepted Article 16, there is no need to give information here concerning family allowances, etc.

Question C

Please indicate what proportion of wage-earners are without protection in respect of wages, either by law or collective agreement.

Question D:

Please provide information on:

– national net average wage[1] (ie. after deduction of social security contributions and taxes[2]);

– national net minimum wage if applicable or the net lowest wages actually paid (ie. after deduction of social security contributions and taxes).[3]

Please provide information, where possible, on:

– the proportion of workers receiving the minimum wage or the lowest wage actually paid (after deduction of social security contributions and taxes);

– the trend in the level of the minimum net wage and/or the lowest wage actually paid compared to national net average wage and any available studies on this subject.

Article 4 para. 2

"With a view to ensuring the effective exercise of the right to a fair remuneration, the Contracting Parties undertake:

to recognise the right of workers to an increased rate of remuneration for overtime work, subject to exceptions in particular cases;"

---

1. In principle the net average wage should be the overall average for all sectors of economic activity. The average wage may be calculated on an annual, monthly, weekly, daily or hourly basis. Wages cover remuneration in cash paid directly and regularly by the employer at the time of each wage payment. This includes normal working hours, overtime and hours not worked but paid, when the pay for these latter are included in the returned earnings. Payments for leave, public holidays and other paid individual absences may be included insofar as the corresponding days or hours are also taken into account to calculate wages per unit of time.
2. The net wage (average and minimum) should be calculated for the standard case of a single worker. Family allowances and social welfare benefits should not be taken into account. Social security contributions should be calculated on the basis of the employee contribution rates laid down by law or collective agreements etc. and withheld by the employer. Taxes are all taxes on earned income. They should be calculated on the assumption that gross earnings represent the only source of income and that there are no special grounds for tax relief other than those associated with the situation of a single worker receiving either the average wage or the minimum wage. Indirect taxes are thus not taken into account.
3. The net minimum wage should be given in units of time comparable to those used for the average wage.

"...The exercise of this right shall be achieved by freely concluded collective agreements, by statutory wage-fixing machinery, or by other means appropriate to national conditions;"

Question A

Please mention what provisions apply according to legislation and collective agreements as regards overtime pay, the method used to calculate the increased rates of remuneration and the categories of work and workers to which they apply.

Please specify what provisions apply in respect of overtime pay on Saturdays, Sundays and other special days or hours (inclunding night work).

Question B

Please mention any special cases for which exceptions are made.

Please indicate, where appropriate, whether measures permitting derogation from legislation in your country regarding daily and weekly working hours (see Article 2 para. 1) have an impact on remuneration or compensation of overtime.

Article 4 para. 3

"With a view to ensuring the effective exercise of the right to a fair remuneration, the Contracting Parties undertake:

to recognise the right of men and women workers to equal pay for work of equal value;"

"...The exercise of this right shall be achieved by freely concluded collective agreements, by statutory wage-fixing machinery, or by other means appropriate to national conditions;"

Question A

Please indicate how the principle of equal pay for work of equal value is applied; state whether the principle applies to all workers.[1]

Question B

Please indicate the progress which has been made in applying this principle.

Question C

Please describe the protection afforded to workers against retaliatory measures, including dismissal.

Please indicate the procedures applied to implement this protection.

---

1. The term "equal pay for work of equal value" in this Form is to be understood in terms of ILO Convention No. 100 (Equal Remuneration), Article 1.

Article 4 para. 4

"With a view to ensuring the effective exercise of the right to a fair remuneration, the Contracting Parties undertake:

to recognise the right of all workers to a reasonable period of notice for termination of employment;"

"... The exercise of this right shall be achieved by freely concluded collective agreements, by statutory wage-fixing machinery, or by other means appropriate to national conditions."

[The Appendix to the Charter stipulates that this provision shall be so understood as not to prohibit immediate dismissal for any serious offence.]

Question A

Please indicate if periods of notice are provided for by legislation, by collective agreements or by practice and if so, indicate the length of such periods, notably in relation to seniority in the enterprise.

Please indicate whether the periods of notice established by legislation can be derogated by collective agreements.

Please indicate the periods of notice applicable to part-time workers and to home workers.

Please indicate in which cases a worker may not be given a notice period.

Please indicate whether provision is made for notice periods in the case of fixed-term contracts which are not renewed.

Question B

Please indicate whether wage-earners may challenge the legality of such notice of termination of employment before a judicial authority.

Article 4 para. 5

"With a view to ensuring the effective exercise of the right to a fair remuneration, the Contracting Parties undertake:

to permit deductions from wages only on the conditions and to the extent prescribed by national laws or regulations or fixed by collective agreements or arbitration awards."

"...The exercise of this right shall be achieved by freely concluded collective agreements, by statutory wage-fixing machinery, or by other means appropriate to national conditions."

[The Appendix to the Charter stipulates that it is understood that a Contracting Party may give the undertaking required in this paragraph if the great majority of workers are not permitted to suffer deductions from wages either by law or through collective agreements or arbitration awards, the exception being those persons not so covered.]

Question A

Please describe how and to what extent observance of this paragraph is ensured in your country, specifying the ways in which this right is exercised, both as regards deductions made by the employer for his own benefit and for the benefit of third parties.

Please indicate whether legislation, regulations or collective agreements provide for the non-seizability of a part of the wage.

Question B

Please state whether the measures described are applicable to all categories of wage-earners. If this is not the case, please give an estimate of the proportion of workers not covered and, if appropriate, give details of the categories concerned.

Article 5: The right to organise

> "With a view to ensuring or promoting the freedom of workers and employers to form local, national or international organisations for the protection of their economic and social interests and to join those organisations, the Contracting Parties undertake that national law shall not be such as to impair, nor shall it be so applied as to impair, this freedom. The extent to which the guarantees provided for in this Article shall apply to the police shall be determined by national laws or regulations. The principle governing the application to the members of the armed forces of these guarantees and the extent to which they shall apply to persons in this category shall equally be determined by national laws or regulations."

Question A

a. Please indicate whether any, and if so what, categories of workers and employers are prohibited by law from forming organisations, or restricted in doing so.

Please indicate, *inter alia*:

– the existence of legislation or special regulations applicable to the forming of organisations by civil servants and other persons employed by the public authorities at central or local level;

– to what extent the rights provided for in this Article apply to members of the armed forces and of the police, explaining in particular the nature and functions of any staff associations which may be available to them;

– whether nationals of other Contracting Parties lawfully resident or working regularly in the territory of your country may join or be a founding member of a trade union. Please indicate in particular whether they may hold positions in the administration or management of a trade union;

    – the eligibility of workers, nationals of other Contracting Parties to the Charter, for election to consultation bodies at the enterprise level such as works councils.

b. Please indicate any conditions of registration or otherwise with which employers' and workers' organisations must comply when they are founded and the provisions with which they must comply in the course of their existence.

c. Please indicate the measures intended to guarantee the exercise of the freedom to organise and in particular those to protect workers' organisations from any interference by employers and by the state. Please indicate how such protection from outside interference applies to employers' organisations.

d. Please indicate, where appropriate, any statutory provisions regarding the affiliation of employers' and workers' organisations with national federations of organisations and with international organisations of the same type.

Question B

a Please describe how the right to join a trade union is protected in law and in practice and indicate whether any, and if so which, categories of workers are prohibited from joining a trade union or restricted in doing so.

b Please indicate whether and how the right of workers not to join a union is protected in law and in practice. Please indicate in particular whether examples exist in practice of an obligation to belong to a trade union (closed shop clauses, etc.) and what are the measures taken in this regard.

Question C

a. Please furnish a complete description of any representativity criteria, ie. any conditions which trade unions must fulfil in order to be considered representative.

b. If such criteria exist, please also give information on the existence and type of appeal against decisions by the authority or authorities responsible for determining whether a trade union is representative or not. Please indicate the functions which are reserved for representative unions in respect of the negotiation and conclusion of collective agreements, participation in the nomination of various types of workers' representatives and participation in consultation bodies.

c. Please reply to the questions under a. and b. in respect of representativity of employers' organisations, except when negotiations at enterprise level are concerned.

Question D

Please indicate under what circumstances and on which conditions trade union representatives have access to the workplace. Please indicate also whether trade unions are entitled to hold meetings on the premises of the enterprise.

Question E

Please give information on the measures taken to ensure protection against reprisals on grounds of trade union activities.

Article 6: Tthe right to bargain collectively

> *Article 6 para. 1*
>
> > *"With a view to ensuring the effective exercise of the right to bargain collectively, the Contracting Parties undertake:*
> >
> > *to promote joint consultation between workers and employers;"*

Please indicate the legislative or other steps taken to encourage joint consultation between workers and employers in your country. In what way do the public authorities encourage or participate in such consultation? Please give particulars on the bodies responsible for such consultation, at the national, regional, or local levels as the case may be, and on the procedures entailed, together with information on the issues covered (financial issues, social issues, working conditions, etc.) and on the sectors of the economy to which the procedures apply.

> *Article 6 para. 2*
>
> > *"With a view to ensuring the effective exercise of the right to bargain collectively, the Contracting Parties undetake:*
> >
> > *to promote, where necessary and appropriate, machinery for voluntary negotiations between employers or employers' organisations and workers' organisations, with a view to the regulation of terms and conditions of employment by means of collective agreements;"*

Question A

Please give a description of the existing collective bargaining machinery and its results in both the private and public sector (indications of the number of negotiations and agreements concluded and other indicators or evaluation criteria).

Question B

Please indicate whether and how the law encourages or obliges employers or their organisations to bargain with workers' organisations collectively, and whether and how it encourages or obliges workers' organisations to bargain with employers or their organisations. Please also indicate how the question of union recognition is dealt with.

Question C

Please indicate to what extent, under what conditions, according to which procedures and for which types of subject matter the State can intervene in the process of free collective bargaining. Please indicate where state intervention occurred during the reference period.

Article 6 para. 3

> *"With a view to ensuring the effective exercise of the right to bargain collectively, the Contracting Parties undertake:*
>
> *to promote the establishment and use of appropriate machinery for conciliation and voluntary arbitration for the settlement of labour disputes;"*

Question A

Please describe such machinery as exists by virtue either of law, collective agreements or practice for the settlement of disputes by:

a. conciliation;

b. arbitration or court procedure;

c. other methods of dispute resolution.

Question B

In so far as certain machinery may be compulsory, please describe:

– the sanctions imposed by law or by collective agreements used for its enforcement;

– their significance in practice.

Question C

Please describe the procedures provided, whether by law, staff regulations or practice, for settling disputes between public sector employees and the administration, and show whether existing procedures are open to them.

> *Article 6 para. 4*
>
> *"With a view to ensuring the effective exercise of the right to bargain collectively, the Contracting Parties recognise:*
>
> *the right of workers and employers to collective action in cases of conflicts of interest, including the right to strike, subject to obligations that might arise out of collective agreements previously entered into."*

[The Appendix to the Charter stipulates that it is understood that each Contracting Party may, in so far as it is concerned, regulate the exercise of the right to strike by law, provided that any further restriction that this might place on the right can be justified under the terms of Article 31.]

Question A

Please explain the meaning of collective action in your country specifying what forms of action are recognised (strike, lockout, other forms), what are the permitted objectives of collective action and how the right to collective action is guaranteed.

Question B

Please indicate who is entitled to take collective action (individuals, groups/coalitions of workers, trade unions, employers or employers' organisations, etc.).

Question C

If the right to collective action is restricted, please state what the content of these restrictions, and whether they are related to the purposes pursued or the methods employed by those taking action, or both, and by which authority they may be imposed.

Please also state any procedural requirements pertaining to collective action (eg. notice rules, cooling-off periods, conciliation/arbitration, ballot requirements, quorums, etc.).

Question D

Please indicate whether any existing restrictions to the right to collective action "are prescribed by law and are necessary in a democratic society for the protection of the rights and freedoms of others or for the protection of public interest, national security, public health, or morals" (Article 31 of the Charter).

Question E

Please state the effect of strikes or lockouts on the continuation of the employment contract and any other consequences, eg. deduction from wages, liability, etc.

Question F

Please supply available statistics on strikes and lockouts.

Article 7: The right of children and young persons to protection

Article 7 para. 1

"With a view to ensuring the effective exercise of the right of children and young persons to protection, the Contracting Parties undertake:

to provide that the minimum age of admission to employment shall be 15 years, subject to exceptions for children employed in prescribed light work without harm to their health, morals or education;"

Question A

Please indicate whether the minimum age of admission to employment is regulated by legislation. If so, please send the relevant texts.

Please indicate whether the minimum age of admission to employment applies to all categories of work, including agricultural work, domestic work and work carried out in family enterprises.

Question B

Please state whether your country's legislation dealing with minimum age allows derogations. if so, please state the derogations provided for in general by law or granted by an authority.

Please provide a definition of "light work" and, if appropriate, the list of such of work.

Question C

Please indicate the measures taken to combat illegal child labour and to implement in practice the relevant legislation and regulations.

> *Article 7 para. 2*
>
> *"With a view to ensuring the effective exercise of the right of children and young persons to protection, the Contracting Parties undertake:*
>
> *to provide that a higher minimum age of admission to employment shall be fixed with respect to prescribed occupations regarded as dangerous or unhealthy;"*

Question A

Please indicate for which types of work exists a higher minimum age than the minimum age for admission to employment, and the age for these types of work.

Question B

Please indicate whether any derogations are provided for concerning these types of work.

Question C

Please indicate the measures taken to implement in practice the relevant legislation and regulations.

> *Article 7 para. 3*
>
> *"With a view to ensuring the effective exercise of the right of children and young persons to protection, the Contracting Parties undertake:*
>
> *to provide that persons who are still subject to compulsory education shall not be employed in such work as would deprive them of the full benefit of their education;"*

Question A

Please indicate the age at which education ceases to be compulsory under your country's present legislation.

Question B

Please indicate the statutory maximum duration of any work performed by children still subject to compulsory education before or after school hours and during weekends and school holidays.

Please indicate the nature of the work performed by these children.

Question C

Please indicate the measures taken to implement in practice the relevant legislation and regulations.

> *Article 7 para. 4*
>
> *"With a view to ensuring the effective exercise of the right of children and young persons to protection, the Contracting Parties undertake:*
>
> *to provide that the working hours of persons under 16 years of age shall be limited in accordance with the needs of their development, and particularly with their need for vocational training;"*

Question A

Please indicate the extent of this limitation, whether it follows from legislative, administrative, or contractual provisions or from practice.

Question B

Please indicate if any workers are not covered by provisions of this nature, whether contained in legislation, collective agreements or other measures and, if so:

a. please provide statistics showing what proportion of all workers is not covered;

b. please give the reasons for which certain workers are not covered;

c. please indicate what special measures have been taken on behalf of workers under sixteen years who do not benefit from any limitation of their hours of work.

Question C

Please indicate the measures taken to implement in practice the relevant legislation and regulations.

Question D

Please indicate whether the measures described apply to all categories of young people at work. If this is not the case, please give an estimate of the proportion of young people not covered and, if possible, indicate the categories concerned.

Question E

Please indicate, where appropriate, why certain workers are not covered, and whether special measures have been taken on their behalf.

Article 7 para. 5

"With a view to ensuring the effective exercise of the right of children and young persons to protection, the Contracting Parties undertake:

to recognise the right of young workers and apprentices to a fair wage or other appropriate allowances;"

Question A

Please indicate the general rules applying to the wages of young workers and to the appropriate allowances of apprentices.

Question B

Please give available statistical information on the level of wages for young workers and on the appropriate allowances for apprentices.

Article 7 para. 6

"With a view to ensuring the effective exercise of the right of children and young persons to protection, the Contracting Parties undertake:

to provide that the time spent by young persons in vocational training during the normal working hours with the consent of the employer shall be treated as forming part of the working day;"

Question A

Please indicate the relevant regulations or collective agreements providing that the hours spent by young persons in their vocational training during normal working hours with the consent of the employer shall be treated as forming part of the working day, and specify, as far as possible, the time allowed to young persons for this purpose.

Question B

Please indicate whether the time devoted to vocational training is paid and on what basis.

Question C

Please indicate whether the measures described apply to all categories of young people at work. If this is not the case, please give an estimate of the proportion of young people not covered and, if possible, indicate the categories concerned.

Question D

Please indicate, where appropriate, why certain workers are not covered, and whether special measures have been taken on their behalf.

Question E

Please indicate the measures taken to implement in practice the relevant legislation and regulations.

Article 7 para. 7

"With a view to ensuring the effective exercise of the right of children and young persons to protection, the Contracting Parties undertake:

to provide that employed persons under 18 years of age shall be entitled to not less than three weeks' annual holiday with pay;"

Question A

Please indicate the minimum duration of annual holiday with pay for workers under eighteen years of age.

Question B

Please indicate how this provision is implemented in your country.

Question C

Please indicate whether the measures described are applicable to all categories of workers under eighteen years of age. If this is not the case, please give an estimate of the proportion of those not covered and, if possible, indicate the categories concerned.

Question D

Please indicate where appropriate why certain workers under eighteen years of age are not covered, and whether special measures have been taken on their behalf.

Question E

Please indicate the measures taken to implement in practice the relevant legislation and regulations.

Article 7 para. 8

"With a view to ensuring the effective exercise of the right of children and young persons to protection, the Contracting Parties undertake:

to provide that persons under 18 years of age shall not be employed in night work with the exception of certain occupations provided for by national laws or regulations;"

[The Appendix to the Charter stipulates that it is understood that a Contracting Party may give the undertaking required in this paragraph if it fulfils the spirit of the undertaking by providing by law that the great majority of persons under 18 years of age shall not be employed in night work.]

Question A

Please indicate the hours to which the term "night work" applies in your country's regulations for the purpose of such prohibition.

Question B

Please list the types of night work which persons under eighteen years of age are authorised to perform either generally or with special permission.

Question C

Please describe the scope of these exceptions and, in particular, the maximum duration and the age under which such derogations cannot be made.

Question D

Please indicate the hours during which night work by young persons is prohibited in all circumstances.

Question E

Please indicate whether the measures described are applicable to all categories of workers under eighteen. If this is not the case, please give an estimate of the proportion of those not covered and, if possible, indicate the categories concerned.

Question F

Please indicate the measures taken to implement in practice the relevant legislation and regulations.

Article 7 para. 9

"With a view to ensuring the effective exercise of the right of children and young persons to protection, the Contracting Parties undertake:

to provide that persons under 18 years of age employed in occupations prescribed by national laws or regulations shall be subject to regular medical control;"

Question A

Please indicate in which occupations regular medical examinations are stipulated for persons under eighteen years of age.

Question B

Please indicate the conditions in which and how often these examinations are made.

Question C

Please indicate the measures taken to implement in practice the relevant legislation and regulations

Article 7 para. 10

"With a view to ensuring the effective exercise of the right of children and young persons to protection, the Contracting Parties undertake:

> *to ensure special protection against physical and moral dangers to which children and young persons are exposed, and particularly against those resulting directly or indirectly from their work."*

Question A

Please describe the work which is considered, either directly or indirectly, as constituting a danger to the health or morals of young persons.

Question B

Please describe the measures to protect young persons who are in fact exposed to physical or moral danger at their work.

Please describe, in particular, the measures taken (stopping of work, transfer, vocational guidance, etc.) when a physical disorder is noted in young persons in the course of their work.

Question C

Please give a summary of the measures taken in order to protect young people outside work.

Question D

Please indicate the measures taken to protect children and young persons against all forms of violence, exploitation or ill-treatment (including sexual abuse) to which they may be subjected, including within the family.

Please indicate the extent of the problem (if possible, with data) and the measures taken or planned in order to guarantee children and young persons the protection to which they are entitled, including not only preventive but also other measures. Please also describe the preventive measures taken against smoking, drug and alcohol abuse, including multiple addiction, as well as against sexually transmitted diseases.

Question E

Please supply all relevant information concerning the bodies responsible for supervising the application of these provisions (in particular the social service and judicial bodies) and how they function, and on the methods employed to carry out such supervision (enquiries, etc.)

Article 8: The right of employed women to protection

> *Article 8 para. 1*
>
> > *"With a view to ensuring the effective exercise of the right of employed women to protection, the Contracting Parties undertake:*

> *to provide either by paid leave, by adequate social security benefits or by benefits from public funds for women to take leave before and after child-birth up to a total of at least 12 weeks;"*

Question A

Please indicate the length of maternity leave, showing, where appropriate, its division before and after confinement.

Question B

Please indicate whether in some cases the total duration of leave before and after confinement is less than twelve weeks.

Question C

Please indicate whether the benefits during maternity leave are provided in the form of paid leave (if normal pay is reduced, please indicate the amount), under a social security system or from public funds, stating whether the payment of benefits is subject to conditions and if so, which.

Question D

Please indicate, in circumstances where part or all of benefits payable during maternity leave are not covered by paid leave, the amount of social security benefits or benefits from public funds in monetary terms and, as appropriate, as a percentage of the wages previously paid to the worker.

Question E

Please indicate any sanctions that may be imposed on an employer failing to observe this provision, and state whether the employed woman has the option of voluntarily giving up all or part of her maternity leave.

Question F

Please indicate the protection to which women employed on fixed-term contracts in your country are entitled, including nationals of the other Contracting Parties to the Charter.

> *Article 8 para. 2*
>
> *"With a view to ensuring the effective exercise of the right of employed women to protection, the Contracting Parties undertake:*
>
> *to consider it as unlawful for an employer to give a woman notice of dismissal during her absence on maternity leave or to give her notice of dismissal at such a time that the notice would expire during such absence;"*

Question A

Please indicate what arrangements exist to give effect to this provision.

Question B

Please also indicate the sanctions provided for dismissals in breach of this provision.

Question C

Please indicate if reinstatement is ensured in cases of dismissal in breach of this provision and, in the exceptional cases where this is not possible, the amounts of compensation awarded.

Question D

Please indicate the protection to which women employed on fixed-term contracts in your country are entitled, including nationals of the other Contracting Parties to the Charter.

Article 8 para. 3

"With a view to ensuring the effective exercise of the right of employed women to protection, the Contracting Parties undertake:

to provide that mothers who are nursing their infants shall be entitled to sufficient time off for this purpose;"

Please indicate the rules which apply in this respect, stating whether time off for breastfeeding is considered as working hours and paid as such.

Article 8 para. 4

"With a view to ensuring the effective exercise of the right of employed women to protection, the Contracting Parties undertake:

a. to regulate the employment of women workers on night work in industrial employment;

b. to prohibit the employment of women workers in underground mining, and, as appropriate, on all other work which is unsuitable for them by reason of its dangerous, unhealthy, or arduous nature."

Question A

Please give details of regulations on the employment of women on night work in industry, in particular as regards the content of regulations on night work of women who are pregnant, have just given birth or are breastfeeding their children, and stating in particular the hours to which the term "night work" applies.

Question B

Please give details of measures to prohibit the employment of women workers in underground mining.

Question C

Please indicate what other occupations of the kind referred to in sub-paragraph b of this paragraph are prohibited and the measures taken to give effect to such extension.

Question D

Please give particulars of any authorised exceptions.

Article 9: The right to vocational guidance

> "With a view to ensuring the effective exercise of the right to vocational guidance, the Contracting Parties undertake to provide or promote, as necessary, a service which will assist all persons, including the handicapped, to solve problems related to occupational choice and progress, with due regard to the individual's characteristics and their relation to occupational opportunity: this assistance should be available free of charge, both to young persons, including school children, and to adults."

Question A

Please give a description of the service - its functions, organisation and operation - specifying in particular:

a. whether access to services is free of charge;

b. whether vocational guidance work is carried out in the public or private sectors;

c. the measures taken to supply all persons with adequate information on the choice of employment;

d. the measures taken to ensure a close link between vocational guidance and training on the one hand and employment on the other;[1]

e. the measures in hand for improving the services;

f. the details of special measures to assist disabled persons.

Question B

Please indicate the measures taken in the field of vocational guidance to promote occupational and social advancement.

---

1. If your country has accepted Article 10 para. 1, it is not necessary to describe these measures here.

Question C

Please indicate the types of information available in the vocational guidance services and the means employed to disseminate this information.

Question D

Please indicate:

a. the total amount of public expenditure devoted to vocational guidance services during the reference period;

b. the number of specialised staff of the vocational guidance services and their qualifications (teachers, psychologists, administrators, etc.);

c. the number of persons benefiting from vocational guidance broken down by age, sex and educational background;

d. the geographical and institutional distribution of vocational guidance services.

Question E

Please indicate whether equality of access to vocational guidance is ensured for all those interested, including nationals of the other Contracting Parties to the Charter lawfully resident or working regularly in your territory, and disabled persons.

Article 10: The right to vocational training

Article 10 para. 1

"With a view to ensuring the effective exercise of the right to vocational training, the Contracting Parties undertake:

to provide or promote, as necessary, the technical and vocational training of all persons, including the handicapped, in consultation with employers' and workers' organisations, and to grant facilities for access to higher technical and university education, based solely on individual aptitude;"

Question A

Please give an account of the functions, organisation, operation and financing of the services designed to provide vocational training for all persons including disabled persons,[1] specifying in particular:

a the rules laid down by legislation, collective agreements or carried out otherwise;

b. the total amount of public expenditure devoted to vocational training;

---

1. If your country has accepted Article 15, it is not necessary to describe here the services for disabled persons.

265

c. the number of vocational and technical training institutions (at elementary and advanced levels);

d. the number of teachers in such schools in the last school year;

e. the number of pupils, full-time and part-time in such schools in the last school year.

Question B

Please indicate how the arrangements for vocational training are provided with reference to the various types of vocational activity and, if data are available, to age and to sex.

Question C

Please state what measures are taken to ensure a close link between vocational guidance and training on the one hand and employment on the other.[1]

Question D

Please indicate the methods adopted by your government with a view to providing access to higher technical education and university education on the basis of the sole criterion of individual aptitude.

Question E

Please indicate whether equality of access to vocational training opportunities is ensured for all those interested, including nationals of the other Contracting Parties to the Charter lawfully resident or working regularly in your territory, and disabled persons.

Article 10 para. 2

"With a view to ensuring the effective exercise of the right to vocational training, the Contracting Parties undertake:

to provide or promote a system of apprenticeship and other systematic arrangements for training young boys and girls in their various employments."

Question A

Please give an account of the legal framework and the functions, organisation, operation and financing of apprenticeships and/or other systems for training young boys and girls in various jobs in your country.

Question B

Please give an account of the measures taken to implement this provision, stating approximately, if possible, the number of young persons benefiting from training systems.

---

1. If your country has accepted Article 9, it is not necessary to describe these measures here.

Question C

Please indicate how the arrangements for vocational training are divided between the various types of vocational activity.

Question D

Please describe any measures under which private apprenticeship schemes are assisted out of public funds.

Question E

Please indicate whether the measures described are applicable to all categories of young boys and girls likely to benefit from and wishing to undertake apprenticeship or vocational training. If this is not the case, please give an estimate of the proportion of those not covered and, if possible, indicate the categories concerned.

Question F

Please indicate whether equality of access to apprenticeship training is ensured for all those interested, including nationals of the other Contracting Parties to the Charter lawfully resident or working regularly in your territory, and disabled persons.

Article 10 para. 3

"With a view to ensuring the effective exercise of the right to vocational training, the Contracting Parties undertake:

to provide or promote, as necessary:

a. adequate and readily available training facilities for adult workers;

b. special facilities for the re-training of adult workers needed as a result of technological development or new trends in employment."

Question A

Please give details of the facilities provided for the training and retraining of adult workers, in particular the arrangements for retraining redundant workers and workers affected by economic and technological change.

Question B

Please indicate how the arrangements for vocational training are divided between the various types of vocational activity.

Question C

Please state whether the measures described are applicable to all categories of interested workers likely to benefit from and in need of training or retraining facilities. If this is not the case, please give an estimate of the proportion of those not covered and, if appropriate, give details of the categories concerned.

267

Question D

Please indicate the approximate number of adult workers who have participated in training or retraining measures.

Question E

Please describe special measures to assist adult women wishing to take up or resume employment.

Question F

Please indicate whether equality of access to adult training and retraining is ensured for all those interested, including nationals of the other Contracting Parties to the Charter lawfully resident or working regularly in your territory, and disabled persons.

Article 10 para. 4

> *"With a view to ensuring the effective exercise of the right to vocational training, the Contracting Parties undertake:*
>
> *to encourage the full utilisation of the facilities provided by appropriate measures such as:*
>
> a. *reducing or abolishing any fees or charges;*
>
> b. *granting financial assistance in appropriate cases;*
>
> c. *including in the normal working hours time spent on supplementary training taken by the worker, at the request of his employer, during employment;*
>
> d. *ensuring, through adequate supervision, in consultation with the employers' and workers' organisations, the efficiency of apprenticeship and other training arrangements for young workers, and the adequate protection of young workers generally."*

Question A

Please give a brief account of any fees or charges imposed in respect of vocational training and indicate, where appropriate, the measures taken to reduce or abolish such fees or charges.

Question B

Please describe the system existing in your country for providing financial assistance (allowances, grants, loans, etc.) to participants in vocational training. Please indicate also the nature of the financial assistance provided (amounts, duration, eligibility criteria, etc.).

Please indicate whether equal treatment in respect of financial assistance is ensured for nationals of all the Contracting Parties to the Charter lawfully resident or working regularly in your territory.

Question C

Please indicate the measures taken to include time spent on training taken by workers, at the request of their employer, in the normal working hours.

Question D

Please indicate the supervision and evaluation measures taken in consultation with the social partners to ensure the efficiency of apprenticeship and other training arrangements for young workers.

Question E

Please indicate if the provision of sub-paragraphs (a), (b) and (c) of Article 10 para. 4 are applicable to the great majority of the persons concerned.

Article 11: The right to protection of health

> *General aspects[1]*

Question A

Please indicate the forms of ill-health which at present raise the greatest public health problems in your country by reason of their frequency, gravity and any sequels.

Please indicate what illnesses were the main causes of death.

Question B

Please describe the measures aimed at ensuring universal access to health care. Please also indicate on what conditions the various health services are made available to the whole of your country, describing the geographical distribution of these services.

Question C[2]

Please indicate how public health services are organised in your country and state, if possible:

a. the number of private or public preventative and screening clinics (if possible distinguishing between general or specialised, particularly in the fields of tuberculosis, sexually transmitted diseases, AIDS, mental health, mother and child welfare, etc.) and the annual attendance of them making special mention of services for schoolchildren;

b. the regular health examinations arranged for the population in general or for a part thereof, and their intervals;

---

1. States having accepted one or more paragraphs of Article 11 are invited to respond to the questions under this heading.
2. If the statistical information requested under this provision is available from publications of Eurostat, WHO or OECD you are invited to refer to the relevant publication.

c. the number of general hospitals and public or private establishments for specialised treatment (especially for tuberculosis, psychiatry – including day hospital –, cancer, after-care, functional and occupational rehabilitation). Give the respective proportions of public and private establishments. Please indicate the number of beds available (or of places in case of day hospitals or rehabilitation clinics accepting out-patients);

d. the number per 1 000 persons of doctors, dentists, midwives and nurses, indicating, if possible, the situation in urban and rural areas;

e. the number of pharmacies per 1 000 persons and if possible their geographical distribution;

f. Please indicate the percentage of GDP allocated to health expenditure.

Article 11 para. 1

"With a view to ensuring the effective exercise of the right to protection of health, the Contracting Parties undertake, either directly or in co-operation with public or private organisations, to take appropriate measures designed inter alia:

to remove as far as possible the causes of ill-health."

Question A

Please indicate infant and perinatal mortality rates for the reference period concerned.

Please indicate the life expectancy at birth in your country.

Question B

Please describe any special measures taken to protect the health of:

a. pregnant women, mothers and babies;

b. children and adolescents;[1]

c. the elderly;

d. Disadvantaged persons or groups (for example the homeless, families with many children, drug addicts and the unemployed, etc.).

Please supply information on all measures taken to protect the reproductive health of all persons, in particular adolescents.

Article 11 para. 2

"With a view to ensuring the effective exercise of the right to protection of health, the Contracting Parties undertake, either directly or in co-operation with public or private organisations, to take appropriate measures designed inter alia:

---

1. If your country has accepted paragraphs 9 and 10 of Article 7, it is not necessary to repeat here the information given thereon.

> *to provide advisory and educational facilities for the promotion of health and the encouragement of individual responsibility in matters of health;"*

Question A

Please indicate what advisory and screening services exist:

a. for schools;

b. for other groups.

Question B

Please describe any measures taken to further health education, including information campaigns.

> *Article 11 para. 3*
>
> *"With a view to ensuring the effective exercise of the right to protection of health, the Contracting Parties undertake, either directly or in co-operation with public or private organisations, to take appropriate measures designed inter alia:*
>
> *to prevent as far as possible epidemic, endemic and other diseases."*

Question A

Please indicate what measures other than those mentioned above are taken to prevent epidemic, endemic and other diseases (compulsory or optional vaccination, disinfection, epidemics policy).

Question B

Please indicate what general measures are taken in the public health field, such as:

a. - prevention of air pollution,
  - prevention of water pollution,
  - prevention of soil pollution;

b. protection against radioactive contamination;

c. protection against noise pollution;

d. food hygiene inspection;

e. minimum housing standards;

f. measures taken to combat smoking, alcohol and drug abuse, including multiple addiction, as well as against sexually transmitted diseases.

Article 12: The right to social security

> *Article 12 para. 1*
>
> *"With a view to ensuring the effective exercise of the right to social security, the Contracting Parties undertake:*
>
> *to establish or maintain a system of social security."*

Please indicate the measures taken to give effect to this undertaking, specifying the nature of the existing system, in particular funding arrangements, giving information allowing the percentage of the population covered and the level of benefits to be determined.

Article 12 para. 2

"With a view to ensuring the effective exercise of the right to social security, the Contracting Parties undertake:

to maintain the social security system at a satisfactory level at least equal to that required for ratification of International Labour Convention (No. 102) concerning Minimum Standards of Social Security."

Question A

Please indicate the branches of social security in which the social security system in force in your country fulfils or goes beyond the requirements of International Labour Convention No. 102.

Question B

With regard to the branches of the social security system in force in your country which do not reach the level provided for in that Convention, please indicate the differences between your established standards and those of the Convention.

Article 12 para. 3

"With a view to ensuring the effective exercise of the right to social security, the Contracting Parties undertake:

to endeavour to raise progressively the system of social security to a higher level."

Question A

Please describe any measures taken with a view to fix the social security standards at a higher level and in particular any measures taking the system to a level higher than that of the International Labour Convention No. 102 (Social Security – Minimum Standards).

Please also provide information in relation to the standards of the European Code of Social Security and its Protocol.

Question B

As far as any other changes in the social security field are concerned, especially in so far as they are not aimed at bringing the system to a higher level, please include the following elements:

– the nature of the changes (field of application, conditions for granting allowances, amounts of allowance, lengths, etc.);
– the reasons given for the changes, the framework of social and economic policy they come within and their adequacy in the situation which gave rise to them;

- the extent of the changes introduced (categories and numbers of people concerned, levels of allowances before and after alteration);
- the existence of measures for those who find themselves in a situation of need as a result of the changes made (this information can be submitted under Article 13);
- the results obtained by such changes.

Article 12 para. 4

"With a view to ensuring the effective exercise of the right to social security, the Contracting Parties undertake:

to take steps, by the conclusion of appropriate bilateral and multilateral agreements, or by other means, and subject to the conditions laid down in such agreements, in order to ensure:

a. equal treatment with their own nationals of the nationals of other Contracting Parties in respect of social security rights, including the retention of benefits arising out of social security legislation, whatever movements the persons protected may undertake between the territories of the Contracting Parties;

b. the granting, maintenance and resumption of social security rights by such means as the accumulation of insurance or employment periods completed under the legislation of each of the Contracting Parties."

[The Appendix to the Charter states that the words: "... and subject to the conditions laid down in such agreements ..." in the introduction to this paragraph are taken to imply inter alia that with regard to benefits which are available independently of any insurance contribution a Contracting Party may require the completion of a prescribed period of residence before granting such benefits to nations of other Contracting Parties.]

Question A

Please give the list of bilateral and multilateral agreements as provided for in this provision and indicate how they allow, for the various social security benefits, the implementation of principles provided for in sub-paragraphs a) and b).

Question B

Please indicate whether, in the absence of any bilateral or multilateral agreements, the nationals of other Contracting Parties concerned are granted the implementation of the principles provided for in sub-paragraphs a) and b) for the various social security benefits.

Question C

Please indicate the length of the prescribed period of residence before nationals of Contracting Parties become eligible for benefits which are available independently of any contribution.

Article 13: The right to social and medical assistance

Article 13 para. 1

"With a view to ensuring the effective exercise of the right to social and medical assistance, the Contracting Parties undertake:

to ensure that any person who is without adequate resources and who is unable to secure such resources either by his own efforts or from other sources, in particular by benefits under a social security scheme, be granted adequate assistance, and, in case of sickness, the care necessitated by his condition."

Question A

Please describe the general organisation of the current public social and medical assistance schemes.

Question B

Please provide detailed information on the different types of social and medical assistance, specifying for each one:

— its form (benefits in cash and/or in kind);

— the categories of persons covered and the number of persons who were in receipt of assistance during the reference period;

— the conditions for the granting of assistance, the criteria used to assess need, the procedure for determining whether a person is without adequate resources, and the body which decides when assistance is to be granted;

— as far as possible, information demonstrating the adequacy of the assistance with respect to the cost of living.

Question C

Please indicate the means by which the right to assistance is secured, indicating whether individuals may uphold their right before an independent body.

Question D

Please give the amount of public funds (central government or local authorities) allocated to social and medical assistance as well as the percentage of GDP this represents, and, if possible, give an estimation of the amount of private funds devoted to assistance.

Article 13 para. 2

"With a view to ensuring the effective exercice of the right to social and medical assistance, the Contracting Parties undertake:

"to ensure that persons receiving such assistance shall not, for that reason, suffer from a diminution of their political or social rights."

Please indicate briefly how this Article is implemented and what measures are used to ensure in particular, the absence of any direct or indirect diminution of political or social rights.

Article 13 para. 3

> *"With a view to ensuring the effective exercise of the right to social and medical assistance, the Contracting Parties undertake:*
>
> *to provide that everyone may receive by appropriate public or private services such advice and personal help as may be required to prevent, to remove, or to alleviate personal or family want."*

Please describe the main services covered by this provision, especially the manner in which they are organised and operate, including their geographic distribution.

Please give as far as possible information about:

— the staff responsible for providing advice and personal help, as well as an indication of their qualifications and duties;

— measures aimed to ensure an adequate response to the needs of individuals and families.

Article 13 para. 4

> *"With a view to ensuring the effective exercise of the right to social and medical assistance, the Contracting Parties undertake:*
>
> *to apply the provisions referred to in paragraphs 1, 2 and 3 of this Article on an equal footing with their nationals to nationals of other Contracting Parties lawfully within their territories, in accordance with their obligations under the European Convention on Social and Medical Assistance, signed at Paris on 11th December 1953."*

[The Appendix to the Charter stipulates that Governments not parties to the European Convention on Social and Medical Assistance may ratify the Social Charter in respect of this paragraph provided that they grant to national of other Contracting parties a treatment which is in conformity with the provisions of the said Convention.]

Please indicate the guarantees which ensure conformity with this provision. Please describe more specifically the provisions which ensure that any repatriation of nationals of other Contracting Parties who are legally within the territory on the sole ground that they are in need of assistance is carried out according to the conditions laid down in Article 6 to 10 of the European Convention on Social and Medical Assistance 1953.

275

Article 14: The right to benefit from social welfare services

Article 14 para. 1

"With a view to ensuring the effective exercise of the right to benefit from social welfare services, the Contracting Parties undertake:

to promote or provide services which, by using methods of social work, would contribute to the welfare and development of both individuals and groups in the community, and to their adjustment to the social environment."

Question A

Please describe the measures taken to apply this provision and list the principal social services of the type mentioned, describing their functions and the target groups they serve.

Question B

Please describe the organisation and administration, the financial resources and working methods of these services, their financial and other relations to the organs of social security and the qualifications of the staff employed by these services.

Question C

Please state what measures have been taken to promote these services during the reference period, whether the individuals are entitled by law to their use or whether those administering have a discretion in granting or withholding them. Please indicate also whether there is a right of appeal against decisions to grant or withhold services.

Article 14 para. 2

"With a view to ensuring the effective exercise of the right to benefit from social welfare services, the Contracting Parties undertake:

to encourage the participation of individuals and voluntary or other organisations in the establishment and maintenance of such services."

Please indicate the measures taken to provide for or to encourage the participation of individuals and charitable organisations and other appropriate organisations in the establishment and maintenance of such services.[1]

---

1. If paragraph 1 of this Article has been accepted it is sufficient here to supplement the reply concerning that paragraph.

Article 15: The right of physically or mentally disabled persons to vocational training, rehabilitation and social resettlement

> *Article 15 para. 1*
>
> *"With a view to ensuring the effective exercise of the right of the physically or mentally disabled to vocational training, rehabilitation and resettlement, the Contracting Parties undertake:*
>
> *to take adequate measures for the provision of training facilities, including, where necessary, specialised institutions, public or private."*

Question A

Please indicate the criteria applied to grant disabled status and give an estimation of the total number of disabled persons as well as the number of disabled persons of working age.

Question B

Please describe the measures taken to give effect to this Article, in favour respectively of physically and mentally disabled persons through vocational training within the framework of general schemes, wherever possible, or within specialised public or private institutions. Please provide information in particular regarding:

a. assessment of the vocational skills of disabled persons (frequency, practical skills) and criteria used to assess the prospects of rehabilitation of a disabled person;

b. adjustment of the methods of vocational rehabilitation in accordance with the needs of the labour market.

Question C

Please specify:

a. the number and nature of the principal specialised institutions giving suitable training and the total number of places available;

b. the number of persons undergoing such training;

c. the number of staff and their qualifications.

> *Article 15 para. 2*
>
> *"With a view to ensuring the effective exercise of the right of the physically or mentally disabled to vocational training, rehabilitation and resettlement, the Contracting Parties undertake:*
>
> *to take adequate measures for the placing of disabled persons in employment, such as specialised placing services, facilities for sheltered employment and measures to encourage employers to admit disabled persons to employment."*

Question A

Please describe the measures taken to ensure the placement and, if appropriate, the employment of physically or mentally disabled persons (for instance quotas, financial subsidies, etc.).

Question B

Please indicate the number (actual or approximate) of physically or mentally disabled persons who during the reference period found paid employment (whether in specialised institutions or not).

Article 16: The right of the family to social, legal and economic protection

> *"With a view to ensuring the necessary conditions for the full development of the family, which is a fundamental unit of society, the Contracting Parties undertake to promote the economic, legal and social protection of family life by such means as social and family benefits, fiscal arrangements, provision of family housing, benefits for the newly married, and other appropriate means."*

Question A

Please mention if the legislation in your country provides specifically for the legal protection of the family, bearing in particular on equality in law between spouses, on family relationships and on marital conflict, and also any special measures to facilitate solutions other than divorce to such conflicts.

Please describe the marital property regimes existing in your country.

Question B

Please describe the economic measures taken on behalf of the welfare of the family in your country:

— by the award of benefits in cash[1] (eg. family allowances) which ensure, permanently, financial compensation, at least in part for family expenses, indicating the manner and the levels in which such benefits are given (with relevant statistical data) as well as the number of persons concerned (percentage of the population);

— by the award of occasional benefits in cash or in kind other than social and medical assistance benefits, intended to give material assistance to families in certain specific circumstances (eg. marriage, setting up or tenancy of housing appropriate to the size of the family, etc.), giving wherever possible, statistical information on the above;

— by alleviating certain expenses (eg. tax relief for family and children, special transport rates for families). In so far as tax relief is

---

1. If your country has accepted Article 12 para. 4 it is not necessary to describe here the measures taken to ensure equal treatment in respect of allocation of family benefits forming part of social security.

concerned, please specify whether tax concessions vary according to the number of children, and if so, how and to what extent;

— by measures of aid to the newly married.

Question C

Please indicate whether in your country there exists social and/or cultural services of particular interest to the family, such as advice to families (either to the whole family or to its members, eg. to mothers, pregnant women, children of various ages), home-help services, family holiday homes, etc.

Please indicate the childminding services available to families, in particular crèches, nurseries and after-school and holiday schemes for children.

Please give a general description of the organisation and facilities of these services. In your answer please distinguish between public and private services and between services available free or against payment. Please give relevant statistical data.

Question D

Please indicate if the legislation in your country provides for family representation on advisory or administrative bodies with a view to defending family interests.

Question E

Please indicate what measures have been taken to promote the construction of family housing, and supply full statistics of the work accomplished.

Question F

Please indicate the measures taken in the field of family planning information.

Question G

If your country publishes official statistics concerning the composition of the family and its economic and social position, please provide a summary of the latest available statistics. In so far as the socio-economic position is concerned, describe the manner in which socio-economic categories are classified in your country.

Article 17: The right of mothers and children to social and economic protection

> *"With a view to ensuring the effective exercise of the right of mothers and children to social and economic protection, the Contracting Parties will take all appropriate and necessary measures to that end, including the establishment or maintenance of appropriate institutions or services."*

Question A

Please indicate the measures taken to give effect to this provision by giving a list of the field covered by the measures of social and economic protection adopted in your country in respect of:

a. mothers,

b. children,

and the institutions or services which contribute to this protection.

Please supply statistics showing the percentage of mothers and children who benefit from such protection.

Question B

Please describe the provision which exist in your country to guarantee to women not covered by any social security scheme the necessary financial assistance during a reasonable period before and after confinement as well as medical care or other adequate care during confinement.[1]

Question C

Please indicate what measures have been taken to protect single mothers.

Question D

Please indicate whether your legislation makes provision for:

a. procedure for the establishment of the paternity or maternity of children born out of wedlock. if appropriate, state the reasons why some categories of children cannot benefit from these procedures and describe any special measures taken on behalf of these categories;

b. liability for the maintenance of children born out of wedlock, and whether the rules applicable differ from those for legitimate children;

c. special arrangements for the guardianship and custody of children born out of wedlock;

d. the legitimisation of children born out of wedlock;

e. special rules for the inheritance right of children born out of wedlock.

Question E

Please describe the measures in force in your country with regard to adoption. How close does the status of the adopted child come to that of a legitimate child?

---

1. If this information has been supplied in reply to the questions relating to Article 16, a simple reference will suffice here.

Question F

Please describe:

a. the steps taken in your country to ensure adequate protection for orphans and children whose parents cannot act as their guardians;

b. how homeless children are cared for in your country:

- in special institutions? If so, please describe the living conditions in these institutions;

- in foster families?

Question G

Please indicate the measures taken in legislation and in practice to protect children against physical and moral dangers, ill-treatment, unacceptable physical punishment, violence and sexual abuse. Please indicate whether psycho-social services exist for children victims of such treatment.[1]

Question H

Please indicate how the legal representation of children is ensured, notably in case of conflict with or between the parents or the persons in charge of the child; are children entitled to be heard in person in court, and if so, from what age and on what issues.

Question I

Please indicate if your legislation provides for special institutions or special courts (possibly child tribunals or special procedures) to deal with young offenders.

Please indicate what is the age of criminal responsibility at which sanctions can be applied; the penalties available and the conditions under which they are carried out, notably for penalties involving restrictions on liberty. Please also indicate the measures of protection, education and treatment and the care provided as a means of prevention or as an alternative to detention, as well as the measures to minimise the risk for vulnerable young people.

Article 18: The right to engage in a gainful occupation in the territory of other Contracting Parties

Article 18 para. 1

"With a view to ensuring the effective exercise of the right to engage in a gainful occupation in the territory of any other Contracting Party, the Contracting Parties undertake:

to apply existing regulations in a spirit of liberality."

---

1. If part of the response is given under Article 7 para. 10, a simple reference will suffice here.

281

Question A

How is this paragraph observed in your country, both with regard to wage-earners and with regard to others?

Question B

Please indicate the number of permits granted compared with the number of applications made.

Question C

Please state whether your country applies restrictions to the right to engage in a gainful occupation by nationals of other states and if so, please mention the grounds.

Article 18 para. 2

"With a view to ensuring the effective exercise of the right to engage in a gainful occupation in the territory of any other Contracting Party, the Contracting Parties undertake:

to simplify existing formalities and to reduce or abolish chancery dues and other charges payable by foreign workers or their employers."

Question A

Please describe the formalities which must be observed by nationals of the other Contracting Parties and the members of their families or by their employers, with regard to their residence in the country and the exercise of an occupation, whether they are seeking paid employment or wish to engage as self-employed, distinguishing between wage-earners or salaried employees, self-employed traders or craftsmen, heads of agricultural or non-agricultural concerns, various professions.

Please state what derogations have been made to the rules normally applicable and with regard to what categories of persons.

Question B

Please indicate what chancery dues or other charges are payable by foreign workers or their employers.

Question C

Please indicate the steps taken to simplify the formalities described in Question A and to reduce the charges referred to in Question B.

Article 18 para. 3

"With a view to ensuring the effective exercise of the right to engage in a gainful occupation in the territory of any other Contracting Party, the Contracting Parties undertake:

to liberalise, individually or collectively, regulations governing the employment of foreign workers."

Question A

Please specify whether, and if so under which conditions, a foreign workers may:

a. change his place of occupation;

b. change his occupation;

c. claim the renewal of the permit.

Question B

Please describe the situation of the holder of a work permit of he loses or gives up his job while the permit is still valid.

Question C

Please indicate the other steps taken to apply this provision of the Charter.

> *Article 18 para. 4*
>
> *"With a view to ensuring the effective exercise of the right to engage in a gainful occupation in the territory of any other Contracting Party, the Contracting Parties undertake:*
>
> *the right of their nationals to leave the country to engage in a gainful occupation in the territories of the other Contracting Parties."*

Please indicate whether there are any restrictions or special conditions affecting the right of such persons to leave the country for this reason and, if so, what the regulations are.

> *Article 19: The right of migrant workers and their families to protection and assistance*
>
> *Article 19 para. 1*
>
> *"With a view to ensuring the effective exercise of the right of migrant workers and their families to protection and assistance in the territory of any other Contracting Party, the Contracting Parties undertake:*
>
> *to maintain or to satisfy themselves that there are maintained adequate and free services to assist such workers, particularly in obtaining accurate information, and to take all appropriate steps, so far as national laws and regulations permit, against misleading propaganda relating to emigration and immigration."*

Question A

Please indicate how the free services to assist migrant workers are organised and operated.

Question B

Please indicate whether national laws and regulations provide for action to combat misleading propaganda relating to emigration and immigrating, and mention any measures that it has been judged suitable to take.

Question C

Please indicate whether information is available for migrant workers in their own language.

Article 19 para. 2

"With a view to ensuring the effective exercise of the right of migrant workers and their families to protection and assistance in the territory of any other Contracting Party, the Contracting Parties undertake:

to adopt appropriate measures within their own jurisdiction to facilitate the departure, journey and reception of such workers and their families, and to provide, within their own jurisdiction, appropriate services for health, medical attention and good hygienic conditions during the journey."

Question A

Please give details of measures to facilitate the departure, travel and reception of migrant workers and of administrative formalities on departure and arrival.

Question B

Please indicate how the medical and health services referred to in this paragraph are organised and function.

Article 19 para. 3

"With a view to ensuring the effective exercise of the right of migrant workers and their families to protection and assistance in the territory of any other Contracting Party, the Contracting Parties undertake:

to promote co-operation, as appropriate, between social services, public and private, in emigration and immigration countries."

Please describe the measures taken to ensure collaboration between the services mentioned of immigration and emigration countries, distinguishing between the social services of the countries of origin or destination of migrant workers which are Contracting Parties.

Article 19 para. 4

"With a view to ensuring the effective exercise of the right of migrant workers and their families to protection and assistance in the territory of any other Contracting Party, the Contracting Parties undertake:

to secure for such workers lawfully within their territories, insofar as such matters are regulated by law or regulations or are subject to the control of administrative authorities, treatment not less favourable than that of their own nationals in respect of the following matters:

a. *remuneration and other employment and working conditions;*

b *membership of trade unions and enjoyment of the benefits of collective bargaining;*

c. *accommodation."*

Question A

Please indicate how the laws, regulations and administrative measures enacted in your country ensure in practice that migrant workers receive no less favourable treatment than your own nationals with regard to the advantages mentioned in this paragraph.

Question B

Please indicate in particular how discrimination is avoided between foreigners and nationals in access to housing.

Article 19 para. 5

"With a view to ensuring the effective exercise of the right of migrant workers and their families to protection and assistance in the territory of any other Contracting Party, the Contracting Parties undertake:

to secure for such workers lawfully within their territories treatment not less favourable than that of their own nationals with regard to employment taxes, dues or contributions payable in respect of employed persons."

Please describe how the requirements of this paragraph are observed in your country.

Article 19 para. 6

"With a view to ensuring the effective exercise of the right of migrant workers and their families to protection and assistance in the territory of any other Contracting Party, the Contracting Parties undertake:

to facilitate as far as possible the reunion of the family of a foreign worker permitted to establish himself in the territory."

[The Appendix to the Charter stipulates that for the purpose of this provision, the term "family of a foreign worker" is understood to mean at least his wife and dependent children under the age of 21 years.]

Question A

Please indicate how the reunion of migrant workers' families is facilitated, particularly by measures taken in regard to accommodation.

Question B

Please indicate which members of the family are taken into account when considering family reunion.

Please indicate the age limit for admission into the territory for the purpose of family reunion of children of migrant workers.

Question C

Please indicate whether it is possible to refuse permission to enter the country in which a migrant worker is already established to a member of his family by reason of that member's physical or mental health.

Article 19 para. 7

"With a view to ensuring the effective exercise of the right of migrant workers and their families to protection and assistance in the territory of any other Contracting Party, the Contracting Parties undertake:

to secure for such workers lawfully within their territories treatment not less favourable than that of their own nationals in respect of legal proceedings relating to matters referred to in this Article."

Please indicate whether the forms of legal assistance available to indigent nationals (exemption from costs or their payment or part-payment from public funds) are also available to migrant workers and their families.

Article 19 para. 8

"With a view to ensuring the effective exercise of the right of migrant workers and their families to protection and assistance in the territory of any other Contracting Party, the Contracting Parties undertake:

to secure that such workers lawfully residing within their territories are not expelled unless they endanger national security or offend against public interest or morality."

Question A

Please indicate the regulations applicable to the expulsion of migrant workers specifying in particular the grounds for expulsion and the procedures observed.

Question B

Please specify what possibilities of appeal are available against such expulsion orders.

Article 19 para. 9

> "With a view to ensuring the effective exercise of the right of migrant workers and their families to protection and assistance in the territory of any other Contracting Party, the Contracting Parties undertake:
>
> to permit, within legal limits, the transfer of such parts of the earnings and savings of such workers as they may desire."

Please indicate the limits within which migrant workers may transfer their earnings and savings.

Article 19 para. 10

> "With a view to ensuring the effective exercise of the right of migrant workers and their families to protection and assistance in the territory of any other Contracting Party, the Contracting Parties undertake:
>
> to extend the protection and assistance provided for in this Article to self-employed migrants insofar as such measures apply."

Please indicate the extent to which the relevant provisions of paragraphs 1 to 9 of Article 19 apply to self-employed migrant workers.

Please specify in particular whether the protective measures and the assistance provided for by these provisions are applied on the same conditions as for employees and whether they guarantee equal treatment with nationals exercising the same occupation.

D. Form for the application of the Additional Protocol of 5 May 1988

Text adopted by the Committee of Ministers at the 485th meeting of the Ministers' Deputies on 28 May 1991

Report of the Government of...[1]

for the period...............................to.. in pursuance of Article 6 of the Protocol to the European Social Charter, on the measures taken to give effect to the accepted provisions of the Protocol to the European Social Charter, the instrument of ratification or approval of which was deposited on ....

The report also covers the application of such provisions in the following territories for whose international relations ....is responsible, to which, in conformity with Article 9, they have been declared applicable:

In accordance with Article 8 of the Protocol and Article 23 of the Charter, copies of this report in the .... language have been communicated to .... on...

The reports drawn up on the basis of this form should give, for each accepted provision of the Protocol, full information on the measures adopted to ensure its application, mentioning in particular:

1. any laws or regulations, collective agreements or other provisions relevant to its application;

2. any court decisions on question of principle relating to these provisions;

3. any factual information making it possible to assess the extent to which these provisions are applied, in particular in relation to the questions specified in this form.

A Contracting Party's report should be accompanied by the relevant laws and regulations relating to the subject matter. These may be sent in their original language by the Contracting Parties may be asked to supply a translation.

The Contracting Parties may, when considered useful, attach reports submitted in pursuance of any particular ILO convention to their report.

---

1. To be completed in English or French.

The information asked for, especially statistics should in principle refer to the period covered by the report.

If complete statistics are lacking, governments may naturally supply data or estimates based on *ad hoc* studies, specialised or sample surveys or other scientifically approved methods.

The replies of the governments should specify:

a. whether they are only concerned with the situation of nationals or whether they apply equally to the national of other Contracting Parties (see Appendix to the Protocol);

b. whether they are valid for the national territory in its entirely, including the other territories (if any) to which the Protocol applies by virtue of Article 9;

c. whether they apply to all categories of persons included in the scope of the provisions.

The Contracting Parties are asked, in their first report, to answer all the questions and, in subsequent reports, to update information given previously. However, to avoid repetition, answers may consist in a reference to a part of the report concerning a particular provision of the Charter.

Article 1: Right to equal opportunities and equal treatment in matters of employment and occupations without discrimination on grounds of sex

"1. With a view to ensuring the effective exercise of the right to equal opportunities and equal treatment in matters of employment and occupation without discrimination on the grounds of sex, the Parties undertake to recognise that right and to take appropriate measures to ensure or promotion its application in the following fields:

 – access to employment, protection against dismissal and occupational resettlement;

 – vocational guidance, training and rehabilitation;

 – terms of employment and working conditions, including remuneration;

 – career development, including promotion.

2. Provisions concerning the protection of women, particularly as regards pregnancy, confinement and the post-natal period, shall be to deemed to be discrimination as referred to in paragraph 1 of this article.

3. Paragraph 1 of this article shall not prevent the adoption of specific measures aimed at removing *de facto* inequalities.

4. Occupational activities which, by reason of their mature or the context in which they are carried out, can be entrusted only to persons of a particular sex may be excluded from the scope of this article or some of its provision."

[The Appendix to the Protocol states that:

Article 1

It is understood that social security matters, as well as other provisions relating to unemployment benefit, old age benefit and survivor's benefit, may be excluded from the scope of this article.

Article 1 para. 4

The provision is not to be interpreted as requiring the Parties to embody in laws or regulations a list of occupations which, by reason of their nature or the context in which they are carries out, may be reserved to persons of a particular sex.]

A. Please state the specific provisions in statues, examples of significant collective agreements, etc. which, in your country, forbid direct and indirect discrimination on grounds of sex in the areas covered by paragraph 1 of Article 1.

B. Please describe all significant case law and other decisions in the field covered by paragraph 1 of Article 1.

C. Please state the guarantees provided for the recognition of the right to equal treatment to which male and female workers are entitled, in particular the protection provided against possible retaliatory measures taken by an employer following a complaint or legal proceedings for discrimination.

D. Please state the measures taken and the machinery established in your country to guarantee or promote in practice equality of opportunity and equal treatment. This information should be specified according to the various areas listed in paragraph 1 of Article 1.

E. Please supply information on de facto situation which, in your country, constitute inequalities in matters covered by paragraph 1 of Article 1 and state the specific measures taken to remedy those situations.

F. Please indicate if, in your country, social security matters and the other provision listed in the Appendix are excluded from the scope of the Protocol.

G. Please state the specific measures taken in accordance with Article 1, paragraph 2, to protect women in employment or occupations, particularly with respect to pregnancy, confinement and the post-natal period.

H. Please state whether other specific measures for protecting women[1] or men in matters covered by paragraph 1 of Article 1 exist and explain the reasons for such measures and their scope.

I. Please indicate whether there are occupations (if so, which ones) that are reserved exclusively for one or other sex, by specifying if it is because of the nature of the activity or the conditions in which it is carried out.

Article 2: Right to information and consultation

"1. With a view to ensuring the effective exercise of the right of workers to be informed and consulted within the undertaking, the Parties undertake to adopt or encourage measures enabling workers or their representatives, in accordance with national legislation and practice:

   a. to be informed regularly or at the appropriate time and in a comprehensible way about the economic and financial situation of the undertaking employing them, on the understanding that the disclosure of certain information which could be prejudicial to the undertaking may be refused or subject to confidentiality; and

   b. to be consulted in good time on proposed decision which could substantially affect the interests of workers, particularly on those decisions which could have an important impact on the employment situation in the undertaking.

2. The Parties may exclude from the field of application of paragraph 1 of this article those undertakings employing less than a certain number of workers to be determined by national legislation or practice."

[The Appendix to the Protocol states that:

Articles 2 and 3:

1. For the purpose of the application of these articles, the term "workers' representatives" means persons who are recognised as such under national legislation or practice.

2. The term "national legislation and practice" embraces as the case may be, in addition to laws and regulations, collective agreements, other agreements between employers and workers' representatives, customs, as well as relevant case law.

3. For the purpose of the application of these articles, the term "undertaking" is understood as referring to as set of tangible and intangible components, with or without legal personality, formed

---

1. These specific measures are not limited to those provided for in Article 8 of the Charter.

to produce goods or provide services for financial gain and with power to determine its own market policy.

4. It is understood that religious communities and their institutions may be excluded from the application of these articles, even if these institutions are "undertakings" within meaning of paragraph 3. Establishments pursuing activities which are inspired by certain ideals or guided by certain moral concepts, ideals and concepts, which are protected by national legislation, may be excluded from the application of these articles to such an extent as is necessary to protect the orientation of the undertaking.

5. It is understood that, where in a State the rights set out in Articles 2 and 3 are exercised in the various establishments of the undertaking, the Party concerned is to be considered as fulfilling the obligations deriving from these provisions.]

A. Please state if workers in undertakings are informed and informed and consulted directly or through their representatives and, in the latter case, how such representatives are appointed at the various levels (workshop, establishment, undertaking, etc.).

B. Please describe the structures, procedures and arrangements for information and consultation in your country with all necessary information concerning the level at which they operate, whether they are compulsory or optional, their frequency, etc.

C. Please state the nature of the information and of the consultation provided for by legislation, examples of significant collective agreements or by other means, and whether they take place at the level of the undertaking or of the establishment.

D. Please state the specified number or numbers of workers below which undertakings are not required to comply with the provisions relating to the information and consultation of workers.

E. If some workers are not covered by provisions of this type prescribed by legislation, collective agreements or other appropriate measures, please indicate the proportion of workers not so covered (see Article 7 of the protocol and the relevant provision in the Appendix).

F. Please state whether undertakings other than those specified in paragraph 2 of Article 2 are excluded from the application of this provision in the meaning of the Appendix to the Protocol (Article 2 and 3, paragraph 4) and state the nature of such undertakings and their sectors of activity.

Article 3: Right to take part in the determination and improvement of the working conditions and working environment

"1. With a view to ensuring the effective exercise of the right of workers to take part in the determination and improvement of the working conditions and working environment in the undertaking, the parties undertake to adopt or encourage measures enabling workers or their representatives, in accordance with national legislation and practice, to contribute:

    a. to the determination and the improvement of the working conditions, work organisation and working environment;

    b. to the protection of health and safety within the undertaking;

    c. to the organisation of social and socio-cultural services and facilities within the undertaking;

    d. to the supervision of the observance of regulations on these matters.

2.   The Parties may exclude from the field of application of paragraph 1 of the article those undertakings employing less than a certain number of workers to be determined by national legislation or practice".

[The Appendix to the Protocol states that:

Articles 2 and 3

1.   For the purpose of the application of these articles, the term "workers' representatives" means persons who are recognised as such under national legislation or practice.

2.   The term "national legislation and practice" embraces as the case be, in addition t laws and regulations, collective agreements, other agreements between employers and workers' representatives, customs, as well as relevant case law.

3.   For the purpose of the application of these articles, the term "undertaking" is understood as referring to as set of tangible and intangible components, with or without legal personality, formed to produce goods or provide services for financial gain and with power to determine its own market policy.

4.   It is understood that religious communities and their institutions may be excluded from the application of these articles, even if these institutions are "undertakings" within the meaning of paragraph 3. Establishments pursing activities which are inspired by certain ideals or guided by certain moral concepts, ideals and concepts which are protected by national legislation, may be excluded from the application of these articles to such an extent as its necessary to protect the orientation of the undertaking.

5.   It is understood that, where in a state the rights set out in Articles 2 and 3 are exercised in the various establishments of the undertaking, the Party concerned is to be considered as fulfilling the obligations deriving from these provisions.]

A. Please state if workers participate directly or through their representatives in the determination and improvement of the working conditions and the working environment and, in the latter case, how such representatives are appointed at the various levels (workshop, establishment, undertaking, etc.).

B. Please give general description of the structures, procedures and arrangements for workers to take part in determining the work conditions in undertakings in general and, when appropriate, in the various activity sectors of undertakings. This information should be specified according to each of the various areas referred to in paragraph 1 of Article 3 of the Protocol. If appropriate, please describe at what levels within the undertaking these rights are exercised and describe how.

C. Please state if workers' participation concerns all of the areas covered by Article 3, paragraph 1, of the Protocol.

D. Please state the number or numbers of workers below which undertakings are not required to make provision for the participation of workers in the determination of their working conditions.

E. If some workers are not covered by provisions of this type prescribed by legislation, collective agreements or other measures, please state the proportion of workers not so covered (see Article 7 of the Protocol and the relevant provision in the Appendix).

F. Please state whether undertakings other than those specified in paragraph 2 of Article 3 are excluded from the application of this provision in the meaning of the Appendix to the Protocol (Articles 2 and 3, paragraph 4) and indicate their nature and the sector of activity involved.

Article 4, paragraph 1: Right of elderly persons to social protection

"With a view to ensuring the effective exercise of the right of elderly persons to social protection, the parties undertake to adopt or encourage, either directly or in co-operation with public or private organisations, appropriate measures designed in particular:

1. to enable elderly persons to remain full members of society for as long as possible, by means of:

    a. adequate resources enabling them to lead a decent life and play an active part in public, social and cultural life;

    b. provision of information about services and facilities available for elderly persons and their opportunities to make use of them."

[The Appendix to the Protocol states that:

·   For the purpose of the application of this paragraph, the term "for as long as possible" refers to the elderly person's physical, psychological and intellectual capacities.]

A. Please describe the measures of social protection and the social services existing in your country to enable elderly persons to remain full members of society as long as possible.

B. Please indicate the measures taken to ensure that elderly persons have adequate resources within the meaning of this paragraph.

C. Please indicate by which ways information about the services and facilities available for elderly persons are provided to the persons concerned.

Article 4, paragraph 2: Right of elderly persons to social protection

"With a view to ensuring the effective exercise of the right of elderly persons to social protection, the Parties undertake to adopt or encourage, either directly or in co-operation with public or private organisations, appropriate measures designed in particular:

(...)

2. to enable elderly persons to choose their life-style freely and to lead independent lives in their familiar surroundings for as long as they wish and are able, by means of:

    a. provision of housing suited to their needs and their state of health or if adequate support for adapting their housing;

    b. the health care and the services necessitated by their state."

A. Please describe the existing public and, where appropriate, private services and the measures taken to ensure the application of this provision.

B. If private services exist, please describe the forms of co-operation between public and private services in the area covered by this provision.

Article 4, paragraph 3: Right of elderly persons to social protection

"With a view to ensuring the effective exercise of the right of elderly persons to social protection, the Parties undertake to adopt or encourage, either directly or in co-operation with public or private organisations, appropriate measures designed in particular:

(...)

3. to guarantee elderly persons living in institutions appropriate support, while respecting their privacy, and participation in decisions concerning living conditions in the institution."

A. Please indicate what for of assistance is granted to elderly persons living in institutions.

B. Please indicate how the inspection of these institutions on compliance with Article 4, paragraph 3, is carried out.

C. Please indicate the measures taken to guarantee respect for the privacy of elderly persons in institutions and their participation in decisions concerning living conditions in such institutions.

E. Form for the reports submitted in pursuance of the revised European Social Charter[1]

(To be completed in English or French)

For the period .... to ....

made by the Government of............................in accordance with Article C of the Revised European Social Charter and Article 21 of the European Social Charter, on the measures taken to give effect to the accepted provisions of the Revised European Social Charter, the instrument of ratification or approval of which was deposited on ....

This report also covers the application of such provisions in the following non-metropolitan territories to which, in conformity with Article L, they have been declared applicable: ....

In accordance with Article C of the Revised Social Charter and Article 23 of the European Social Charter, copies of this report have been communicated to ....
....[1]

The reports drawn up on the basis of this Form should give, for each accepted provision of the Revised European Social Charter, any useful information on measures adopted to ensure its application, mentioning in particular:

1. any laws or regulations, collective agreements or other provisions that contribute to such application;

2. any judicial decisions on questions of principle relating to these provisions;

3. any factual information enabling an evaluation of the extent to which these provisions are applied; this concerns particularly questions specified in this Form.

The Parties' reports should be accompanied by the principal laws and regulations on which the application of the accepted provisions of the Revised Charter is based. These may be sent in their original language and translation in one of the official languages of the Council of Europe may be asked for in exceptional circumstances.

---

1. Adopted by the Committee of Ministers on 17 January 2001 at the 737th meeting of the Ministers Deputies.
2 Please state whether you have received any observations from these national organisations of employers and workers, and supply those they have asked you to transmit. The information provided would be usefully supplemented by your communicating a summary of all other observations, to which you might add any comments that you consider useful.

The replies of the governments should, wherever appropriate, specify explicitly:

a. whether they are only concerned with the situation of nationals or whether they apply equally to the nationals of the other Parties (see Appendix to the Revised Charter, points 1 and 2);

b. whether they are valid for the national territory in its entirety, including the non-metropolitan territories if any to which the Revised Charter applies by virtue of Article 34;

c. whether they apply to all categories of persons included in the scope of the provision.

A state bound by obligations under certain International Labour Conventions may find it sufficient to supply a copy of the relevant reports submitted to the ILO on the application of these conventions in so far as the latter cover the same field of application and the same reference period as the relevant provision of the Charter.

The information required, especially statistics, should, unless otherwise stated, be supplied for the period covered by the report.

Where statistics are requested for any provision, it is understood that, if complete statistics are lacking, governments may supply data or estimates based on *ad hoc* studies, specialised or sample surveys, or other scientifically valid methods, whenever they consider the information so collected to be useful.

The report should as far as possible be submitted by E-mail to the address social.charter@coe.int or be appended by a diskette in Word format. If this is not possible, the Parties are requested to submit their reports in five copies and the appendices in two copies.

Parties ar requested:

– *as far as the first report is concerned:*

to reply to all questions appearing in this Form[1];

– *as far as subsequent reports are concerned:*

to update the information given in the previous report.

The secretariat is invited to distribute with this form a working document – that will be regularly updated – indicating the provisions of the United Nations, the ILO, the WHO, the European Union and the Council of Europe corresponding to the different articles of the Charter and a summary presentation of the different control mechanisms.

---

1. Unless the information has already been provided in the report submitted in pursuance of the European Social Charter and that there have been no subsequent changes in the situation.

Article 1: The right to work

Article 1 para. 1

"With a view to ensuring the effective exercise of the right to work, the Parties undertake:

to accept as one of their primary aims and responsibilities the achievement and maintenance of as high and stable a level of employment as possible, with a view to the attainment of full employment;"

Question A

Please indicate the policy followed by your government in attempting to reach and maintain full employment. Please supplement with details of the measures and programmes implemented to achieve as high and stable a level of employment as possible.

Please indicate, if possible, the trend in total employment policy expenditure over the past five years, including the relative shares of "active" (job creation, training, etc.) and "passive" (financial compensation, etc.) measures.

Please indicate the active policy measures taken in order to favour access to employment of groups most exposed to or affected by unemployment (eg. women, the young,[1] older workers, the long-term unemployed,[2] the disabled, immigrants and/or ethnic minorities). Please give indications on the number of beneficiaries from these measures and information, if possible, on their impact on employment.

Question B

Please indicate the trends in employment[3] covering all sectors of the economy. In connection with this, indicate as far as possible, the activity rate,[4] the employment rate[5] and the breakdown of employment by region, by sex, by age, by employment status (employed, self-employed), by type of employment (full time and part time, permanent and fixed term, temporary), and by sector of activity.

Please give the trend of the figures and percentages of unemployed in your country, including the proportion of unemployed to the total

---

1. Aged between fifteen and twenty-four.
2. Persons without employment for over one year and seeking employment.
3. Reference is made to the definition of employment adopted by the Thirteenth International Conference of Labour Statisticians (Geneva, 1982) or any further versions.
4. The activity rate represents the total labour force as a percentage of the population aged 15 years and over and living in private households. The labour force is defined as the sum of persons in employment plus the unemployed.
5. The employment rate represents persons in employment as a percentage of the population aged 15-64 years and living in private households.

labour force. Please give a break-down of the unemployed by region, category, sex, age and by length of unemployment.

Question C

Please indicate the trend in the number and the nature of vacant jobs in your country.

Article 1 para. 2

"With a view to ensuring the effective exercise of the right to work, the Parties undertake:

to protect effectively the right of the worker to earn his living in an occupation freely entered upon;"

[The Appendix to the Charter stipulates that this provision shall not be interpreted as prohibiting or authorising any union security clause or practice.]

Elimination of all forms of discrimination in employment

Question A

Please give information concerning legislative or other measures taken to ensure the elimination of all discrimination in employment which might be based on sex, social or national origin, political opinion, religion, race, colour or age and to promote effectively equal opportunities in seeking employment and in taking up an occupation.[1]

Please give information in this respect on existing sanctions and remedies in cases of discrimination in employment.

Question B

Please indicate any methods adopted:

a. to seek the co-operation of employers' and workers' organisations and other appropriate bodies in promoting the acceptance and observance of the above policy of non-discrimination;

b. to ensure the acceptance and observance of the above policy through educational efforts.

Question C

Please indicate the guarantees, including applicable sanctions and remedies, which prevent any discrimination in regard to members of workers' organisations at the time of engagement, promotion or dismissal.

---

1. The term "discrimination" in this Form is to be understood in terms of ILO Convention No. 111 (Discrimination, Employment, Occupations), Article 1.

Prohibition of forced labour

Question D

Please indicate whether any form of forced or compulsory labour is authorised or tolerated.[1]

Question E

If so, please describe the nature and scope of any such labour and indicate the extent to which recourse has been had thereto during the reference period.

Question F

Please indicate what measures are being taken to secure the complete abolition of forced or compulsory labour and the date by which these measures will be fully implemented.

Question G

Please give information concerning the conditions under which work is carried out in prison establishments.

> *Article 1 para. 3*
> *"With a view to ensuring the effective exercise of the right to work, the Parties undertake:*
> *to establish or maintain free employment services for all workers;"*

Question A

Please describe the operation of free employment services available in your country, indicating the age, sex and nature of occupation of persons placed by them in employment and persons seeking employment.

Please indicate as far as possible the number of vacancies, the placement rate and the duration of unemployment of persons placed.

Question B

Please describe the organisation of public employment services in your country indicating the accompanying measures for the unemployed, and where appropriate, the steps taken to revise the geographical distribution of local and regional employment centres and to redeploy resources when the changing patterns of economic activity and of population so warrant.

Question C

If both public and private free employment services exist in your country, please describe the steps taken to co-ordinate such services,

---

1. The term "forced or compulsory labour" in this Form is to be understood in terms of ILO Convention No. 29 (Forced Labour), Article 2.

and to determine the conditions governing the operation of private employment agencies.

Question D

Please indicate whether and how the participation of representatives of employers and workers in the organisation and operation of the employment services and in the development of employment services policy is provided for.

Question E

Please indicate what legislation or administrative guarantees are provided to ensure that these services are available to all.

Article 1 para. 4

"With a view to ensuring the effective exercise of the right to work, the Parties undertake:

to provide or promote appropriate vocational guidance, training and rehabilitation."

Please indicate, illustrating with relevant data as far as possible, what measures have been taken to provide or promote:

a.   vocational guidance;[1]

b.   vocational training;[2]

c.   vocational rehabilitation;[3]

with the aim of giving everyone the possibility of earning his living in an occupation freely entered upon.

Please indicate whether equal access is ensured for all those interested, including nationals of the other Contracting Parties to the Charter lawfully resident or working regularly in your territory, and disabled people.

Article 2: The right to just condition s of work

Article 2 paras. 1 to 7

Please indicate, for Article 2 as a whole, the rules applying to workers in atypical employment relationships (fixed-term contracts, part-time, replacements, temporaries, etc.).

---

1. If your country has accepted Article 9, it is not necessary to describe the vocational guidance services here.
2. If your country has accepted Article 10, it is not necessary to describe the vocational training services here.
3. If your country has accepted Article 15, it is not necessary to describe the rehabilitation services for physically or mentally handicapped persons.

Article 2 para. 1

"With a view to ensuring the effective exercise of the right to just conditions of work, the Parties undertake:

to provide for reasonable daily and weekly working hours, the working week to be progressively reduced to the extent that the increase of productivity and other relevant factors permit;"

Question A

Please indicate what statutory provisions apply in respect of the number of working hours, daily and weekly and the duration of the daily rest period.

Question B

Please indicate what rules concerning normal working hours and overtime are usual in collective agreements, and what is the scope of these rules.

Question C

Please indicate the average working hours in practice for each major professional category.

Question D

Please indicate to what extent working hours have been reduced by legislation, by collective agreements, or in practice during the reference period and, in particular, as a result of increased productivity.

Question E

Please describe, where appropriate, any measures permitting derogations from legislation in your country regarding daily and weekly working hours and the duration of the daily rest period (see also Article 2 paras. 2, 3 and 5).

Please indicate the reference period to which such measures may be applied.

Please indicate whether any such measures are implemented by legislation or by collective agreement and in the latter case, at what level these agreements are concluded and whether only representative trade unions are entitled to conduct negotiations in this respect.

Question F

If some workers are not covered by provisions of this nature, whether contained in legislation, collective agreements or other measures, please state what proportion of all workers is not so covered (see Article I of the revised Social Charter).

Article 2 para. 2

"With a view to ensuring the effective exercise of the right to just conditions of work, the Parties undertake:

to provide for public holidays with pay;"

Question A

Please indicate the number of public holidays with pay laid down by legislation, stipulated by collective agreement or established by practice during the last calendar year.

Question B

Please indicate what rules apply to public holidays with pay according to legislation, collective agreements or practice.

Please describe, where appropriate, whether measures permitting derogation from legislation in your country regarding daily and weekly working hours have an impact on rules pertaining to public holidays with pay.

Question C

If some workers are not covered by provisions of this nature, whether contained in legislation, collective agreements, or other measures, please state what proportion of all workers is not so covered (see Article I of the revised Social Charter).

Article 2 para. 3

"With a view to ensuring the effective exercise of the right to just conditions of work, the Parties undertake:

to provide for a minimum of four weeks' annual holiday with pay;"

Question A

Please indicate the length of annual holidays under legislative provisions or collective agreements; please also indicate the minimum period of employment entitling workers to annual holidays.

Please describe, where appropriate, whether measures permitting derogation from statutory rules in your country regarding daily and weekly working hours have an impact on rules pertaining to the duration of annual holidays.

Question B

Please indicate the effect of incapacity for work through illness or injury during all or part of annual holiday on the entitlement to annual holidays.

Question C

Please indicate if it is possible for workers to renounce their annual holiday.

Question D

Please indicate the customary practice where legislation or collective agreements do not apply.

Question E

If some workers are not covered by provisions of this nature, whether contained in legislation, collective agreements or other measures, please state what proportion of all workers is not covered (see Article I of the revised Social Charter).

> *Article 2 para. 4*
>
> *"With a view to ensuring the effective exercise of the right to just conditions of work, the Parties undertake:*
>
> *to eliminate risks in inherently dangerous or unhealthy occupations, and where it has not yet been possible to eliminate or reduce sufficiently these risks, to provide for either a reduction of working hours or additional paid holidays for workers engaged in such occupations;"*

Question A

Please indicate the policies and the legislative measures taken to eliminate or to reduce the inherent risks of dangerous or unhealthy occupations. Please also describe the procedures for periodic review and evaluation.

Question B

Please state the occupations regarded as dangerous or unhealthy. If a list exists of these occupations, please supply it.

Question C

Where it has not yet been possible to eliminate or reduce sufficiently these risks, please state what provisions apply under legislation or collective agreements or otherwise in practice as regards reduced working hours or additional paid holidays in relation to this provision of the revised Charter.

Question D

If some workers are not covered by provisions of this nature, whether contained in legislation, collective agreements or other measures, please state what proportion of all workers concerned is not covered (see Article I of the revised Social Charter).

> *Article 2 para. 5*
>
> *"With a view to ensuring the effective exercise of the right to just conditions of work, the Parties undertake:*

> *to ensure a weekly rest period which shall, as far as possible, coincide with the day recognised by tradition or custom in the country or region concerned as a day of rest."*

Question A

Please indicate what provisions apply according to legislation, collective agreements or otherwise in practice as regards weekly rest periods.

Please indicate whether postponement of the weekly rest period is provided for these provisions and, if so, please indicate under what circumstances and over what period of reference.

Please indicate, where appropriate, whether measures derogating from statutory rules in your country regarding daily and weekly working time have an impact on rules relating to the weekly rest period.

Question B

Please indicate what measures have been taken to ensure that workers obtain their weekly rest period in accordance with this paragraph.

Question C

If some workers are not covered by provisions of this nature, whether contained in legislation, collective agreements or other measures, please state what proportion of all workers is not covered (see Article I of the revised Social Charter).

> *Article 2 para. 6*
>
> *"With a view to ensuring the effective exercise of the right to just conditions of work, the Parties undertake:*
>
> *to ensure that workers are informed in written form, as soon as possible, and in any event not later than two months after the date of commencing their employment, of the essential aspects of the contract or employment relationship;"*

Question A

Please indicate the rules (in legislation, collective agreements) or other provisions which apply for informing workers in writing of the essential aspects of their contract or employment relationship.

Please describe the content and form of this information, as well as the point at which it must be communicated in writing.

Please indicate how rules or other measures are applied in practice.

Question B

If the rules are not of a general nature (Appendix to the revised Social Charter), please indicate the exceptions and referring to item b of the Appendix, please state the reason for their exclusion (see Article I of the revised Social Charter).

Article 2 para. 7

> *"With a view to ensuring the effective exercise of the right to just conditions of work, the Parties undertake:*
>
> *to ensure that workers performing night work benefit from measures which take account of the special nature of the work".*

Question A

Please indicate the rules (legislation, collective agreements or in practice) in force which ensure that workers performing night work benefit from measures to take account of the special nature of the work (medical examinations, breaks, compensatory time off, access to company services, inspections, circumstances in which it is possible to transfer to day work, etc.). Please indicate in particular the hours to which the term "night work" applies.

Question B

Please indicate the proportion of any workers who are not covered (see Article I of the revised Social Charter).

Article 3: The right to safe and healthy working conditions

Article 3 paras. 1 to 4

Please indicate how organisations of employers and workers are consulted by the authorities on the measures required to implement each of the paragraphs of Article 3 (procedure and level of consultation, content and frequency of consultation).

Article 3 para. 1

> *"With a view to ensuring the effective exercise of the right to safe and healthy working conditions, the Parties undertake, in consultation with employers' and workers' organisations:*
>
> *to formulate, implement and periodically review a coherent national policy on occupational health and the working environment. The primary aim of this policy shall be to improve occupational safety and health and to prevent accidents and injury to health arising out of, linked with or occurring in the course of work, particularly by minimising the causes of hazards inherent in the working environment;"*

Please describe policy in the field of occupational safety, occupational health and the working environment and the measures taken to improve occupational safety and health and to prevent health and safety risks. Please describe also the measures of implementation of this policy as well as procedures for its periodic review and evaluation.

Article 3 para. 2

> *"With a view to ensuring the effective exercise of the right to safe and healthy working conditions, the Contracting Parties undertake, in consultation with employers' and workers' organisations:*
>
> *to issue safety and health regulations;"*

Question A

Please list the principal legislative or administrative provisions issued in order to protect the physical and mental health and safety of workers, indicating clearly:

a. their material scope of application (risks covered and the preventive and protective measure provided for) and;

b. their personal scope of application (whatever the legal status – employees or not – and whatever their sector of activity, including home workers and domestic staff).

Please specify the rules adopted to ensure that workers under atypical employment contracts enjoy the same level of protection as other workers in an enterprise.

Question B

Please indicate the special measures taken to protect the health and safety of workers engaged in dangerous or unhealthy work.

Article 3 para. 3

> *"With a view to ensuring the effective exercise of the right to safe and healthy working conditions, the Contracting Parties undertake, in consultation with employers' and workers' organisations:*
>
> *to provide for the enforcement of such regulations by measures of supervision."*

Question A

Please indicate the methods applied by the Labour Inspectorate to enforce health and safety regulations and please also give information, inter alia, statistical, on:

a. the places of work, including the home, subjected to the control of the Labour Inspection, indicating the categories of enterprises exempted from this control;

b. the number of control visits carried out;

c. the proportion of workers covered by these visits.

Question B

Please describe the system of civil and penal sanctions guaranteeing the application of health and safety regulations and also provide information on violations committed:

a. the number of violations;

b. the sectors in which they have been identified;

c. the action, including judicial, taken in this respect.

Question C

Please provide statistical information on occupational accidents, including fatal accidents, and on occupational diseases by sectors of activity specifying what proportion of the labour force is covered by the statistics. Please describe also the preventive measures taken in each sector.

> *Article 3 para. 4*
>
> *"With a view to ensuring the effective exercise of the right to safe and healthy working conditions, the Parties undertake, in consultation with employers' and workers' organisations:*
>
> *to promote the progressive development of occupational health services for all workers with essentially preventive and advisory functions".*

Question A

Please indicate whether occupational health services (health, security and occupational health services) exist in all companies and in all sectors. If not, please state whether plans have been made to establish them, when they will be implemented in practice and/or whether provision is made for inter-company services.

Question B

Please describe the functions, organisation and operation of occupational health services.

> *Article 4: The right to a fair remuneration*
>
> > *Article 4 para. 1*
> >
> > *"With a view to ensuring the effective exercise of the right to a fair remuneration, the Contracting Parties undertake:*
> >
> > *to recognise the right of workers to a remuneration such as will give them and their families a decent standard of living;"*
> >
> > *"...The exercise of this right shall be achieved by freely concluded collective agreements, by statutory wage-fixing machinery, or by other means appropriate to national conditions;"*

Question A

Please state what methods are provided and what measures are taken to provide workers with a fair wage, having regard to national living standards and particularly to the changes in the cost of living index and in national income.[1]

---

1. If your country has accepted Article 16, there is no need to give information here concerning family allowances, etc.

Question B

Please specify if these include methods for fixing minimum wage standards by law or collective agreements.

Question C

Please indicate what proportion of wage-earners are without protection in respect of wages, either by law or collective agreement.

Question D

Please provide information on:

- national net average wage[1] (ie. after deduction of social security contributions and taxes[2]);

- national net minimum wage if applicable or the net lowest wages actually paid (ie. after deduction of social security contributions and taxes).[3]

Please provide information, where possible, on:

- the proportion of workers receiving the minimum wage or the lowest wage actually paid (after deduction of social security contributions and taxes);

- the trend in the level of the minimum net wage and/or the lowest wage actually paid compared to national net average wage and any available studies on this subject.

Article 4 para. 2

"With a view to ensuring the effective exercise of the right to a fair remuneration, the Parties undertake:

---

1. In principle the net average wage should be the overall average for all sectors of economic activity. The average wage may be calculated on an annual, monthly, weekly, daily or hourly basis. Wages cover remuneration in cash paid directly and regularly by the employer at the time of each wage payment. This includes normal working hours, overtime and hours not worked but paid, when the pay for these latter are included in the returned earnings. Payments for leave, public holidays and other paid individual absences may be included insofar as the corresponding days or hours are also taken into account to calculate wages per unit of time.
2. The net wage (average and minimum) should be calculated for the standard case of a single worker. Family allowances and social welfare benefits should not be taken into account. Social security contributions should be calculated on the basis of the employee contribution rates laid down by law or collective agreements etc. and withheld by the employer. Taxes are all taxes on earned income. They should be calculated on the assumption that gross earnings represent the only source of income and that there are no special grounds for tax relief other than those associated with the situation of a single worker receiving either the average wage or the minimum wage. Indirect taxes are thus not taken into account.
3. The net minimum wage should be given in units of time comparable to those used for the average wage.

> *to recognise the right of workers to an increased rate of remuneration for overtime work, subject to exceptions in particular cases;"*
>
> *"...The exercise of this right shall be achieved by freely concluded collective agreements, by statutory wage-fixing machinery, or by other means appropriate to national conditions;"*

Question A

Please mention what provisions apply according to legislation and collective agreements as regards overtime pay, the method used to calculate the increased rates of remuneration and the categories of work and workers to which they apply.

Please specify what provisions apply in respect of overtime pay on Saturdays, Sundays and other special days or hours (including night work).

Question B

Please mention any special cases for which exceptions are made.

Please indicate, where appropriate, whether measures permitting derogation from legislation in your country regarding daily and weekly working hours (see Article 2 para. 1) have an impact on remuneration or compensation of overtime.

> *Article 4 para. 3*
>
> *"With a view to ensuring the effective exercise of the right to a fair remuneration, the Parties undertake:*
>
> *to recognise the right of men and women workers to equal pay for work of equal value;"*
>
> *"...The exercise of this right shall be achieved by freely concluded collective agreements, by statutory wage-fixing machinery, or by other means appropriate to national conditions;"*

Question A

Please indicate how the principle of equal pay for work of equal value is applied; state whether the principle applies to all workers.[1]

Question B

Please indicate the progress which has been made in applying this principle.

Question C

Please describe the protection afforded to workers against retaliatory measures, including dismissal.

---

1. The term "equal pay for work of equal value" in this Form is to be understood in terms of ILO Convention No. 100 (Equal Remuneration), Article 1

Please indicate the procedures applied to implement this protection.

Article 4 para. 4

> *"With a view to ensuring the effective exercise of the right to a fair remuneration, the Parties undertake:*
>
> *to recognise the right of all workers to a reasonable period of notice for termination of employment;"*
>
> *"... The exercise of this right shall be achieved by freely concluded collective agreements, by statutory wage-fixing machinery, or by other means appropriate to national conditions."*

[The Appendix to the revised Charter stipulates that this provision shall be so understood as not to prohibit immediate dismissal for any serious offence.]

Question A

Please indicate if periods of notice are provided for by legislation, by collective agreements or by practice and if so, indicate the length of such periods, notably in relation to seniority in the enterprise.

Please indicate whether the periods of notice established by legislation can be derogated by collective agreements.

Please indicate the periods of notice applicable to part-time workers and to home workers.

Please indicate in which cases a worker may not be given a notice period.

Please indicate whether provision is made for notice periods in the case of fixed-term contracts which are not renewed.

Question B

Please indicate whether wage-earners may challenge the legality of such notice of termination of employment before a judicial authority.

Article 4 para. 5

> *"With a view to ensuring the effective exercise of the right to a fair remuneration, the Parties undertake:*
>
> *to permit deductions from wages only under conditions and to the extent prescribed by national laws or regulations or fixed by collective agreements or arbitration awards."*
>
> *"...The exercise of this right shall be achieved by freely concluded collective agreements, by statutory wage-fixing machinery, or by other means appropriate to national conditions."*

[The Appendix to the revised Charter stipulates that it is understood that a Contracting Party may give the undertaking required in this paragraph if the great majority of workers are not permitted to suffer deductions from wages either by law or through collective agreements or arbitration awards, the exception being those persons not so covered.]

Question A

Please describe how and to what extent observance of this paragraph is ensured in your country, specifying the ways in which this right is exercised, both as regards deductions made by the employer for his own benefit and for the benefit of third parties.

Please indicate whether legislation, regulations or collective agreements provide for the non-seizability of a part of the wage.

Question B

Please state whether the measures described are applicable to all categories of wage-earners. If this is not the case, please give an estimate of the proportion of workers not covered and, if appropriate, give details of the categories concerned.

Article 5: The right to organise

> *"With a view to ensuring or promoting the freedom of workers and employers to form local, national or international organisations for the protection of their economic and social interests and to join those organisations, the Contracting Parties undertake that national law shall not be such as to impair, nor shall it be so applied as to impair, this freedom. The extent to which the guarantees provided for in this Article shall apply to the police shall be determined by national laws or regulations. The principle governing the application to the members of the armed forces of these guarantees and the extent to which they shall apply to persons in this category shall equally be determined by national laws or regulations."*

Question A

a. Please indicate whether any, and if so what, categories of workers and employers are prohibited by law from forming organisations, or restricted in doing so.

Please indicate, *inter alia*:

– the existence of legislation or special regulations applicable to the forming of organisations by civil servants and other persons employed by the public authorities at central or local level;

– to what extent the rights provided for in this Article apply to members of the armed forces and of the police, explaining in particular the nature and functions of any staff associations which may be available to them;

– whether nationals of other Contracting Parties lawfully resident or working regularly in the territory of your country may join or be a founding member of a trade union. Please indicate in particular whether they may hold positions in the administration or management of a trade union;

– the eligibility of workers, nationals of other Contracting Parties, for election to consultation bodies at the enterprise level such as works councils.

b. Please indicate any conditions of registration or otherwise with which employers' and workers' organisations must comply when they are founded and the provisions with which they must comply in the course of their existence.

c. Please indicate the measures intended to guarantee the exercise of the freedom to organise and in particular those to protect workers' organisations from any interference by employers and by the state. Please indicate how such protection from outside interference applies to employers' organisations.

d. Please indicate, where appropriate, any statutory provisions regarding the affiliation of employers' and workers' organisations with national federations of organisations and with international organisations of the same type.

Question B

Please describe how the right to join a trade union is protected in law and in practice and indicate whether any, and if so which, categories of workers are prohibited from joining a trade union or restricted in doing so.

Please indicate whether and how the right of workers not to join a union is protected in law and in practice. Please indicate in particular whether examples exist in practice of an obligation to belong to a trade union (closed shop clauses, etc.) and what are the measures taken in this regard.

Question C

a. Please furnish a complete description of any representativity criteria, ie. any conditions which trade unions must fulfil in order to be considered representative.

b. If such criteria exist, please also give information on the existence and type of appeal against decisions by the authority or authorities responsible for determining whether a trade union is representative or not. Please indicate the functions which are reserved for representative unions in respect of the negotiation and conclusion of collective agreements, participation in the nomination of various types of workers' representatives and participation in consultation bodies.

c. Please reply to the questions under a. and b. in respect of representativity of employers' organisations, except when negotiations at enterprise level are concerned.

Question D

Please indicate under what circumstances and on which conditions trade union representatives have access to the workplace. Please indicate also whether trade unions are entitled to hold meetings on the premises of the enterprise.

Question E

Please give information on the measures taken to ensure protection against reprisals on grounds of trade union activities.

Article 6: The right to bargain collectively

> *Article 6 para. 1*
>
> *"With a view to ensuring the effective exercise of the right to bargain collectively, the Parties undertake:*
>
> *to promote joint consultation between workers and employers;"*

Please indicate the legislative or other steps taken to encourage joint consultation between workers and employers in your country. In what way do the public authorities encourage or participate in such consultation? Please give particulars on the bodies responsible for such consultation, at the national, regional, or local levels as the case may be, and on the procedures entailed, together with information on the issues covered (financial issues, social issues, working conditions, etc.) and on the sectors of the economy to which the procedures apply.

> *Article 6 para. 2*
>
> *"With a view to ensuring the effective exercise of the right to bargain collectively, the Parties undertake:*
>
> *to promote, where necessary and appropriate, machinery for voluntary negotiations between employers or employers' organisations and workers' organisations, with a view to the regulation of terms and conditions of employment by means of collective agreements;"*

Question A

Please give a description of the existing collective bargaining machinery and its results in both the private and public sector (indications of the number of negotiations and agreements concluded and other indicators or evaluation criteria).

Question B

Please indicate whether and how the law encourages or obliges employers or their organisations to bargain with workers' organisations collectively, and whether and how it encourages or obliges workers' organisations to bargain with employers or their organisations. Please also indicate how the question of union recognition is dealt with.

Question C

Please indicate to what extent, under what conditions, according to which procedures and for which types of subject matter the State can intervene in the process of free collective bargaining. Please indicate where state intervention occurred during the reference period.

Article 6 para. 3

"With a view to ensuring the effective exercise of the right to bargain collectively, the Parties undertake:

to promote the establishment and use of appropriate machinery for conciliation and voluntary arbitration for the settlement of labour disputes;"

Question A

Please describe such machinery as exists by virtue either of law, collective agreements or practice for the settlement of disputes by:

a. conciliation;

b. arbitration or court procedure;

c. other methods of dispute resolution.

Question B

In so far as certain machinery may be compulsory, please describe:

- the sanctions imposed by law or by collective agreements used for its enforcement;

- their significance in practice.

Question C

Please describe the procedures provided, whether by law, staff regulations or practice, for settling disputes between public sector employees and the administration, and show whether existing procedures are open to them.

Article 6 para. 4

"With a view to ensuring the effective exercise of the right to bargain collectively, the Parties recognise:

the right of workers and employers to collective action in cases of conflicts of interest, including the right to strike, subject to obligations that might arise out of collective agreements previously entered into."

[The Appendix to the revised Charter stipulates that it is understood that each Contracting Party may, in so far as it is concerned, regulate the exercise of the right to strike by law, provided that any further restriction that this might place on the right can be justified under the terms of Article G of the revised Charter.]

Question A

Please explain the meaning of collective action in your country spec-ifying what forms of action are recognised (strike, lockout, other forms), what are the permitted objectives of collective action and how the right to collective action is guaranteed.

Question B

Please indicate who is entitled to take collective action (individuals, groups/coalitions of workers, trade unions, employers or employers' organisations, etc.).

Question C

If the right to collective action is restricted, please state the content of these restrictions, and whether they are related to the purposes pur-sued or the methods employed by those taking action, or both, and by which authority they may be imposed.

Please also state any procedural requirements pertaining to collective action (eg. notice rules, cooling-off periods, conciliation/arbitration, ballot requirements, quorums, etc.).

Question D

Please indicate whether any existing restrictions to the right to col-lective action "are prescribed by law and are necessary in a democra-tic society for the protection of the rights and freedoms of others or for the protection of public interest, national security, public health, or morals" (Article G of the revised Charter).

Question E

Please state the effect of strikes or lockouts on the continuation of the employment contract and any other consequences, eg. deduction from wages, liability, etc.

Question F

Please supply available statistics on strikes and lockouts.

Article 7: The right of children and young persons to protection

Article 7 para. 1

"With a view to ensuring the effective exercise of the right of chil-dren and young persons to protection, the Parties undertake:

to provide that the minimum age of admission to employment shall be 15 years, subject to exceptions for children employed in prescribed light work without harm to their health, morals or education;"

Question A

Please indicate whether the minimum age of admission to employment is regulated by legislation. If so, please send the relevant texts.

Please indicate whether the minimum age of admission to employment applies to all categories of work, including agricultural work, domestic work and work carried out in family enterprises.

Question B

Please state whether your country's legislation dealing with minimum age allows derogations. if so, please state the derogations provided for in general by law or granted by an authority.

Please provide a definition of "light work" and, if appropriate, the list of such of work.

Question C

Please indicate the measures taken to combat illegal child labour and to implement in practice the relevant legislation and regulations.

> *Article 7 para. 2*
>
> *"With a view to ensuring the effective exercise of the right of children and young persons to protection, the Parties undertake:*
>
> *to provide that the minimum age of admission to employment shall be 18 years with respect to prescribed occupations regarded as dangerous or unhealthy;"*

Question A

Please state the occupations which are regarded as dangerous or unhealthy for the purpose of this provision. Specify whether a minimum age of admission of at least eighteen years is stipulated for each of these occupations.

Question B

Please indicate whether, in accordance with the Appendix, the law allows for derogations where the work concerned is necessary for their vocational training. If so, please indicate the type of work involved. Please indicate also how such work is supervised by the competent authorities and how the health and safety of the young workers concerned is protected.

Question C

Please indicate the measures taken to implement in practice the relevant legislation and regulations.

> *Article 7 para. 3*
>
> *"With a view to ensuring the effective exercise of the right of children and young persons to protection, the Parties undertake:*

> *to provide that persons who are still subject to compulsory edu-*
> *cation shall not be employed in such work as would deprive them*
> *of the full benefit of their education;"*

Question A

Please indicate the age at which education ceases to be compulsory under your country's present legislation.

Question B

Please indicate the statutory maximum duration of any work performed by children still subject to compulsory education before or after school hours and during weekends and school holidays.

Please indicate the nature of the work performed by these children.

Question C

Please indicate the measures taken to implement in practice the relevant legislation and regulations.

> *Article 7 para. 4*
>
> *"With a view to ensuring the effective exercise of the right of chil-*
> *dren and young persons to protection, the Parties undertake:*
>
> *to provide that the working hours of persons under 18 years of*
> *age shall be limited in accordance with the needs of their devel-*
> *opment, and particularly with their need for vocational training;"*

Question A

Please indicate the extent of this limitation, whether it follows from legislative, administrative, or contractual provisions or from practice.

Question B

Please indicate if any workers are not covered by provisions of this nature, whether contained in legislation, collective agreements or other measures and, if so:

a. please provide statistics showing what proportion of all workers is not covered;

b. please give the reasons for which certain workers are not covered;

c. please state what special measures have been taken on behalf of workers under eighteen years who do not benefit from any limitation of their hours of work.

Question C

Please indicate the measures taken to implement in practice the relevant legislation and regulations.

Question D

Please indicate whether the measures described apply to all categories of young people at work. If this is not the case, please give an estimate

319

of the proportion of young people not covered and, if possible, indicate the categories concerned.

Question E

Please indicate, where appropriate, why certain workers are not covered, and whether special measures have been taken on their behalf.

Article 7 para 5

"With a view to ensuring the effective exercise of the right of children and young persons to protection, the Parties undertake:

to recognise the right of young workers and apprentices to a fair wage or other appropriate allowances;"

Question A

Please indicate the general rules applying to the wages of young workers and to the appropriate allowances of apprentices.

Question B

Please give available statistical information on the level of wages for young workers and on the appropriate allowances for apprentices.

Article 7 para. 6

"With a view to ensuring the effective exercise of the right of children and young persons to protection, the Parties undertake:

to provide that the time spent by young persons in vocational training during the normal working hours with the consent of the employer shall be treated as forming part of the working day;"

Question A

Please indicate the relevant regulations or collective agreements providing that the hours spent by young persons in their vocational training during normal working hours with the consent of the employer shall be treated as forming part of the working day, and specify, as far as possible, the time allowed to young persons for this purpose.

Question B

Please indicate whether the time devoted to vocational training is paid and on what basis.

Question C

Please indicate whether the measures described apply to all categories of young people at work. If this is not the case, please give an estimate of the proportion of young people not covered and, if possible, indicate the categories concerned.

Question D

Please indicate, where appropriate, why certain workers are not covered, and whether special measures have been taken on their behalf.

Question E

Please indicate the measures taken to implement in practice the relevant legislation and regulations.

> *Article 7 para. 7*[1]
>
> *"With a view to ensuring the effective exercise of the right of children and young persons to protection, the Parties undertake:*
>
> *to provide that employed persons of under 18 years of age shall be entitled to a minimum of four weeks' annual holiday with pay;"*

Question A

Please indicate the minimum duration of annual holiday with pay for workers under eighteen years of age.

Question B

Please indicate how this provision is implemented in your country.

Question C

Please indicate whether the measures described are applicable to all categories of workers under eighteen years of age. If this is not the case, please give an estimate of the proportion of those not covered and, if possible, indicate the categories concerned.

Question D

Please indicate where appropriate why certain workers under eighteen years of age are not covered, and whether special measures have been taken on their behalf.

Question E

Please indicate the measures taken to implement in practice the relevant legislation and regulations.

> *Article 7 para. 8*
>
> *"With a view to ensuring the effective exercise of the right of children and young persons to protection, the Parties undertake:*
>
> *to provide that persons under 18 years of age shall not be employed in night work with the exception of certain occupations provided for by national laws or regulations;"*

---

1. If you have answered the question under Article 2 para. 3, it is not necessary to answer this question.

[The Appendix to the revised Charter stipulates that it is understood that a Contracting Party may give the undertaking required in this paragraph if it fulfils the spirit of the undertaking by providing by law that the great majority of persons under 18 years of age shall not be employed in night work.]

Question A

Please indicate the hours to which the term "night work" applies in your country's regulations for the purpose of such prohibition.

Question B

Please list the types of night work which persons under eighteen years of age are authorised to perform either generally or with special permission.

Question C

Please describe the scope of these exceptions and, in particular, the maximum duration and the age under which such derogations cannot be made.

Question D

Please indicate the hours during which night work by young persons is prohibited in all circumstances.

Question E

Please indicate whether the measures described are applicable to all categories of workers under eighteen. If this is not the case, please give an estimate of the proportion of those not covered and, if possible, indicate the categories concerned.

Question F

Please indicate the measures taken to implement in practice the relevant legislation and regulations.

Article 7 para. 9

"With a view to ensuring the effective exercise of the right of children and young persons to protection, the Parties undertake:

to provide that persons under 18 years of age employed in occupations prescribed by national laws or regulations shall be subject to regular medical control;"

Question A

Please indicate in which occupations regular medical examinations are stipulated for persons under eighteen years of age.

Question B

Please indicate the conditions in which and how often these examinations are made.

Question C

Please indicate the measures taken to implement in practice the relevant legislation and regulations

Article 7 para. 10

"With a view to ensuring the effective exercise of the right of children and young persons to protection, the Parties undertake:

to ensure special protection against physical and moral dangers to which children and young persons are exposed, and particularly against those resulting directly or indirectly from their work."

Question A

Please describe the work which is considered, either directly or indirectly, as constituting a danger to the health or morals of young persons.

Question B

Please describe the measures to protect young persons who are in fact exposed to physical or moral danger at their work.

Please describe, in particular, the measures taken (stopping of work, transfer, vocational guidance, etc.) when a physical disorder is noted in young persons in the course of their work.

Question C

Please give a summary of the measures taken in order to protect young people outside work.

Question D

Please indicate the measures taken to protect children and young persons against all forms of violence, exploitation or ill-treatment (including sexual abuse) to which they may be subjected, including within the family.

Please indicate the extent of the problem (if possible, with data) and the measures taken or planned in order to guarantee children and young persons the protection to which they are entitled, including not only preventive but also other measures. Please also describe the preventive measures taken against smoking, drug and alcohol abuse, including multiple addiction, as well as against sexually transmitted diseases.

Question E

Please supply all relevant information concerning the bodies responsible for supervising the application of these provisions (in particular the social service and judicial bodies) and how they function, and on the methods employed to carry out such supervision (enquiries, etc.)

Article 8: The right of employed women to protection of maternity

Article 8 para. 1

"With a view to ensuring the effective exercise of the right of employed women to protection of maternity, the Parties undertake:

to provide either by paid leave, by adequate social security benefits or by benefits from public funds for employed women to take leave before and after childbirth up to a total of at least 14 weeks;"

Question A

Please indicate the length of maternity leave, showing, where appropriate, its division before and after confinement.

Question B

Please indicate whether in some cases the total duration of leave before and after confinement may be less than fourteen weeks.

Question C

Please indicate whether the benefits during maternity leave are provided in the form of paid leave (if normal pay is reduced, please indicate the amount), under a social security system or from public funds, stating whether the payment of benefits is subject to conditions and if so, which.

Question D

Please indicate, in circumstances where part or all of benefits payable during maternity leave are not covered by paid leave, the amount of social security benefits or benefits from public funds in monetary terms and, as appropriate, as a percentage of the wages previously paid to the worker.

Question E

Please indicate any sanctions that may be imposed on an employer failing to observe this provision, and state whether the employed woman has the option of voluntarily giving up all or part of her maternity leave.

Question F

Please indicate the protection to which women employed on fixed-term contracts in your country are entitled, including nationals of the other Contracting Parties to the Charter.

Article 8 para. 2

"With a view to ensuring the effective exercise of the right of employed women to protection of maternity, the Parties undertake:

> *to consider it as unlawful for an employer to give a woman notice of dismissal during the period from the time she notifies her employer that she is pregnant until the end of her maternity leave, or to give her notice of dismissal at such a time that the notice would expire during such a period;"*

Question A

Please indicate what arrangements exist to give effect to this provision.

Question B

Please also indicate the sanctions provided for dismissals in breach of this provision.

Question C

Please indicate if reinstatement is ensured in cases of dismissal in breach of this provision and, in the exceptional cases where this is not possible, the amounts of compensation awarded.

Question D

Please indicate the protection to which women employed on fixed-term contracts in your country are entitled, including nationals of the other Contracting Parties to the Charter.

> *Article 8 para. 3*
>
> *"With a view to ensuring the effective exercise of the right of employed women to protection of maternity, the Parties undertake:*
>
> *to provide that mothers who are nursing their infants shall be entitled to sufficient time off for this purpose;"*

Please indicate the rules which apply in this respect, stating whether time off for breastfeeding is considered as working hours and paid as such.

> *Article 8 para 4*
>
> *"With a view to ensuring the effective exercise of the right of employed women to protection of maternity, the Parties undertake:*
>
> *to regulate the employment in night work of pregnant women, women who have recently given birth and women nursing their infants;"*

Please give details on the regulations of night work of pregnant women, women who recently have given birth or who are nursing their infants and stating in particular the hours to which the term "night work" applies.

Article 8 para. 5

"With a view to ensuring the effective exercise of the right of
employed women to protection of maternity, the Parties undertake:

to prohibit the employment of pregnant women, women who have
recently given birth or who are nursing their infants in underground mining and all other work which is unsuitable by reason
of its dangerous, unhealthy or arduous nature and to take appropriate measures to protect the employment rights of these women".

Question A

Please give details of measures to prohibit the employment of pregnant women, women who have recently given birth or who are nursing their infants in underground mining.

Please indicate the point in time when this protection takes effect and
ceases. Please indicate the measures taken to protect the employment
rights of these women.

Question B

Please indicate what other kind of unsuitable occupations by reason
of its dangerous, unhealthy or arduous nature are prohibited and
what measures are taken to give effect to such prohibition.

Please indicate the point in time when this protection takes effect and
ceases. Please indicate the measures taken to protect the employment
rights of these women.

Question C

Please give details of any authorised exceptions.

Article 9: The right to vocational guidance

"With a view to ensuring the effective exercise of the right to vocational guidance, the Parties undertake to provide or promote, as
necessary, a service which will assist all persons, including the
handicapped, to solve problems related to occupational choice
and progress, with due regard to the individual's characteristics
and their relation to occupational opportunity: this assistance
should be available free of charge, both to young persons, including schoolchildren, and to adults."

Question A

Please give a description of the service – its functions, organisation
and operation – specifying in particular:

a. whether access to services is free of charge;

b. whether vocational guidance work is carried out in the public or
private sectors;

c. the measures taken to supply all persons with adequate information on the choice of employment;

d. the measures taken to ensure a close link between vocational guidance and training on the one hand and employment on the other;[1]

e. the measures in hand for improving the services;

f. the details of special measures to assist disabled persons.

Question B

Please indicate the measures taken in the field of vocational guidance to promote occupational and social advancement.

Question C

Please indicate the types of information available in the vocational guidance services and the means employed to disseminate this information.

Question D

Please indicate:

a. the total amount of public expenditure devoted to vocational guidance services during the reference period;

b. the number of specialised staff of the vocational guidance services and their qualifications (teachers, psychologists, administrators, etc.);

c. the number of persons benefiting from vocational guidance broken down by age, sex and educational background;

d. the geographical and institutional distribution of vocational guidance services.

Question E

Please indicate whether equality of access to vocational guidance is ensured for all those interested, including nationals of the other Contracting Parties to the Charter lawfully resident or working regularly in your territory, and disabled persons.

Article 10: The right to vocational training

> *Article 10 para. 1*
>
> *"With a view to ensuring the effective exercise of the right to vocational training, the Parties undertake:*
>
> *to provide or promote, as necessary, the technical and vocational training of all persons, including the handicapped, in consultation with employers' and workers' organisations, and to grant*

---

1. If your country has accepted Article 10 para. 1, it is not necessary to describe these measures here.

327

> *facilities for access to higher technical and university education, based solely on individual aptitude;"*

Question A

Please give an account of the functions, organisation, operation and financing of the services designed to provide vocational training for all persons including those with disabilities,[1] specifying in particular:

a. the rules laid down by legislation, collective agreements or carried out otherwise;

b. the total amount of public expenditure devoted to vocational training;

c. the number of vocational and technical training institutions (at elementary and advanced levels);

d. the number of teachers in such schools in the last school year;

e. the number of pupils, full-time and part-time in such schools in the last school year.

Question B

Please indicate how the arrangements for vocational training are provided with reference to the various types of vocational activity and, if data are available, to age and to sex.

Question C

Please state what measures are taken to ensure a close link between vocational guidance and training on the one hand and employment on the other.[2]

Question D

Please indicate the methods adopted by your government with a view to providing access to higher technical education and university education on the basis of the sole criterion of individual aptitude.

Question E

Please indicate whether equality of access to vocational training opportunities is ensured for all those interested, including nationals of the other Contracting Parties to the Charter lawfully resident or working regularly in your territory, and disabled persons.

Article 10 para. 2

> *"With a view to ensuring the effective exercise of the right to vocational training, the Parties undertake:*
>
> *to provide or promote a system of apprenticeship and other systematic arrangements for training young boys and girls in their various employments."*

---

1. If your country has accepted Article 15, it is not necessary to describe the services for persons with disabilities here.
2. If your country has accepted Article 9, it is not necessary to describe these measures here.

Question A

Please give an account of the legal framework and the functions, organisation, operation and financing of apprenticeships and/or other systems for training young boys and girls in various jobs in your country.

Question B

Please give an account of the measures taken to implement this provision, stating approximately, if possible, the number of young persons benefiting from training systems.

Question C

Please indicate how the arrangements for vocational training are divided between the various types of vocational activity.

Question D

Please describe any measures under which private apprenticeship schemes are assisted out of public funds.

Question E

Please indicate whether the measures described are applicable to all categories of young boys and girls likely to benefit from and wishing to undertake apprenticeship or vocational training. If this is not the case, please give an estimate of the proportion of those not covered and, if possible, indicate the categories concerned.

Question F

Please indicate whether equality of access to apprenticeship training is ensured for all those interested, including nationals of the other Contracting Parties to the Charter lawfully resident or working regularly in your territory, and disabled persons.

Article 10 para. 3

"With a view to ensuring the effective exercise of the right to vocational training, the Parties undertake:

to provide or promote, as necessary:

a. adequate and readily available training facilities for adult workers;

b. special facilities for the retraining of adult workers needed as a result of technological development or new trends in employment;"

Question A

Please give details of the facilities provided for the training and retraining of adult workers, in particular the arrangements for retraining redundant workers and workers affected by economic and technological change.

Question B

Please indicate how the arrangements for vocational training are divided between the various types of vocational activity.

Question C

Please state whether the measures described are applicable to all categories of interested workers likely to benefit from and in need of training or retraining facilities. If this is not the case, please give an estimate of the proportion of those not covered and, if appropriate, give details of the categories concerned.

Question D

Please indicate the approximate number of adult workers who have participated in training or retraining measures.

Question E

Please describe special measures to assist adult women wishing to take up or resume employment.

Question F

Please indicate whether equality of access to adult training and retraining is ensured for all those interested, including nationals of the other Contracting Parties to the Charter lawfully resident or working regularly in your territory, and disabled persons.

Article 10 para. 4

"With a view to ensuring the effective exercise of the right to vocational training, the Parties undertake;

to provide or promote, as necessary, special measures for the retraining and reintegration of the long-term unemployed;"

Please indicate the special measures taken to provide or promote the retraining and reintegration of long-term unemployed, including as far as possible information on the number of participants and the results achieved.

Article 10 para. 5

"With a view to ensuring the effective exercise of the right to vocational training, the Parties undertake:

to encourage the full utilisation of the facilities provided by appropriate measures such as:

a. reducing or abolishing any fees or charges;

b. granting financial assistance in appropriate cases;

c. including in the normal working hours time spent on supplementary training taken by the worker, at the request of his employer, during employment;

d. *ensuring, through adequate supervision, in consultation with the employers' and workers' organisations, the efficiency of apprenticeship and other training arrangements for young workers, and the adequate protection of young workers generally."*

Question A

Please give a brief account of any fees or charges imposed in respect of vocational training and indicate, where appropriate, the measures taken to reduce or abolish such fees or charges.

Question B

Please describe the system existing in your country for providing financial assistance (allowances, grants, loans, etc.) to participants in vocational training. Please indicate also the nature of the financial assistance provided (amounts, duration, eligibility criteria, etc.).

Please indicate whether equal treatment in respect of financial assistance is ensured for nationals of all the Contracting Parties to the Charter lawfully resident or working regularly in your territory.

Question C

Please indicate the measures taken to include time spent on training taken by workers, at the request of their employer, in the normal working hours.

Question D

Please indicate the supervision and evaluation measures taken in consultation with the social partners to ensure the efficiency of apprenticeship and other training arrangements for young workers.

Question E

Please indicate if the provision of sub-paragraphs (a), (b) and (c) of Article 10 para. 4 are applicable to the great majority of the persons concerned.

Article 11: The right to protection of health

General aspects[1]

Question A

Please indicate the forms of ill-health which at present raise the greatest public health problems in your country by reason of their frequency, gravity and any sequels.

Please indicate what illnesses were the main causes of death.

---

1. States having accepted one or more paragraphs of Article 11 are invited to respond to the questions under this heading.

Question B

Please describe the measures aimed at ensuring universal access to health care. Please also indicate on what conditions the various health services are made available to the whole of your country, describing the geographical distribution of these services.

Question C[1]

Please indicate how public health services are organised in your country and state, if possible:

a. the number of private or public preventative and screening clinics (if possible distinguishing between general or specialised, particularly in the fields of tuberculosis, sexually transmitted diseases, AIDS, mental health, mother and child welfare, etc.) and the annual attendance of them making special mention of services for schoolchildren;

b. the regular health examinations arranged for the population in general or for a part thereof, and their intervals;

c. the number of general hospitals and public or private establishments for specialised treatment (especially for tuberculosis, psychiatry – including day hospital –, cancer, after-care, functional and occupational rehabilitation). Give the respective proportions of public and private establishments. Please indicate the number of beds available (or of places in case of day hospitals or rehabilitation clinics accepting out-patients);

d. the number per 1 000 persons of doctors, dentists, midwives and nurses, indicating, if possible, the situation in urban and rural areas;

e. the number of pharmacies per 1 000 persons and if possible their geographical distribution;

f. Please indicate the percentage of GDP allocated to health expenditure.

> *Article 11 para. 1*
>
> *"With a view to ensuring the effective exercise of the right to protection of health, the Parties undertake, either directly or in cooperation with public or private organisations, to take appropriate measures designed inter alia:*
>
> *to remove as far as possible the causes of ill-health."*

Question A

Please indicate infant and perinatal mortality rates for the reference period concerned.

---

1. If the statistical information requested under this provision is available from publications of Eurostat, WHO or OECD you are invited to refer to the relevant publication

Please indicate the life expectancy at birth in your country.

Question B

Please describe any special measures taken to protect the health of:

a. pregnant women, mothers and babies;

b. children and adolescents;[1]

c. the elderly;

d. disadvantaged persons or groups (for example the homeless, families with many children, drug addicts and the unemployed, etc.).

Please supply information on all measures taken to protect the reproductive health of all persons, in particular adolescents.

> *Article 11 para. 2*
>
> *"With a view to ensuring the effective exercise of the right to protection of health, the Parties undertake, either directly or in co-operation with public or private organisations, to take appropriate measures designed inter alia:*
>
> *to provide advisory and educational facilities for the promotion of health and the encouragement of individual responsibility in matters of health;"*

Question A

Please indicate what advisory and screening services exist:

a. for schools;

b. for other groups.

Question B

Please describe any measures taken to further health education, including information campaigns.

> *Article 11 para 3*
>
> *"With a view to ensuring the effective exercise of the right to protection of health, the Parties undertake, either directly or in co-operation with public or private organisations, to take appropriate measures designed inter alia:*
>
> *to prevent as far as possible epidemic, endemic and other diseases, as well as accidents."*

Question A

Please indicate what measures other than those mentioned above are taken to prevent epidemic, endemic and other diseases (compulsory or optional vaccination, disinfection, epidemics policy).

---

1. If your country has accepted paragraphs 9 and 10 of Article 7, it is not necessary to repeat the information given thereon here.

Question B

Please indicate what general measures are taken in the public health field, such as:

a. – prevention of air pollution,

   – prevention of water pollution,

   – prevention of soil pollution;

b. protection against radioactive contamination;

c. protection against noise pollution;

d. food hygiene inspection;

e. minimum housing standards;

f. measures taken to combat smoking, alcohol and drug abuse, including multiple addiction, as well as against sexually transmitted diseases.

Article 12: The right to social security

   Article 12 para. 1

     "With a view to ensuring the effective exercise of the right to social security, the Parties undertake:

     to establish or maintain a system of social security;"

Please indicate the measures taken to give effect to this undertaking, specifying the nature of the existing system, in particular funding arrangements, giving information allowing the percentage of the population covered and the level of benefits to be determined.

   Article 12 para. 2

     "With a view to ensuring the effective exercise of the right to social security, the Contracting Parties undertake:

     to maintain the social security system at a satisfactory level at least equal to that necessary for the ratification of the European Code of Social Security;"

Question A

Please specify the branches of social security in which the social security system in force in your country fulfils (or goes beyond) the requirements of the European Code of Social Security.

Question B

With regard to the branches of the social security system in force which do not reach the level provided for in the Code, please indicate the differences between your established standards and those of the Code.

Article 12 para. 3

"With a view to ensuring the effective exercise of the right to social security, the Parties undertake:

to endeavour to raise progressively the system of social security to a higher level;"

Question A

Please describe any measures taken to establish higher social security standards, in particular any measures raising the system to a higher level than that of the European Code of Social Security.

Please also provide information in relation to the standards of the Protocol to the European Code of Social Security and/or the revised European Code of Social Security.

Question B

As far as any other changes in the social security field are concerned, especially in so far as they are not aimed at bringing the system to a higher level, please include the following elements:

– the nature of the changes (field of application, conditions for granting allowances, amounts of allowance, lengths, etc.);

– the reasons given for the changes, the framework of social and economic policy they come within and their adequacy in the situation which gave rise to them;

– the extent of the changes introduced (categories and numbers of people concerned, levels of allowances before and after alteration);

– the existence of measures for those who find themselves in a situation of need as a result of the changes made (this information can be submitted under Article 13);

– the results obtained by such changes.

Article 12 para. 4

"With a view to ensuring the effective exercise of the right to social security, the Parties undertake:

to take steps, by the conclusion of appropriate bilateral and multilateral agreements, or by other means, and subject to the conditions laid down in such agreements, in order to ensure:

a. equal treatment with their own nationals of the nationals of other Parties in respect of social security rights, including the retention of benefits arising out of social security legislation, whatever movements the persons protected may undertake between the territories of the Parties;

b. the granting, maintenance and resumption of social security rights by such means as the accumulation of insurance or employment periods completed under the legislation of each of the Parties."

[The Appendix to the Charter states that the words: "... and subject to the conditions laid down in such agreements ..." in the introduction to this paragraph are taken to imply inter alia that with regard to benefits which are available independently of any insurance contribution a Contracting Party may require the completion of a prescribed period of residence before granting such benefits to nationals of other Contracting Parties.]

Question A

Please give the list of bilateral and multilateral agreements as provided for in this provision and indicate how they allow, for the various social security benefits, the implementation of the principles provided for in sub-paragraphs a) and b).

Question B

Please indicate whether, in the absence of any bilateral or multilateral agreements, the nationals of other Contracting Parties concerned are granted the implementation of the principles provided for in sub-paragraphs a) and b) for the various social security benefits.

Question C

Please indicate the length of the prescribed period of residence before nationals of the other Contracting Parties become eligible for benefits which are available independently of any contribution.

Article 13: The right to social and medical assistance

> *Article 13 para. 1*
>
> *"With a view to ensuring the effective exercise of the right to social and medical assistance, the Parties undertake:*
>
> *to ensure that any person who is without adequate resources and who is unable to secure such resources either by his own efforts or from other sources, in particular by benefits under a social security scheme, be granted adequate assistance, and, in case of sickness, the care necessitated by his condition;"*

Question A

Please describe the general organisation of the current public social and medical assistance schemes.

Question B

Please provide detailed information on the different types of social and medical assistance, specifying for each one:

– its form (benefits in cash and/or in kind);

– the categories of persons covered and the number of persons who were in receipt of assistance during the reference period;

- the conditions for the granting of assistance, the criteria used to assess need, the procedure for determining whether a person is without adequate resources, and the body which decides when assistance is to be granted;
- as far as possible, information demonstrating the adequacy of the assistance with respect to the cost of living.

Question C

Please indicate the means by which the right to assistance is secured, indicating whether individuals may uphold their right before an independent body.

Question D

Please give the amount of public funds (central government or local authorities) allocated to social and medical assistance as well as the percentage of GDP this represents, and, if possible, give an estimation of the amount of private funds devoted to assistance.

Article 13 para. 2

"With a view to ensuring the effective exercise of the right to social and medical assistance, the Parties undertake:

to ensure that persons receiving such assistance shall not, for that reason, suffer from a diminution of their political or social rights;"

Please indicate briefly how this Article is implemented and what measures are used to ensure in particular, the absence of any direct or indirect diminution of political or social rights.

Article 13 para. 3

"With a view to ensuring the effective exercise of the right to social and medical assistance, the Parties undertake:

to provide that everyone may receive by appropriate public or private services such advice and personal help as may be required to prevent, to remove, or to alleviate personal or family want;"

Please describe the main services covered by this provision, especially the manner in which they are organised and operate, including their geographic distribution.

Please give as far as possible information about:

- the staff responsible for providing advice and personal help, as well as an indication of their qualifications and duties;
- measures aimed to ensure an adequate response to the needs of individuals and families.

Article 13 para. 4

"With a view to ensuring the effective exercise of the right to social and medical assistance, the Parties undertake:

337

to apply the provisions referred to in paragraphs 1, 2 and 3 of this Article on an equal footing with their nationals to nationals of other Contracting Parties lawfully within their territories, in accordance with their obligations under the European Convention on Social and Medical Assistance, signed at Paris on 11th December 1953."

[The Appendix to the Charter stipulates that Governments not parties to the European Convention on Social and Medical Assistance may ratify the Social Charter in respect of this paragraph provided that they grant to national of other Contracting parties a treatment which is in conformity with the provisions of the said Convention.]

Please indicate the guarantees which ensure conformity with this provision. Please describe more specifically the provisions which ensure that any repatriation of nationals of other Contracting Parties who are legally within the territory on the sole ground that they are in need of assistance is carried out according to the conditions laid down in Article 6 to 10 of the European Convention on Social and Medical Assistance 1953.

Article 14: The right to benefit from social welfare services

Article 14 para. 1

"With a view to ensuring the effective exercise of the right to benefit from social welfare services, the Parties undertake:

to promote or provide services which, by using methods of social work, would contribute to the welfare and development of both individuals and groups in the community, and to their adjustment to the social environment;"

Question A

Please describe the measures taken to apply this provision and list the principal social services of the type mentioned, describing their functions and the target groups they serve.

Question B

Please describe the organisation and administration, the financial resources and working methods of these services, their financial and other relations to the organs of social security and the qualifications of the staff employed by these services.

Question C

Please state what measures have been taken to promote these services during the reference period, whether the individuals are entitled by law to their use or whether those administering have a discretion in granting or withholding them. Please indicate also whether there is a right of appeal against decisions to grant or withhold services.

Article 14 para. 2

"With a view to ensuring the effective exercise of the right to benefit from social welfare services, the Parties undertake:

to encourage the participation of individuals and voluntary or other organisations in the establishment and maintenance of such services."

Please indicate the measures taken to provide for or to encourage the participation of individuals and charitable organisations and other appropriate organisations in the establishment and maintenance of such services.[1]

Article 15: The right of persons with disabilities to independence, social integration and participation in the life of the community

Article 15 para. 1

"With a view to ensuring to persons with disabilities, irrespective of age and the nature and origin of their disabilities, the effective exercise of the right to independence, social integration and participation in the life of the community, the Parties undertake, in particular:

to take the necessary measures to provide persons with disabilities with guidance, education and vocational training in the framework of general schemes wherever possible or , where this is not possible, through specialised bodies, public or private;"

Question A

Please indicate the criteria applied to grant disabled status and give an estimation of the total number of persons with disabilities as well as the number of persons with disabilities of working age.

Question B

Please describe the measures taken to provide persons with disabilities with education, guidance and vocational training in the framework of general schemes wherever possible or, where this is not possible, through specialised bodies, public or private, and provide information on the following points:

a. assessment of the skills of persons with disabilities and criteria used to assess the prospects of rehabilitation of persons with disabilities;

b. organisation of education for persons with disabilities in ordinary schools and/or specialised schools (access, number of persons and establishments);

---

1. If paragraph 1 of this Article has been accepted it is sufficient to supplement the reply concerning that paragraph here.

c. organisation of vocational guidance for persons with disabilities (access, number of persons with disabilities receiving guidance through mainstream or specialist provision);

d. organisation of vocational training (access, number of persons with disabilities receiving vocational training through mainstream or specialist provision);

e. adjustment of the methods of vocational rehabilitation in accordance with the needs of the labour market;

f. financial assistance available to persons with disabilities undertaking vocational rehabilitation.

Question C

Please specify whether the measures mentioned above are available to all persons with disabilities irrespective of age, the nature and origin of their disability.

Question D

Please specify:

a. the number and nature of the principal institutions giving general education, guidance and vocational training and the number of places available;

b. the number of persons undergoing such training;

c. the number of staff, their qualifications and the measures taken to ensure their expertise;

d. the organisation of co-operation between general and specialised services.

Article 15 para. 2

"With a view to ensuring to persons with disabilities, irrespective of age and the nature and origin of their disabilities, the effective exercise of the right to independence, social integration and participation in the life of the community, the Parties undertake, in particular:

to promote their access to employment through all measures tending to encourage employers to hire and keep in employment persons with disabilities in the ordinary working environment and to adjust the working conditions to the needs of the disabled or, where this is not possible by reason of the disability, by arranging for or creating sheltered employment according to the level of disability. In certain cases, such measures may require recourse to specialised placement and support services;"

Question A

Please describe the measures taken to promote the employment of persons with disabilities in an ordinary working environment and in particular the measures concerning the placing of persons with disabilities; incentives for employers to hire persons with disabilities and, where appropriate, measures obliging employers to adjust working conditions. Please provide information on employment obligation for persons with disabilities.

Please specify the measures to ensure the retention of persons with disabilities in employment (duty of occupational redeployment for persons who become disabled following an accident at work or an occupational disease, ban on dismissal of workers because of their disability, obligation for employers to adjust working conditions, provision of support for persons with disabilities to start their own business, etc.).

Question B

Please indicate the number (or an approximation) of persons with disabilities who during the reference period found paid employment (whether in specialised institutions or not; in the public or private sector).

Question C

Please provide information on sheltered employment structures (type, capacity, pay rates for persons with disabilities working there). Please indicate the opportunities which exist to transfer from sheltered employment to open employment.

> *Article 15 para. 3*
>
> *"With a view to ensuring to persons with disabilities, irrespective of age and the nature and origin of their disabilities, the effective exercise of the right to independence, social integration and participation in the life of the community, the Parties undertake, in particular:*
>
> *to promote their full social integration and participation in the life of the community in particular through measures, including technical aids, aiming to overcome barriers to communication and mobility and enabling access to transport, housing, cultural activities and leisure."*

Question A

Please indicate how national policy promotes the independence, the full integration and participation in the life of the community of persons with disabilities. Please describe in particular how this applies to children with disabilities.

Question B

Please describe:

a. the measures taken to overcome barriers to communication and mobility;

b. the measures taken to enable access to transport, housing, cultural activities and leisure for persons with disabilities.

Question C

Please indicate how organisations representing or assisting persons with disabilities are consulted or involved in the formulation and implementation of the social integration policies for persons with disabilities.

Article 16: The right of the family to social, legal and economic protection

> "With a view to ensuring the necessary conditions for the full development of the family, which is a fundamental unit of society, the Parties undertake to promote the economic, legal and social protection of family life by such means as social and family benefits, fiscal arrangements, provision of family housing, benefits for the newly married and other appropriate means."

Question A

Please mention if the legislation in your country provides specifically for the legal protection of the family, bearing in particular on equality in law between spouses, on family relationships and on marital conflict, and also any special measures to facilitate solutions other than divorce to such conflicts.

Please describe the marital property regimes existing in your country.

Question B

Please describe the economic measures taken on behalf of the welfare of the family[1]:

a. by the award of benefits in cash[2] (eg. family allowances) which permanently ensure financial compensation, at least in part, for family burdens, indicating the manner and the levels in which such benefits are given (with relevant figures) as well as the number of persons concerned (percentage of the population);

b. by the award of occasional benefits in cash or in kind other than social and medical assistance benefits, intended to give material assistance to families in certain specific circumstances (e.g. marriage, setting up or tenancy of housing appropriate to the size of the family group) giving, wherever possible, statistical information;

c. by alleviating certain expenses (eg. tax relief for family and children, special transport rates for families). In so far as tax relief is

---

1. This question also covers the situation of single-parent families.
2. If your country has accepted Article 12 para. 4 it is not necessary to describe the measures taken to ensure equal treatment in respect of allocation of family benefits forming part of social security. If your country has accepted Article 31 para. 3, it is unnecessary to describe measures concerning housing benefits.

concerned, please specify whether tax concessions vary according to the number of children; and if so, how and to what extent;

d. by assistance to the newly married;

e. by providing the necessary financial assistance to women who are not covered by a social security system for a reasonable period before and after confinement, as well as medical care or other adequate care during childbirth[1].

Question C

Please indicate whether in your country there exists social and/or cultural services of particular interest to the family, such as advice to families (either to the whole family or to its members, eg. to mothers, pregnant women, children of various ages), home-help services, family holiday homes, etc.

Please indicate the childminding services available to families, in particular crèches, nurseries and after-school and holiday schemes for children.

Please give a general description of the organisation and facilities of these services. In your answer please distinguish between public and private services and between services available free or against payment. Please give relevant statistical data.

Question D

Please indicate whether legislation or other provisions in your country provide for protection of victims of violence or sexual abuse within the household.

Please indicate whether there are regulations and measures to prevent the risk of ill-treatment and to support and rehabilitate the victims.

Question E

Please indicate if the legislation in your country provides for family representation on advisory or administrative bodies with a view to defending family interests.

Question F

Please indicate what measures have been taken to promote the construction of family housing, and supply full statistics of the work accomplished.

Question G

Please indicate the measures taken in the field of family planning information.

---

1. This question has been taken from the 1981 Form for reports under Article 17 of the Charter.

Question H

If your country publishes official statistics concerning the composition of the family and its economic and social position, please provide a summary of the latest available statistics. In so far as the socio-economic position is concerned, describe the manner in which socio-economic categories are classified in your country.

Article 17: The right of children and young persons to social, legal and economic protection

Article 17 para. 1

> *"With a view to ensuring the effective exercise of the right of children and young persons to grow up in an environment which encourages the full development of their personality and of their physical and mental capacities, the Parties undertake, either directly or in co-operation with public and private organisations, to take all appropriate and necessary measures designed:*
>
> a. *to ensure that children and young persons, taking account of the rights and duties of their parents, have the care, the assistance, the education and the training they need, in particular by providing for the establishment or maintenance of institutions and services sufficient and adequate for this purpose;*
>
> b. *to protect children and young persons against negligence, violence or exploitation;*
>
> c. *to provide protection and special aid from the state for children and young persons temporarily or definitively deprived of their family's support;"*

Question A

Please state whether your legislation makes provision for:

a. procedure for the establishment of the paternity or maternity of children born out of wedlock. If appropriate, state the reasons why some categories of children cannot benefit from these procedures and describe any special measures taken on behalf of these categories;

b. liability for the maintenance of children born out of wedlock, and whether the rules applicable differ from those for children born within marriage;

c. special arrangements for the guardianship and custody of children born out of wedlock;

d. the legitimisation of children born out of wedlock;

e. special rules for the inheritance right of children born out of wedlock.

Question B

Please describe the measures in force with regard to adoption. How close does the status of the adopted child come to that of the biological child ?

Question C

Please indicate how the legal representation of children is ensured, notably in case of conflict with or between the parents or the persons in charge of the child. Are children entitled to be heard and have their views taken into account during legal proceedings? If so, from what age and on which issues?

Question D

Please indicate if your legislation provides for special institutions or special courts (possibly child tribunals or special procedures) to deal with young offenders.

Please indicate what is the age of criminal responsibility, at which sanctions can be applied; the penalties available and the conditions under which they are carried out, notably for penalties involving restrictions on liberty. Please also indicate the measures of protection, education and treatment and the care provided as a means of prevention or as an alternative to detention, as well as the measures to minimise the risk for vulnerable young people.

Question E[1]

a. Please indicate the preventive measures taken to protect the health of children and young persons.

b. Please describe primary and specialised health services available to children and young persons, including psychiatric care.

Question F

a. Please describe the provision of child day-care services, especially in terms of capacity, staffing, funding and accessibility.

b. Please indicate whether any socio-medical services are provided through schools and day-care services, and measures ensuring adequate nutrition of children and young persons.

Question G

Please indicate compensatory measures (educational, social assistance, leisure, etc.) taken to protect children and young persons with special needs, including those with disabilities. Please also indicate whether your country provides early intervention to facilitate these persons integration into society on reaching adulthood.

---

1. It is not necessary to answer this question if the information has been provided under Article 11.

Question H

Please indicate the age limit for individual entitlement of young persons to social security or social assistance benefits. Please state whether any exceptions are made, for example, in relation to children in institutions.

Question I[1]

Please indicate the measures taken in legislation and in practice to protect children and young persons against physical and moral dangers, ill-treatment, corporal punishment, negligence, exploitation, violence and sexual abuse. Please indicate whether psycho-social services or other services (shelters, telephone hotlines) exist for children victims of such treatment.

Question J

a. Please indicate the support, including financial support, offered to foster families. Please state the number of children and young persons living in foster families in your country.

b. Please indicate the number of places and children in residential care, as well as the living conditions in these establishments (nutrition, health services, recreational facilities, privacy and communication with family and friends);

c. Please describe the arrangements made for inspection of standards in residential care.

d. Please indicate the criteria according to which parental rights and duties may be abrogated, and to which children may be separated from their families and placed in the care of third parties. Please indicate how the right of both children and parents to express their opinions in such circumstances is secured.

Question K

Please indicate the role of private organisations in providing care and assistance to children and young persons, and the legal framework governing their activities, in particular with respect to state inspection.

Question L

Please provide information on the level of public expenditure, as well as the number and qualifications of staff in this field.

Article 17 para 2

"With a view to ensuring the effective exercise of the right of children and young persons to grow up in an environment which encourages the full development of their personality and of their

---

1. If your country has accepted Article 7 para. 10, it is not necessary to repeat the information given thereon here.

physical and mental capacities, the Parties undertake, either directly or in co-operation with public and private organisations, to take all appropriate and necessary measures designed:

to provide to children and young persons a free primary and secondary education as well as to encourage regular attendance at schools".

Question A

Please indicate whether free primary and secondary education is universally available in your country. Please indicate the extent to which mainstream education is open to children and young persons with disabilities.

Question B

Please indicate as far as possible the extent of truancy in primary and secondary schools.

Please indicate what measures are taken to encourage regular attendance and what sanctions exist for truancy.

Question C

Please indicate any measures or initiatives to encourage regular attendance in favour of children and young persons from minority groups (eg. ethnic or linguistic minorities) and vulnerable groups (eg. those with disabilities, those suffering from dyslexia, those in long-term care, those from disadvantaged backgrounds).

Question D

Please indicate what proportion of children and young persons complete the secondary education cycle successfully and the existing possibilities for those for whom it is not the case.

Article 18: The right to engage in a gainful occupation in the territory of other parties

Article 18 para. 1

"With a view to ensuring the effective exercise of the right to engage in a gainful occupation in the territory of any other Party, the Parties undertake:

to apply existing regulations in a spirit of liberality;"

Question A

How is this paragraph observed in your country, both with regard to wage-earners and with regard to others?

Question B

Please indicate the number of permits granted compared with the number of applications made.

Question C

Please state whether your country applies restrictions to the right to engage in a gainful occupation by nationals of other states and if so, please mention the grounds.

> *Article 18 para. 2*
>
> *"With a view to ensuring the effective exercise of the right to engage in a gainful occupation in the territory of any other Party, the Parties undertake:*
>
> *to simplify existing formalities and to reduce or abolish chancery dues and other charges payable by foreign workers or their employers;"*

Question A

Please describe the formalities which must be observed by nationals of the other Contracting Parties and the members of their families or by their employers, with regard to their residence in the country and the exercise of an occupation, whether they are seeking paid employment or wish to engage as self-employed, distinguishing between wage-earners or salaried employees, self-employed traders or craftsmen, heads of agricultural or non-agricultural concerns, various professions.

Please state what derogations have been made to the rules normally applicable and with regard to what categories of persons.

Question B

Please indicate what chancery dues or other charges are payable by foreign workers or their employers.

Question C

Please indicate the steps taken to simplify the formalities described in Question A and to reduce the charges referred to in Question B.

> *Article 18 para. 3*
>
> *"With a view to ensuring the effective exercise of the right to engage in a gainful occupation in the territory of any other Party, the Parties undertake:*
>
> *to liberalise, individually or collectively, regulations governing the employment of foreign workers;"*

Question A

Please specify whether, and if so under which conditions, a foreign worker may:

a. change his place of occupation;

b. change his occupation;

c. claim the renewal of the permit.

Question B

Please describe the situation of the holder of a work permit of he loses or gives up his job while the permit is still valid.

Question C

Please indicate the other steps taken to apply this provision of the Charter.

Article 18 para. 4

"With a view to ensuring the effective exercise of the right to engage in a gainful occupation in the territory of any other Party, the Parties undertake:

the right of their nationals to leave the country to engage in a gainful occupation in the territories of the other Parties."

Please indicate whether there are any restrictions or special conditions affecting the right of such persons to leave the country for this reason and, if so, what the regulations are.

Article 19: The right of migrant workers and their families to protection and assistance

Article 19 para. 1

"With a view to ensuring the effective exercise of the right of migrant workers and their families to protection and assistance in the territory of any other Party, the Parties undertake:

to maintain or to satisfy themselves that there are maintained adequate and free services to assist such workers, particularly in obtaining accurate information, and to take all appropriate steps, so far as national laws and regulations permit, against misleading propaganda relating to emigration and immigration;"

Question A

Please indicate how the free services to assist migrant workers are organised and operated.

Question B

Please indicate whether national laws and regulations provide for action to combat misleading propaganda relating to emigration and immigrating, and mention any measures that it has been judged suitable to take.

Question C

Please indicate whether information is available for migrant workers in their own language.

Article 19 para. 2

"With a view to ensuring the effective exercise of the right of migrant workers and their families to protection and assistance in the territory of any other Party, the Parties undertake:

to adopt appropriate measures within their own jurisdiction to facilitate the departure, journey and reception of such workers and their families, and to provide, within their own jurisdiction, appropriate services for health, medical attention and good hygienic conditions during the journey;"

Question A

Please give details of measures to facilitate the departure, travel and reception of migrant workers and of administrative formalities on departure and arrival.

Question B

Please indicate how the medical and health services referred to in this paragraph are organised and function.

Article 19 para. 3

"With a view to ensuring the effective exercise of the right of migrant workers and their families to protection and assistance in the territory of any other Party, the Parties undertake:

to promote co-operation, as appropriate, between social services, public and private, in emigration and immigration countries;"

Please describe the measures taken to ensure collaboration between the services mentioned of immigration and emigration countries, distinguishing between the social services of the countries of origin or destination of migrant workers which are Contracting Parties.

Article 19 para. 4

"With a view to ensuring the effective exercise of the right of migrant workers and their families to protection and assistance in the territory of any other Party, the Parties undertake:

to secure for such workers lawfully within their territories, insofar as such matters are regulated by law or regulations or are subject to the control of administrative authorities, treatment not less favourable than that of their own nationals in respect of the following matters:

a. *remuneration and other employment and working conditions;*

b. *membership of trade unions and enjoyment of the benefits of collective bargaining;*

c. *accommodation;"*

Question A

Please indicate how the laws, regulations and administrative measures enacted in your country ensure in practice that migrant workers receive no less favourable treatment than your own nationals with regard to the advantages mentioned in this paragraph.

Question B

Please indicate in particular how discrimination is avoided between foreigners and nationals in access to housing.

Article 19 para. 5

"With a view to ensuring the effective exercise of the right of migrant workers and their families to protection and assistance in the territory of any other Party, the Parties undertake:

to secure for such workers lawfully within their territories treatment not less favourable than that of their own nationals with regard to employment taxes, dues or contributions payable in respect of employed persons;"

Please describe how the requirements of this paragraph are observed in your country.

Article 19 para. 6

"With a view to ensuring the effective exercise of the right of migrant workers and their families to protection and assistance in the territory of any other Party, the Parties undertake:

to facilitate as far as possible the reunion of the family of a foreign worker permitted to establish himself in the territory;"

[The Appendix to the revised Charter stipulates that for the purpose of applying this provision, the term "family of a foreign worker" is understood to mean at least the worker's spouse and unmarried children, as long as the latter are considered to be minors by the receiving State and are dependent on the migrant worker.]

Question A

Please indicate how the reunion of migrant workers' families is facilitated, particularly by measures taken in regard to accommodation.

Question B

Please indicate which members of the family are taken into account when considering family reunion.

Please indicate the age limit for admission into the territory for the purpose of family reunion of children of migrant workers.

Question C

Please indicate whether it is possible to refuse permission to enter the country in which a migrant worker is already established to a member of his family by reason of that member's physical or mental health.

Article 19 para. 7

"With a view to ensuring the effective exercise of the right of migrant workers and their families to protection and assistance in the territory of any other Party, the Parties undertake:

to secure for such workers lawfully within their territories treatment not less favourable than that of their own nationals in respect of legal proceedings relating to matters referred to in this Article;"

Please indicate whether the forms of legal assistance available to indigent nationals (exemption from costs or their payment or part-payment from public funds) are also available to migrant workers and their families.

Article 19 para. 8

"With a view to ensuring the effective exercise of the right of migrant workers and their families to protection and assistance in the territory of any other Party, the Parties undertake:

to secure that such workers lawfully residing within their territories are not expelled unless they endanger national security or offend against public interest or morality;"

Question A

Please indicate the regulations applicable to the expulsion of migrant workers specifying in particular the grounds for expulsion and the procedures observed.

Question B

Please specify what possibilities of appeal are available against such expulsion orders.

Article 19 para. 9

"With a view to ensuring the effective exercise of the right of migrant workers and their families to protection and assistance in the territory of any other Party, the Parties undertake:

to permit, within legal limits, the transfer of such parts of the earnings and savings of such workers as they may desire;"

Please indicate the limits within which migrant workers may transfer their earnings and savings.

Article 19 para. 10

> "With a view to ensuring the effective exercise of the right of migrant workers and their families to protection and assistance in the territory of any other Party, the Parties undertake:
>
> to extend the protection and assistance provided for in this Article to self-employed migrants insofar as such measures apply;"

Please indicate the extent to which the relevant provisions of paragraphs 1 to 9 of Article 19 apply to self-employed migrant workers.

Please specify in particular whether the protective measures and the assistance provided for by these provisions are applied on the same conditions as for employees and whether they guarantee equal treatment with nationals exercising the same occupation.

Article 19 para. 11

> "With a view to ensuring the effective exercise of the right of migrant workers and their families to protection and assistance in the territory of any other Party, the Parties undertake:
>
> to promote and facilitate, the teaching of the national language of the receiving state or, if there are several, one of these languages, to migrant workers and members of their families;"

Please indicate the measures taken to promote and facilitate the teaching of the national language (or languages) of the receiving state to the migrant worker and his/her family, in particular:

a. the number and nature of the principal institutions especially in terms of capacity, staffing, funding and accessibility;

b. the number of persons undergoing such teaching.

Article 19 para. 12

> "With a view to ensuring the effective exercise of the right of migrant workers and their families to protection and assistance in the territory of any other Party, the Parties undertake:
>
> to promote and facilitate, as far as practicable, the teaching of the migrant worker's mother tongue to the children of the migrant worker."

Please indicate the measures taken to promote and facilitate the teaching of migrant workers' mother tongues to their children, in particular:

a. the number and nature of the principal institutions, especially in terms of capacity, staffing, funding and accessibility;

b. the number of children undergoing such teaching.

Article 20: The right to equal opportunities and equal treatment in matters of employment and occupation without discrimination on the grounds of sex

"With a view to ensuring the effective exercise of the right to equal opportunities and equal treatment in matters of employment and occupation without discrimination on the grounds of sex, the Parties undertake to recognise that right and to take appropriate measures to ensure or promote its application in the following fields:

a. *access to employment, protection against dismissal and occupational reintegration;*

b. *vocational guidance, training, retraining and rehabilitation;*

c. *terms of employment and working conditions, including remuneration;*

d. *career development, including promotion".*

Question A

Please state how the rights contained in this provision have been protected in legislation. This information should be specified according to the areas listed in paragraph 1 of Article 20.

Question B

Please indicate whether legislation provides a right for a worker to take legal action before a court or other competent authority in order to ensure the effective implementation and exercise of his rights under this provision. The information shall cover the four areas specified in the provision.

Question C

Please state whether clauses in collective agreements and employment contracts that contravene the principles of non-discrimination may be declared null and void and according to which procedure.

Question D

Please describe which safeguards legislation provides against gender discrimination and against retaliatory measures undertaken by the employer. Please state how it provides for the rectification of the situation (reinstatement in cases of dismissal, financial compensation, etc.). Please indicate also whether there are other sanctions against an employer who is guilty of such discrimination.

Question E

Please describe who has the burden of proof in cases of alleged gender discrimination in your country and whether this issue is regulated in legislation or case law. If the latter is the case, please enclose some decisions based on this case law.

Question F

Please describe the specific measures to prevent discrimination against women in matters of employment and occupation, particularly in cases of pregnancy, confinement and during the post-natal period.

Question G

Please indicate whether there are occupations (if so, which ones) that are reserved exclusively for one or other sex, specifying whether this is due to the nature of the activity or the conditions in which it is carried out.

Question H

Please indicate whether measures of positive action in favour of one gender aimed at removing de facto inequalities are allowed under the legislation and, if so, whether such measures were taken during the reference period.

Question I

Please provide information on the situation in practice covering the four areas specified in the provision, ie. on:

a. the employment situation of both sexes (ie. the number of men and women who are in employment, unemployed, working part-time or on fixed-term contracts or other forms of temporary contracts);

b. access to and participation in vocational guidance, training, retraining and rehabilitation and the extent to which women train for jobs which have traditionally been occupied by men and vice versa;

c. differences in terms of employment and working conditions, including remuneration (with an indication of the differences between full-time workers on permanent contracts and part-time workers or workers on fixed-term contracts or other forms of temporary contracts);

d. differences in career advancement between the sexes in the various sectors of the economy.

Question J

Please indicate what active policies carried out by your authorities to achieve equal opportunities and equal treatment in employment and what practical measures have been taken to implement these policies.

Question K

Please indicate if social security matters as well as provisions concerning unemployment benefit, old age benefit and survivor's benefit are considered to be within the scope of this provision.

Article 21: The right to information and consultation

"With a view to ensuring the effective exercise of the right of workers to be informed and consulted within the undertaking, the Parties undertake to adopt or encourage measures enabling workers or their representatives, in accordance with national legislation and practice:

a. to be informed regularly or at the appropriate time and in a comprehensible way about the economic and financial situation of the undertaking employing them, on the understanding that the disclosure of certain information which could be prejudicial to the undertaking may be refused or subject to confidentiality; and

b. to be consulted in good time on proposed decisions which could substantially affect the interests of workers, particularly on those decisions which could have an important impact on the employment situation in the undertaking."

Question A

Please describe the rules and/or the mechanisms whereby the right of workers to information and consultation within the undertaking either directly or through their representatives is guaranteed, for example through legislation, collective agreements or other means.

Please indicate by whom and on what basis the workers' representatives are designated.

Question B

Please indicate the nature of the information to be supplied on the economic and financial situation of the undertaking, and its frequency. Please indicate the nature and substance of the consultation on decisions which might affect workers' interests, as well the timing. If the rules are determined by collective agreement, please provide information concerning the main agreements.

Question C

Please indicate any exceptions applying to the obligation to supply information, whether they concern a right to refuse to give certain information or confidentiality rules referred to in Article 21 para. a.

Question D[1]

If some workers are not covered by provisions of this type either by legislation, collective agreements or other measures, please indicate the percentage of workers not so covered.

---

1. See Article I and the appendix thereto.

Question E[1]

Please indicate whether certain undertakings are excluded from the obligation of information and consultation on the grounds that they employ less than a certain number of workers. If so, please state the specified number of workers below which undertakings are not required to comply with this provision.

Question F

Please indicate whether there are certain undertakings, such as religious undertakings or other undertakings within the meaning of paragraph 4 of the appendix to Article 21, excluded from the rights guaranteed in this provision. If so please provide details on this subject.

Question G

Please describe the legal remedies available to workers or their representatives who consider that their rights under this provision have not been respected, and please indicate the applicable sanctions.

Article 22: The right to take part in the determination and improvement of the working conditions and working environment

> *"With a view to ensuring the effective exercise of the right of workers to take part in the determination and improvement of the working conditions and working environment in the undertaking, the Parties undertake to adopt or encourage measures enabling workers or their representatives, in accordance with national legislation and practice, to contribute:*
>
> a. *to the determination and the improvement of the working conditions, work organisation and working environment;*
>
> b. *to the protection of health and safety within the undertaking;*
>
> c. *to the organisation of social and socio-cultural services and facilities within the undertaking;*
>
> d. *to the supervision of the observance of regulations on these matters."*

Question A

Please describe the rules and/or the mechanisms whereby the right of workers to information and consultation within the undertaking either directly or through their representatives is guaranteed, for example through legislation, collective agreements or other means.

Please indicate by whom and on what basis the workers' representatives are designated.

---

1. See paragraph 6 of the appendix to Article 21.

Question B

Please state whether workers' participation concerns all of the areas covered by Article 22:

– the determination and improvement of the working conditions, work organisation and working environment;

– the protection of health and safety within the undertaking;

– the organisation of social and socio-cultural services within the undertaking;

– the supervision of the observance of regulations on these matters.

Question C[1]

If some workers are not covered by provisions of this type either by legislation, collective agreements or other measures, please indicate the proportion of workers not so covered.

Question D[2]

Please indicate whether certain undertakings are excluded from the obligations contained in Article 22 on the grounds that they employ less than a certain number of workers. If so, please state the specified number of workers below which undertakings are not required to comply with these provisions.

Question E

Please indicate whether there are certain undertakings, such as religious undertakings or other undertakings within the meaning of para. 4 of the appendix to Article 22, excluded from the rights guaranteed in this provision. If so please provide details on this subject.

Question F

Please describe the legal remedies available to workers or their representatives who consider that their rights under this provision have not been respected. Please indicate the applicable sanctions.

Article 23: The right of elderly persons to social protection

> *"With a view to ensuring the effective exercise of the right of elderly persons to social protection, the Parties undertake to adopt or encourage, either directly or in co-operation with public or private organisations, appropriate measures designed in particular:*
>
> *– to enable elderly persons to remain full members of society for as long as possible, by means of:*
>
> *a. adequate resources enabling them to lead a decent life and play an active part in public, social and cultural life;*

---

1. See Article I and the appendix thereto.
2. See paragraph 6 of the appendix to Article 22.

b. *provision of information about services and facilities available for elderly persons and their opportunities to make use of them;*

– *to enable elderly persons to choose their life-style freely and to lead independent lives in their familiar surrounding for as long as they wish and are able, by means of:*

a. *provision of housing suited to their needs and their state of health or of adequate support for adapting their housing;*

b. *the health care and the services necessitated by their state;*

– *to guarantee elderly persons living in institutions appropriate support, while respecting their privacy, and participation in decisions concerning living conditions in the institution."*

Question A

Please describe the measures of social protection and the social services in your country to enable elderly persons to remain full members of society as long as possible.

Question B

Please indicate the measures taken to ensure that elderly persons have adequate monetary and non-monetary resources within the meaning of this provision.

Question C

Please provide information on total public expenditure during the reference period on social protection and social services for the elderly.

Question D

Please indicate by which ways information about the services and facilities available for elderly persons are provided to the persons concerned.

Question E

Please describe the measures taken to enable elderly persons to choose their life-style freely and to lead independent lives in their familiar surroundings for as long as they wish and are able, in particular by means of:

a. provision of housing suited to their needs and their state of health or adequate support for adapting their housing;

b. the health care and any other services in the home necessitated by their state.

Question F

If private services exist, please describe the forms of co-operation between public and private services in the are covered by this provision.

Question G

Please provide information on the number of elderly living in institutions, public or private, giving as far as possible the number of institutions and their staff and on the availability of places in relation to the number of applications. Please also indicate what form of assistance is granted to elderly persons living in institutions (eg. covering the costs of their stay).

Question H

Please provide information on any regulations applicable to institutions for the elderly, public or private, including procedures observed when institutionalising elderly persons.

Please indicate how control of these institutions is carried out.

Question I

Please indicate the measures taken to guarantee respect for the privacy of elderly persons in institutions and their participation in decisions concerning living conditions in such institutions.

Article 24: The right to protection in cases of termination of employment

> *"With a view to ensuring the effective exercise of the right of workers to protection in cases of termination of employment, the Parties undertake to recognise:*
>
> a. *the right of all workers not to have their employment terminated without valid reasons for such termination connected with their capacity or conduct or based on the operational requirements of the undertaking, establishment or service;*
>
> b. *the right of workers whose employment is terminated without valid reason to adequate compensation or other appropriate relief.*
>
> *To this end, the Parties undertake to ensure that a worker who considers that his employment has been terminated without a valid reason shall have the right to appeal to an impartial body."*

Question A

Please state the valid grounds for termination of employment provided by national legislation and whether national legislation prohibits certain cases of termination of employment[1].

Please specify whether these grounds appear in legislation or regulations or whether they are derived from court decisions or other sources and provide examples of case law on this point.

---

1. See paras. 1 and 3 of the Appendix to Article 24.

Please state whether termination of employment is notified in writing, and if so, whether the employer is required to state the reasons for dismissal in the notification.

Please state what are the workers' rights in cases of unilateral amendments by the employer to the substantive conditions of the employment contract.

Question B

Please state whether workers who consider that they have been dismissed without valid reason have a right of appeal to a tribunal or an impartial authority.

Please indicate the time-limit which workers must observe to exercise this right of appeal.

Please state where the burden of proof lies.

Question C

If the court or tribunal to which the appeal lies considers that the termination of employment is unjustified, please indicate whether the worker is entitled to adequate damages (and describe how the level of damages is determined) or to any other form of compensation (and indicate what such compensation consists of).

Inasmuch as the remedy for unfair or unlawful termination of employment is monetary, please indicate:

a. whether this applies to all enterprises, regardless of their size;

b. whether there is a minimum level of damages;

c. whether the choice of damages (instead of reinstatement) is left to the worker, the employer or the court.

Question D

Please list the categories of workers excluded from this protection and indicate how they are in conformity with item 2 of the Appendix to Article 24.

If workers who are employed under a fixed-term contract are excluded (item 2 of the Appendix to Article 24) from this protection, please provide a definition of a fixed-term contract.

If there is a trial period of employment for this protection, please indicate its length.

Article 25: The right of workers to the protection of their claims in the event of the insolency of their employer

> "With a view to ensuring the effective exercise of the right of workers to the protection of their claims in the event of the insolvency of their employer, the Parties undertake to provide that workers'

claims arising from contracts of employment or employment relationships be guaranteed by a guarantee institution or by any other effective form of protection."

Question A

Please indicate whether workers' claims in the event of the insolvency of their employer, are secured by means of a guarantee institution, a privilege, a combination thereof or by other means.

Question B

Please state how the term "insolvency" has been defined and to which situations it has been applied.

Question C[1]

Please indicate which claims are protected in case of the insolvency of the employer.

Question D

Please indicate whether there are any categories of workers not covered by the protection offered in this field by reason of the special nature of their employment relationship.

Question E

Please indicate whether workers' claims are limited to a prescribed amount. If so, state what the amount is and how it is determined.

Article 26: The right to dignity at work

Please indicate how organisations of employers and workers are consulted by the authorities on the measures required to implement each of the paragraphs of Article 26 (procedure and level of consultation, content, and frequency of consultation).

Article 26 para. 1

"With a view to ensuring the effective exercise of the right of all workers to protection of their dignity at work, the Parties undertake, in consultation with employers' and workers' organisations:

to promote awareness, information and prevention of sexual harassment in the workplace or in relation to work and to take all appropriate measures to protect workers from such conduct;"

Question A

Please indicate which forms of behaviour are considered as sexual harassment.

---

1. See paragraph 3 of the appendix to Article 25.

Question B

Please indicate what awareness-raising, information and preventive activities to counter sexual harassment at work or in relation to work are carried out (eg. description, target groups, expenditure, etc.).

Please indicate the role of the employer in preventing and combating sexual harassment. Please provide details with regard to training schemes, publications and infrastructures that exist and that employers put into place in order to effectively combat sexually harassing behaviour.

Please indicate any specialised infrastructures to receive and deal with complaints against such behaviour (eg. ombudsman, counselling, etc.).

Question C

Please describe any protective measures undertaken to prevent sexual harassment in the workplace and indicate whether any sanctions are provided by law against such behaviour (in particular financial and other compensation).

Please give details on the relevant court procedures, indicating where the burden of proof lies.

Please indicate the employers' liabilities in case of recorded sexual harassment at the workplace.

Question D

Please indicate if reinstatement is provided in cases of dismissal or voluntary resignation as a result of sexual harassment at work or in relation to work and in cases where reinstatement is not possible, please indicate the amount of the damages awarded. Please specify the measures provided to combat any form of retaliation following a sexual harassment claim.

Article 26 para. 2

"With a view to ensuring the effective exercise of the right of all workers to protection of their dignity at work, the Parties undertake, in consultation with employers' and workers' organisations:

to promote awareness, information and prevention of recurrent reprehensible or distinctly negative and offensive actions directed against individual workers in the workplace or in relation to work and to take all appropriate measures to protect workers from such conduct".

Question A

Please indicate which forms of behaviour are considered as reprehensible or distinctly negative and offensive actions directed against individual workers.

Question B

Please indicate any prejudicial actions against workers' dignity other than sexual harassment, which are recognised and combated through different measures such as legislation, regulations, collective agreements, etc.

Question C

Please answer the questions B to D of paragraph 1 with respect to reprehensible or distinctly negative and offensive actions directed against workers other than sexual harassment.

Article 27: The right of workers with family responsabilities to equal opportunities and equal treatment

Article 27 para. 1[1]:

> *"With a view to ensuring the exercise of the right to equal opportunity and treatment for men and women workers with family responsibilities and between such workers and other workers, the Parties undertake:*
>
> *to take appropriate measures:*
>
> a. *to enable workers with family responsibilities to enter and remain in employment, as well as to re-enter employment after an absence due to those responsibilities, including measures in the field of vocational guidance and training;*
>
> b. *to take account of their needs in terms of conditions of employment and social security;*
>
> c. *to develop or promote services, public or private in particular child daycare services and other childcare arrangements;"*

Question A

Please describe the measures taken to implement this provision, in particular the measures taken in the field of vocational guidance and training, including retraining.

Question B

Please describe the measures taken to implement this provision, especially measures concerning the length and organisation of working time.

Please indicate the measures taken to allow workers with family responsibilities who so wish to work part-time and to allow them to return to full-time employment. Where appropriate, please describe the rules applying to these different forms of work, their supervision and the applicable social protection (please specify in particular qual-

---

1. See appendix to Article 27.

ifying conditions for social security, the benefits which these workers may claim, etc.).

Question C

Please indicate the services (public or private, in particular child day-care services and other childcare arrangements) available to workers with family responsibilities, stating their nature and capacity.

Please indicate how the quality of these services is assured (approval procedure, supervisory system, staff training, etc.) as well as access (cost and geographical location across the national territory).

Please indicate the measures taken to promote access to these services for low-income families.

Article 27 para. 2

"With a view to ensuring the exercise of the right to equal opportunity and treatment for men and women workers with family responsibilities and between such workers and other workers, the Parties undertake:

to provide a possibility for either parent to obtain, during a period after maternity leave, parental leave to take care of a child, the duration and conditions of which should be determined by national legislation, collective agreements or practice;"

Please indicate the statutory provisions or other provisions that ensure parental leave. Where collective agreements are concerned, please indicate the sectors in which such leave is provided. Please indicate the length of this leave and the practical conditions governing it (eligibility, apportionment, payment).

Please provide information on the extent to which men and women take parental leave. Please indicate if the two parents may take parental leave at the same time.

Article 27 para. 3

"With a view to ensuring the exercise of the right to equal opportunity and treatment for men and women workers with family responsibilities and between such workers and other workers, the Parties undertake:

to ensure that family responsibilities shall not, as such, constitute a valid reason for termination of employment".

Please indicate the statutory provisions that ensure the application of this provision and provide any relevant decisions delivered by the competent national courts.

Please specify the guarantees provided for a person dismissed because of their family responsibilities.

Article 28: The right of workers' representatives to protection in the undertaking and facilities to be accorded to them

"With a view to ensuring the effective exercise of the right of workers' representatives to carry out their functions, the Parties undertake to ensures that in the undertaking:

a. *they enjoy effective protection against acts prejudicial to them, including dismissal, based on their status or activities as workers' representatives within the undertaking;*

b. *they are afforded such facilities as may be appropriate in order to enable them to carry out their functions promptly and efficiently, account being taken of the industrial relations system of the country and the needs, size and capabilities of the undertaking concerned".*

Question A

Please indicate all forms of worker representation in the undertaking provided in law, with details on any variations which may apply by economic sector or size of undertaking and indicate how workers' representatives are designated.

Question B

Please indicate how effective protection is ensured to workers' representatives in the undertaking against any act prejudicial to them on the grounds of their status or activities as workers' representatives in the undertaking (general or specific legal provisions, etc.).

Question C

Please describe the legal remedies available to workers' representatives who consider they have suffered acts prejudicial to them on the grounds of their status or activities as workers' representatives. In these cases please indicate where the burden of proof lies.

Question D

Please indicate the facilities provided for in law, in collective agreements or in practice for workers' representatives to enable them to carry out their functions promptly and efficiently. Please describe any additional provision made in collective agreements, and provide representative examples. Please indicate also any restrictions or exemptions permitted in law or commonly accepted in collective agreements.

Article 29: The right to information and consultation in collective redundancy procedures

"With a view to ensuring the effective exercise of the right of workers to be informed and consulted in situations of collective redundancies, the Parties undertake to ensure that employers shall inform and consult workers' representatives, in good time prior to such collective redundancies, on ways and means of avoiding*

> *collective redundancies or limiting their occurrence and mitigating their consequences, for example by recourse to accompanying social measures aimed, in particular, at aid for the redeployment or retraining of the workers concerned."*

Question A

Please state whether, and if so, how collective redundancy is defined in national law.

Question B

Please describe the procedures pertaining to information and consultation of workers' representatives and indicate in particular:

a. whether information and consultation should take place prior to collective redundancies and, if so, whether this requirement is respected in practice;

b. the types of workers' representatives (elected representatives and/or union representatives) informed and consulted, specifying what is the situation in enterprises where the number of employees does not attain the minimum requiring the establishment of a representative body of workers;

c. the various stages of the information and consultation procedures;

d. how consultation contributes to avoiding or reducing collective redundancies or to mitigating their consequences specifying in particular whether it must result in an agreement and what are the obligations of the employer with a view to enabling workers' representatives to put forward proposals.

Question C

Please indicate what are the sanctions provided for in cases where information and consultation procedures are not complied with. Please also indicate the means of appeal available to workers' representatives in case of default by the employer as well as the possibilities of intervention by the public authorities.

Please indicate the courses of action open to workers on an individual basis in cases of breach of the rules relating to collective dismissals, as well as the consequences of such a breach in their regard.

Article 30: The right to protection against poverty and social exclusion
> *"With a view to ensuring the effective exercise of the right to protection against poverty and social exclusion, the Parties undertake:*
>
> a. *to take measures within the framework of an overall and co-ordinated approach to promote the effective access of persons who live or risk living in a situation of social exclusion or poverty, as well as their families, to, in particular, employment, housing, training, education, culture and social and medical assistance;*

b. *to review these measures with a view to their adaptation if necessary."*

Question A

If there is an official poverty line please describe its main methodological features. If not, please indicate the methodology followed or criteria used to measure poverty.

Please indicate the methodology followed or criteria used to measure social exclusion.

Please provide information taken from studies or enquiries concerning the nature and extent of poverty and social exclusion showing the number of persons and/or households who are socially excluded or live in poverty (if possible broken down according to sex, age, family characteristics, regional situations, etc.).

Question B

Please describe the global and co-ordinated approach taken to prevent and combat poverty and social exclusion, indicating:

a. the measures implemented in particular to promote the employment of persons who are, or who risk being in a situation of poverty or social exclusion;[1]

b. the methodology and level of funding devoted to this policy;

c. the number of beneficiaries and the results obtained.

Question C

Please provide information on whether and how poverty and social exclusion measures are monitored and evaluated with a view to their adaptation if necessary.

Question D

Please indicate whether and how the social partners and the relevant non-governmental organisations participate in the formulation, implementation, evaluation and adaptation of measures to combat poverty and social exclusion.

Article 31: The right to housing

Article 31 para. 1

"With a view to ensuring the effective exercise of the right to housing, the Parties undertake to take measures designed:

to promote access to housing of an adequate standard;"

---

1. The reply may contain references to information submitted under other provisions of the revised Social Charter.

Question A

Please indicate whether there is a right to adequate housing. If so, please indicate the legal basis, supply the relevant texts and describe any significant case law.

Question B

Please indicate the measures taken to promote access to adequate housing especially for:

a. families, particularly single-parent families and large families;

b. vulnerable groups such as persons with disabilities and elderly persons;

c. homeless persons;

d. migrants.

Question C

Please indicate whether there is a nationality condition, or a length of residence requirement, imposed on beneficiaries of state schemes in this field. Please indicate whether nationals from other Parties are subject to any additional conditions of eligibility.

Question D

Please indicate the level of state funding in this area, the various forms of housing aid, the number of applicants and the number of beneficiaries.

Question E

Please describe the obligatory standards that apply in relation to housing quality.

Please provide information on the extent to which sub-standard dwellings exist. Please indicate what measures are taken to improve housing standards, especially in public-owned housing stock.

Please describe the means by which compliance with housing standards is ensured in practice.

> *Article 31 para. 2*
>
> *"With a view to ensuring the effective exercise of the right to housing, the Parties undertake to take measures designed:*
>
> *to prevent and reduce homelessness with a view to its gradual elimination;"*

Question A

Please provide where possible information on the number of homeless persons, indicating where possible the number of children and young persons, elderly persons, persons with disabilities, and nationals of other Parties.

Question B

Please indicate what measures are taken to prevent homelessness. Please indicate the total expenditure reserved for this purpose.

Please describe existing legal protection in cases of eviction for non-payment of rent and repossession.

Question C[1]

Please indicate what measures are taken to reduce homelessness, with particular emphasis on long-term solutions to this problem.

Please indicate whether there is a right to adequate housing. If so, please indicate the legal basis, supply the relevant texts and describe any significant case law.

Please indicate the role of voluntary organisations in this field.

> *Article 31 para. 3*
>
> *"With a view to ensuring the effective exercise of the right to housing, the Parties undertake to take measures designed:*
>
> *to make the price of housing accessible to those without adequate resources."*

Question A

Please describe the measures taken in your country to make the price of housing accessible to those without adequate resources (housing benefit, reduced-rate loans, tenancy buy-out options, etc.). Please indicate the amounts of public funds reserved for this purpose.

Question B

Please indicate the criteria applied to identify persons without adequate resources.

Please indicate whether, where a person meets the criteria, they are entitled to assistance in accessing housing as of right. Please indicate whether they may challenge an unfavourable decision before the courts on both procedural and substantive grounds.

Please indicate the number of persons who apply for such assistance and the number who benefit.

Question C

Please indicate whether there is preferential treatment for any group such as homeless persons, large families, persons with disabilities, elderly persons, single parents, and migrant workers.[2]

---

1. Reference may be made to information supplied under Article 31 para. 1.
2. Reference may be made to information supplied under Article 31 para. 1.

Question D

Please indicate whether nationals of other Parties are subject to any additional conditions.

Question E

Please indicate annual trends in housing prices (sale and rental), including significant regional variations where appropriate.

IX. Supervision of the application of the European Social Charter

A. Supervision relating to the reports submitted under Article 21 of the Charter

1. First supervision cycle

Committee of Independent Experts – Conclusions I (1970, 281 p., ISBN: 92-871-0177-9)

Governmental Committee First report (1971, 60 p. ref: CG/Ch. Soc(70)24 Final)

Consultative Assembly of the Council of Europe (Twenty-third ordinary session)

Opinion No. 57 (1971)[1] on the application of the European Social Charter

The Assembly,

1. Having regard to Part IV of the European Social Charter, and particularly to Articles 28 and 29;

2. After examining the report of the independent experts, and having regard, in addition, to the first report of the Governmental Committee on the European Social Charter transmitted to the Assembly for information by the Committee of Ministers;

3. Considering that, in playing its part in the supervision of the application of the European Social Charter, the Assembly is free to express its own opinion on the reports of the independent or government experts forwarded to it;

4. Noting that none of the national organisations of employers and trade unions referred to in Articles 23 and 24 of the Charter have made any comments on the governmental reports, requests the Committee of Ministers to invite governments to promote the effective application of those articles;

5. Considering that the independent experts must be praised for the remarkable legal work they have accomplished and for the way in which they fulfilled their obligations, and that approval should be given of the procedure and the method adopted by them and of the way in which they have approached the task assigned to them of making an independent and objective appraisal of the conformity of the national legislation, regulations and practices of the

---

1. Assembly debate on 14 May 1971 (7th sitting) (see Doc. 2943, report of the Committee on Social and Health Questions).
   Text adopted by the Assembly on 14 May 1971 (7th sitting).

States concerned with the provisions of the Charter which those States solemnly undertook to observe at the time of ratification;

6. Considering that the independent experts, in the terms laid down for them under Part I of the Charter, are particularly well qualified to appraise, for the purely legal point of view, the compatibility of national regulations and practices with the provisions of the Charter, and that it lies within their province to propose that observations and recommendations should be sent to the States concerned;

7. Emphasises that the comments and the proposals for recommendations made by the Committee of Independent Experts are fully justified in terms of the objective findings set out in their report, and that they should, in principle, be communicated to that governments concerned with a reminder that the undertakings entered into must be fully observed, as is the case with any treaty, if the way is not to be opened up to the gradual deterioration of the instrument of international law which the Charter represents;

8. Recognising that in the early stages of the application of the Charter the governments concerned may have interpreted some of its provisions in a way which was not fully in accord with the obligations they entail;

9. Convinced, nevertheless, that the procedure for the supervision of the application of the Charter will ensure the uniform interpretation of the undertakings embodied in it;

10. Persuaded that the provisions of the Charter should not, save where specifically stated in the Charter itself, and in conformity with the general principles of public international law, be regarded as a mere reiteration of undertakings contained in other legal instruments of a treaty nature which are not only applied in a different context and subscribed to by a group of States other than those of the Council of Europe, as for example International Labour Convention No. 100 concerning equal remunerations for men and women workers for work of equal value, but which also occur in political contexts other than that constituted by the States contracting to the Charter;

11. Considering that the role of the independent experts is to make a legal examination of the States' reports in order to ascertain whether or not national regulations conform to the accepted provisions, without regard for any considerations of interpretation bound up with the interests of political expediency;

12. Recalling its Recommendation 454 (1966) on the uniform interpretation of treaties, and emphasising that, there being no obligation to ratify, the rules ratified must be formally observed, and that, in the absence of any provision to the contrary in the Charter itself, its provisions must be interpreted in the same way

by all the States concerned, since otherwise there would cease to be any internationally agreed commitment,

13. Requests the Committee of Ministers to transmit this opinion and the accompanying explanatory memorandum to all member States, and not only to those directly concerned;

14. Proposes that, in the special circumstances governing this initial stage of the supervision of the application of the Charter, the Committee of Ministers should forward the independent experts' conclusions to the States concerned in toto, commending the comments contained therein as well as the proposals for recommendations to their attention, and calling upon them to take full note of them, so that when examining subsequent biennial reports the independent experts may be able to see that national rules and practices conform to the terms of the Charter;

15. Urges that also in future the conclusions of the independent experts, as well as the report of the Governmental Committee, be transmitted to it, as soon as each of these documents is available, so that it may examine them in detail with a view to accomplishing the task entrusted to it under the terms of Articles 28 and 29 of the Charter.

16. Considers that Article 22 of the Charter should be implemented immediately so that the various bodies may have at their disposal all the information they need in order to appraise the progressive application of the Charter, in pursuance of Part 1 and of Article 20 (3).

Committee of Ministers

Resolution (71) 30
(Adopted by the Ministers' Deputies on 12 November 1971)

The Committee of Ministers,

Having regard to the European Social Charter, and in particular to the provisions of Part IV thereof;

Having taken note of the Conclusions of the Committee of Independent Experts and of the valuable observations on which they are based, the report of the Governmental Committee on the European Social Charter, and the opinion of the Consultative Assembly on the supervision of the application of the Charter;

Expressing its satisfaction with the manner in which the Committee of Independent Experts and the Governmental Committee carried out their respective functions, and its appreciation of the interest shown by the Consultative Assembly;

Recalling that the procedure which has just been completed covered for the first time the entire system which has been established to consider the comprehensive reports which Contracting Parties rendered under the provisions of Article 21 of the Charter, and, in consequence, considering that it would not be opportune for it to make a judgement at this stage on the different observations formulated in this context,

Decides:

I.   in accordance with the report of the Governmental Committee, not to address at this stage any recommendations to the Contracting Parties to the European Social Charter;

II. to transmit to the governments of the Contracting Parties the report of the Governmental Committee and the opinion of the Assembly;

III. to transmit also to the same governments the Conclusions of the Committee of Independent Experts including the analysis made by that committee, offering useful guidance which may assist in achieving the full application of the principles enshrined in the European Social Charter.

2. Second supervision cycle

Committee of Independent Experts – Conclusions II (1971, 232 p., ISBN: 92-871-0178-7)

Governmental Committee Second report (1972, 31 p., ref: CG/Ch. Soc(72)40)

Consultative Assembly of the Council of Europe (Twenty-fifth ordinary session)

Opinion No. 64 (1973)[1] *on the application of the European Social Charter*

The Assembly,

1.   Having regard to Part IV of the Social Charter; particularly to Articles 28 and 29;

2.   After examining the conclusions of the Committee of Independent Experts on the supervision of the application of the Charter for 1968-69, and having regard to the second report of the Governmental Committee on the European Social Charter, transmitted to the Assembly in pursuance of the Committee of Ministers' decision of 12 November 1971;

3.   Recalling its opinion No. 57 (1971), on the application of the European Social Charter for the period 1965-67;

4.   Emphasising the importance of the European Social Charter for the achievement of the aims laid down for the Council of Europe in Statute;

---

1. Assembly debate on 26 September 1973 (10th sitting) (see Doc. 3276 revised, report of the Committee on Social and Health Questions). Text adopted by the Assembly on 26 September 1973 (10th sitting).

5. Considering that the Committee of Independent Experts, set up under Articles 24 and 25 of the Charter, has a major part to play, in accordance with these articles, in supervising the application of the Charter by States that have adhered thereto;

6. Considering that the Committee of Independent Experts is to be congratulated yet again on the excellent fashion in which it has fulfilled its functions;

7. Considering that one of the tasks of this committee of experts, which is responsible under the Charter for examining reports sent to the Secretary General of the Council of Europe by the Contracting Parties and submitting its conclusions therein, is to consider how the various provisions of the Charter should be interpreted, and that it may make proposals for recommendations which, after being examined by the Governmental Committee on the European Social Charter and by the Assembly, are submitted to the Committee of Ministers, with which it lies to take the necessary decisions in pursuance of Article 29 of the Charter;

8. Considering that, while the final decision rests with the Committee of Ministers, the other bodies that have a part to play in the supervision procedure may make to the Committee of Ministers any proposals for the implementation of Article 29;

9. Considering that the experts' interpretations of the various provisions of the Charter are to be regarded as highly authoritative opinions, not to be disregarded without overriding reasons;

10. Considering that the provisions of the Social Charter, which is an international treaty, are binding on all States that have accepted them and must be interpreted in a uniform fashion by all the States concerned;

11. Considering that the experts' report shows that the government reports received at the end of the second 2-year period are distinctly better and more comprehensive than the first reports, and that a number of States have amended their legislation and administrative regulations in order to comply with their obligations under the Social Charter, or are preparing to do so;

12. Expressing satisfaction at the progress achieved as a result of the supervision procedure since the Charter came into force;

13. Noting that the experts' comments are thus a driving force in the improvement of social legislation in States that have ratified the Charter, and serve as a valuable aid to these States in their striving for social progress.

14. Having taken note of the proposals for recommendations presented by the Committee of Independent Experts, and considering that Article 29 of the Charter should in principle be applied

whenever a State has failed, in whole or in part, to comply with one of the provisions of the Charter accepted by it;

15. Considering, however, that when the States in question are clearly endeavouring to make good any gaps in their laws or imperfections in their practice, or when these gaps are of minor importance, it does not seem expedient automatically to address formal recommendations to the States concerned, and considering that in such cases the Committee of Ministers might submit the experts' observations in the form of "suggestions", reserving the right to make recommendations at a later stage if the situation remains unchanged;

16. Considering that the procedure has already been facilitated by the fact that the committee of experts has adopted the practice of instructing the Secretariat to seek further information from governments whenever it is unable to ascertain for certain whether or not a State has satisfied the undertakings entered into, but that such a practice is unnecessary in cases where the committee already possesses perfectly clear information showing a failure to comply with one of the provisions accepted;

17. Recalling that, as previously suggested by the governmental committee and the Assembly, the Committee of Ministers decided by Resolution (71) 30 not to make any recommendations to Contracting Parties at a stage when the procedure covered for the first time the entire system established for the examination of reports, but considering that the situation is different now that the second period of supervision has been completed;

18. Considering, therefore, that recommendations should now be made to various States on the application of certain provisions of the Charter;

19. Considering that, as statistics are essential for effective supervision, governments should do everything possible to furnish the supervisory bodies with the statistical data they need to carry out their tasks, and that such statistics should not be regarded as confidential;

20. Considering that the time has also come to implement Article 22 of the Charter, so that Contracting Parties may be asked to provide, on lines indicated by the Committee of Ministers, reports on certain of the provisions of the Charter not yet accepted by them,

21. Requests that the Committee of Ministers transmit this opinion and the accompanying explanatory memorandum to all member states;

22. Proposes that the Committee of Ministers make recommendations to the States in question on the application of certain particularly important provisions of the Charter, namely Article 1 (2), Article 2 (1), (3), (4) and (5), Article 3 (2), Article 5 and Article 6 (4),

on the lines indicated in the explanatory memorandum to this opinion;

23. Proposes to the Committee of Ministers that the proposals for recommendations drawn up by the Committee of Independent Experts be transmitted to the States concerned in the form of suggestions, except where otherwise specified in the accompanying explanatory memorandum;

24. Proposes that the Committee of Ministers implement the procedure set forth in Article 22 of the Charter, particularly as regards the application of Articles 4 (3), 7 (1) and 8;

25. Urges that the national organisations of employers and trade unions referred to in Article 23 of the Charter make use of the right conferred on them therein, and requests that the Committee of Ministers ask governments to approach such organisations to that end.

Committee of Ministers

Resolution (74) on the implementation of the European Social Charter during the period 1968-69
(Adopted by the Committee of Ministers on 29 May 1974 at the 232nd meeting of the Ministers' Deputies)

The Committee of Ministers,

Having regard to the European Social Charter and in particular to the provisions of Part IV thereof;

Having taken note with satisfaction of the second report of the Governmental Committee to which Conclusions II of the Committee of Independent Experts are appended, as well as of Opinion No. 64 of the Consultative Assembly, concerning the first report submitted by the Government of Cyprus and the reports submitted by Sweden and the United Kingdom, for the period 1968-69;

Acting in pursuance of Article 29 of the Charter,

1. Decides to transmit to the governments of these states Conclusions II of the Committee of Independent Experts, the second report of the Governmental Committee, as well as Opinion No. 64 of the Consultative Assembly;

2. Draws the attention of the governments of these states to the observations formulated in the documents mentioned under 1 above, especially as regards the action required to make their national legislation and practice comply with the obligations deriving from the Charter.

3. Third supervision cycle

Committee of Independent Experts – Conclusions III (1973, 260 p., ISBN: 92-871-0181-7)

Governmental Committee Third report (1974, 18 p., ref: CG/Ch. Soc(74)14)

Parliamentary Assembly of the Council of Europe (twenty-seventh ordinary session)

> *Opinion No. 71 (1975)[1] on the third period of supervision of the application of the European Social Charter*

The Assembly,

1. Having regard to Part IV of the European Social Charter, and especially to Articles 28 and 29;

2. Having examined the conclusions of the Committee of Independent Experts on the supervision of the application of the Charter during the period 1970-71, and having also taken the third report of the Governmental Committee on the European Social Charter into consideration;

3. Recalling the terms of its Opinions No. 57 (1971) and No. 64 (1973), on the supervision of the application of the Charter over the first two 2-year periods,

4. Expresses its acute disappointment that the Committee of Ministers should have taken virtually no action to implement the most important proposals contained in the Assembly's opinion and, in particular, made no recommendations to Contracting Parties under Article 29 of the Charter, nor even any precise suggestion regarding the failure of certain national laws or practices to comply with the provisions of the Social Charter accepted by those Contracting Parties;

5. Again emphasises that the interpretations given by the independent experts are to be regarded as highly authoritative opinions, from which one should not depart without overriding reasons;

6. Urges the Committee of Ministers most strongly to make recommendations to the following states for the strict application of the Social Charter:

   – Austria, on the application of Article 8 paragraph 2, and Article 19, paragraph 6

   – Cyprus, on the application of Article 12, paragraph 2;

   – Denmark, on the application of Article 8, paragraph 1;

---

1. Assembly debate on 22 April 1975 (3rd sitting) (see Doc. 3592, report of the Committee on Social and Health Questions).
Text adopted by the Assembly on 22 April 1975 (3rd sitting).

- Ireland, on the application of Article 1, paragraph 2, Article 8, paragraph 1, and Article 18, paragraphs 2 and 3;

- Italy, on the application of Article 8, paragraph 2, and Article 13, paragraph 1;

- Norway, on the application of Article 19, paragraph 6;

- the United Kingdom on the application of Article 8, paragraph 1, Article 19 paragraphs 2 and 3, and Article 19, paragraph 6;

7. Proposes that the Committee of Ministers should invite the states concerned to make their national legislation and practice conform to the provisions of the Charter in the instances referred to in the preceding paragraph, and appoint a period at the end of which they would be required to report on the measures taken to that end;

8. Proposes that the Committee of Ministers should communicate to the states concerned, by way of suggestions, the other observations of the Committee of Independent Experts, and in particular to Italy, Norway and Sweden those relating to the application of Article 4, paragraph 3, of the Charter, concerning the right of men and women workers to equal pay for work of equal value;

9. Reiterates its proposal that the Committee of Ministers should put into practice the procedure provided for in Article 22 of the Charter;

10. Expressly draws the attention of the Committee of Ministers to the considerations set out in the explanatory memorandum to this opinion (Doc. 3592), and in particular to paragraphs 25-27[1]

---

1. 25. The Governmental Committee suggests ways in which the workload of Contracting Parties and the supervisory organs could be reduced without amendment to the Charter of prejudice to its implementation.
It proposes that supervision of provisions accepted in Part II of the Charter be spread over six years, a detailed study being made of only one third of the provisions every two years. Every two years governments would be asked to submit a detailed report only on the accepted provisions which were to be thoroughly examined by the supervisory organs in the course of the period in question; in respect of other accepted provisions, they would supply a brief general report in which, if they wished, they could include information about any changes they considered important which had occurred since the previous biennial report. The initial report of any new Contracting Party would, of course, deal in detail with all provisions accepted.
This proposal is highly interesting in so far as it would enable the supervisory bodies to deal more effectively with the many problems arising out of the interpretation and application of the Charter. Whereas it is the task of the committee of experts to study the application of all the provisions in the Charter, neither the Assembly nor the Governmental Committee can do the same and are obliged to confine themselves to a necessarily arbitrary selection. It would therefore be an advantage if the supervisory authorities could concentrate their attention on only some of the provisions in the Charter, so that its application could be studied in stages.

(see next page)

383

which concern modifications to the machinery for supervision of the European Social Charter, and requests that the Committee of Ministers submit officially to the Committee of Independent Experts the proposals of the Governmental Committee in this respect and communicate the conclusions of the Committee of Independent Experts on the matter to the Assembly in order to enable it to give a final opinion on the question.

(continued)

However, important reservations must be made in respect of the Governmental Committee's proposal. First, whenever the committee of experts asked the governments concerned to provide additional information, they should do so in their following report, not six years later. Secondly, the system of biennial reporting is expressly laid down in the Charter and it should in theory cover all provisions that have been accepted. Accordingly, if the Governmental Committee's proposal is put into practice, the states concerned should still inform the Council of Europe organs of any important changes since the preceding report, even if these related to clauses which were not being studied in detail during the period of supervision in question; the provision of such information should therefore continue to be compulsory, and not become optional.

As regards the idea of dividing the Charter's articles into three groups, the Governmental Committee recommends that, in view of the connections between articles, this should be done as follows:
– first 2-year period: Articles 1-4, 9, 10 and 15;
– second 2-year period: Articles 5-8, 18 and 19;
– third 2-year period: Articles 11-14, 16 and 17.

This division is acceptable, but again with the proviso that states should not limit their reports to the provisions under consideration for the period in question but should merely deal in greater detail in their reports with the matters covered by such provisions (which would also enable the supervisory organs to give a fuller opinion on those matters); they should still be required to provide essential information on the other subjects, especially if any changes had occurred in the situation.

26. In addition, the Governmental Committee proposes that reports submitted under Article 22 should be considered at the same time and in connection with the same groups of articles as the more detailed reports presented under Article 21. The Assembly will no doubt be able to support this proposal.

27. The Governmental Committee also wishes the questionnaires sent to governments to be simplified and suggests that, when reporting in accordance with Article 22, governments should no longer have to describe the situation but merely explain why they have not accepted the provision or provisions in question.

The Assembly will undoubtedly appreciate that national administrations should want some simplification of the possibly tedious work devolving on them under Article 21 of the Charter. But it should bear in mind that the Committee of Independent Experts has frequently been unable to assess whether a state has honoured its obligations under the Charter because the information provided by the state's government has not been precise or detailed enough. If the questionnaires are simplified, the situation may become even worse. The Committee of Ministers should therefore be put on its guard against such simplification.

As for the Governmental Committee's proposal, on reporting under Article 22, not only does it appear inexpedient but its compatibility with this provision of the Charter is questionable. If governments were merely asked to state

(see next page)

Committee of Ministers

Resolution (75) 26 on the implementation of the European Social Charter during the period 1970-71 (third cycle of supervision) (Adopted by the Committee of Ministers on 17 October 1975 at the 249th meeting of the Ministers' Deputies)

The Committee of Ministers,

Having regard to the European Social Charter and in particular the provisions of Part IV thereof;

Having noted the Governmental Committee's third report, to which are appended Conclusions III of the Committee of Independent Experts, and Opinion No. 71 of the Consultative Assembly, concerning the first report from the Government of Austria, the second report from the Government of Cyprus and the third series of reports from the Governments of Denmark, the Federal Republic of Germany, Ireland, Italy, Norway, Sweden and the United Kingdom for the period 1970-71;

Acting in accordance with Article 29 of the Charter,

1. Decides to forward to the governments of these states Conclusions III of the Committee of Independent Experts, the Governmental Committee's third report and the Consultative Assembly's Opinion No. 71;

2. Draws the attention of the governments of these states to the comments contained in the documents mentioned in paragraph 1 above, and in particular to items 6, 7 and 8 of the Assembly's opinion, concerning the steps necessary to bring national legislation and practice more closely into line with the obligations ensuing from the Charter.

(continued)

the reasons why they had not accepted this or that provision in the Charter, they would not have to provide any of the desired information on the way in which they were actually applying the Charter's principles, whether or not they had formally accepted them. The Charter specifies that States must provide "reports", not rules laid down in the Charter. The reports have to be sent to employers' organisations and trade unions, and considered by the Committee of Independent Experts, in pursuance of Articles 23 and 24 of the Charter. The conclusions of the committee of experts, which must also deal with the reports, are then submitted to the Assembly and the Governmental Committee for examination. This examination would, however, be very incomplete if, as regards provisions not accepted, it were to be confined to governments' reasons for not accepting such provisions. Besides, if it were necessary for governments merely to state their reasons, it is hard to see why the Charter should have provided for periodic reporting on the subject. It would have been enough to ask governments to give their explanations when ratifying the Charter. The Assembly must therefore urge the Committee of Ministers to ensure that Article 22 is given full effect and that the "reports concerning provisions which are not accepted" (heading of Article 22) are similar in structure to the "reports concerning accepted provisions" (heading of Article 21).

4. Fourth supervision cycle

Committee of Independent Experts – Conclusions IV (1975, 315 p., ISBN: 92-871-0183-3)

Governmental Committee Fourth report (1976, 12 p. ref: CG/Ch. Soc(76)6 Final)

Parliamentary Assembly of the Council of Europe (twenty-ninth ordinary session)

> *Opinion No. 83 (1977)*[1] *on the fourth period of supervision of the application of the European Social Charter*

The Assembly,

1. Having regard to Part IV of the European Social Charter, and especially to Articles 28 and 29;

2. Having examined the conclusions of the Committee of Independent Experts relating to the supervision of the application of the Charter during the period 1972-73, and having also taken the fourth report of the Governmental Committee on the European Social Charter into consideration;

3. Recalling the terms of its previous opinions on the supervision of the application of the Charter over the first three two-year periods, and in particular its Opinion No. 71 (1975), concerning the third cycle of supervision;

4. Welcoming the progress made with the effective application of the Charter by the contracting parties, but finding that in a number of states such application still leaves something to be desired;

5. Welcoming also a recent decision of the Committee of Ministers to put into effect the procedure set out in Article 22 of the Charter, which envisages the submission of reports concerning the provisions of the Charter which contracting parties have not accepted;

6. Whereas the implementation of a whole series of measures advocated by the Charter is of particular importance in a period of recession,

7. Regrets once again that the Committee of Ministers has so far made no formal recommendation to the contracting parties in accordance with Article 29 of the Charter, even in cases where a provision accepted by a contracting party has not been applied;

---

1. Text adopted by the Assembly by the tacit adoption procedure on 26 April 1977. See Doc. 3949, report of the Committee on Social and Health Questions.

8. Recommends that the Committee of Ministers make recommendations to the following states for the strict application of the European Social Charter in respect of the articles mentioned:

   - Austria (Article 8.1);
   - Denmark (Article 8.1);
   - Ireland (Article 2.4 and Article 8.1);
   - Italy (Article 13.1);
   - Norway (Article 19.6);
   - the United Kingdom (Article 8.1 and Article 19.4 and 6);

9. Proposes that the Committee of Ministers, in accordance with Article 29, invite the states concerned to make their legislation and practice conform to the provisions of the Charter in the instances referred to in the preceding paragraph, and appoint a period at the end of which they would be required to report on the measures taken to that end;

10. Proposes that the Committee of Ministers communicate to the states concerned, by way of suggestions, the other observations of the Committee of Independent Experts, and in particular to Austria, Italy, Norway and Sweden those relating to the application of Article 4.3 of the Charter, on the right of men and women workers to equal pay for work of equal value.

Committee of Ministers

> *Resolution (78) 9 on the implementation of the European Social Charter during the period 1972-73 (fourth cycle of supervision) (Adopted by the Committee of Ministers on 2 March 1978 at the 284th meeting of the Ministers' Deputies)*

The Committee of Ministers,

Having regard to the European Social Charter and in particular the provisions of Part IV thereof;

Having noted the Governmental Committee's fourth report, to which are appended Conclusions I of the Committee of Independent Experts, and Opinion No. 83 of the Consultative Assembly concerning the second report from the Government of Austria, the third report from the Government of Cyprus and the fourth series of reports from the Governments of Denmark, the Federal Republic of Germany, Ireland, Italy, Norway, Sweden and the United Kingdom for the period 1972-73;

Acting in accordance with Article 29 of the charter,

1. Decides to forward to the governments of these states Conclusions I of the Committee of Independent Experts, the Governmental Committee's fourth report and the Consultative Assembly's Opinion No. 83;

2. Draws the attention of the governments of these states to the comments contained in the documents mentioned in paragraph 1 above, and in particular to items 8, 9 and 10 of the Assembly's opinion, concerning the steps necessary to bring national legislation and practice more closely into line with the obligations ensuing from the charter.

5. Fifth supervision cycle

Committee of Independent Experts – Conclusions V (1977, 259 p., ISBN: 92-871-0185-X)

Governmental Committee Fifth report (1979, 22 p., ref: CG/Ch. Soc(78)11 Final)

Parliamentary Assembly of the Council of Europe (thirty-first ordinary session)

> *Opinion No. 95 (1971)*[1] *on the fifth period of supervision (1974-75) of the application of the European Social Charter*

The Assembly,

1. Having regard to Part IV of the European Social Charter, and in particular to Articles 28 and 29, dealing with consultation of the Assembly on its application;

2. Having examined the conclusions of the Committee of Independent Experts regarding the supervision of application of the Charter, and particularly Article 4, paragraph 3, Article 5, Article 6 and Article 7, paragraphs 1, 2, 3, and 4, during the period 1974-75 and having also considered the Fifth Report of the Governmental Committee on the European Social Charter;

3. Expressing its satisfaction that the application of the Charter is still being progressively improved by the adoption in various states of laws, regulations and practices bringing national rules into line with the provisions of the Charter;

4. Noting, however, with regret that the Charter is not always fully implemented by states which have ratified it, and regretting the fact that the Committee of Ministers has never made full use of Article 29 of the Social Charter to address recommendations to Contracting Parties who fail to respect their obligations;

5. Agreeing with the committee of experts on the need, at a time of recession, to attach special importance to the provisions of the Charter in connection with action to counter underemployment and unemployment, particularly among young people, and to improve the situation of migrant workers.

---

1. Text adopted by the Standing Committee, acting on behalf of the Assembly, on 28 June 1979. See Doc. 4371, report of the Committee on Social and Health Questions.

6. Considering that it is also important that Contracting Parties be urged to devote their full attention to the proper application of the Charter with regard to equal pay for male and female workers, the right to organise and bargain collectively, and the right of children and adolescents to protection.

7. Recommendations that the Committee of Ministers, with a view to improving the application of the European Social Charter, address recommendations to those countries, namely Austria, Cyprus, Denmark, the Federal Republic of Germany, Ireland, Italy, Norway, Sweden and the United Kingdom, who to some extent do not respect their obligations under it, and further invite early ramifications from the nine member states who have not yet done so.

Committee of Ministers

Resolution ChS (80) 1 concerning the implementation of the European Social Charter during the period 1974-75 (fifth cycle of supervision) (Adopted by the Committee of Ministers on 11 June 1980 at the 320th meeting of the Ministers' Deputies)

The Committee of Ministers, under the terms of Article 29 of the European Social Charter,

Having regard to the European Social Charter and in particular to the provisions of Part IV thereof;

Having taken note of the 5th report of the Governmental Committee, to which Conclusions V of the Committee of Independent Experts are appended, and of Opinion No. 95 of the Consultative Assembly on the 3rd report submitted by the Government of Austria, the 4th report submitted by the Government of Cyprus, the 1st report submitted by the Government of France and the 5th reports submitted by the Governments of Denmark, the Federal Republic of Germany, Ireland, Italy, Norway, Sweden and the United Kingdom for the period 1974-75,

1. Decides to communicate to the governments of these states Conclusions V of the Committee of Independent Experts, the 5th report of the Governmental Committee, and Consultative Assembly Opinion No. 95;

2. Draws the attention of the governments of these states to the observations made in the documents mentioned in paragraph 1 above, in particular those considerations in paragraph 6 of the aforementioned Assembly opinion relating to equal pay for men and women workers (Article 4, paragraph 3, of the Charter), the right to organise (Article 5) and the right of children and young persons to protection (Article 7), concerning which steps may have to be taken in order to bring domestic legislation and practice more fully into line with the obligations ensuing from the Charter.

6. Sixth supervision cycle

Committee of Independent Experts – Conclusions VI (1979, 233 p., ISBN: 92-871-0187-6) and Addendum (1983, 19 p., ISBN: 92-871-0228-7)

Governmental Committee Sixth report (1980, 14 p. ref: T-SG(80)9)

Parliamentary Assembly of the Council of Europe (thirty-third ordinary session)

Opinion No. 106 (1981)[1] *on the sixth period of supervision of the application of the European Social Charter*

The Assembly,

1. Considering that in 1981 the twentieth anniversary of the signature of the European Social Charter will be celebrated;

2. Welcoming in this respect the work already started by the member governments for updating the Social Charter in compliance with Recommendation 839 of the Parliamentary Assembly;

3. Having regard to Part IV of the European Social Charter, and in particular to Articles 28 and 29, dealing with consultation of the Assembly on its application;

4. Having examined the conclusions of the Committee of Independent Experts regarding the supervision of the application of the Charter during the period 1976-77, and particularly Article 1, paragraph 1, Article 1, paragraph 4, in conjunction with Articles 9, 10 and 15, Article 12, and Article 19, paragraphs 4, 6, 8 and 10, and having also considered the sixth report of the Governmental Committee on the European Social Charter;

5. Welcoming the fact that more states have ratified the Social Charter, that other states already bound by the instrument have accepted further obligations, and that the application of the Charter has further improved, thanks to the adoption in various states of new laws, regulations and practices bringing national rules into line with the provisions of the Charter;

6. Noting, however, with regret that the provisions accepted by the states which have ratified the Charter are not always fully applied, and that the Committee of Ministers, whilst having communicated Opinion No. 95 (1979) of the Assembly to the Contracting Parties and having drawn the attention of the governments of these states to the observations made in the opinion, concerning which steps might have to be taken to bring legislation and practice more fully in line with the obligations ensuing from the Charter, has not so far made any specific recommendations to the

---

1. Text adopted by the Standing Committee, acting on behalf of the Assembly, on 1 July 1981. See Doc. 4736, report of the Committee on Social and Health Questions.

governments of Contracting Parties who fail fully to respect their obligations;

7. Considering that it is still necessary, in view of the persistence of the recession, to give special attention to those provisions of the Charter which concern the achievement of full employment, in order to counter unemployment and underemployment, particularly among young people, women and immigrant workers, and to ensure that governments do their utmost to foster vocational guidance, vocational training and vocational resettlement of both nationals and immigrants.

8. Recommends that the Committee of Ministers, with a view to improving the application of the Charter, address recommendations to those countries which do not fully comply with the instrument, and in particular:

a. recommend that the governments of all Contracting Parties adopt policies aimed at achieving and maintaining as high and stable a level of employment as possible, with a view to the attainment of full employment in accordance with Article 1, paragraph 1, of the Charter;

b. address recommendations:

   i. to the Federal Republic of Germany, concerning the application of Article 1, paragraph 4, and Article 10, paragraphs 1 and 2;

   ii. to Austria, Denmark, France, Iceland, Italy, and Norway, to urge them to conclude whatever agreements are necessary to make good certain shortcomings observed in the application of Article 12, paragraph 4;

   iii. to Denmark, the Federal Republic of Germany, Ireland and the United Kingdom, concerning the application of Article 18, paragraphs 2 and 3; to France, concerning the application of Article 18, paragraph 3;

   iv. to France and to the United Kingdom, concerning the application of Article 19, paragraph 4;

   v. to Austria and the United Kingdom, concerning the application of Article 19, paragraph 6;

   vi. to the Federal Republic of Germany, Ireland, Sweden and the United Kingdom, concerning the application of Article 19, paragraph 8;

9. Invites the Committee of Ministers to revise without delay the supervision procedure of the Charter, so as to reduce the time-lag between reference periods of the control and adoption of the final resolutions, which is at present inadmissibly long and, therefore, diminishes the accuracy of the work of the supervision instances.

Committee of Ministers

> *Resolution ChS (82) 1 concerning the implementation of the European Social Charter during the period 1976-77 (sixth cycle of supervision) (Adopted by the Committee of Ministers on 26 March 1982 at the 345th meeting of the Ministers' Deputies)*

The Committee of Ministers,

Referring to the European Social Charter and in particular to the provisions of Part IV thereof;

Having regard to Article 29 of the Charter;

Having taken note of the 6th report of the Governmental Committee set up under Article 27, to which Conclusions V of the Committee of Independent Experts are appended, and of Opinion No. 106 of the Consultative Assembly on the 4th report submitted by the Government of Austria, the 5th report submitted by the Government of Cyprus, the 2nd report submitted by the Government of France and the 6th reports submitted by the Governments of Denmark, The Federal Republic of Germany, Ireland, Italy, Norway, Sweden and the United Kingdom for the period 1976-77,

1. Observes that all these states apply to a very large extent the provisions of the Charter which they have accepted;

2. Decides to communicate to the governments of these states Conclusions V of the Committee of Independent Experts, the 6th report of the Governmental Committee and Consultative Assembly Opinion No. 106;

3. Draws the attention of the governments of these states to the observations made in the documents mentioned in paragraph 2 above, in particular those considerations in paragraph 8 of the aforementioned Assembly Opinion on re-establishing, achieving or maintaining full employment (Article 1, paragraph 1, of the Charter), certain aspects of the international co-ordination of social security systems (Article 12, paragraph 4), the employment of certain categories of migrant workers (Article 18, paragraphs 2 and 3), the situation of certain categories of migrant workers in respect of equality of treatment (Article 19, paragraph 4), certain aspects of family reunion of migrant workers (Article 19, paragraph 6) and of their protection against expulsion (Article 19, paragraph 8), in regard to which steps may have to be taken with a view to bringing domestic legislation, regulations and practice more fully into line with the obligations arising from the Charter.

7. Seventh supervision cycle

Committee of Independent Experts – Conclusions VII (1981, 205 p., ISBN: 92-871-0189-2)

Governmental Committee Seventh report (1982, 27 p., ref: T-SG(82)3)

Parliamentary Assembly of the Council of Europe (thirty-fourth ordinary session)

> *Opinion No. 113 (1983)*[1] *on the seventh period of supervision of the application of the European Social Charter*

The Assembly,

1. Having regard to Part IV of the European Social Charter, notably Articles 28 and 29 on consultation with the Assembly on the application of the Charter;

2. Having examined the conclusions of the Committee of Independent Experts concerning the supervision and application of the Charter during the period 1978-79, and having taken into consideration the 7th Report of the Governmental Committee of the European Social Charter;

3. Noting with satisfaction that all the states which submitted their two-yearly reports for the seventh supervision period have made further progress in the application of the Charter by virtue of the adoption of new statutory requirements and governmental or administrative decisions, and the opening of negotiations between a number of states with a view to new bilateral international agreements;

4. Regretting that no national workers' organisations availed themselves of the right, conferred on such organisations by Article 23 of the Charter, to submit comments on the two-yearly reports by the governments of their respective countries, and that only one employers' organisation submitted such comments;

5. Observing that, despite progress in the application of the Charter by the Contracting Parties, some of the provisions they accepted are still not fully implemented;

6. Observing also that, although there are still certain differences of opinion between the Committee of Independent Experts and the Governmental Committee on the interpretation and application of several provisions of the Charter, the two supervisory bodies expressed convergent views on several issues, ad both admitted that various states were not fully implementing a number of provisions of the Charter;

---

1. Assembly debate on 28 January 1983 (28th Sitting) (see Doc. 4983, report of the Committee on Social and Health Questions). Text adopted by the Assembly on 28 January 1983 (28th sitting).

7. Considering it necessary, for the purpose of ensuring effective supervision and observance of the undertakings given, to draw the attention of the governments of the states in question, pursuant to Article 29 of the Charter, specifically to the application of those provisions of the Charter which both the Committee of Independent Experts and the Governmental Committee consider are not being fully complied with,

8. Accordingly recommends that the Committee of Ministers make specific recommendations, with a view to improving the application of the Charter, to the following states:

    a. Cyprus, Ireland and Italy, in respect of the application of Article 3, paragraph 1; Italy in respect of the application of Article 3, paragraph 2;

    b. Austria and Italy, in respect of the application of Article 8, paragraph 2; Italy and Sweden in respect of the application of Article 8, paragraph 3;

    c. Austria, in respect of the application of Article 10, paragraph 2;

    d. Italy and the United Kingdom, in respect of the application of Article 13, paragraph 1;

    e. The United Kingdom, in respect of the application of Article 15, paragraph 1;

    f. Austria and the United Kingdom, in respect of the application of Article 19, paragraph 6.

Committee of Ministers

> *Resolution ChS (83)1 concerning the implementation of the European Social Charter during the period 1978-79 (seventh period of supervision)*
> *(Adopted by the Committee of Ministers on 23 March 1983 at the 357th meeting of the Ministers' Deputies)*

The Committee of Ministers,

Referring to the European Social Charter and in particular to the provisions of Part IV thereof;

Having regard to Article 29 of the Charter;

Having taken note of the 7th report of the Governmental Committee set up under Article 27 to which Conclusions VII of the Committee of Independent Experts are appended, and of Opinion No. 113 of the Consultative Assembly on the 5th report submitted by the Government of Austria, the 5th report submitted by the Government of Cyprus, the 3rd report submitted by the Government of France and the 7th reports submitted by the Governments of Denmark, the Federal Republic of Germany, Ireland, Italy, Norway, Sweden and the United Kingdom for the period 1978-79,

1. Considers that all these states apply to a very large extent the provisions of the Charter which they have accepted;

2. Decides to communicate to the governments of these states Conclusions VII of the Committee of Independent Experts, the 7th report of the Governmental Committee and Consultative Assembly Opinion No. 113;

3. Draws the attention of the governments of the states concerned to cases not entirely in conformity with the Charter and dealing with the shortness of certain periods of notice for termination of employment (Article 4, paragraph 4, of the Charter), some aspects of the exercise by migrant workers of the right to organise (Article 5 of the Charter), some regulations in respect of the prohibition of children's employment (Article 7, paragraph 1, of the Charter), the access of young foreign boys and girls to apprenticeship facilities (Article 10, paragraph 2, of the Charter) and certain aspects of the family reunion of migrant workers (Article 19, paragraph 6, of the Charter) in regard to which steps may have to be taken with a view to bringing domestic legislation, regulations and practice more fully into line with the obligations arising from the Charter.

8. Eighth supervision cycle

Committee of Independent Experts – Conclusions VIII (1984, 368 p., ISBN: 92-871-0295-3) and Addendum (1985, 23 p., ISBN: 92-871-0786-6)

Governmental Committee Seventh report (1985, 24 p., ref: T-SG(84)17)

Parliamentary Assembly of the Council of Europe (thirty-sixth ordinary session)

> *Opinion No. 121 (1985)*[1] *on the eighth period of supervision of the application of the European Social Charter*

The Assembly,

1. Having regard to Part IV of the European Social Charter, notably Articles 28 and 29 on consultation with the Assembly on the application of the Charter;

2. Having examined the conclusions of the Committee of Independent Experts concerning the supervision and application of the Charter during the period 1980-81 (eighth period of supervision), and having taken into consideration the 8th report of the Governmental Committee of the European Social Charter;

3. Noting that the states bound by the Charter have again made substantial efforts during this period to ensure more satisfactory

---

1. Text adopted by the Standing Committee, acting on behalf of the Assembly, on 22 March 1985. See Doc. 5374, report of the Committee on Social and Health Questions.

application of the principles enshrined in this instrument, and that a number of laws and regulations have been adopted which confirm the Charter's beneficial influence for the pursuit of social progress in the member countries of the Council of Europe;

4. Regretting, however, that the economic crisis has prompted certain states to reduce the level of social protection despite the undertakings contracted by them, in particular where the rights of migrant workers are concerned;

5. Noting that, in other fields too, not all the Contracting Parties are complying fully with their undertakings;

6. Considering it necessary, for the purpose of ensuring effective supervision and observance of the undertakings given, to draw the attention of the governments of the states in question, pursuant to Article 29 of the Charter, specifically to the application of certain provisions of the Charter which are not being fully complied with;

7. Considering also that, taking into account the present economic crisis and its effects on employment and working conditions, all member states should be reminded of the need to give full application to the measures of Articles 1, 3, 10 and 12 of the Charter;

8. Considering, further, that, twenty years after the entry into force of the European Social Charter, the organs of the Council of Europe should make a special effort to draw the attention of those member states which are not yet bound by the Charter to the importance of this instrument, which is to social affairs what the European Convention on Human Rights is to the protection of civil and political rights,

9. Accordingly recommends that the Committee of Ministers make specific recommendations, according to Article 29 of the European Social Charter, with a view to improving the application of the Charter, to the following member states:

   a. Cyprus, Ireland and the United Kingdom in respect of Article 5;

   b. Denmark, Ireland and the United Kingdom in respect of Article 8, paragraph 1;

   c. the Federal Republic of Germany, Austria, Norway, the United Kingdom in respect of Article 19, paragraph 6;

10. Recommends also that the Committee of Ministers draw the attention of all states bound by the Charter to the need to give full application to the measures of Articles 1, 3, 10 and 12 of the Charter;

11. Requests the Committee of Ministers to ask the governments of those member countries that have not yet ratified the European

Social Charter (Belgium, Liechtenstein, Luxembourg, Malta, Portugal, Switzerland and Turkey, some of which have not yet signed it) to take note of this opinion and take whatever steps are necessary in order to remove any obstacles to ratification and to inform the Committee of Ministers before the end of 1985 of the provisions foreseen for the ratification of the Social Charter in the near future.

Committee of Ministers

Resolution ChS (85) 1 concerning the implementation of the European Social Charter during the period 1980-81 (eighth period of super- vision)
(Adopted by the Committee of Ministers on 21 June 1985 at the 387th meeting of the Minister's Deputies)

The Committee of Ministers,

Referring to the European Social Charter and in particular to the pro- visions of Part IV thereof;

Having regard to Article 29 of the Charter;

Having taken note of the 8th report of the Governmental Committee set up under Article 27, to which Conclusions VIII of the Committee of Independent Experts are appended, and of Opinion No. 121 of the Consultative Assembly on the 6th report submitted by the Government of Austria, the 7th report submitted by the Government of Cyprus, the 4th report submitted by the Government of France, and the 8th reports submitted by the Governments of Denmark, the Federal Republic of Germany, Ireland, Italy, Norway, Sweden and the United Kingdom, the first reports submitted by the Governments of the Netherlands and Spain for the periods 22 May 1980-31 December 1981 and 5 June 1980-31 December 1981 respectively,

1. Considers that all these states apply to a very large extent the pro- visions of the Charter which they have accepted;

2. Decides to communicate to the governments of these states Conclusions VIII of the Committee of Independent Experts, the 8th report of the Governmental Committee and Consultative Assembly Opinion No. 121;

3. Draws the attention of the governments of the states concerned to cases not entirely in conformity with the Charter and relating to Articles 5, 8, paragraph 1, and 19, paragraph 6, in regard to which steps may have to be taken with a view to bringing domes- tic legislation, regulations and practice more fully into line with the obligations arising from the Charter.

9. Ninth supervision cycle – first group of states

Committee of Independent Experts – Conclusions IX-1 (1985, 174 p., ISBN: 92-871-0788-2)

Governmental Committee Ninth report (I) (1986, 41 p., ref: T-SG(86)1)

Parliamentary Assembly of the Council of Europe (thirty-eighth ordinary session)

> *Opinion No. 128 (1986)*[1] *on the ninth supervision cycle of the application of the European Social Charter*

The Assembly,

1. Considering that the system for supervising the application of the European Social Charter, as designed and operated particularly at Committee of Ministers level, is far from generally satisfactory in the eyes of the Assembly, despite the few positive changes made in recent years;

2. Having regard to Part IV of the European Social Charter, in particular to Articles 28 and 29, which require the Assembly to be consulted on its application;

3. Having examined the conclusions of the Committee of Independent Experts on supervision of the application of the Charter during the period 1982-83 (ninth supervision cycle) in six of the contracting states (Denmark, Iceland, Norway, the Netherlands, the United Kingdom and Sweden), and having also taken into consideration the 9th report of the Governmental Committee of the European Social Charter;

4. Welcoming the increasing convergence between the conclusions of the Committee of Independent Experts and those of the Governmental Committee;

5. Noting with satisfaction that, as during the previous supervision cycles, further progress has been made on several points in the various countries towards the achievement of the European Social Charter's objectives through the adoption of statutes, regulations and practices ensuring better application of the Charter;

6. Noting once again, however, that whereas well advised measures have been taken in several countries with a view to counteracting the effects of the economic crisis, such as the adoption of arrangements to improve the vocational training of young people, there has been no such improvement in other cases, as evidenced, for

---

1. Text adopted by the Standing Committee, acting on behalf of the Assembly, on 3 July 1986. See Doc. 5576, report of the Social and Health Affairs Committee.

example, by certain measures to reduce the earnings of young people;

7. Considering that the time has come to draw the attention of governments to the special importance which should be attached to observance of undertakings given under the European Social Charter, in particular as regards the protection of young people (Article 7) and the abolition of all discrimination between men and women at work (Article 1, paragraph 2, and Article 4, paragraph 3), and to call on them to remove all deficiencies noted in the application of these provisions;

8. Considering also that the states bound by the charter which have not yet fully accepted its provisions relating to the above-mentioned problems, namely Article 7 on the protection of children and young persons and Article 4, paragraph 3, on equal pay for men and women for work of equal value, should be called on to implement the necessary procedures for the acceptance of those provisions;

9. Regretting that *vis-à-vis* the member states which have not yet ratified the Social Charter the Committee of Ministers has taken no action to secure such ratification,

10. Accordingly recommends that the Committee of Ministers:

i.   ask those member states which have not yet ratified the Social Charter to indicate why they have not yet done so and to ratify it in a reasonably near future;

ii. make specific recommendations to the following member states in accordance with Article 29 of the Social Charter:

    a. Sweden, as regards the application of Article 7, paragraph 1;

    b. the Netherlands, the United Kingdom and Sweden, as regards the application of Article 7, paragraph 3;

    c. the Netherlands and the United Kingdom and Sweden, as regards the application of Article 7, paragraph 5;

    d. Norway, as regards the application of Article 7, paragraph 6;

    e. Sweden, as regards the application of Article 7, paragraph 9;

11. Likewise recommends that the Committee of Ministers draw the attention of all contracting states to the desirability of implementing the necessary procedures for the acceptance (in cases where they have not yet been accepted) of the provisions for the Article 7, paragraphs 1 to 10, and Article 4, paragraph 3, of the charter, as well as to the need to give full effect to those provisions and to those of Article 1, paragraph 2, which has already been accepted by all contracting states;

12. Reiterates its intention to seek means of supplementing the supervision of the Social Charter by a more thorough political examination of current social policies, notably by the introduction of the "social balance sheets" already proposed in its Recommendation 1022 and envisaged in the Secretary General's draft medium-term plan.

Committee of Ministers

Resolution ChS (88) 1 concerning the implementation of the European Social Charter during the period 1982-83 (ninth supervision cycle – first group of states)
(Adopted by the Committee of Ministers on 26 April 1988 at the 416th meeting of the Ministers' Deputies)

The Committee of Ministers,

Referring to the European Social Charter and in particular to the provisions of Part IV thereof;

Having regard to Article 29 of the Charter;

Considering the 3rd report submitted by the Government of Iceland, the 2nd report submitted by the Government of the Netherlands and the 9th reports submitted by the Governments of Denmark, Norway, Sweden and the United Kingdom;

Considering Conclusions IX of the Committee of Independent Experts appointed under Article 25 of the Charter, the 9th report of the Governmental Committee appointed under Article 27 of the Charter and Opinion No.128 (1986) of the Parliamentary Assembly,

Draws the attention of the governments of the states listed above to the various considerations set out in the aforementioned documents; and,

On the basis of the 9th report of the Governmental Committee and in accordance with Article 29 of the Charter.

Recommends the governments concerned to take account, in an appropriate manner, of the various observations made in that report.

10. Ninth supervision cycle – second group of states

Committee of Independent Experts – Conclusions IX-2 (1986, 160 p. ISBN: 92-871-0901-X) and Addendum (1987, 51 p., ISBN: 92-871-0989-3)

Governmental Committee Ninth report (II) (1987, 42 p., (no ref.))

Parliamentary Assembly of the Council of Europe (thirty-ninth ordinary session)

Opinion No. 137 (1988)[1] *on the second stage of the ninth supervision cycle of the application of the European Social Charter*

The Assembly,

1. Having regard to Part IV of the European Social Charter, in particular to Articles 28 and 29, which require the Assembly to be consulted on the application of the Charter;

2. Having examined the conclusions of the Committee of Independent Experts on supervision of the application of the Charter during the period 1982-84 (ninth supervision cycle) in seven of the contracting states (Austria, Cyprus, the Federal Republic of Germany, France, Ireland, Italy and Spain), and having also taken into consideration the 9th report of the Governmental Committee of the European Social Charter;

3. Welcoming the convergence in several instances between the conclusions of the Committee of Independent Experts and those of the Governmental Committee as a very positive development, but deploring, on the other hand, the many instances in which the Governmental Committee did not join the Independent Experts in their conclusions, but rather deferred the adoption of its own conclusions and, in interpretation session which implies the risk of diverging interpretations.

4. Noting with satisfaction that, as during the previous supervision cycles, further progress has been made on several points in the various countries towards the achievement of the European Social Charter's objective through the adoption of statutes, regulations and practices ensuring a better application of the Charter;

5. Noting once again, however, that, whereas well-advised measures have been taken in several countries with a view to counteracting the effects of the economic crisis, such as the adoption of arrangements to improve the vocational training of young people, there has been no such improvement in other cases, as evidenced, for example, by certain measures to reduce the earnings of young people and by the delay in measures to protect children and juveniles against work and working hours which jeopardise their education and vocational training;

6. Noting that, in other fields too, not all the contracting states whose reports have been examined, are complying fully with their undertakings;

---

1. Text adopted by the Standing Committee, acting on behalf of the Assembly, on 23 March 1988. See Doc. 5816, report of the Social and Health Affairs Committee.

7. Considering that the time has come to draw the attention of governments to the special importance which should be attached to the observance of undertakings given under the European Social Charter, in particular as regards the protection of young people (Article 7) and the abolition of all discrimination between men and women at work (Article 1, paragraph 2 and Article 4, paragraph 3), and to call on them to remove all deficiencies noted in the application of these provisions;

8. Considering also that the states bound by the Charter which have not yet fully accepted its provisions relating to the above-mentioned problems, namely Article 7 on the protection of children and young persons, and Article 4, paragraph 3, on equal pay for men and women for work of equal value, should be called on to implement the necessary procedures for the acceptance of those provisions;

9. Regretting that *vis-à-vis* the member states which have not yet ratified the European Social Charter, the Committee of Ministers has taken no specific action to secure such ratification;

10. Considering that it is necessary, for the purpose of ensuring the full observance and an effective supervision of the Charter, that the Committee of Ministers specifically draw the attention of the governments of the contracting states in question, pursuant to Article 29 of the Charter, to certain provisions of the Charter which have not been fully complied with;

11. Expressing therefore its great disappointment that, until now, the Committee of Ministers has never acted upon the Assembly's recommendation to make specific recommendations to certain contracting states in accordance with Article 29 of the Charter, not even in cases where the Assembly's recommendation was based upon the convergent conclusions of the Committee of Independent Experts and the Governmental Committee;

12. Noting with regret that none of the national employers' organisations and the trade unions referred to in Articles 23 and 24 of the Charter has made any comments on the governments' reports;

13. Reiterating its intention to seek means of supplementing the supervision of the European Social Charter by a more thorough political examination of current social policies;

14. Welcoming the adoption of the additional protocol to the Charter by the Committee of Ministers during their 81st Session as a first step towards a further extension of the rights guaranteed by the Charter, and the progress made in the discussions within the Committee of Ministers on the possibilities of further improving the supervision system, and expressing the hope that these efforts

will be continued and that the Assembly will be consulted in time on any proposal on these matters,

15. Accordingly, recommends that the Committee of Ministers:

i. ask those member states which have not yet ratified the European Social Charter (Belgium, Liechtenstein, Luxembourg, Malta, Portugal, Switzerland and Turkey) to submit a report to the Committee of Ministers before the end of 1988 stating the difficulties which prevent or delay ratification;

ii. apply Article 22 positively and dynamically by asking the Contracting Parties to submit reports on the reasons why they are unable to accept additional provisions, so that ratification may result in the acceptance of all provisions within a reasonable time;

iii. draw, more specifically, the attention of the governments of the following member states to the desirability of implementing the necessary procedures for the acceptance of Article 4, paragraph 3, and Article 7, to the extent that they have not yet accepted these provisions:

    a. Austria, as regards Article 7, paragraphs 1 and 6;

    b. Cyprus, as regards Article 4, paragraph 3, and Article 7, paragraphs 1 to 10

    c. the Federal Republic of Germany, as regards Article 7, paragraph 1;

    d. Ireland, as regards Article 4, paragraph 3, and Article 7, paragraphs 1, 7 and 9;

iv. make specific recommendations to the following member states in accordance with Article 29 of the European Social Charter:

    a. France, as regards the application of Article 1, paragraph 2, and Article 7, paragraphs 1 and 3;

    b. Ireland as regards the application of Article 1, paragraph 2, and Article 7, paragraphs 3, 4 and 5;

    c. Italy, as regards the application of Article 1, paragraph 2, and Article 7, paragraphs 1, 3 and 4;

v. draw the attention of all contracting states to the fact that, for an effective supervision of the application of the Charter, it is necessary that the biennial reports are submitted in time, and that they contain all relevant information, including the additional information requested during the previous supervision cycle;

vi. invite governments to promote the effective application of Articles 23 and 24 as an intermediate stage to full participation of national employers' organisations and trade unions in the supervision cycle at the level of the Governmental Committee.

Committee of Ministers

Resolution ChS (88) 2 concerning the implementation of the European Social Charter during the period 1982-84 (ninth supervision cycle – second group of states)
(Adopted by the Committee of Ministers on 13 June 1988 at the 418th meeting of the Ministers' Deputies)

The Committee of Ministers,

Referring to the European Social Charter and in particular to the provisions of Part IV thereof;

Having regard to Article 29 of the Charter;

Considering the 2nd report submitted by the Government of Spain, the 5th report submitted by the Government of France, the 7th report submitted by the Government of Austria, the 8th report submitted by the Government of Cyprus and the 9th reports submitted by the Governments of the Federal Republic of Germany, Ireland and Italy;

Considering Conclusions IX-2 (and addendum) of the Committee of Independent Experts appointed under Article 25 of the Charter, the 9th report (II) of the Governmental Committee appointed under Article 27 of the Charter and Opinion No. 137 (1988) of the Consultative Assembly,

Draws the attention of the governments of the states listed above to the various considerations set out in the aforementioned documents; and,

On the basis of the 9th report (II) of the Governmental Committee and in accordance with Article 29 of the Charter,

Recommends the governments concerned to take account, in an appropriate manner, of the various observations made in that report.

11. Tenth supervision cycle – first group of states

Committee of Independent Experts – Conclusions X-1 (1987, 222 p. ISBN: 92-871-1075-1) and Addendum (1990, 13 p. ISBN: 92-871-1837-X)

Governmental Committee Tenth report (I) (1987, 44 p. (no ref.))

Parliamentary Assembly of the Council of Europe (forty-first ordinary session)

Opinion No. 145 (1989)[1] on the first stage of the tenth supervision cycle of the application of the European Social Charter

The Assembly,

1. Having regard to Part IV of the European Social Charter, in particular to Articles 29 and 29, which require the Assembly to be consulted on the application of the Charter;

---

1. Assembly debate on 9 May 1989 (3rd sitting) (see Doc. 6030, report of the Social, Health and Family Affairs Committee, Rapporteur: Mr Bohl). Text adopted by the Assembly on 9 May 1989 (3rd sitting).

2. Having examined the conclusions of the Committee of Independent Experts on supervision of the application of the Charter during the period 1984-85 (tenth supervision cycle) in seven of the contracting states (Denmark, Greece, Iceland, Norway, the Netherlands, Sweden and the United Kingdom), and having also taken into consideration the tenth report (I) of the Governmental Committee of the European Social Charter;

3. Welcoming the convergence in several instances between the conclusions of the Committee of Independent Experts and those of the Governmental Committee, but deploring, however, the many instances in which the Governmental Committee did not joint the Independent Experts in their conclusions, but deviated from them or deferred its own conclusions, and deploring also the instances in which the Governmental committee deviated from the interpretation of charter provisions given by the Committee of Independent Experts;

4. Noting with satisfaction that, as during the previous supervision cycles, further progress has been made on several points in the various countries towards the achievement of the European Social Charter's objectives through the adoption of statutes, regulations and practices ensuring a better application of the Charter;

5. Noting also with satisfaction that, in many countries, various policies have been introduced to combat unemployment, in particular, unemployment of young people, women, older workers, migrant workers and the disabled;

6. Noting, however, that in spite of such policies the unemployment rate – in particular, the youth unemployment rate – is still very high in some countries;

7. Noting with regret that not all the contracting states, whose reports have been examined, are complying fully with their undertakings under the Charter;

8. Drawing attention, in particular, to the unsatisfactory situation concerning respect for the obligation to protect effectively the right of the worker to earn his living in an occupation freely entered upon (Article 1, paragraph 2, of the Charter), which should be considered as one of the basic rights of workers;

9. Noting also the problems which still occur with regard to respect for the right to collective action in case of labour conflicts, including the right to strike (Article 6, paragraph 4), and stressing the fact that collective action, an essential element of freedom of association, is recognised in international law as one of the fundamental rights of workers, and that accordingly states should make every effort to prevent infringements thereof;

10. Considering also that those contracting states which have not yet accepted all the provisions of the Charter should be called upon to implement the necessary procedures for their acceptance;

11. Regretting that, *vis-à-vis* those member states which have not yet ratified the Social Charter, the Committee of Ministers has taken no specific action to secure ratification;

12. Stressing once again that, in order to ensure full observance of the Charter and effective supervision of its application, the Committee of Ministers should draw the attention of the governments of the contracting states specifically to those provisions which they have not fully complied with, by making the necessary recommendations pursuant to Article 29 of the Charter;

13. Expressing therefore its great disappointment that the Committee of Ministers has still not acted upon the Assembly's recommendation that specific recommendations should be made to certain contracting states in accordance with Article 29 of the Charter, not even in cases where the Assembly's recommendation was based upon convergent conclusions of the Committee of Independent Experts and the Governmental Committee; and desirous that the Committee of Ministers initiate discussions to amend its voting procedure under Article 29 of the Charter to enable it to perform its functions under that article in a more effective way;

14. Noting with satisfaction that, in this phase of the tenth supervision cycle, some national employers' organisations and trade unions, as provided for in Articles 23 and 24 of the Charter, have made comments on the governmental reports, and expressing the hope that more national organisations will in the future make use of the opportunities made available to them under Article 23;

15. Reiterating its intention to highlight efforts at seeking ways and means to improve the implementation of the Charter,

16. Accordingly recommends that the Committee of Ministers:

i. ask those member states which have not yet accepted the Social Charter (Belgium, Liechtenstein, Luxembourg, Portugal, San Marino, Switzerland and Turkey) to submit reports to the Committee of Ministers before the end of 1989 stating the difficulties which prevent or delay signature or ratification;

ii. include the Additional Protocol in the group of core provisions which must be accepted upon ratification of the Charter;

iii apply Article 22 positively and dynamically, so that this procedure may result in the acceptance of all provisions within a reasonable time;

iv. draw the specific attention of the governments of the following contracting states to the desirability of implementing the necessary procedures for the acceptance of the provisions of the Charter examined by the Assembly, to the extent that they have not yet accepted them;

   – Denmark, as regards Article 4, paragraph 4, and Article 7, paragraph 9;

   – Greece, as regards Article 6, paragraph 4;

   – Iceland, as regards Article 7, paragraph 9;

   – Norway, as regards Article 7, paragraph 9;

v. make specific recommendations to the following member states in accordance with Article 29 of the Social Charter;

   – Denmark as regards the application of Article 6, paragraph 4;

   – Greece, as regards the application of Article 1, paragraph 2;

   – Iceland, as regards the application of Article 1, paragraph 2, and Article 6, paragraph 4;

   – the Netherlands, as regards the application of Article 1, paragraph 2, Article 3, paragraph 1, and Article 4, paragraph 4;

   – Sweden, as regards the application of Article 7, paragraph 9;

   – the United Kingdom, as regards the application of Article 1, paragraph 2, Article 4, paragraph 4, and Article 6, paragraph 4;

vi. draw the attention of all contracting states to the fact that effective supervision of the application of the application of the Charter depends on having biennial reports submitted in time and containing all relevant information, including the additional information requested during the previous supervision cycle;

vii. invite governments to promote the effective application of Articles 23 and 24 as an intermediate stage to full participation of national employers' organisations and trade unions in the supervision cycle at the level of the Governmental Committee;

viii. convene an international conference on the revision of the European Social Charter, which should focus on the desirability and feasibility of both modifying and supplementing the substantive rights contained in the Charter, and of revising its supervisory mechanism, taking also into account developments within the European Community;

ix. pending the outcome of this conference, strengthen the resources and instruments of the Committee of Independent Experts – including the provision of an adequate secretariat – to enable it to perform its functions more efficiently and effectively.

Committee of Ministers

> *Resolution ChS (89) 1 concerning the implementation of the European Social Charter during the period 1984-85 (tenth supervision cycle – first group of states)*
> *(Adopted by the Committee of Ministers on 13 September 1989 at the 428th meeting of the Ministers' Deputies)*

The Committee of Ministers,

Referring to the European Charter and in particular to the provisions of Part IV thereof;

Having regard to Article 29 of the Charter;

Considering the reports presented by the Governments of Denmark, Greece, Iceland, the Netherlands, Norway, Sweden and the United Kingdom for the period from 1 January 1984 to 31 December 1985;

Considering Conclusions X-1 of the Committee of Independent Experts appointed under Article 25 of the Charter, the 10th report (I) of the Governmental Committee appointed under Article 27 of the Charter and Assembly Opinion No. 145 (1989),

Draws the attention of the governments of the states listed above to the various considerations set out in the aforementioned documents; and,

On the basis of the 10th report (I) of the Governmental Committee and in accordance with Article 29 of the Charter,

Recommends the governments concerned to take account, in an appropriate manner, of the various observations made in that report.

12. Tenth supervision cycle – second group of states

Committee of Independent Experts – Conclusions X-2 (1988, 210 p. ISBN: 92-871-1619-9)

Governmental Committee Tenth report (II) (1989, 43 p. (no ref.))

Parliamentary Assembly of the Council of Europe (forty-second ordinary session)

> *Opinion No. 149 (1990)[1] on the application of the Social Charter of the Council of Europe (tenth cycle: phase 2)*

1. In the periodical opinions which it is given the opportunity to present on the application of the Social Charter,[2] the Assembly

---

1. Text adopted by the Assembly, under the tacit adoption procedure, on 8 May 1990. See Doc. 6201 and addendum, report of the Social, Health and Family Affairs Committee, Rapporteur: Mr Bohl.
2. Under Article 28 of the Social Charter.

usually focuses on respect shown for the specific obligations by which Contracting Parties consider themselves formally bound.

2. 1989, however, was a most exceptional year. Events in central and eastern Europe led the Assembly to draw attention to the Social Charter of the Council of Europe "as an instrument of dialogue and *rapprochement*" with the countries concerned (Recommendation 1107). In the field of social policy, the year was marked by a strong but unsuccessful[1] effort to produce a "social charter" for the European Community. The Assembly commented on and sought to influence the direction of this effort in its Resolutions 915 and 931.[2]

3. A side-effect of this effort was to throw light on the value of the Social Charter of the Council of Europe as a statement of principles governing the aims of policy, in contrast to its value as a statement of formal obligations.

3.1. As a statement of social policy principles, the Social Charter of the Council of Europe "embodies a wider range of rights, fuller standards and a more all-embracing view of social protection" (Resolution 931) than anything the European Community looked like coming up with in the course of last year.

3.2. Nine of the twelve Community states already subscribe to these aims, and it is understood by the Assembly that the governments of the other three are currently promoting their countries' accession.

3.3. Social policy initiatives will continue to be taken within the Community (notably in regard to the health and safety of people at work), yet nothing could be more judicious nor in tune with the views of Resolution 931) than to work towards the realisation of a "European social area" which encompasses all countries of the Council of Europe, including those of the Community and EFTA, and extends potentially to those of Eastern and Central Europe which are showing interest in stronger relations with the European institutions.

4. Accordingly, the Assembly has called (Resolution 931) for accession by the European Community to the Social Charter of the Council of Europe on the grounds: a. that the latter instrument, suitably adapted, needs to be brought into a proper relationship with Community law; b. that a broader and richer basis would thereby be afforded for social action and policy throughout the Community (in conformity with the "principle of subsidiarity"); and c. that this is in the interest of the wider Europe which is emerging.

---

1. In so far as it was impossible to reach unanimous agreement between all member states of the Community.
2. Further to the substantive discussions of the Utrecht Symposium (25-26 April 1989) and the Syracuse Hearing (19-20 October 1989).

5. The Assembly has attached great importance to its involvement in the procedures of the Social Charter. It has always marked its appreciation of the work of the committees of independent experts and governmental representatives. I would wish to do so again in respect of the reports/conclusions of these two committees which are currently transmitted for opinion to it on the tenth supervision cycle 1985-86 for Austria, Cyprus, France, the Federal Republic of Germany, Ireland, Italy and Spain.

6. But, on this occasion, the Assembly's presentation of specific comments (see below) on the information and interpretations developed under the procedures of the Social Charter in respect of the period and countries concerned should not be allowed to deflect attention from what is now essential: revision of procedures with a view to the accession of the European Community and to an opening-up towards central and eastern Europe.

7. The Assembly is aware of the many legal difficulties which will have to be resolved. These difficulties must not serve as a pretext for inaction.

8. In its Resolution 931, the Assembly called for discussions to be set in train between the European Community and the Council of Europe. It transmits herewith to the Committee of Ministers its opinion that the time is ripe for the next "quadripartite" meeting (see Recommendation 1107) to set up a "study group" in whatever form might be judged most appropriate.

9. Meanwhile, the Assembly, according to the prescribed procedure of Part IV of the Charter, transmits to the Committee of Ministers the following observations.

10.1. Satisfactory progress has been made in some member states. For example, in Cyprus, a maternity protection law was adopted in 1987, modelled to some extent on the provisions of Article 8 of the Charter. In Austria, as from 1 July 1988, following an amendment to legislation on the employment of foreigners, young second-generation foreigners are henceforth exempt from the obligation of getting a work permit in order to follow training-courses.

10.2. As noted, however, by the Committee of Independent Experts and sometimes by the Governmental Committee, certain weaknesses are evident in the application of certain provisions, to which the Committee of Ministers should draw the attention of the states concerned:

a. Article 1, paragraph 2, on the prohibition of forced labour

In France, in Ireland and in Italy, sailors in the merchant navy are subject to penal sanctions in certain cases when the safety of the ship and people aboard are not affected; the national legislative provisions in question, although in practice obsolete, remain none the less in force and should be formally abolished.

b. Article 7, paragraph 3, on the full respect of school obligation

In Austria, in France, in Ireland and in Italy, there continue to be certain gaps in the legislative or regulatory protection for children of school age who are working in family undertakings, principally in agriculture.

c. Article 8, paragraph 2, on protection against unjustified dismissal of women at work

There continue to be anomalies in the legislations of Austria and Italy, which in effect do not protect, in every case, domestic employees against dismissal for reasons of pregnancies.

10.3. In conclusion, the Assembly would wish to register its concern that there are still three member states of the European Community among those which have not yet ratified the Charter (Belgium, Finland, Liechtenstein, Luxembourg, Portugal, San Marino, Switzerland), particularly considering that, in the perspective of Community Membership and participation, it would seem necessary that the twelve states in question at least subscribe to a "minimal platform" consisting of the same articles and provisions.

Committee of Ministers

Resolution ChS (90) 1 concerning the implementation of the European Social Charter during the period 1985-86 (tenth supervision cycle – second group of states)
(Adopted by the Committee of Ministers on 12 September 1990 at the meeting of the Ministers' Deputies)

The Committee of Ministers,

Referring to the European Social Charter and in particular to the provisions of Part IV thereof;

Having regard to Article 29 of the Charter;

Considering the reports presented by the Governments of Austria, Cyprus, the Federal Republic of Germany, France, Ireland, Italy and Spain for the period from 1 January 1985 to 31 December 1986;

Considering Conclusions X-2 of the Committee of Independent Experts appointed under Article 27 of the Charter Assembly Opinion No. 149 (1990),

Draws the attention of the governments of the states listed above to the various considerations set out in the aforementioned documents; and,

411

On the basis of the 10th report (II) of the Governmental Committee and in accordance with Article 29 of the Charter.

Recommends the governments concerned to take account, in an appropriate manner, of the various observations made in that report.

13. Eleventh supervision cycle – first group of states

Committee of Independent Experts – Conclusions XI-1 (1989, 237 p. ISBN: 92-871-1742-X)

Governmental Committee Eleventh report (I) (1990, 134 p. (no ref.))

Parliamentary Assembly of the Council of Europe (forty-second ordinary session)

Opinion No. 156 (1991)[1] *on the eleventh supervision cycle of the application of the Council of Europe's European Social Charter*

1. The Parliamentary Assembly's involvement in the procedure for supervision of the Social Charter (see Part IV of the Charter, Articles 28 and 29) gives it an opportunity of pointing out that the Social Charter and the European Convention on Human Rights, of which the first enshrines social and economic rights, and the second mainly civil and political rights, must be seen as being of equal importance, closely linked and complementary.

2. The Assembly is convinced that giving the Social Charter a new impetus is both highly desirable on the eve of the European Community's Single Market, and politically opportune in view of the changes in central and eastern Europe and the emphasis laid on the economic and social justice aspects of the CSCE process in the Paris Charter.

3. None the less, there remains a striking contrast between the status accorded to the European Social Charter and that accorded to the European Convention on Human Rights by member states, both in their ratification of those texts and in the means and resources which they devote to making them work. The Social Charter has not received its due, and the public at large knows little of its content; moreover, its supervisory procedure is not in keeping either with its value or its content.

4. If the notion of a "European social area" is to have any real credibility, the social rights recognised in the Charter must be made the central element of social policy in all the democratic states of western and eastern Europe, and all the Community states must accept them forthwith, thus removing any doubts concerning

---

1. Text adopted by the Standing Committee, acting on behalf of the Assembly, on 11 March 1991. See Doc. 6395, report on the Social, Health and Family Affairs Committee, Rapporteur: Mr Beix.

their determination to open up towards the so-called "post-communist" societies.

5.   The Assembly accordingly:

i.   welcomes the launching by the Committee of Ministers, in the wake of the informal Ministerial Conference on Human Rights (Rome, 5 November 1990), of a process of reflection and consultation designed to improve both the Charter and its workings;

ii.   recalls its numerous, earlier proposals on this question, particularly concerning the supervision procedure (see Recommendation 839 (1978), and declares its active support for this initiative and its desire to contribute constructively to it.

6.   Within this context and without there being any need to await the outcome of the action taken to revitalise the Charter, the Assembly asks the Committee of Ministers;

i.   to urge all member states which have not yet done so, and all new member states to sign the Social Charter, thus indicating their acceptance of the social values and rights which it enshrines and protects, and their wish to form part of a single European social area;

ii.   to take practical action to secure even partial ratification of the Charter by states which have not yet done so, using all appropriate means for that purpose, including regular, formal examination of the reasons given by these states for non-ratification, and the legal validity of these reasons.

7.   Accordingly, and having examined Conclusions XI-1 of the Committee of Independent Experts of the European Social Charter and the corresponding report of the Governmental Committee, the Assembly asks the Committee of Ministers to make use of the powers given to it by Article 29 and:

i.   while noting with satisfaction the social progress recorded in the various states concerned, to urge these states to respect all their commitments under the Charter, as defined by the Committee of Independent Experts;

ii.   to urge, in particular, each of the states concerned to ensure at the earliest possible date:

   a. that all employed or self-employed men and women in industry, farming, the service industries and all other sectors of activity have safe and healthy working conditions (Article 3 of the Charter), bearing in mind our growing awareness of the health risks caused by the environment (including the working environment), technological change, the increased presence of women on the labour-market, etc.;

b. that all women can genuinely reconcile their desire to have children with the exercise of a professional activity, by granting them maternity or parental leave in conditions which preserve their living standards, acquired rights and legitimate professional aspirations, protect them against unlawful dismissal and respect the physical integrity and health of mothers, as well as the health and interests of children (Article 8 of the Charter);

c. that the right to family life does not remain a dead letter, but is granted in practice to all migrant workers in Europe through effective and generous application of Article 19, paragraph 6, of the Charter, the elimination between Contracting Parties of all direct or indirect obstacles to family reunion, and the extension of this basic right to all aliens lawfully resident in their territory, as urged in the appendix to the Social Charter.

Committee of Ministers

Resolution ChS (91) 1 concerning the implementation of the European Social Charter during the period 1986-87 (eleventh supervision cycle – 1st group of states)
(Adopted by the Committee of Ministers on 23 May 1991 at the 458th meeting of the Ministers' Deputies)

The Committee of Ministers,

Referring to the European Social Charter and in particular to the provisions of Part IV thereof;

Having regard to Article 29 of the Charter;

Considering the reports presented by the Governments of Denmark, Greece, Iceland, the Netherlands, Norway, Sweden and the United Kingdom for the period from 1 January 1986 to 31 December 1987;

Considering Conclusions XI-1 of the Committee of Independent Experts appointed under Article 25 of the Charter, the 11th report (I) of the Governmental Committee appointed under Article 27 of the Charter and Assembly Opinion No. 156 (1991).

Draws the attention of the governments of the states listed above to the various considerations set out in the aforementioned documents; and,

On the basis of the 11th report (I) of the Governmental Committee and in accordance with Article 29 of the Charter,

Recommends the governments concerned to take account, in an appropriate manner, of the various observations made in the report.

14. Eleventh supervision cycle – second group of states

Committee of Independent Experts – Conclusions XI-2 (1991, 215 p., ISBN: 92-871-1904-X) and Addendum (1991, 60 p. ISBN: 92-871-1943-0)

Governmental Committee Eleventh report (II) and Addendum to the 10th report (1992, 99 p., ISBN: 92-871-2030-7)

Committee of Ministers

> *Resolution ChS (92) 2 on the implementation of the European Social Charter during the period 1987-88 (11th cycle of supervision – second group of states) and during the period 1984-85 in the Netherlands Antilles (10th supervision cycle)*
> *(Adopted by the Committee of Ministers on 15 December 1992 at the 485th meeting of the Ministers' Deputies*

The Committee of Ministers,

Referring to the European Social Charter, in particular to the provisions of Part IV thereof;

Having regard to Article 29 of the Charter,

Considering the reports submitted by the Governments of Austria, Cyprus, France, Germany, Ireland, Italy and Spain for the period from 1 January 1984 to 31 December 1985;

Considering the report submitted by the Government of the Netherlands on the Netherlands Antilles for the period from 1 January 1984 to 31 December 1985;

Considering Conclusions XI-2, the Addendum to Conclusions X-1 of the Committee of Independent Experts appointed under Article 25 of the Charter as well as the 11th report (II) and the Addendum to the 10th report (I) (Netherlands Antilles) of the Governmental Committee appointed under Article 27 of the Charter;

Recalling the request made, both to the States Parties to the Charter and the supervisory bodies, by the Ministers participating in the Ministerial Conference on the European Social Charter held in Turin on 21-22 October 1991, on the occasion of the 30th anniversary of the Charter, and by the Committee of Ministers in its decision of 11 December 1991, "to envisage the application of certain of the measures provided for in this Protocol [the Amending Protocol] before its entry into force, in so far as the text of the Charter will allow";

Noting also that the Parliamentary Assembly, in a letter dated 3 September 1992 from its President to the Chairman of the Committee of Ministers, has decided to abstain from communicating its views on a particular set of conclusions of the Committee of Independent Experts as provided for under Article 28 of the Charter and to use these conclusions as a basis for periodical social policy debates to be held by the Assembly in accordance with Article 6 of the Amending Protocol to the European Social Charter,

Noting that the conclusion of the debate on sever poverty and social exclusion, held on 7 October 1992 by the Assembly, at the third part of its 44th Ordinary Session, reflect the views of the Assembly on the eleventh supervision cycle of the application of the Charter (second group of states) for the period 1987-88 (Order No. 482),

Draws the attention of the governments listed above to the various considerations set out in the aforementioned documents; and,

On the basis of the 11th report (II) and of the Addendum to the 10th report (I) (Netherlands Antilles) of the Governmental Committee and in accordance with Article 29 of the Charter;

Recommends the governments concerned to take account, in an appropriate manner, of all the various observations made in the reports.

15. Twelfth supervision cycle – first group of states

Committee of Independent Experts – Conclusions XII-1 (1992, 355 p., ISBN: 92-871-2067-6)

Governmental Committee Twelfth report (I) (1993, 146 p., ISBN: 92-871-2268-7)

Committee of Ministers

> *Resolution ChS (93) 1 on the implementation of the European Social Charter during the period 1988-1989 (12th cycle of supervision – first group of states)*
> *(Adopted by the Committee of Ministers on 7 September 1993 at the 497th meeting of the Ministers' Deputies)*

The Committee of Ministers, in its composition restricted to Contracting Parties to the European Social Charter,[1]

Referring to the European Social Charter, in particular to the provisions of Part IV thereof;

Having regard to Article 29 of the Charter,

Considering the reports submitted by the Governments of Denmark, Greece, Iceland, the Netherlands, Norway, Sweden and the United Kingdom for the period from 1 January 1988 to 31 December 1989;

Considering Conclusions XII-1 of the Committee of Independent Experts appointed under Article 25 of the Charter and the 12th report (I) of the Governmental Committee appointed under Article 27 of the Charter;

---

1. Austria, Belgium, Cyprus, Denmark, Finland, France, Germany, Greece, Iceland, Ireland, Italy, Luxembourg, Malta, the Netherlands, Norway, Portugal, Spain, Sweden, Turkey and the United Kingdom.

Recalling the request made, both to the Contracting Parties to the Charter and the supervisory bodies, by the Ministers participating in the Ministerial Conference on the European Social Charter held in Turin on 21-22 October 1991, on the occasion of the 30th anniversary of the Charter, and by the Committee of Ministers in its decision of 11 December 1991, "to envisage the application of certain of the measures provided for in this Protocol (the Amending Protocol) before its entry into force, in so far as the text of the Charter will allow";

Noting that the Governmental Committee, in view of this request has decided, in accordance with Article 4 of the Amending Protocol, to select, in the light of the reports of the Committee of Independent Experts and of the Contracting Parties and on the basis of social, economic and other policy considerations, the situations which should, in its view, be the subject of recommendations to each Contracting Party;

Noting also that the Parliamentary Assembly, in a letter from its President to the Chairman of the Committee of Ministers of 3 September 1992, has decided to abstain from communicating its views on a particular set of conclusions of the Committee of Independent Experts as provided for under Article 28 of the Charter and to use these conclusions as a basis for periodical social policy debates to be held by the Assembly in accordance with Article 6 of the Amending Protocol,

Draws the attention of the governments concerned to the recommendations adopted for the 12th cycle of supervision following the proposals made by the Governmental Committee;

Recommends in addition the governments of the first group of states to take account, in an appropriate manner, of all the various observations made in the Conclusions of the Committee of Independent Experts and the report of the Governmental Committee.

Committee of Ministers

> *Recommendation No. R ChS (93) 1 on the application of the European Social Charter by Greece during the period 1988-89 (12th supervision cycle)*
> *(Adopted by the Committee of Ministers on 7 September 1993 at the 497th meeting of the Ministers' Deputies)*

The Committee of Ministers, in its composition restricted to Contracting Parties to the European Social Charter,[1]

Referring to the European Social Charter, in particular Part IV thereof;

---

1. Austria, Belgium, Cyprus, Denmark, Finland, France, Germany, Greece, Iceland, Ireland, Italy, Luxembourg, Malta, the Netherlands, Norway, Portugal, Spain, Sweden, Turkey and the United Kingdom.

Whereas the European Social Charter, signed in Turin on 18 October 1961, came into force on 6 July 1984 with respect to Greece;

Whereas, in accordance with Article 20, Greece has accepted sixty-seven out of the seventy-two provisions contained in the Charter;

Whereas the Government of Greece submitted in 1990 its 3rd report on those provisions of the Charter which it has accepted, and whereas this report has been examined in accordance with Articles 24 to 27 of the Charter;

Having examined Conclusions XII-1 of the Committee of Independent Experts appointed under Article 25 of the Charter and the 12th report (I) of the Governmental Committee appointed under Article 27 of the Charter;

Having noted that in respect of Article 1, paragraph 2 (prohibition against forced labour), the Committee of Independent Experts adopted a negative conclusion as:

- Section 64 of Decree 1400/1973 provides that the length of the compulsory period of service for career officers who have followed several training courses may be up to 25 years;

- the Merchant Navy Penal and Disciplinary Code and Act No. 3276/1944 on collective bargaining in the merchant navy provides for a possibility for penal sanctions against seamen in certain cases not involving the safety of the vessel or of the persons aboard;

Having noted finally that in respect of Article 13, paragraph 4 (equal treatment with respect to social and medical assistance), a recommendation had been proposed as:

- "pension" for those aged over 68 is restricted to Greek nationals;

- Legislative Decree 57/1973, which provides that social assistance is granted to foreigners resident in Greece on an equal footing with Greek nationals, also provides that in order to be considered a resident in Greece a foreign national must have been lawfully present in Greece for at least six months,

Observes that the Governmental Committee in accordance with Article 29 of the Charter has proposed that an individual recommendation be addressed to Greece in relation to Article 1, paragraph 2, Article 13, paragraph 1 and Article 13, paragraph 4;

Recommends the Greek Government to take account, in an appropriate manner, of the negative conclusions of the Committee of Independent Experts and invites it to provide information in its next report on the measures it has taken to this effect.

Committee of Ministers

> *Recommendation No. R ChS (93) 2 on the application of the European Social Charter by Norway during the period 1988-89 (12th supervision cycle)*
> *(Adopted by the Committee of Ministers on 7 September 1993 at the 497th meeting of the Ministers' Deputies)*

The Committee of Ministers, in its composition restricted to Contracting Parties to the European Social Charter,[1]

Referring to the European Social Charter, in particular Part IV thereof;

Whereas the European Social Charter, signed in Turin on 18 October 1961, came into force on 26 February 1965 with respect to Norway;

Whereas, in accordance with Article 20, Norway has accepted sixty out of the seventy-two provisions contained in the Charter;

Whereas the Government of Norway submitted in 1990 its 12th report on the provisions of the Charter which it has accepted, and whereas this report has been examined in accordance with Articles 24 to 27 of the Charter;

Having examined Conclusions XII-1 of the Committee of Independent Experts appointed under Article 25 of the Charter and the 12th report (I) of the Governmental Committee appointed under Article 27 of the Charter;

Having noted that in respect of Article 6, paragraph 4 (the right to collective action), that according to the Committee of Independent Experts the use of compulsory arbitration in the case of a strike by nurses was not justified under Article 31 of the Charter, as no emergency operation had been cancelled or postponed and as the government intervened at the very beginning of the strike, before its effect could be validly assessed. The Committee of Independent Experts also considered that the apparent absence of any limitation on the government's power to intervene in strike action and the consequent absence of any protection for workers constituted a breach of this provision;

Observes that the Governmental Committee in accordance with Article 29 of the Charter has proposed that an individual recommendation be addressed to Norway in relation to Article 6, paragraph 4; and underlined in this respect that legislative intervention in the right to strike is justified under the Charter, only if the restrictions in question are in conformity with Article 31 of the Charter and could, consequently, not have been applied in respect of the nurses' strike in the circumstances, even though the strike affected a sensitive sector, as the emergency services were not adversely affected and no serious social problems had occurred;

---

1. Austria, Belgium, Cyprus, Denmark, Finland, France, Germany, Greece, Iceland, Ireland, Italy, Luxembourg, Malta, the Netherlands, Norway, Portugal, Spain, Sweden, Turkey and the United Kingdom.

Recommends the Norwegian Government to inform the Parliament of the obligations arising out of Article 6, paragraph 4, of the Charter and to abstain from proposing legislative intervention beyond the limits set by Article 31 of the Charter;

Having noted also that in respect of Article 7, paragraph 3 (the right of children and young persons to protection – the full benefit of compulsory education), that the Committee of Independent Experts found that, although the total number of working hours and school hours for children over the age of 13 who are still subject to compulsory education could not exceed eight hours a day, taking into consideration the duration of classes, it is possible for children to engage in an occupational activity nineteen hours per week. The Committee of Independent Experts considered a total of forty-nine hours work at school and out of school to be excessive for children of that age;

Observes that the Governmental Committee has likewise proposed that an individual recommendation be addressed to Norway in relation to Article 7, paragraph 3,

Recommends the Norwegian Government in this respect to clarify and to amend the regulations governing the working hours of children over the age of 13 who are still subject to compulsory education.

Committee of Ministers

> *Recommendation No. R ChS (93) 3 on the application of the European Social Charter by the United Kingdom during the period 1988-89 (12th supervision cycle)*
> *(Adopted by the Committee of Ministers on 7 September 1993 at the 497th meeting of the Ministers' Deputies)*

The Committee of Ministers, in its composition restricted to Contracting Parties to the European Social Charter,[1]

Referring to the European Social Charter, in particular Part IV thereof;

Whereas the European Social Charter, signed in Turin on 18 October 1961, came into force on 26 February 1965 with respect to the United Kingdom;

Whereas, in accordance with Article 20, the United Kingdom has accepted sixty out of the seventy-two provisions contained in the Charter;

Whereas the Government of the United Kingdom submitted in 1990 its 12th report on the provisions of the Charter which it has accepted, and whereas this report has been examined in accordance with Articles 24 to 27 of the Charter;

---

1. Austria, Belgium, Cyprus, Denmark, Finland, France, Germany, Greece, Iceland, Ireland, Italy, Luxembourg, Malta, the Netherlands, Norway, Portugal, Spain, Sweden, Turkey and the United Kingdom.

Having examined Conclusions XII-1 of the Committee of Independent Experts appointed under Article 25 of the Charter and the 12th report (I) of the Governmental Committee appointed under Article 27 of the Charter;

Having noted that in respect of Article 6, paragraph 4 (the right to collective action) that the Committee of Independent Experts had reached a negative conclusion as legislation allows an employer to dismiss all employees who take part in strikes, and to re-hire striking workers on a selective basis three months after their dismissal (Section 62 of the 1978 Protection of Employment (Consolidation) Act;

Observes that the Governmental Committee in accordance with Article 29 of the Charter has proposed that an individual recommendation be addressed to the United Kingdom in relation to Article 6, paragraph 4;

Having noted also in respect of Article 8, paragraph 1 (the right of employed women to protection – maternity leave) that the Committee of independent Experts concluded negatively as the amount of maternity benefits was not considered sufficient;

Observes that the Governmental Committee has likewise proposed that an individual recommendation be addressed to the United Kingdom in relation to Article 8, paragraph 1, while underlining that the low amount of maternity benefits in practice puts pressure on women not to benefit from their right to maternity leave;

Recommends the Government of the United Kingdom to take account, in an appropriate manner, of the negative conclusions of the Committee of Independent Experts and invites it to provide information in its next report on the measures it has taken to this effect.

16. Twelfth supervision cycle – second group of states

Committee of Independent Experts – Conclusions XII-2 (1993, 347 p., ISBN: 92-871-2243-1)

*Governmental Committee Twelfth report (II) (*1995, 138 p., ISBN: 92-871-2628-3)

Committee of Ministers

> *Resolution ChS (94) 1 on the implementation of the European Social Charter during the period 1989-90 (12th cycle of supervision – second group of states)*
> *(Adopted by the Committee of Ministers on 8 April 1994 at the 511th meeting of the Ministers' Deputies*

The Committee of Ministers, in its composition restricted to Contracting Parties to the European Social Charter,[1]

---

1. Austria, Belgium, Cyprus, Denmark, Finland, France, Germany, Greece, Iceland, Ireland, Italy, Luxembourg, Malta, the Netherlands, Norway, Portugal, Spain, Sweden, Turkey and the United Kingdom.

Referring to the European Social Charter, in particular to the provisions of Part IV thereof;

Having regard to Article 29 of the Charter,

Considering the reports submitted by the Governments of Austria, Cyprus, France, Germany, Italy, Malta and Spain for the period from 1 January 1989 to 31 December 1990;

Considering Conclusions XII-2 of the Committee of Independent Experts appointed under Article 25 of the Charter and the 12th report (II) of the Governmental Committee appointed under Article 27 of the Charter;

Recalling the request made, both to the States Parties to the Charter and the supervisory bodies, by the Ministers participating in the Ministerial Conference on the European Social Charter held in Turin on 21-22 October 1991, on the occasion of the 30th anniversary of the Charter, and by the Committee of Ministers in its decision of 11 December 1991, "to envisage the application of certain of the measures provided for in this Protocol (the Amending Protocol) before its entry into force, in so far as the text of the Charter will allow";

Noting that the Governmental Committee, in view of this request has decided, in accordance with Article 4 of the Amending Protocol, to select, in the light of the reports of the Committee of Independent Experts and of the Contracting Parties and on the basis of social, economic and other policy considerations, the situations which should, in its view, be the subject of recommendations to each Contracting Party;

Noting also that the Parliamentary Assembly, in a letter from its President to the Chairman of the Committee of Ministers of 3 September 1992, has decided to abstain from communicating its views on a particular set of conclusions of the Committee of Independent Experts as provided for under Article 28 of the Charter and to use these conclusions as a basis for periodical social policy debates to be held by the Assembly in accordance with Article 6 of the Amending Protocol,

Draws the attention of the governments concerned to the recommendations adopted for the 12th cycle of supervision following the proposals made by the Governmental Committee;

Recommends in addition the governments of the second group of states to take account, in an appropriate manner, of all the various observations made in the Conclusions of the Committee of Independent Experts and the report of the Governmental Committee.

Committee of Ministers

> *Recommendation No. R ChS (94) 1 on the application of the European Social Charter by Austria during the period 1989-90 (12th supervision cycle)*
>
> *(Adopted by the Committee of Ministers on 8 April 1994 at the 511th meeting of the Ministers' Deputies)*

The Committee of Ministers, in its composition restricted to Contracting Parties to the European Social Charter,[1]

Referring to the European Social Charter, in particular Part IV thereof;

Whereas the European Social Charter, signed in Turin on 18 October 1961, came into force on 28 November 1969 with respect to Austria;

Whereas, in accordance with Article 20, Austria has accepted sixty-two out of the seventy-two provisions contained in the Charter;

Whereas the Government of Austria submitted in 1991 its 10th report on the provisions of the Charter which it has accepted, and whereas this report has been examined in accordance with Articles 24 to 27 of the Charter;

Having examined Conclusions XII-2 of the Committee of Independent Experts appointed under Article 25 of the Charter and the 12th report (II) of the Governmental Committee appointed under Article 27 of the Charter;

Having noted that in respect of Article 5 (the right to organise), that the Committee of Independent Experts had reached a negative conclusion as workers in enterprises with fewer than five employees are not protected against dismissal on grounds of trade union activities;

Observes that the Governmental Committee in accordance with Article 29 of the Charter has proposed that an individual recommendation be addressed to Austria in relation to Article 5;

Having noted also in respect of Article 8, paragraph 2 (illegality of dismissal during maternity leave) that the Committee of independent Experts concluded negatively as the Austrian legislation allows for domestic employees to be dismissed from the end of the fifth month of pregnancy,

Observes that the Governmental Committee has likewise proposed that an individual recommendation be addressed to Austria in relation to Article 8, paragraph 2, while underlining that women are most vulnerable in terms of job security during maternity leave;

---

1. Austria, Belgium, Cyprus, Denmark, Finland, France, Germany, Greece, Iceland, Ireland, Italy, Luxembourg, Malta, the Netherlands, Norway, Portugal, Spain, Sweden, Turkey and the United Kingdom.

Recommends the Government of Austria, to take account, in an appropriate manner, of the negative conclusions of the Committee of Independent Experts and invites it to provide information in its next report on the measures it has taken to this effect.

Committee of Ministers

> *Recommendation No. R ChS (94) 2 on the application of the European Social Charter by France during the period 1989-90 (12th supervision cycle)*
>
> *(Adopted by the Committee of Ministers on 8 April 1994 at the 511th meeting of the Ministers' Deputies)*

The Committee of Ministers, in its composition restricted to Contracting Parties to the European Social Charter,[1]

Referring to the European Social Charter, in particular Part IV thereof;

Whereas the European Social Charter, signed in Turin on 18 October 1961, came into force on 8 April 1973 with respect to France;

Whereas, in accordance with Article 20, France has accepted all seventy-two provisions contained in the Charter;

Whereas the Government of France submitted in 1991 its 8th report on the provisions of the Charter which it has accepted, and whereas this report has been examined in accordance with Articles 24 to 27 of the Charter;

Having examined Conclusions XII-2 of the Committee of Independent Experts appointed under Article 25 of the Charter and the 12th report (II) of the Governmental Committee appointed under Article 27 of the Charter;

Having noted that in respect of Article 1, paragraph 2 (prohibition against forced labour) the Committee of Independent Experts had reached a negative conclusion as:

– Sections 39, paragraph 4 and 59, paragraph 1 of the Disciplinary and Penal Code of the Merchant Navy, providing a possibility for penal sanctions against seamen in certain cases not involving the safety of the vessel or the life or health of those on board, had still not been repealed,

Observes that the Governmental Committee in accordance with Article 29 of the Charter has proposed that an individual recommendation be addressed to France in relation to Article 1, paragraph 2;

---

1. Austria, Belgium, Cyprus, Denmark, Finland, France, Germany, Greece, Iceland, Ireland, Italy, Luxembourg, Malta, the Netherlands, Norway, Portugal, Spain, Sweden, Turkey and the United Kingdom.

Recommends the French Government to take account, in an appropriate manner, of the negative conclusions of the Committee of Independent Experts and invites it to provide information in its next report on the measures it has taken to this effect.

Committee of Ministers

> *Recommendation No. R ChS (94) 3 on the application of the European Social Charter by Germany during the period 1989-90 (12th supervision cycle)*
> *(Adopted by the Committee of Ministers on 8 April 1994 at the 511th meeting of the Ministers' Deputies)*

The Committee of Ministers, in its composition restricted to Contracting Parties to the European Social Charter,[1]

Referring to the European Social Charter, in particular Part IV thereof;

Whereas the European Social Charter, signed in Turin on 18 October 1961, came into force on 26 February 1965 with respect to Germany;

Whereas, in accordance with Article 20, Germany has accepted sixty-seven out of the seventy-two provisions contained in the Charter;

Whereas the Government of Germany submitted in 1991 its 12th report on the provisions of the Charter which it has accepted, and whereas this report has been examined in accordance with Articles 24 to 27 of the Charter;

Having examined Conclusions XII-2 of the Committee of Independent Experts appointed under Article 25 of the Charter and the 12th report (II) of the Governmental Committee appointed under Article 27 of the Charter;

Having noted that in respect of Article 19, paragraph 6 (the right of migrant workers to family reunion), that the Committee of Independent Experts had reached a negative conclusion as:

- the age limit for the entry of children of migrant workers nationals of non-European Community Contracting Parties to the Charter for purposes of family reunion was sixteen years instead of twenty-one, as provided for in the Appendix to the Charter;

- family reunion was not allowed in the case of young persons with only one parent resident in Germany, and;

- second generation migrant workers must have been resident in Germany for at least eight years and have been married for at

---

1. Austria, Belgium, Cyprus, Denmark, Finland, France, Germany, Greece, Iceland, Ireland, Italy, Luxembourg, Malta, the Netherlands, Norway, Portugal, Spain, Sweden, Turkey and the United Kingdom.

least one year in order for their spouses to be allowed to enter Germany for purposes of family reunion;

Observes that the Governmental Committee, while pointing out that it has made a proposal to the Committee on the European Social Charter (Charte-Rel), to lower the age limit for family reunion provided for in the Appendix to Article 19 para. 6 of the Charter to eighteen years, has proposed, in accordance with Article 29 of the Charter, that an individual recommendation be addressed to Germany under Article 19 para. 6 to amend its legislation in order to allow all children under eighteen years of age of migrant workers legally resident in Germany and the spouses of second generation migrant workers legally resident in Germany, to enter this country for purposes of family reunion;

Recommends the Government of Germany, to take account, in an appropriate manner, of the negative conclusions of the Committee of Independent Experts and invites it to provide information in its next report on the measures it has taken to this effect.

Committee of Ministers

> *Recommendation No. R ChS (94) 4 on the application of the European Social Charter by Italy during the period 1989-90 (12th supervision cycle)*
> *(Adopted by the Committee of Ministers on 8 April 1994 at the 511th meeting of the Ministers' Deputies)*

The Committee of Ministers, in its composition restricted to Contracting Parties to the European Social Charter,[1]

Referring to the European Social Charter, in particular Part IV thereof;

Whereas the European Social Charter, signed in Turin on 18 October 1961, came into force on 21 November 1965 with respect to Italy;

Whereas, in accordance with Article 20, Italy has accepted all seventy-two provisions contained in the Charter;

Whereas the Government of Italy submitted in 1991 its 12th report on the provisions of the Charter which it has accepted, and whereas this report has been examined in accordance with Articles 24 to 27 of the Charter;

Having examined Conclusions XII-2 of the Committee of Independent Experts appointed under Article 25 of the Charter and the 12th report (II) of the Governmental Committee appointed under Article 27 of the Charter;

---

1. Austria, Belgium, Cyprus, Denmark, Finland, France, Germany, Greece, Iceland, Ireland, Italy, Luxembourg, Malta, the Netherlands, Norway, Portugal, Spain, Sweden, Turkey and the United Kingdom.

Having noted that in respect of Article 1, paragraph 2 (prohibition against forced labour) the Committee of Independent Experts had reached a negative conclusion as Sections 1091 and 1094 of the Navigation Code provide for penal sanctions for seamen and civil aviation staff who desert their posts or refuse to obey orders in certain cases not involving the safety of the vessel or aeroplane or of the persons aboard;

Having noted also that in respect of Article 3 para. 2 (provision for the enforcement of safety and health regulations by measures of supervision), the Committee of Independent Experts had not received statistical information on the activities of the local health units enabling it to change its previous negative conclusion;

Having noted further that as regards Article 4 para. 4 (reasonable notice of termination of employment), the Committee of Independent Experts had adopted a negative conclusion as the periods of notice were insufficient in certain branches of activity;

Having noted also that as regards Article 4 para. 5 (limitation of deduction from wages), the Committee of Independent Experts had adopted a negative conclusion as no regulation of deductions from wages for workers' debts to their employers had been introduced;

Having noted as well that in respect of Article 7 para. 1 (minimum age of admission to employment), the Committee of Independent Experts had adopted a negative conclusion as there was no prohibition of employment of young persons under fifteen years of age in agriculture and domestic work;

Having noted also that in respect of Article 8 paras. 1, 2 and 3 (paid maternity leave; illegality of dismissal during maternity leave; time-off for nursing mothers), the Committee of Independent Experts had adopted negative conclusions as domestic employees:

- were not entitled to maternity cash benefits if they were dismissed during pregnancy;
- were not protected by a ban on dismissal during maternity leave or at such a time that the notice of dismissal would expire during such leave;

and as domestic employees and home workers:

- were not entitled to nursing breaks;

Having noted finally that as regards Article 13 para. 1 (social and medical assistance for those in need), the Committee of Independent Experts had adopted a negative conclusion as there was no entitlement as of right to social assistance, with the possibility of appeal to an independent body of appeal, such as a court;

Observes that the Governmental Committee in accordance with Article 29 of the Charter has proposed that an individual recommendation be addressed to Italy in relation to Article 1 para. 2, Article 3

427

para. 2, Article 4 paras. 4 and 5, Article 7 para. 1, Article 8 para. 1, 2 and 3, and Article 13 para. 1;

Observes that in respect of Article 3 para. 2, the Governmental Committee has proposed that the recommendation should invite Italy to provide the information needed for the Committee of Independent Experts to arrive at a positive conclusion;

Observes also that in respect of Article 7 para. 1, the Governmental Committee has proposed that the recommendation should invite Italy to amend its legislation so as to restrict the authorisation of employment of young persons aged under fifteen to cases of light work;

Recommends the Italian Government to take account, in an appropriate manner, of the negative conclusions of the Committee of Independent Experts, as well as the proposals of the Governmental Committee, and invites it to provide information in its next report on the measures it has taken to this effect.

Committee of Ministers

> *Recommendation No. R ChS (94) 5 on the application of the European Social Charter by Spain during the period 1989-90 (12th supervision cycle)*
> *(Adopted by the Committee of Ministers on 8 April 1994 at the 511th meeting of the Ministers' Deputies)*

The Committee of Ministers, in its composition restricted to Contracting Parties to the European Social Charter,[1]

Referring to the European Social Charter, in particular Part IV thereof;

Whereas the European Social Charter, signed in Turin on 18 October 1961, came into force on 5 June 1980 with respect to Spain;

Whereas, in accordance with Article 20, Spain has accepted all seventy-two provisions contained in the Charter;

Whereas the Government of Spain submitted in 1991 its 5th report under the Charter, and whereas this report has been examined in accordance with Articles 24 to 27 of the Charter;

Having examined Conclusions XII-2 of the Committee of Independent of the Governmental Committee appointed under Article 27 of the Charter;

Having noted that in respect of Article 1, paragraph 2 (prohibition against forced labour) the Committee of Independent Experts adopted a negative conclusion as the Act of 22 December 1955 relating to merchant seamen and that of 24 December 1964 (as amended by the

---

1. Austria, Belgium, Cyprus, Denmark, Finland, France, Germany, Greece, Iceland, Ireland, Italy, Luxembourg, Malta, the Netherlands, Norway, Portugal, Spain, Sweden, Turkey and the United Kingdom.

organic law of 1986) relating to airmen, included provisions for criminal sanctions in the event of disciplinary offences, even in those cases where neither the safety of the vessel or aeroplane, nor the life or health of those on board were threatened,

Observes that the Governmental Committee, in accordance with Article 29 of the Charter, has proposed that an individual recommendation be addressed to Spain in relation to Article 1, paragraph 2;

Recommends the Spanish Government to take account, in an appropriate manner, of the negative conclusions of the Committee of Independent Experts and invites it to provide information in its next report on the measures it has taken to this effect.

17. Thirteenth supervision cycle – first part

Committee of Independent Experts – Conclusions XIII-1 (1994, 304 p., ISBN: 92-871-2465-5)

Governmental Committee Thirteenth report (I) (1995, 240 p., ISBN: 92-871-2753-0)

Committee of Ministers

Resolution ChS (95) 1 on the implementation of the European Social Charter during the period 1990-91 (13th supervision cycle – part I) (Adopted by the Committee of Ministers on 22 June 1995 at the 541st meeting of the Ministers' Deputies)

The Committee of Ministers, in its composition restricted to Contracting Parties to the European Social Charter,[1]

Referring to the European Social Charter, in particular to the provisions of Part IV thereof;

Having regard to Article 29 of the Charter;

Considering the reports submitted by the Governments of Denmark, Greece, Iceland, Ireland,[2] the Netherlands, Norway, Sweden, Turkey and the United Kingdom for the period from 1 January 1990 to 31 December 1991, as well as those submitted by the Governments of Austria, Cyprus, France, Italy and Spain for the period from 1 January to 31 December 1991;

Considering Conclusions XIII-1 of the Committee of Independent Experts appointed under Article 25 of the Charter and the 13th report (I) of the Governmental Committee appointed under Article 27 of the Charter;

---

1. Austria, Belgium, Cyprus, Denmark, Finland, France, Germany, Greece, Iceland, Ireland, Italy, Luxembourg, Malta, the Netherlands, Norway, Portugal, Spain, Sweden, Turkey and the United Kingdom.
2. The Irish report also covered the year 1989.

Recalling the request made, both to the States Parties to the Charter and the supervisory bodies, by the ministers participating in the Ministerial Conference on the European Social Charter held in Turin on 21 and 22 October 1991, on the occasion of the thirtieth anniversary of the Charter, and by the Committee of Ministers in its decision of 11 December 1991, "to envisage the application of certain of the measures provided for in this Protocol [the Amending Protocol], before its entry into force, in so far as the text of the Charter will allow";

Noting that the Governmental Committee, in view of this request, has decided, in accordance with Article 4 of the Amending Protocol, to select, in the light of the reports of the Committee of Independent Experts and of the Contracting Parties and on the basis of social, economic and other policy considerations, the situations which should, in its view, be the subject of recommendations to each Contracting Party;

Noting also that the Parliamentary Assembly, in a letter from its President to the Chairman of the Committee of Ministers of 3 September 1992, has decided to abstain from communicating its views on a particular set of conclusions of the Committee of Independent Experts as provided for under Article 28 of the Charter and to use these conclusions as a basis for periodical social policy debates to be held by the Assembly in accordance with Article 6 of the Amending Protocol,

Draws the attention of the governments concerned to the recommendations adopted for the 13th supervision cycle (part I) following the proposals made by the Governmental Committee;

Recommends in addition that these governments take account, in an appropriate manner, of all the various observations made in the conclusions of the Committee of Independent Experts and the report of the Governmental Committee.

Committee of Ministers

Recommendation No. R ChS (95) 1 on the application of the European Social Charter by Austria during the year 1991 (13th supervision cycle – part I)
(Adopted by the Committee of Ministers on 22 June 1995 at the 541st meeting of the Ministers' Deputies)

The Committee of Ministers, in its composition restricted to Contracting Parties to the European Social Charter,[1]

---

1. Austria, Belgium, Cyprus, Denmark, Finland, France, Germany, Greece, Iceland, Ireland, Italy, Luxembourg, Malta, the Netherlands, Norway, Portugal, Spain, Sweden, Turkey and the United Kingdom.

Having regard to the European Social Charter, in particular Part IV thereof;

Whereas the European Social Charter, signed in Turin on 18 October 1961, came into force on 28 November 1969 with respect to Austria;

Whereas, in accordance with Article 20, Austria has accepted sixty-two out of the seventy-two provisions contained in the Charter;

Whereas the Government of Austria submitted in 1992 its 11th report on the provisions of the Charter which it has accepted, and whereas this report has been examined in accordance with Articles 24 to 27 of the Charter;

Having examined Conclusions XIII-1 of the Committee of Independent Experts appointed under Article 25 of the Charter and the 13th report (I) of the Governmental Committee appointed under Article 27 of the Charter;

Having noted in respect of Article 5 (the right to organise) that the Committee of Independent Experts had reached a negative conclusion since the 11th cycle as workers in enterprises with fewer than five employees are not protected against dismissal on grounds of trade union activities,

Recalls that, as proposed by the Governmental Committee in its 12th report (II) it had, on 8 April 1994, issued a recommendation to Austria in relation to Article 5;

Observes that no change had occurred in part I of the 13th cycle,

Recommends the Government of Austria to take account, in an appropriate manner, of the negative conclusion of the Committee of Independent Experts and of this second recommendation of the Committee of Ministers and again invites it to provide information in its next report on the measures it has taken to this effect.

Committee of Ministers

> *Recommendation No. R ChS (95) 2 (on the application of the European Social Charter by Denmark during the period 1990-91 (13th supervision cycle – part I)*
> *(Adopted by the Committee of Ministers on 22 June 1995 at the 541st meeting of the Ministers' Deputies)*

The Committee of Ministers, in its composition restricted to Contracting Parties to the European Social Charter,[1]

---

1. Austria, Belgium, Cyprus, Denmark, Finland, France, Germany, Greece, Iceland, Ireland, Italy, Luxembourg, Malta, the Netherlands, Norway, Portugal, Spain, Sweden, Turkey and the United Kingdom.

431

Having regard to the European Social Charter, in particular Part IV thereof;

Whereas the European Social Charter, signed in Turin on 18 October 1961, came into force on 2 April 1965 with respect to Denmark;

Whereas, in accordance with Article 20, Denmark has accepted forty-five out of the seventy-two provisions contained in the Charter;

Whereas the Government of Denmark submitted in 1992 its 13th report on those provisions of the Charter which it has accepted, and whereas this report has been examined in accordance with Articles 24 to 27 of the Charter;

Having examined Conclusions XIII-1 of the Committee of Independent Experts appointed under Article 25 of the Charter and the 13th report (I) of the Governmental Committee appointed under Article 27 of the Charter;

Having noted that in respect of Article 5 (the right to organise), the Committee of Independent Experts had adopted a negative conclusion as the Danish International Ships' Register interfered with the right freely to join or form organisations, fettering the right of workers to protect their economic and social interests, as well as the right of trade unions to protect their members by limiting the scope of collective agreements;

Having noted also that in respect of Article 6, paragraph 2 (promotion of machinery for voluntary negotiations), the Committee of Independent Experts had adopted a negative conclusion because of the restrictions introduced by the 1988 Act establishing the Danish International Ships' Register on collective bargaining and the unequal treatment for nationals of Contracting Parties in this field;

Having noted as well that in respect of Article 6, paragraph 4 (the right to collective action), the Committee of Independent Experts had adopted a negative conclusion as civil servants were denied the right to strike,

Observes that the Governmental Committee, in accordance with Article 29 of the Charter, has proposed that an individual recommendation be addressed to Denmark in relation to Article 5 and Article 6, paragraphs 2 and 4;

Recommends that the Danish Government take account in an appropriate manner of the negative conclusions of the Committee of Independent Experts, and invites it to provide information in its next report on the measures it has taken to this effect.

Committee of Ministers

> *Recommendation No. R ChS (95) 3 on the application of the European Social Charter by France during the year 1991 (13th supervision cycle – part I)*
>
> *(Adopted by the Committee of Ministers on 22 June 1995 at the 541st meeting of the Ministers' Deputies)*

The Committee of Ministers, in its composition restricted to Contracting Parties to the European Social Charter,[1]

Having regard to the European Social Charter, in particular Part IV thereof;

Whereas the European Social Charter, signed in Turin on 18 October 1961, came into force on 8 April 1973 with respect to France;

Whereas, in accordance with Article 20, France has accepted all seventy-two provisions contained in the Charter;

Whereas the Government of France submitted in 1992 its 9th report under the Charter, and whereas this report has been examined in accordance with Articles 24 to 27 of the Charter;

Having examined Conclusions XIII-1 of the Committee of Independent Experts appointed under Article 25 of the Charter and the 13th report (I) of the Governmental Committee appointed under Article 27 of the Charter;

Having noted that in respect of Article 1, paragraph 2 (prohibition against forced labour), the Committee of Independent Experts had adopted a negative conclusion since the 7th cycle as Sections 39, paragraph 4 and 59, paragraph 1 of the Disciplinary and Penal Code of the Merchant Navy, providing a possibility for penal sanctions against seamen in certain cases not involving the safety of the vessel or the life and health of those on board, had still not been repealed,

Recalls that, as proposed by the Governmental Committee in its 12th report (II) it had, on 8 April 1994 issued a recommendation to France in relation to Article 1, paragraph 2;

Observes that no change occurred in part I of the 13th cycle;

Recommends the French Government to take account, in an appropriate manner, of the negative conclusion of the Committee of Independent Experts and of this second recommendation of the Committee of Ministers and again invites it to provide information in its next report on the measures it has taken to this effect.

---

1. Austria, Belgium, Cyprus, Denmark, Finland, France, Germany, Greece, Iceland, Ireland, Italy, Luxembourg, Malta, the Netherlands, Norway, Portugal, Spain, Sweden, Turkey and the United Kingdom.

Committee of Ministers

> *Recommendation No. R ChS (95) 4 on the application of the European Social Charter by Greece during the period 1990-91 (13th supervision cycle – part I)*
>
> *(Adopted by the Committee of Ministers on 22 June 1995 at the 541st meeting of the Ministers' Deputies)*

The Committee of Ministers, in its composition restricted to Contracting Parties to the European Social Charter,[1]

Having regard to the European Social Charter, in particular Part IV thereof;

Whereas the European Social Charter, signed in Turin on 18 October 1961, came into force on 6 July 1984 with respect to Greece;

Whereas, in accordance with Article 20, Greece has accepted sixty-seven out of the seventy-two provisions contained in the Charter;

Whereas the Government of Greece submitted in 1992 its 4th report on those provisions of the Charter which it has accepted, and whereas this report has been examined in accordance with Articles 24 to 27 of the Charter;

Having examined Conclusions XIII-1 of the Committee of Independent Experts appointed under Article 25 of the Charter and the 13th report (I) of the Governmental Committee appointed under Article 27 of the Charter;

Having noted that in respect of Article 1, paragraph 2 (prohibition against forced labour), the Committee of Independent Experts had adopted a negative conclusion since the 10th cycle as:

- Section 64 of Decree 1400/1973 provides that the length of the compulsory period of service for career officers who have followed several training courses may be up to twenty-five years;

- the provisions for the application of criminal sanctions against seafarers in cases where neither the safety of the vessel nor the lives or health of the persons on board are endangered are still in force (Articles 205, 207 para. 1, 208, 210 para. 1 and 222 of the Code of Public Maritime Law of 1973; Section 4 para. 1 of Act No. 3276/1944 on Collective Bargaining in the Merchant Navy; Section 15 of Act No. 299/1936 on the Settlement of Collective Disputes in the Navy);

---

1. Austria, Belgium, Cyprus, Denmark, Finland, France, Germany, Greece, Iceland, Ireland, Italy, Luxembourg, Malta, the Netherlands, Norway, Portugal, Spain, Sweden, Turkey and the United Kingdom.

Having noted also that in respect of Article 13, paragraph 1 (social and medical assistance for those in need), the Committee of Independent Experts had adopted a negative conclusion since the 12th cycle as there existed neither a right to be granted social assistance in Greece nor the possibility of invoking such a right before an independent body such as a court;

Having noted finally that in respect of Article 13, paragraph 4 (equal treatment with respect to social and medical assistance), a second recommendation had been proposed as:

- "pension" for those aged over 68 is restricted to Greek nationals;
- Legislative Decree 57/1973, which provides that social assistance is granted to foreigners resident in Greece on an equal footing with Greek nationals, also provides that in order to be considered a resident in Greece a foreign national must have been lawfully present in Greece for at least six months,

Recalls that, as proposed by the Governmental Committee in its 12th report (I) it had, on 7 September 1993, issued a recommendation to Greece in relation to Article 1, paragraph 2 and Article 13, paragraphs 1 and 4;

Observes that no change occurred in part I of the 13th cycle;

Recommends the Greek Government to take account, in an appropriate manner, of the negative conclusions of the Committee of Independent Experts and of this second recommendation of the Committee of Ministers and again invites it to provide information in its next report on the measures it has taken to this effect.

Committee of Ministers

> *Recommendation No. R ChS (95) 5 on the application of the European Social Charter by Greece during the period 1990-91 (13th supervision cycle – part I)*
> *(Adopted by the Committee of Ministers on 22 June 1995 at the 541st meeting of the Ministers' Deputies)*

The Committee of Ministers, in its composition restricted to Contracting Parties to the European Social Charter,[1]

Having regard to the European Social Charter, in particular Part IV thereof;

Whereas the European Social Charter, signed in Turin on 18 October 1961, came into force on 6 July 1984 with respect to Greece;

---

1. Austria, Belgium, Cyprus, Denmark, Finland, France, Germany, Greece, Iceland, Ireland, Italy, Luxembourg, Malta, the Netherlands, Norway, Portugal, Spain, Sweden, Turkey and the United Kingdom.

Whereas, in accordance with Article 20, Greece has accepted sixty-seven out of the seventy-two provisions contained in the Charter;

Whereas the Government of Greece submitted in 1992 its 4th report on those provisions of the Charter which it has accepted, and whereas this report has been examined in accordance with Articles 24 to 27 of the Charter;

Having examined Conclusions XIII-1 of the Committee of Independent Experts appointed under Article 25 of the Charter and the 13th report (I) of the Governmental Committee appointed under Article 27 of the Charter;

Having noted in respect of Article 7, paragraphs 1 and 3 (minimum age of admission to employment; safeguarding the full benefit of compulsory education), that the Committee of Independent Experts had adopted negative conclusions as no minimum age for admission to employment exists for children engaged in agricultural, forestry or livestock work of a family nature,

Observes that the Governmental Committee, in accordance with Article 29 of the Charter, has proposed that an individual recommendation be addressed to Greece in relation to Article 7, paragraphs 1 and 3, while underlining that Greece has a considerable rural population and that the provisions in question aimed to protect one of the most vulnerable groups in society;

Having noted also in respect of Article 19, paragraph 1 (free assistance and information services; steps against misleading propaganda on emigration and immigration), the Committee of Independent Experts had adjourned its conclusion for lack of information as the national report did not contain the information requested in the previous conclusion;

Having noted finally that in respect of Article 19, paragraph 8 (security against expulsion), the Committee of Independent Experts had adopted a negative conclusion as there was no right to appeal against a decision of expulsion taken by an "act of government",

Observes that the Governmental Committee has likewise proposed that an individual recommendation be addressed to Greece in relation to Article 19, paragraphs 1 and 8;

Recommends that the Greek Government take account, in an appropriate manner, of the negative and adjourned conclusions of the Committee of Independent Experts, and invites it to provide information in its next report on the measures it has taken to this effect in respect of the negative conclusions as well as to provide the information requested by the Committee of Independent Experts in respect of the adjourned conclusion.

Committee of Ministers

Recommendation No. R ChS (95) 6 on the application of the European Social Charter by Ireland during the period 1989-91 (13th supervision cycle – part I)
(Adopted by the Committee of Ministers on 22 June 1995 at the 541st meeting of the Ministers' Deputies)

The Committee of Ministers, in its composition restricted to Contracting Parties to the European Social Charter,[1]

Having regard to the European Social Charter, in particular Part IV thereof;

Whereas the European Social Charter, signed in Turin on 18 October 1961, came into force on 26 February 1965 with respect to Ireland;

Whereas, in accordance with Article 20, Ireland has accepted sixty-three out of the seventy-two provisions contained in the Charter;

Whereas the Government of Ireland submitted in 1992 its 12th report on the provisions of the Charter which it has accepted, and whereas this report has been examined in accordance with Articles 24 to 27 of the Charter;

Having examined Conclusions XIII-1 of the Committee of Independent Experts appointed under Article 25 of the Charter and the 13th report (I) of the Governmental Committee appointed under Article 27 of the Charter;

Having noted in respect of Article 1, paragraph 2 (prohibition against forced labour), that the Committee of Independent Experts had adopted a negative conclusion as under the Merchant Shipping Act 1894 seamen who fail to rejoin their ship or who do not carry out orders are liable to punishment, which may involve their imprisonment;

Having noted also in respect of Article 4, paragraph 4 (reasonable notice of termination of employment), that the Committee of Independent Experts had adopted a negative conclusion as the minimum notice periods provided for by the 1973 Minimum Notice and Terms of Employment Act were insufficient;

Having noted in addition in respect of Article 6, paragraph 4 (the right to collective action), that the Committee of Independent Experts had adopted a negative conclusion as under Section 16 of the 1875 Conspiracy and Protection of Property Act merchant seamen were not protected from criminal prosecution for conspiracy in respect of acts relating to trade disputes;

---

1. Austria, Belgium, Cyprus, Denmark, Finland, France, Germany, Greece, Iceland, Ireland, Italy, Luxembourg, Malta, the Netherlands, Norway, Portugal, Spain, Sweden, Turkey and the United Kingdom.

Having noted further in respect of Article 7, paragraph 3 (safeguarding the full benefit of compulsory education), that the Committee of Independent Experts had adopted a negative conclusion as:

- the prohibition on employing children still subject to compulsory schooling during the school year does not apply to children related to the employer. For these children there is neither any maximum working day or week (apart from a prohibition on night work and statutory rest periods, which is not sufficient); nor any restriction on their employment in light non-industrial work;

- no restrictions apply during school holidays to children related to the employer (apart from the prohibition on night work and the statutory rest periods);

Having noted finally in respect of Article 19, paragraph 8 (security against expulsion), that the Committee of Independent Experts had adopted a negative conclusion as there was no right of appeal against a deportation order for persons who were neither nationals of member states of the European Community nor of states bound by the European Convention on Establishment,

Observes that the Governmental Committee in accordance with Article 29 of the Charter has proposed that an individual recommendation be addressed to Ireland in relation to Article 1, paragraph 2, Article 4, paragraph 4, Article 6, paragraph 4, Article 7, paragraph 3 and Article 19, paragraph 8;

Recommends that the Irish Government take account, in an appropriate manner, of the negative conclusions of the Committee of Independent Experts, and invites it to provide information in its next report on the measures it has taken to this effect.

Committee of Ministers

> *Recommendation No. R ChS (95) 7 on the application of the European Social Charter by Italy during the year 1991 (13th supervision cycle – part I)*
> *(Adopted by the Committee of Ministers on 22 June 1995 at the 541st meeting of the Ministers' Deputies)*

The Committee of Ministers, in its composition restricted to Contracting Parties to the European Social Charter,[1]

Having regard to the European Social Charter, in particular Part IV thereof;

Whereas the European Social Charter, signed in Turin on 18 October 1961, came into force on 21 November 1965 with respect to Italy;

---

1. Austria, Belgium, Cyprus, Denmark, Finland, France, Germany, Greece, Iceland, Ireland, Italy, Luxembourg, Malta, the Netherlands, Norway, Portugal, Spain, Sweden, Turkey and the United Kingdom.

Whereas, in accordance with Article 20, Italy has accepted all seventy-two provisions contained in the Charter;

Whereas the Government of Italy in 1992 submitted its 13th report under the Charter, and whereas this report has been examined in accordance with Articles 24 to 27 of the Charter;

Having examined Conclusions XIII-1 of the Committee of Independent Experts appointed under Article 25 of the Charter and the 13th report (I) of the Governmental Committee appointed under Article 27 of the Charter;

Having noted that in respect of Article 1, paragraph 2 (prohibition against forced labour), the Committee of Independent Experts had adopted a negative conclusion since the 4th cycle as Sections 1091 and 1094 of the Navigation Code provide for penal sanctions for seamen and civil aviation staff who desert their posts or refuse to obey orders in certain cases not involving the safety of the vessel or aeroplane or of the persons aboard;

Having noted also that in respect of Article 3, paragraph 2 (provision for the enforcement of safety and health regulations by measures of supervision), the Committee of Independent Experts had not received statistical information on the activities of the local health units enabling it to change its conclusion, which was negative since the 6th cycle;

Having noted further that as regards Article 4, paragraph 4 (reasonable notice of termination of employment), the Committee of Independent Experts had adopted a negative conclusion since the 1st cycle as the periods of notice were insufficient in certain branches of activity;

Having noted finally that as regards Article 4, paragraph 5 (limitation of deduction from wages), the Committee of Independent Experts had adopted a negative conclusion since the 8th cycle as no regulation of the deductions from their wages for workers' debts to their employers had been introduced,

Recalls that, as proposed by the Governmental Committee in its 12th report (II) it had on 8 April 1994 issued a recommendation to Italy in relation to Article 1, paragraph 2, Article 3, paragraph 2 and Article 4, paragraphs 4 and 5;

Observes that no change occurred in part I of the 13th cycle;

Observes that in respect of Article 4, paragraph 5, the Governmental Committee has underlined that employers and workers should be involved in the implementation of the principle set forth in the provision;

Recommends the Italian Government to take account, in an appropriate manner, of the negative conclusions of the Committee of Independent Experts and of this second recommendation of the

Committee of Ministers and again invites it to provide information in its next report on the measures it has taken to this effect.

Committee of Ministers

> *Recommendation No. R ChS (95) 8 on the application of the European Social Charter by Italy during the year 1991 (13th supervision cycle – part I)*
> *(Adopted by the Committee of Ministers on 22 June 1995 at the 541st meeting of the Ministers' Deputies)*

The Committee of Ministers, in its composition restricted to Contracting Parties to the European Social Charter,[1]

Having regard to the European Social Charter, in particular Part IV thereof;

Whereas the European Social Charter, signed in Turin on 18 October 1961, came into force on 21 November 1965 with respect to Italy;

Whereas, in accordance with Article 20, Italy has accepted all seventy-two provisions contained in the Charter;

Whereas the Government of Italy in 1992 submitted its 13th report under the Charter, and whereas this report has been examined in accordance with Articles 24 to 27 of the Charter;

Having examined Conclusions XIII-1 of the Committee of Independent Experts appointed under Article 25 of the Charter and the 13th report (I) of the Governmental Committee appointed under Article 27 of the Charter;

Having noted that in respect of Article 3, paragraphs 1 and 2 (issue of safety and health regulations and provision for the enforcement of safety and health regulations by measures of supervision), the Committee of Independent Experts had adopted a negative conclusion as self-employed workers in agriculture, trade and industry, together with members of their families working with them, were not covered by health and safety regulations,

Observes that the Governmental Committee, in accordance with Article 29 of the Charter, has proposed that an individual recommendation be addressed to Italy in relation to Article 3, paragraphs 1 and 2;

Recommends that the Italian Government take account, in an appropriate manner, of the negative conclusions of the Committee of Independent Experts and invites it to provide information in its next report on the measures it has taken to this effect.

---

1. Austria, Belgium, Cyprus, Denmark, Finland, France, Germany, Greece, Iceland, Ireland, Italy, Luxembourg, Malta, the Netherlands, Norway, Portugal, Spain, Sweden, Turkey and the United Kingdom.

Committee of Ministers

> *Recommendation No. R ChS (95) 9 on the application of the European Social Charter by Spain during the year 1991 (13th supervision cycle – part I)*
> *(Adopted by the Committee of Ministers on 22 June 1995 at the 541st meeting of the Ministers' Deputies)*

The Committee of Ministers, in its composition restricted to Contracting Parties to the European Social Charter,[1]

Having regard to the European Social Charter, in particular Part IV thereof;

Whereas the European Social Charter, signed in Turin on 18 October 1961, came into force on 5 June 1980 with respect to Spain;

Whereas, in accordance with Article 20, Spain has accepted all seventy-two provisions contained in the Charter;

Whereas the Government of Spain submitted in 1992 its 6th report under the Charter, and whereas this report has been examined in accordance with Articles 24 to 27 of the Charter;

Having examined Conclusions XIII-1 of the Committee of Independent Experts appointed under Article 25 of the Charter and the 13th report (I) of the Governmental Committee appointed under Article 27 of the Charter;

Having noted that in respect of Article 1, paragraph 2 (prohibition against forced labour), the Committee of Independent Experts adopted a negative conclusion since the 12th cycle as Act No. 359 of 22 December 1955 relating to merchant seamen, and Act No. 209 of 24 December 1964 relating to airmen, included provision for criminal sanctions in the event of disciplinary offences, even in those cases where neither the safety of the vessel or aeroplane, nor the life or health of those on board were threatened,

Recalls that, as proposed by the Governmental Committee in its 12th report (II) it had, on 8 April 1994, issued a recommendation to Spain in relation to Article 1, paragraph 2;

Having noted that Act No. 359 of 22 December 1955 had been abrogated since the recommendation was adopted,

Observes that no change had occurred in part I of the 13th cycle as regards Act No. 209 of 24 December 1964;

Recommends the Spanish Government to take account, in an appropriate manner, of the negative conclusion of the Committee of Independent Experts and of this second recommendation of the

---

1. Austria, Belgium, Cyprus, Denmark, Finland, France, Germany, Greece, Iceland, Ireland, Italy, Luxembourg, Malta, the Netherlands, Norway, Portugal, Spain, Sweden, Turkey and the United Kingdom.

Committee of Ministers on this point and again invites it to provide information in its next report on the measures it has taken to this effect.

Committee of Ministers

> *Recommendation No. R ChS (95) 10 on the application of the European Social Charter by Sweden during the period 1990-91 (13th supervision cycle – part I)*
> *(Adopted by the Committee of Ministers on 22 June 1995 at the 541st meeting of the Ministers' Deputies)*

The Committee of Ministers, in its composition restricted to Contracting Parties to the European Social Charter,[1]

Having regard to the European Social Charter, in particular Part IV thereof;

Whereas the European Social Charter, signed in Turin on 18 October 1961, came into force on 26 February 1965 with respect to Sweden;

Whereas, in accordance with Article 20, Sweden has accepted sixty-two out of the seventy-two provisions contained in the Charter;

Whereas the Government of Sweden submitted in 1992 its 13th report on the provisions of the Charter which it has accepted, and whereas this report has been examined in accordance with Articles 24 to 27 of the Charter;

Having examined Conclusions XIII-1 of the Committee of Independent Experts appointed under Article 25 of the Charter and the 13th report (I) of the Governmental Committee appointed under Article 27 of the Charter;

Having noted also that in respect of Article 19, paragraph 8 (security against expulsion), the Committee of Independent Experts had adopted a negative conclusion because of the absence of a remedy before an independent body in cases of expulsion on grounds of national security,

Observes that the Governmental Committee, in accordance with Article 29 of the Charter, has proposed that an individual recommendation be addressed to Sweden in relation to Article 19, paragraph 8;

Recommends that the Swedish Government take account, in an appropriate manner, of the negative conclusion of the Committee of Independent Experts and invites it to provide information in its next report on the measures it has taken to this effect.

---

1. Austria, Belgium, Cyprus, Denmark, Finland, France, Germany, Greece, Iceland, Ireland, Italy, Luxembourg, Malta, the Netherlands, Norway, Portugal, Spain, Sweden, Turkey and the United Kingdom.

18. Thirteenth supervision cycle – second part

Committee of Independent Experts – Conclusions XIII-2 (1995, 422 p., ISBN: 92-871-2665-8)

Governmental Committee Thirteenth report (II) (1996, 194 p., ISBN: 92-871-28677)

Committee of Ministers

> *Resolution ChS (95) 2 on the implementation of the European Social Charter during the period 1991-92 (13th supervision cycle – part II) (Adopted by the Committee of Ministers on 14 December 1995 at the 552nd meeting of the Ministers' Deputies)*

The Committee of Ministers, in its composition restricted to Contracting Parties to the European Social Charter,[1]

Referring to the European Social Charter, in particular to the provisions of Part IV thereof;

Having regard to Article 29 of the Charter;

Considering the reports submitted by the Governments of Austria, Belgium, Cyprus, Denmark, France, Germany, Greece, Iceland, Ireland, Italy, Malta, the Netherlands, Norway, Spain, Sweden and the United Kingdom;

Considering Conclusions XIII-2 of the Committee of Independent Experts appointed under Article 25 of the Charter and the 13th report (II) of the Governmental Committee appointed under Article 27 of the Charter;

Recalling the request made, both to the Contracting Parties to the Charter and the supervisory bodies, by the ministers participating in the Ministerial Conference on the European Social Charter held in Turin on 21 and 22 October 1991, on the occasion of the thirtieth anniversary of the Charter, and by the Committee of Ministers in its decision of 11 December 1991, "to envisage the application of certain of the measures provided for in this Protocol [the Amending Protocol] before its entry into force, in so far as the text of the Charter will allow";

Noting that the Governmental Committee, in view of this request, has decided, in accordance with Article 4 of the Amending Protocol, to select, in the light of the reports of the Committee of Independent Experts and of the Contracting Parties and on the basis of social, economic and other policy considerations, the situations which should, in its view, be the subject of recommendations to each Contracting Party;

---

1. Austria, Belgium, Cyprus, Denmark, Finland, France, Germany, Greece, Iceland, Ireland, Italy, Luxembourg, Malta, the Netherlands, Norway, Portugal, Spain, Sweden, Turkey and the United Kingdom.

Noting also that the Parliamentary Assembly, in a letter from its President to the Chairman of the Committee of Ministers of 3 September 1992, has decided to abstain from communicating its views on a particular set of conclusions of the Committee of Independent Experts as provided for under Article 28 of the Charter and to use these conclusions as a basis for periodic social policy debates to be held by the Assembly in accordance with Article 6 of the Amending Protocol,

Adopts the recommendations included in the Appendix to the present Resolution;

Reiterates the following recommendations to which no effect has yet been given:

- with regard to Ireland: Article 19 para. 8 (security against expulsion), reference period: 1992;[1]

- with regard to Italy: Article 7 para. 1 (minimum age of admission to employment), and Article 13 para. 1 (social and medical assistance for those in need), reference period: 1991-92;[2]

- with regard to Norway: Article 7 paragraph 3 (safeguarding the full benefit of compulsory education), reference period: 1991-92;[3]

- with regard to Sweden: Article 19 paragraph 8 (security against expulsion), reference period: 1992.[4]

Recommends in addition that governments take account, in an appropriate manner, of all the various observations made in the Conclusions of the Committee of Independent Experts and the report of the Governmental Committee.

Committee of Ministers

Recommendation No. R ChS (95) 11 on the application of the European Social Charter by Greece during the period 1991-92 (13th supervision cycle – part II)
(Adopted by the Committee of Ministers on 14 December 1995 at the 552nd meeting of the Ministers' Deputies)

The Committee of Ministers, in its composition restricted to Contracting Parties to the European Social Charter,[5]

Having regard to the European Social Charter, in particular Part IV thereof;

---

1. Recommendation No. R-ChS (95) 6 of 22 June 1995.
2. Recommendation No. R-ChS (94) 4 of 8 April 1994.
3. Recommendation No. R-ChS (93) 2 of 7 September 1993.
4. Recommendation No. (95) 10 of 22 June 1995.
5. Austria, Belgium, Cyprus, Denmark, Finland, France, Germany, Greece, Iceland, Ireland, Italy, Luxembourg, Malta, the Netherlands, Norway, Portugal, Spain, Sweden, Turkey and the United Kingdom.

Whereas the European Social Charter, signed in Turin on 18 October 1961, came into force on 6 July 1984 with respect to Greece and whereas, in accordance with Article 20, Greece has accepted sixty-seven out of the seventy-two provisions contained in the Charter;

Whereas the Government of Greece submitted in 1993 its 5th report under the Charter, and whereas this report has been examined in accordance with Articles 24 to 27 of the Charter;

Having examined Conclusions XIII-2 of the Committee of Independent Experts appointed under Article 25 of the Charter and the 13th report (I) of the Governmental Committee appointed under Article 27 of the Charter;

Having noted that no steps having been taken to simplify procedures in respect of nationals of Contracting Parties to the Charter, not members of the European Union and not parties to the Agreement on the European Economic Area, the Committee of Independent Experts had adopted a negative conclusion in respect of Article 18 para. 2 (simplifying existing formalities and reducing dues and taxes),

Following a proposal by the Governmental Committee;

Recommends that the Government of Greece take account, in an appropriate manner, of the negative conclusion of the Committee of Independent Experts and requests that it provide information in its next report on the measures it has taken to this effect.

Committee of Ministers

> *Recommendation R ChS (95) 12 on the application of the European Social Charter by Italy during the period 1991-92 (13th supervision cycle – part II)*
> *(Adopted by the Committee of Ministers on 14 December 1995 at the 552nd meeting of the Ministers' Deputies)*

The Committee of Ministers, in its composition restricted to Contracting Parties to the European Social Charter,[1]

Having regard to the European Social Charter, in particular Part IV thereof;

Whereas the European Social Charter, signed in Turin on 18 October 1961, came into force on 21 November 1965 with respect to Italy and whereas, in accordance with Article 20, Italy has accepted all seventy-two provisions contained in the Charter;

---

1. Austria, Belgium, Cyprus, Denmark, Finland, France, Germany, Greece, Iceland, Ireland, Italy, Luxembourg, Malta, the Netherlands, Norway, Portugal, Spain, Sweden, Turkey and the United Kingdom.

Whereas the Government of Italy submitted in 1993 its 14th report under the Charter, and whereas this report has been examined in accordance with Articles 24 to 27 of the Charter;

Having examined Conclusions XIII-2 of the Committee of Independent Experts appointed under Article 25 of the Charter and the 13th report (II) of the Governmental Committee appointed under Article 27 of the Charter;

Having noted that as a result of the lack of legislation sufficiently limiting working hours for young persons under sixteen years of age, the Committee of Independent Experts had adopted a negative conclusion in respect of Article 7 para. 4 (working hours of persons under sixteen years of age),

Following a proposal by the Governmental Committee;

Recommends that the Government of Italy take account, in an appropriate manner, of the negative conclusion of the Committee of Independent Experts and requests that it provide information in its next report on the measures it has taken to this effect.

19. Thirteenth supervision cycle – third part

Committee of Independent Experts – Conclusions XIII-3 (1996, 504 p., ISBN: 92-871-2914-2)

Governmental Committee Thirteenth report (III) (1996, 168 p., ISBN: 92-871-3192-9)

Committee of Ministers

> *Resolution ChS (97)1 on the implementation of the European Social Charter during the period 1992-93 (13th supervision cycle – part III) (Adopted by the Committee of Ministers on 15 January 1997 at the 581st meeting of the Ministers' Deputies)*

The Committee of Ministers, in its composition restricted to Contracting Parties to the European Social Charter,[1]

Referring to the European Social Charter, in particular to the provisions of Part IV thereof;

Having regard to Article 29 of the Charter;

Considering the reports presented by the Governments of Austria, Cyprus, Denmark, Finland, France, Greece, Iceland, Ireland, Italy, Luxembourg, Malta, the Netherlands, Norway, Portugal, Spain, Sweden, Turkey and the United Kingdom;

---

1. Austria, Belgium, Cyprus, Denmark, Finland, France, Germany, Greece, Iceland, Ireland, Italy, Luxembourg, Malta, the Netherlands, Norway, Portugal, Spain, Sweden, Turkey and the United Kingdom.

Considering Conclusions XIII-3 of the Committee of Independent Experts appointed under Article 25 of the Charter and the 13th report (III) of the Governmental Committee appointed under Article 27 of the Charter;

Recalling the request made, both to the Contracting Parties to the Charter and the supervisory bodies, by the ministers participating in the Ministerial Conference on the European Social Charter held in Turin on 21 and 22 October 1991, on the occasion of the thirtieth anniversary of the Charter, and by the Committee of Ministers in its decision of 11 December 1991, "to envisage the application of certain of the measures provided for in this protocol [the amending protocol] before its entry into force, in so far as the text of the Charter will allow";

Noting that the Governmental Committee, in view of this request, has decided, in accordance with Article 4 of the amending protocol, to select, in the light of the reports of the Committee of Independent Experts and of the Contracting Parties and on the basis of social, economic and other policy considerations, the situations which should, in its view, be the subject of recommendations to each Contracting Party,

Draws the attention of the governments concerned to the recommendations adopted for the 13th supervision cycle (Part III), following a proposal by the Governmental Committee;

Reiterates the following recommendations to which no effect has yet been given:

- with regard to France: Article 1, paragraph 2 (prohibition of forced labour) – reference period: 1992-93;[1]

- with regard to Greece: Article 1, paragraph 2 (prohibition of forced labour) – reference period: 1992-93;[2]

- with regard to Italy: Article 1, paragraph 2 (prohibition of forced labour);[3] Article 3, paragraph 2 (supervision of safety and health regulations);[4] and Article 4, paragraph 5 (deduction from wages)[5] – reference period: 1992-93;

Recommends in addition that governments take account, in an appropriate manner, of all the various observations made in the Conclusions of the Committee of Independent Experts and the report of the Governmental Committee.

---

1. Recommendation No. R ChS (94) 2 of 8 April 1994 and Recommendation No. R ChS (95) 3 of 22 June 1995.
2. Recommendation No. R ChS (93) 1 of 7 September 1993 and Recommendation No. R ChS (95) 4 of 22 June 1995.
3. Recommendation No. R ChS (94) 4 of 8 April 1994 and Recommendation No. R ChS (95) 7 of 22 June 1995.
4. *Idem.*
5. *Idem.*

Committee of Ministers

> *Recommendation No. R ChS (97)1 on the application of the European Social Charter by Malta during the year 1993 (13th supervision cycle – part III)*
> *(Adopted by the Committee of Ministers on 15 January 1997 at the 581st meeting of the Ministers' Deputies)*

The Committee of Ministers, in its composition restricted to Contracting Parties to the European Social Charter,[1]

Having regard to the European Social Charter, in particular Part IV thereof;

Whereas the European Social Charter, signed in Turin on 18 October 1961, came into force on 3 November 1988 with respect to Malta and whereas, in accordance with Article 20, Malta has accepted fifty-four of the provisions contained in the Charter;

Whereas the Government of Malta submitted in 1994 its 3rd report on the application of the Charter, and whereas this report has been examined in accordance with Articles 24 to 27 of the Charter;

Having examined Conclusions XIII-3 of the Committee of Independent Experts appointed under Article 25 of the Charter and the 13th report (III) of the Governmental Committee appointed under Article 27 of the Charter;

Having noted that the Committee of Independent Experts had adopted a negative conclusion with regard to Article 5 (right to organise) and 6, paragraph 2 (promotion of machinery for voluntary negotiations) for the following reason: police officers were still obliged to join the Maltese Police Association and were not entitled to become affiliated to another union or similar association;

Following a proposal by the Governmental Committee,

Recommends that the Government of Malta take account, in an appropriate manner, of the negative conclusions of the Committee of Independent Experts and requests that it provide information in its next report on the measures it has taken to this effect.

---

1. Austria, Belgium, Cyprus, Denmark, Finland, France, Germany, Greece, Iceland, Ireland, Italy, Luxembourg, Malta, the Netherlands, Norway, Portugal, Spain, Sweden, Turkey and the United Kingdom.

Committee of Ministers

Recommendation R ChS (97) 2 on the application of the European Social Charter by Turkey during the period 1992-93 (13th supervision cycle – Part III)
(Adopted by the Committee of Ministers on 15 January 1997 at the 581st meeting of the Ministers' Deputies)

The Committee of Ministers, in its composition restricted to Contracting Parties to the European Social Charter,[1]

Having regard to the European Social Charter, in particular Part IV thereof;

Whereas the European Social Charter, signed in Turin on 18 October 1961, came into force on 24 December 1989 with respect to Turkey and whereas, in accordance with Article 20, Turkey has accepted forty-six provisions contained in the Charter;

Whereas the Government of Turkey submitted in 1994 its 2nd report on the application of the Charter, and whereas this report has been examined in accordance with Articles 24 to 27 of the Charter;

Having examined Conclusions XIII-3 of the Committee of Independent Experts appointed under Article 25 of the Charter and the 13th report (III) of the Governmental Committee appointed under Article 27 of the Charter;

Having noted that the Committee of Independent Experts had adopted a negative conclusion with regard to Article 7, paragraph 3 (full benefit of compulsory education), for the following reason: Labour Act No. 1475, Article 67 of which provides for the prohibition of work for children did not apply to children working in some sectors of the economy (agriculture, craftwork, and building work falling within the scope of family businesses, domestic work or work in enterprises which correspond to the law on small commercial and craftwork enterprises);

Following a proposal by the Governmental Committee,

Recommends that the Government of Turkey take account, in an appropriate manner, of the negative conclusion of the Committee of Independent Experts and requests that it provide information in its next report on the measures it has taken to this effect.

---

1. Austria, Belgium, Cyprus, Denmark, Finland, France, Germany, Greece, Iceland, Ireland, Italy, Luxembourg, Malta, the Netherlands, Norway, Portugal, Spain, Sweden, Turkey and the United Kingdom.

Committee of Ministers

> *Recommendation No. R ChS (97) 3 on the application of the European Social Charter by the United Kingdom during the period 1992-93 (13th supervision cycle – Part III)*
> *(Adopted by the Committee of Ministers on 15 January 1997 at the 581st meeting of the Ministers' Deputies)*

The Committee of Ministers, in its composition restricted to Contracting Parties to the European Social Charter,[1]

Having regard to the European Social Charter, in particular Part IV thereof;

Whereas the European Social Charter, signed in Turin on 18 October 1961, came into force on 26 February 1965 with respect to the United Kingdom and whereas, in accordance with Article 20, the United Kingdom has accepted sixty of the provisions contained in the Charter;

Whereas the Government of the United Kingdom submitted in 1994 its 15th report on the application of the Charter, and whereas this report has been examined in accordance with Articles 24 to 27 of the Charter;

Having examined Conclusions XIII-3 of the Committee of Independent Experts appointed under Article 25 of the Charter and the 13th report (III) of the Governmental Committee appointed under Article 27 of the Charter;

Having noted that the Committee of Independent Experts had adopted a negative conclusion:

1. as it considered with regard to Article 1, paragraph 2 (prohibition of forced labour), that Section 30.c of the Merchant Shipping Act of 1970 enabled criminal sanctions to be imposed on striking seamen even when neither the safety of the boat nor the life or health of those on board was threatened;

2. as it considered with regard to Articles 5 (right to organise) and 6, paragraph 2 (promotion of machinery for voluntary negotiations), that Section 13 of the Act of 1993 – which could be used by employers to dissuade workers to become or to remain trade union members – and Sections 64 to 67 of the Act of 1992 – which could result in restrictions on trade unions' liberty to draft their rules of procedure and in heavy financial penalties being imposed upon them – were an infringement on the rights to organise and to bargain collectively;

---

1. Austria, Belgium, Cyprus, Denmark, Finland, France, Germany, Greece, Iceland, Ireland, Italy, Luxembourg, Malta, the Netherlands, Norway, Portugal, Spain, Sweden, Turkey and the United Kingdom.

3. with regard to Article 6, paragraph 4 (right to collective action), because the employer can dismiss all workers who took part in strikes and re-employ them selectively three months after dismissal;

Following a proposal by the Governmental Committee,

Recommends that the Government of the United Kingdom take account, in an appropriate manner, of the negative conclusion of the Committee of Independent Experts and requests that it provide information in its next report on the measures it has taken to this effect.

20. Thirteenth supervision cycle – fourth part

Committee of Independent Experts – Conclusions XIII-4 (1996, 492 p., ISBN: 92-871-3091-4)

Governmental Committee Thirteenth report (IV) and Thirteenth report (V) (1998, 244 p., ISBN: 92-871-3701-3)

Committee of Ministers

> *Resolution ChS (98) 1 on the implementation of the European Social Charter during the period 1993-94 (13th supervision cycle – part IV) (Adopted by the Committee of Ministers on 4 February 1998 at the 617th meeting of the Ministers' Deputies)*

The Committee of Ministers,[1]

Referring to the European Social Charter, in particular to the provisions of Part IV thereof;

Having regard to Article 29 of the Charter;

Considering the reports submitted by the Governments of Austria, Belgium, Cyprus, Denmark, France, Germany, Greece, Iceland, Ireland, Italy, Malta, the Netherlands, Norway, Spain, Sweden, Turkey and the United Kingdom;

Considering Conclusions XIII-4 of the Committee of Independent Experts appointed under Article 25 of the Charter and the 13th report (IV) of the Governmental Committee appointed under Article 27 of the Charter;

---

1. At the 492nd meeting of Ministers' Deputies in April 1993, the Deputies "agreed unanimously to the introduction of the rule whereby only representatives of those states which have ratified the Charter vote in the Committee of Ministers when the latter acts as a control organ of the application of the Charter".
These states are presently Austria, Belgium, Cyprus, Denmark, Finland, France, Germany, Greece, Iceland, Ireland, Italy, Luxembourg, Malta, the Netherlands, Norway, Poland, Portugal, Spain, Sweden, Turkey and the United Kingdom.

Recalling the request made, both to the Contracting Parties to the Charter and the supervisory bodies, by the ministers participating in the Ministerial Conference on the European Social Charter held in Turin on 21 and 22 October 1991, on the occasion of the 30th anniversary of the Charter, and by the Committee of Ministers in its decision of 11 December 1991, to envisage the application of certain of the measures provided for in this Protocol [the Amending Protocol] before its entry into force, in so far as the text of the Charter will allow;

Noting that the Governmental Committee, in view of this request, has decided, in accordance with Article 4 of the Amending Protocol, to select, in the light of the reports of the Committee of Independent Experts and of the Contracting Parties and on the basis of social, economic and other policy considerations, the situations which should, in its view, be the subject of recommendations to each Contracting Party,

Draws the attention of the governments concerned to the recommendations adopted for the 13th supervision cycle (Part IV), following a proposal by the Governmental Committee;

Recommends in addition that governments take account, in an appropriate manner, of all the various observations made in the conclusions of the Committee of Independent Experts and the report of the Governmental Committee.

Committee of Ministers

> *Recommendation No. R ChS (98) 1 on the application of the European Social Charter by France during the period 1993-94 (13th supervision cycle – part IV)*
> *(Adopted by the Committee of Ministers on 4 February 1998 at the 617th meeting of the Ministers' Deputies)*

The Committee of Ministers,[1]

Having regard to the European Social Charter, in particular Part IV thereof;

Whereas the European Social Charter, signed in Turin on 18 October 1961, came into force on 8 April 1973 with respect to France and whereas, in accordance with Article 20, France has accepted seventy-two of the provisions contained in the Charter;

---

1. At the 492nd meeting of Ministers' Deputies in April 1993, the Deputies "agreed unanimously to the introduction of the rule whereby only representatives of those states which have ratified the Charter vote in the Committee of Ministers when the latter acts as a control organ of the application of the Charter".
   These states are presently Austria, Belgium, Cyprus, Denmark, Finland, France, Germany, Greece, Iceland, Ireland, Italy, Luxembourg, Malta, the Netherlands, Norway, Poland, Portugal, Spain, Sweden, Turkey and the United Kingdom.

Whereas the Government of France submitted in 1995 its 11th report on the application of the Charter, and whereas this report has been examined in accordance with Articles 24 to 27 of the Charter;

Having examined Conclusions XIII-4 of the Committee of Independent Experts appointed under Article 25 of the Charter and the 13th report (IV) of the Governmental Committee appointed under Article 27 of the Charter;

Having noted that the Committee of Independent Experts had adopted a negative conclusion with regard to Article 17 (the right of mothers and children to social and economic protection) because of the differences which still exist between the inheritance rights of children born in and out of marriage;

Following a proposal by the Governmental Committee,

Recommends that the Government of France take account, in an appropriate manner, of the negative conclusion of the Committee of Independent Experts and requests that it provide information in its next report on the measures it has taken to this effect.

Committee of Ministers

> *Recommendation No. R ChS (98) 2 on the application of the European Social Charter by Germany during the period 1993-94 (13th supervision cycle – part IV)*
> *(Adopted by the Committee of Ministers on 4 February 1998 at the 617th meeting of the Ministers' Deputies)*

The Committee of Ministers,[1]

Having regard to the European Social Charter, in particular Part IV thereof;

Whereas the European Social Charter, signed in Turin on 18 October 1961, came into force on 26 February 1965 with respect to Germany and whereas, in accordance with Article 20, Germany has accepted sixty-seven provisions contained in the Charter;

Whereas the Government of Germany submitted in 1995 its 14th report on the application of the Charter, and whereas this report has been examined in accordance with Articles 24 to 27 of the Charter;

---

1. At the 492nd meeting of Ministers' Deputies in April 1993, the Deputies "agreed unanimously to the introduction of the rule whereby only representatives of those states which have ratified the Charter vote in the Committee of Ministers when the latter acts as a control organ of the application of the Charter".
   These states are presently Austria, Belgium, Cyprus, Denmark, Finland, France, Germany, Greece, Iceland, Ireland, Italy, Luxembourg, Malta, the Netherlands, Norway, Poland, Portugal, Spain, Sweden, Turkey and the United Kingdom.

Having examined Conclusions XIII-4 of the Committee of Independent Experts appointed under Article 25 of the Charter and the 13th report (IV) of the Governmental Committee appointed under Article 27 of the Charter;

Having noted that the Committee of Independent Experts had adopted a negative conclusion with regard to Article 6 par. 4 (The right to collective action) as all strikes not aimed at achieving a collective agreement and not called or endorsed *(Übernahme)* by a trade union are forbidden in Germany;

Following a proposal by the Governmental Committee,

Recommends that the Government of Germany take account, in an appropriate manner, of the negative conclusion of the Committee of Independent Experts and requests that it provide information in its next report on the measures it has taken to this effect.

Committee of Ministers

> *Recommendation No. R ChS (98) 3 on the application of the European Social Charter by Italy during the period 1993-94 (13th supervision cycle – part IV)*
> *(Adopted by the Committee of Ministers on 4 February 1998 at the 617th meeting of the Ministers' Deputies)*

The Committee of Ministers,[1]

Having regard to the European Social Charter, in particular Part IV thereof;

Whereas the European Social Charter, signed in Turin on 18 October 1961, came into force on 21 November 1965 with respect to Italy and whereas, in accordance with Article 20, Italy has accepted the seventy-two provisions contained in the Charter;

Whereas the Government of Italy submitted in 1995 its 16th report on the application of the Charter, and whereas this report has been examined in accordance with Articles 24 to 27 of the Charter;

Having examined Conclusions XIII-4 of the Committee of Independent Experts appointed under Article 25 of the Charter and the

---

1. At the 492nd meeting of Ministers' Deputies in April 1993, the Deputies "agreed unanimously to the introduction of the rule whereby only representatives of those states which have ratified the Charter vote in the Committee of Ministers when the latter acts as a control organ of the application of the Charter".
These states are presently Austria, Belgium, Cyprus, Denmark, Finland, France, Germany, Greece, Iceland, Ireland, Italy, Luxembourg, Malta, the Netherlands, Norway, Poland, Portugal, Spain, Sweden, Turkey and the United Kingdom.

13th report (IV) of the Governmental Committee appointed under Article 27 of the Charter;

Having noted that the Committee of Independent Experts had adopted a negative conclusion considering Article 7 par. 2 (higher minimum age in certain occupations) as the minimum age for employment in occupations involving exposure to benzene was fixed at 16 years whilst it should be fixed at 18 years;

Following a proposal by the Governmental Committee,

Recommends that the Government of Italy take account, in an appropriate manner, of the negative conclusion of the Committee of Independent Experts and requests that it provide information in its next report on the measures it has taken to this effect.

Committee of Ministers

> *Recommendation No. R ChS (98) 4 on the application of the European Social Charter by Turkey during the period 1993-94 (13th supervision cycle – part IV)*
> *(Adopted by the Committee of Ministers on 4 February 1998 at the 617th meeting of the Ministers' Deputies)*

The Committee of Ministers,[1]

Having regard to the European Social Charter, in particular Part IV thereof;

Whereas the European Social Charter, signed in Turin on 18 October 1961, came into force on 24 December 1989 with respect to Turkey and whereas, in accordance with Article 20, Turkey has accepted forty provisions contained in the Charter;

Whereas the Government of Turkey submitted in 1995 its 3rd report on the application of the Charter, and whereas this report has been examined in accordance with Articles 24 to 27 of the Charter;

Having examined Conclusions XIII-4 of the Committee of Independent Experts appointed under Article 25 of the Charter and the 13th report (IV) of the Governmental Committee appointed under Article 27 of the Charter;

---

1. At the 492nd meeting of Ministers' Deputies in April 1993, the Deputies "agreed unanimously to the introduction of the rule whereby only representatives of those states which have ratified the Charter vote in the Committee of Ministers when the latter acts as a control organ of the application of the Charter".
These states are presently Austria, Belgium, Cyprus, Denmark, Finland, France, Germany, Greece, Iceland, Ireland, Italy, Luxembourg, Malta, the Netherlands, Norway, Poland, Portugal, Spain, Sweden, Turkey and the United Kingdom.

Having noted that the Committee of Independent Experts had adopted a negative conclusion:

1. considering that under Article 11 (the right to protection of health) the measures taken to reduce the particularly high rate of perinatal and infant mortality are not sufficient;

2. considering that under Article 16 (the right of the family to social, legal and economic protection) the proportion of families in receipt of family allowance is small; and that the civil code permits inequality within the couple as spouses as well as parents;

Following a proposal by the Governmental Committee,

Recommends that the Government of Turkey take account, in an appropriate manner, of the negative conclusion of the Committee of Independent Experts and requests that it provide information in its next report on the measures it has taken to this effect.

21. Thirteenth supervision cycle – fifth part

Committee of Independent Experts – Conclusions XIII-5 (1997, 350 p., ISBN: 92-871-3464-2)

Governmental Committee Thirteenth report (IV) and Thirteenth report (V) (1998, 244 p., ISBN: 92-871-3701-3)

Committee of Ministers

> *Resolution ChS (98) 2 on the implementation of the European Social Charter during the period 1994-95 (13th supervision cycle – part V) (Adopted by the Committee of Ministers on 2 July 1998 at the 638th meeting of the Ministers' Deputies)*

The Committee of Ministers,[1]

Referring to the European Social Charter, in particular to the provisions of Part V thereof;

Having regard to Article 29 of the Charter;

Considering the reports on the European Social Charter submitted by the Governments of Finland, Luxembourg, Portugal (period of reference 1994-1995) and the reports on the Additional Protocol of 1988

---

1. At the 492nd meeting of Ministers' Deputies in April 1993, the Deputies "agreed unanimously to the introduction of the rule whereby only representatives of those states which have ratified the Charter vote in the Committee of Ministers when the latter acts as a control organ of the application of the Charter".
These states are presently Austria, Belgium, Cyprus, Denmark, Finland, France, Germany, Greece, Iceland, Ireland, Italy, Luxembourg, Malta, the Netherlands, Norway, Poland, Portugal, Spain, Sweden, Turkey and the United Kingdom.

submitted by the Governments of Finland, Italy, Norway, the Netherlands and Sweden (period of reference 1994-1995);

Considering Conclusions XIII-5 of the Committee of Independent Experts appointed under Article 25 of the Charter and the 13th report (V) of the Governmental Committee appointed under Article 27 of the Charter;

Recalling the request made, both to the Contracting Parties to the Charter and the supervisory bodies, by the ministers participating in the Ministerial Conference on the European Social Charter held in Turin on 21 and 22 October 1991, on the occasion of the 30th anniversary of the Charter, and by the Committee of Ministers in its decision of 11 December 1991, "to envisage the application of certain of the measures provided for in this Protocol [the Amending Protocol] before its entry into force, in so far as the text of the Charter will allow";

Noting that the Governmental Committee, in view of this request, has decided, in accordance with Article 4 of the Amending Protocol, to select, in the light of the reports of the Committee of Independent Experts and of the Contracting Parties and on the basis of social, economic and other policy considerations, the situations which should, in its view, be the subject of recommendations to each Contracting Party;

Draws the attention of the governments concerned to the recommendation adopted for the 13th supervision cycle (Part V), following a proposal by the Governmental Committee;

Recommends in addition that governments take account, in an appropriate manner, of all the various observations made in the Conclusions of the Committee of Independent Experts and the report of the Governmental Committee.

---

1. At the 492nd meeting of Ministers' Deputies in April 1993, the Deputies "agreed unanimously to the introduction of the rule whereby only representatives of those states which have ratified the Charter vote in the Committee of Ministers when the latter acts as a control organ of the application of the Charter".
These states are presently Austria, Belgium, Cyprus, Denmark, Finland, France, Germany, Greece, Iceland, Ireland, Italy, Luxembourg, Malta, the Netherlands, Norway, Poland, Portugal, Spain, Sweden, Turkey and the United Kingdom.

Committee of Ministers

> *Recommendation No. R ChS (98) 5 on the application of the European Social Charter by Portugal during the period 1994-95 (13th supervision cycle – part V)*
> *(Adopted by the Committee of Ministers on 2 July 1998 at the 638th meeting of the Ministers' Deputies)*

The Committee of Ministers,[1]

Having regard to the European Social Charter, in particular Part V thereof;

Whereas the European Social Charter, signed in Turin on 18 October 1961, came into force on 30 October 1991 with respect to Portugal and whereas, in accordance with Article 20, Portugal has accepted seventy-two of the provisions contained in the Charter;

Whereas the Government of Portugal submitted in 1996 its 2nd report on the application of the Charter, and whereas this report has been examined in accordance with Articles 24 to 27 of the Charter;

Having examined Conclusions XIII-5 of the Committee of Independent Experts appointed under Article 25 of the Charter and the 13th report (V) of the Governmental Committee appointed under Article 27 of the Charter;

Having noted that the Committee of Independent Experts had adopted a negative conclusion with regard to Article 7 (minimum age of admission to employment) for the following reason: while the legislation was effectively in conformity with Article 7, paragraph 1 in law, in view of the extent of the violations of its provisions in practice during the reference period, the situation in Portugal was not in keeping with Article 7, paragraph 1;

Following a proposal by the Governmental Committee, which took into consideration the numerous legal and practical measures deployed by the Portuguese authorities to combat illegal child labour, which noted that Portugal had ratified most of the relevant international instruments on the protection of children, thereby clearly

---

1. At the 492nd meeting of Ministers' Deputies in April 1993, the Deputies "agreed unanimously to the introduction of the rule whereby only representatives of those states which have ratified the Charter vote in the Committee of Ministers when the latter acts as a control organ of the application of the Charter".
These states are presently Austria, Belgium, Cyprus, Denmark, Finland, France, Germany, Greece, Iceland, Ireland, Italy, Luxembourg, Malta, the Netherlands, Norway, Poland, Portugal, Spain, Sweden, Turkey and the United Kingdom.

demonstrating its political commitment to human rights and in particular children's rights; and which considered that it was its duty as a supervisory body of the Charter, clearly to mark its determination to combat illegal child labour,

Recommends that the Government of Portugal take into account, in an appropriate manner, the negative conclusion of the Committee of Independent Experts and requests that it provide information in its next report on the measures it has taken to this effect.

22. Fourteenth supervision cycle – first part

Committee of Independent Experts – Conclusions XIV-1 Volumes 1 and 2 (1998, 860 p., ISBN: 92-871-3634-3)

Governmental Committee Fourteenth report (I) and Fourteenth report (II) (1998, 290 p., ISBN: 92-871-4086-3)

Committee of Ministers

> *Resolution ChS (99) 2 on the implementation of the European Social Charter during the period 1994-96 (14th supervision cycle – part I) (Adopted by the Committee of Ministers on 4 March 1999 at the 662nd meeting of the Ministers' Deputies)*

The Committee of Ministers,[1]

Referring to the European Social Charter, in particular to the provisions of Part V thereof;

Having regard to Article 29 of the Charter;

Considering the reports on the European Social Charter submitted by the Governments of Austria, Belgium, Cyprus, Denmark, Finland, France, Germany, Greece, Iceland, Ireland, Italy, Luxembourg, Malta, the Netherlands, Norway, Portugal, Spain, Sweden, Turkey and the United Kingdom (period of reference 1995-96);

Considering Conclusions XIV-1 of the Committee of Independent Experts appointed under Article 25 of the Charter and the 14th report (I) of the Governmental Committee appointed under Article 27 of the Charter;

---

1. At the 492nd meeting of Ministers' Deputies in April 1993, the Deputies "agreed unanimously to the introduction of the rule whereby only representatives of those states which have ratified the Charter vote in the Committee of Ministers when the latter acts as a control organ of the application of the Charter".
   These states are presently Austria, Belgium, Cyprus, Denmark, Finland, France, Germany, Greece, Iceland, Ireland, Italy, Luxembourg, Malta, the Netherlands, Norway, Poland, Portugal, Spain, Sweden, Turkey and the United Kingdom.

Recalling the request made, both to the Contracting Parties to the Charter and the supervisory bodies, by the ministers participating in the Ministerial Conference on the European Social Charter held in Turin on 21 and 22 October 1991, on the occasion of the thirtieth anniversary of the Charter, and by the Committee of Ministers in its decision of 11 December 1991, "to envisage the application of certain of the measures provided for in this Protocol [the Amending Protocol] before its entry into force, in so far as the text of the Charter will allow";

Noting that the Governmental Committee, in view of this request, has decided, in accordance with Article 4 of the Amending Protocol, to select, in the light of the reports of the Committee of Independent Experts and of the Contracting Parties and on the basis of social, economic and other policy considerations, the situations which should, in its view, be the subject of recommendations to each Contracting Party;

Draws the attention of the Governments concerned to the Recommendations adopted for the 14th supervision cycle (Part I), following a proposal by the Governmental Committee;[1]

Renews the following Recommendation which has not yet come into effect:

- relating to Greece: article 1 para. 2 (prohibition of forced labour), reference period: 1992-1993[2]

- relating to Germany: article 19 para.6 (right of migrant workers to family reunion), reference period: 1989-1990[3]

- relating to Ireland: article 19 para. 8 (Security against expulsion), reference period 1989-1990[4]

Recommends in addition that governments take account, in an appropriate manner, of all the various observations made in the Conclusions of the Committee of Independent Experts and the report of the Governmental Committee.

---

1. When adopting this Resolution at their 662nd meeting (2-8 March 1999), the Deputies agreed to postpone to their 671st meeting (19-20 May 1999) consideration of the draft individual recommendation on the application of the European Social Charter by Denmark proposed by the Governmental Committee. At the 671st meeting and the 686th meeting (27 Ocober 1999) the Deputies agreed to postpone examination of this matter to a future meeting.
2. Recommendation No. R ChS (93) 1 of 7 September 1993 and Recommendation No. R ChS (95) 4 of 22 June 1995.
3. Recommendation No. R Chs (94) 3 of 8 April 1994.
4. Recommendation No. R Chs (95) 6 of 22 June 1995.

Committee of Ministers

Recommendation No. R ChS (99) 1 on the application of the European Social Charter by Austria during the period 1994-96 (14th supervision cycle – part I)
(Adopted by the Committee of Ministers on 4 March 1999 at the 662nd meeting of the Ministers' Deputies)

The Committee of Ministers,[1]

Having regard to the European Social Charter, in particular Part V thereof;

Whereas the European Social Charter, signed in Turin on 18 October 1961, came into force on 28 November 1969 with respect to Austria whereas, in accordance with Article 20, Austria has accepted 62 of the provisions contained in the Charter;

Whereas the Government of Austria submitted in 1997 its 15th report on the application of the Charter, and whereas this report has been examined in accordance with Articles 24 to 27 of the Charter;

Having examined Conclusions XIV-1 of the Committee of Independent Experts appointed under Article 25 of the Charter and the 14th report (I) of the Governmental Committee appointed under Article 27 of the Charter;

Having noted that the Committee of Independent Experts had adopted a negative conclusion with regard to Article 5 for the following reasons:

- Only nationals of states members of the European Union or parties to the Agreement on the European Economic Area may be elected to works' councils. Thus, during the reference period, Cypriot, Maltese and Turkish nationals of Contracting Parties to the Charter were not eligible to works' councils;

Following a proposal by the Governmental Committee,

Recommends that the Government of Austria take account, in an appropriate manner, of the negative conclusion of the Committee of Independent Experts and requests that it provide information in its next report on the measures it has taken to this effect.

---

1. At the 492nd meeting of Ministers' Deputies in April 1993, the Deputies "agreed unanimously to the introduction of the rule whereby only representatives of those states which have ratified the Charter vote in the Committee of Ministers when the latter acts as a control organ of the application of the Charter".
These states are presently Austria, Belgium, Cyprus, Denmark, Finland, France, Germany, Greece, Iceland, Ireland, Italy, Luxembourg, Malta, the Netherlands, Norway, Poland, Portugal, Spain, Sweden, Turkey and the United Kingdom.

Committee of Ministers

Recommendation No. R ChS (99) 2 on the application of the European Social Charter by Ireland during the period 1994-96 (14th supervision cycle – part I)
(Adopted by the Committee of Ministers on 4 March 1999 at the 662nd meeting of the Ministers' Deputies)

The Committee of Ministers,[1]

Having regard to the European Social Charter, in particular Part V thereof;

Whereas the European Social Charter, signed in Turin on 18 October 1961, came into force on 26 February 1965 with respect to Ireland and whereas, in accordance with Article 20, Ireland has accepted 63 of the provisions contained in the Charter;

Whereas the Government of Ireland submitted in 1998 its 16th report on the application of the Charter, and whereas this report has been examined in accordance with Articles 24 to 27 of the Charter;

Having examined Conclusions XIV-1 of the Committee of Independent Experts appointed under Article 25 of the Charter and the 14th report (I) of the Governmental Committee appointed under Article 27 of the Charter;

Having noted that the Committee of Independent Experts had adopted a negative conclusion with regard to Articles 5 and 6 para. 2 for the following reasons:

- The conditions for obtaining a negotiation licence are considered at variance with the Charter: to engage in collective bargaining, a trade union must have a negotiation licence, which is granted *inter alia* if the union: is registered (except for foreign-based trade unions); demonstrates that it has not less than 1,000 members resident in the state; deposits with the High Court a sum of money which varies according to the size of the union. Only authorised trade unions, their members and officials are entitled to protection against civil liability in respect of acts done in furtherance of a trade dispute and to certain advantages under the employment protection legislation accrue to authorised trade unions and their members.

---

1. At the 492nd meeting of Ministers' Deputies in April 1993, the Deputies "agreed unanimously to the introduction of the rule whereby only representatives of those states which have ratified the Charter vote in the Committee of Ministers when the latter acts as a control organ of the application of the Charter".
These states are presently Austria, Belgium, Cyprus, Denmark, Finland, France, Germany, Greece, Iceland, Ireland, Italy, Luxembourg, Malta, the Netherlands, Norway, Poland, Portugal, Spain, Sweden, Turkey and the United Kingdom.

Neither law nor practice comply with the Charter in relation to the right not to join a trade union. Both pre- and post-entry closed shop agreements exist in Ireland. The Courts have not ruled definitively on the constitutionality of either the pre-entry closed shop or the post-entry closed shop as it is applied to newly recruited employees;

Following a proposal by the Governmental Committee,

Recommends that the Government of Ireland take account, in an appropriate manner, of the negative conclusion of the Committee of Independent Experts and requests that it provide information in its next report on the measures it has taken to this effect.

23. Fourteenth supervision cycle – second part

Committee of Independent Experts – Conclusions XIV-2 Volumes 1 and 2 (1998, 828 p., ISBN: 92-871-3792-7)

Governmental Committee Fourteenth report (I) and Fourteenth report (II) (1999, 290 p., ISBN: 92-871-4086-3)

Committee of Ministers

> *Resolution ChS (99) 3 on the implementation of the European Social Charter (Articles 2, 3, 4, 9, 10 and 15) during the period 1993-1996 (14th supervision cycle – part II)*
> *(Adopted by the Committee of Ministers on 27 October 1999 at the 686th meeting of the Ministers' Deputies)*

The Committee of Ministers,

Referring to the European Social Charter, in particular to the provisions of Part V thereof;

Having regard to Article 29 of the Charter;

Considering the reports on the European Social Charter submitted by the Governments of Austria, Belgium, Cyprus, Denmark, Finland, France, Germany, Greece, Iceland, Ireland, Italy, Luxembourg, Malta, the Netherlands, Norway, Portugal, Spain, Sweden, Turkey and the United Kingdom, and concerning Articles 2, 3, 4, 9, 10 and 15 (period of reference 1993-96);

Considering Conclusions XIV-2 of the Committee of Independent Experts appointed under Article 25 of the Charter and the 14th report (II) of the Governmental Committee appointed under Article 27 of the Charter;

Recalling the request made, both to the Contracting Parties to the Charter and the supervisory bodies, by the ministers participating in the Ministerial Conference on the European Social Charter held in Turin on 21 and 22 October 1991, on the occasion of the thirtieth anniversary of the European Social Charter, and by the Committee of Ministers in its decision of 11 December 1991, "to envisage the application of certain of the measures provided for in this Protocol [the Amending Protocol] before its entry into force, in so far as the text of the Charter will allow";

Noting that the Governmental Committee, in view of this request, has decided, in accordance with Article 4 of the Amending Protocol, to select, in the light of the reports of the Committee of Independent Experts and of the Contracting Parties and on the basis of social, economic and other policy considerations, the situations which should, in its view, be the subject of recommendations to each Contracting Party,

Draws the attention of the Governments concerned to the Recommendation adopted for the 14th supervision cycle (part II), following a proposal by the Governmental Committee;

Recommends in addition that governments take account, in an appropriate manner, of all the various observations made in the Conclusions of the Committee of Independent Experts and the report of the Governmental Committee

Committee of Ministers

> *Recommendation No. R ChS (99) 3 on the application of the European Social Charter by Turkey during the period 1993-96 (14th supervision cycle – part II)*
> *(Adopted by the Committee of Ministers on 27 October 1999 at the 686th meeting of the Ministers' Deputies)*

The Committee of Ministers,

Having regard to the European Social Charter, in particular Part V thereof;

Whereas the European Social Charter, signed in Turin on 18 October 1961, came into force on 24 December 1989 with respect to Turkey whereas, in accordance with Article 20, Turkey has accepted 46 of the provisions contained in the Charter;

Whereas the Government of Turkey submitted in 1998 its 5th report on the application of the Charter (concerning Articles 2, 3, 4, 9, 10 and 15), and whereas this report has been examined in accordance with Articles 24 to 27 of the Charter;

Having examined Conclusions XIV-2 of the Committee of Independent Experts appointed under Article 25 of the Charter and the 14th report (II) of the Governmental Committee appointed under Article 27 of the Charter;

Having noted that the Committee of Independent Experts had adopted a negative conclusion with regard to Article 4 para. 3 for the following reasons:

- The situation is not in conformity with this provision as national legislation (Labour Act No. 1475) does not set out the principle of equal pay for work of equal value. It provides only in fact for equal pay within the framework of "work of a similar nature" with "equal efficiency".

- In addition, the financial compensation provided (six weeks' salary for workers employed for less than six months and twenty-four weeks' salary for workers with over three years' service) in cases of dismissal for claims of equal pay is not sufficient to dissuade employers from firing workers or to represent acceptable financial compensation for workers.

- Moreover, certain sectors of the economy not covered by the Labour Act (domestic services or craft work carried out at home by members of a same family or their close relatives) do not benefit from any specific protection with respect to equal pay.

Following a proposal by the Governmental Committee,

Recommends that the Government of Turkey take account, in an appropriate manner, of the negative conclusion of the Committee of Independent Experts and requests that it provide information in its next report on the measures it has taken to this effect.

24. Fifteenth supervision cycle – first part

European Committee of Social Rights – Conclusions XV-1 (2000, 715 p.; ISBN: Volume 1: 92-871-4266-1, Volume 2: 92-871-4269-6), Addendum (Ireland, Luxembourg, the Netherlands, Dutch Antilles and Poland) (2000, 202 p.; ISBN: 92-871-4438-9) and Addendum (Germany) (2001, 63 p.; ISBN: 92-978-4642-8)

Governmental Committee – Fifteenth report and Addendum (Germany)

The Committee of Ministers

Resolution ResChS(2001)5 on the implementation of the European Social Charter (Articles 1, 5, 6, 12, 13, 16 and 19) during the period 1997-1998 (15th supervision cycle – part I), (adopted by the Committee of Ministers on 7 February 2001 at the 740th meeting of the Ministers Deputies)

The Committee of Ministers[1]

Referring to the European Social Charter, in particular to the provisions of Part V thereof;

Having regard to Article 29 of the Charter;

Considering the reports on the European Social Charter, submitted by the governments of Austria, Belgium, Cyprus, Denmark, Finland, France, Greece, Iceland, Ireland, Italy, Luxembourg, Malta, the Netherlands, Norway, Poland, Portugal, Spain, Sweden, Turkey and the United Kingdom (period of reference 1997-1998);

Considering Conclusions XV-1 of the European Committee of Social Rights appointed under Article 25 of the and the 15th report (I) of the Governmental Committee appointed under Article 27 of the Charter;

Recalling the request made, both to the Contracting Parties to the Charter and the supervisory bodies, by the ministers participating in the Ministerial conference on the European Social Charter held in Turin on 21 and 22 October 1991, on the occasion of the thirtieth anniversary of the European Social Charter, and by the Committee of Ministers in its decision of 11 December 1991, "to envisage the application of certain of the measures provided for in this Protocol the amending Protocol before its entry into force, in so far as the text of the Charter will allow";

Noting that the Governmental Committee, in view of this request, has decided, in accordance with Article 4 of [the Amending Protocol], to select, in light of the reports of the European Committee of Social Rights and of the Contracting Parties and on the basis of social, economic and other policy considerations, the situations which should in its view, be the subject of recommendations to each Contracting Party;

Draws the attention of the Governments concerned to the Recommendations adopted for the 15th supervision cycle (part I), following a proposal by the Governmental Committee;

Renews the following recommendations which have not yet been implemented:

---

1. At the 492nd meeting of Ministers' Deputies in April 1993, the Deputies "agreed unanimously to the introduction of the rule whereby only representatives of those states which have ratified the Charter vote in the Committee of Ministers when the latter acts as a control organ of the application of the Charter". The states having ratified the Charter or the revised Charter are Austria, Belgium, Bulgaria, Cyprus, the Czech Republic, Denmark, Estonia, Finland, France, Germany, Greece, Hungary, Iceland, Ireland, Italy, Luxembourg, Malta, the Netherlands, Norway, Poland, Portugal, Romania, Slovakia, Slovenia, Spain, Sweden, Turkey and the United Kingdom.

- in respect of Austria: Article 5 (equality of treatment);[1]

- in respect of Ireland: Articles 5 and 6 paragraph 2 (negotiation licence) and Article 19 paragraph 8 (procedural guarantees);[2]

- in respect of Turkey: Article 16 (equality between spouses)[3]

Recommends in addition that governments take account, in an appropriate manner, of all various observations made in the Conclusions of the European Committee of Social Rights and the report of the Governmental Committee.

Committee of Ministers

Recommendation RecChS(2001)2 on the application of the European Social Charter by Ireland during the period 1997-1998, (15th Supervision cycle – part I)
(Adopted by the Committee of Ministers on 7 February 2001 at the 740th meeting of the Ministers' Deputies)

The Committee of Ministers,[4]

Having regard to the European Social Charter, in particular Part V thereof;

Whereas the European Social Charter, signed in Turin on 18 October 1961, came into force on 26 February 1965 with respect to Ireland and whereas, in accordance with Article 20, Ireland has accepted sixty-three of the provisions contained in the Charter;

Whereas the Government of Ireland submitted in 2000 in its 18th report on the application of the Charter, and whereas this report has been examined in accordance with articles 24 to 27 of the Charter;

Having examined Conclusions XV-1 of the European Committee of Social Rights, the Committee of Independent Experts appointed under Article 25 of the Charter and the 15th report (I) of the Governmental Committee appointed under Article 27 of the Charter;

---

1. Recommendation No. R ChS(99)1 of 4 March 1999.
2. Recommendation No. R ChS(99)2 of March 4 1999 (Articles 5 and 6 paragraph 2) and Recommendation No. R ChS(95)6 of 22 June 1995.
3. Recommendation No. R ChS(98)4 of 4 February 1998.
4. At the 492nd meeting of Ministers' Deputies in April 1993, the Deputies "agreed unanimously to the introduction of the rule whereby only representatives of those states which have ratified the Charter vote in the Committee of Ministers when the latter acts as a control organ of the application of the Charter". The states having ratified the Charter or the revised Charter are Austria, Belgium, Bulgaria, Cyprus, the Czech Republic, Denmark, Estonia, Finland, France, Germany, Greece, Hungary, Iceland, Ireland, Italy, Luxembourg, Malta, the Netherlands, Norway, Poland, Portugal, Romania, Slovakia, Slovenia, Spain, Sweden, Turkey and the United Kingdom.

Having noted that the European Committee of Social Rights had adopted a negative conclusion with regard to Article 6 paragraph 4 for the following reasons:

– only trade unions authorised to negotiate (that is, holding a negotiation license) and their members are afforded immunity against civil action in the event of a strike;

– under the Unfair Dismissals Act 1977 as amended an employer may dismiss all employees for taking part in strike action;

Following a proposal by the Governmental Committee:

Recommends that the Government of Ireland takes account, in an appropriate manner, of the negative conclusion of the European Committee of Social Rights and requests that it provide information in its next report on the measures it had taken to this effect.

Committee of Ministers

> *Recommendation RecChS(2001)3 on the application of the European Social Charter by Malta during the period 1997-1998, (15th Supervision cycle – part I)*
> *(Adopted by the Committee of Ministers on 7 February 2001 at the 740th meeting of the Ministers' Deputies)*

The Committee of Ministers,[1]

Referring to the European Social Charter, in particular to the provisions of Part V thereof;

Whereas the European Social Charter, signed in Turin on 18 October 1961, came into force on 3 November 1989 with respect to Malta and whereas, in accordance with Article 20, Malta has accepted fifty-four of the provisions contained in the Charter;

Whereas the Government of Malta submitted in 1999 in its 7th report on the application of the Charter, and whereas this report has been examined in accordance with Articles 24 to 27 of the Charter;

Having examined Conclusions XV-1 of the European Committee of Social Rights, the Committee of Independent Experts appointed under Article 25 of the Charter and the 15th report (I) of the Governmental Committee appointed under Article 27 of the Charter;

---

1. At the 492nd meeting of Ministers' Deputies in April 1993, the Deputies "agreed unanimously to the introduction of the rule whereby only representatives of those states which have ratified the Charter vote in the Committee of Ministers when the latter acts as a control organ of the application of the Charter". The states having ratified the Charter or the revised Charter are Austria, Belgium, Bulgaria, Cyprus, the Czech Republic, Denmark, Estonia, Finland, France, Germany, Greece, Hungary, Iceland, Ireland, Italy, Luxembourg, Malta, the Netherlands, Norway, Poland, Portugal, Romania, Slovakia, Slovenia, Spain, Sweden, Turkey and the United Kingdom.

Having noted that the European Committee of Social Rights had adopted a negative conclusion with regard to Articles 5 (the right to organise) and 6 paragraph 2 (promotion of machinery for voluntary negotiations) for the following reasons:

- the 1961 Police Ordinance prohibits members of the Police from joining a trade union or other similar organisation other than the Malta Police Association which has very limited rights and as membership of the association is compulsory and as the excessive restrictions on trade union rights in the police force infringe the right to bargain collectively in this sector,

Following a proposal by the Governmental Committee:

Recommends that the Government of Malta takes account, in an appropriate manner, of the negative conclusion of the European Committee of Social Rights and requests that it provide information in its next report on the measures it had taken to this effect.

Addendum to Resolution ResChS(2001)5 on the implementation of the European Social Charter during the period 1997-1998 (15th supervision cycle – part I)
(Adopted by the Committee of Ministers on 5 September 2001 at the 762nd meeting of the Ministers' Deputies)

The Committee of Ministers[1],

Referring to the European Social Charter, in particular to the provisions of Part V thereof;

Having regard to Article 29 of the Charter;

Having regard to Resolution ResChS(2001)5 on the implementation of the European Social Charter during the period 1997-1998 (fifteenth supervision cycle – part I) adopted by the Committee of Ministers on 7 February 2001;

Considering the report on the European Social Charter submitted by the Government of Germany (period of reference 1997-1998);

Considering the Addendum to Conclusions XV-1 (Germany) of the European Committee of Social Rights appointed under Article 25 of the Charter and the Addendum to the 15th report (I) of the Governmental Committee appointed under Article 27 of the Charter;

---

1. At the 492nd meeting of the Ministers' Deputies in April 1993, the Deputies "agreed unanimously to the introduction of the rule whereby only representatives of those states which have ratified the Charter vote in the Committee of Ministers when the latter acts as a control organ of the application of the Charter".
The states having ratified the Charter or the revised Charter are Austria, Belgium, Cyprus, the Czech Republic, Denmark, Estonia, Finland, France, Germany, Greece, Hungary, Iceland, Ireland, Italy, Lithuania, Luxembourg, Malta, the Netherlands, Norway, Poland, Portugal, Romania, Slovakia, Slovenia, Sweden, Turkey and the United Kingdom.

Decides to add in the paragraph "Renews the following recommendations which have not yet been implemented" the following:

"– in respect of Germany: Article 19 para. 6 (family reunion)"[1].

---

1. Recommendation No. R ChS(94)3 of 8 April 1994 and Resolution No. Res ChS(99)2 of 4 March 1999.

B. Supervision relating to reports submitted under Article 22 of the Social Charter

1. First exercise

First report on certain provisions of the Charter which have not been accepted (1981, 28 p.)

Parliamentary Assembly of the Council of Europe (thirty-fourth ordinary session)

> *Opinion No. 111 (1982)[1] on some provisions of the European Social Charter which have not been accepted*

The Assembly,

1. Noting that in recent years some of the signatories to the Social Charter have declared themselves bound by provisions of the Charter which they did not accept when ratifying it;

2. Noting, however, that a large number of provisions have still not been accepted (780 acceptances of a total of 72 provisions by 13 Contracting Parties, as against 156 non-acceptances, including non-acceptances of important provisions) (see appendix);

3. Welcoming the Committee of Ministers' decision to implement for the first time the procedure provided for in Article 22 of the Social Charter and consequently ask the Contracting Parties to report on certain non-accepted provisions;

4. Considering that this procedure is designed, on the one hand, to complement the procedure relating to accepted provisions for the purpose of assessing the state of the Contracting Parties' legislation and practice with regard to the Charter as a whole and, on the other hand, to promote acceptance of further provisions of the Charter;

5. Having examined the national reports and the reports of the Committee of Independent Experts and the governmental committee on the same subject, and noted that the committees' views converge in various respects;

6. Noting that the initial implementation of Article 22 relates to Article 4, paragraph 3 (right of men and women workers to equal

---

1. Text adopted by the Standing Committee, acting on behalf of the Assembly, on 2 July 1982. See Doc. 4917, report of the Committee on Social and Health Questions.

pay for work of equal value), Article 7, paragraph 1 (prohibition of child labour; fixing of a minimum age for admission to employment), Article 8, paragraph 1 (maternity leave) and Article 8, paragraph 2 (prohibition of dismissal during maternity leave);

7. Noting that the legislation of some of the Contracting Parties very nearly fulfils the conditions governing acceptance of the aforementioned provisions, whereas the situation elsewhere still seems incompatible with the Charter's requirements;

8. Being of the opinion that the Assembly should also take this opportunity of urging states which have not yet signed or ratified the Charter to speed up necessary amendments to their legislation with a view to joining the group of thirteen Contracting Parties as soon as possible. As Articles 21 and 22 require reviews of the situation of accepting states, fairness demands that similar pressure be brought to bear on the eight states not yet bound by the Charter. Although, as the preamble states, practice in countries with systems of customary law may prove difficult to reconcile with practice in countries with systems of statute law, the fact remains that the future of the European Social Charter depends on the participation of all states;

9. Recommends that the Committee of Ministers:

    i. ask the governments of states whose de jure or de facto situation is relatively close to meeting the requirements of the Charter to adopt measures enabling them to accept the provisions referred to in paragraph 6 above;

    ii. ask the governments of states whose legislation or practice are still far short of the level of social protection required by the Charter to consider gradually approximating their standards to the requirements for acceptance of the relevant provisions;

    iii. ask the governments of Belgium, Greece, Liechtenstein, Luxembourg, Malta, Portugal, Switzerland and Turkey, which have not yet ratified the Social Charter, to note this opinion and do everything possible to upgrade their legislation as necessary with a view to ratifying the Charter;

10. Asks the Committee of Ministers to continue to implement Article 22 regularly, while henceforth consulting the Assembly in the selection of the provisions on which national reports are to be submitted;

11. Hereby confirms its commitment to the principles of the Social Charter, which effectively safeguard fundamental rights and freedoms.

Committee of Ministers

Resolution ChS (83) 2 on certain non-accepted provisions of the European Social Charter
(Adopted by the Committee of Ministers on 23 March 1983 at the 357th meeting of the Ministers' Deputies)

The Committee of Ministers,

Referring to the European Social Charter and particularly to the provisions of Part IV thereof;

Having regard to Article 29 of the Charter;

Acting in the context of the examination of the first reports submitted under Article 22 – Reports on non-accepted provisions – concerning the following articles:
- Article 4, paragraph 3,
- Article 7, paragraph 1,
- Article 8, paragraph 1,
- Article 8, paragraph 2;

Having taken note of the first report containing the conclusions of the Governmental Committee of the European Social Charter on certain provisions of the Charter which have not been accepted, to which is appended the first report of the Committee of Independent Experts concerning these same provisions, and Assembly Opinion No. 111 (1982), prepared from the reports submitted by the Governments of Austria, Cyprus, Denmark, the Federal Republic of Germany, Ireland, Norway, Sweden and the United Kingdom.

Resolves to transmit the three aforesaid documents to the governments of these states, calling their attention to the passages concerning them and in particular to paragraphs 9.i and 9.ii of Opinion No. 111.

2. Second exercise

Second report on certain provisions of the Charter which have not been accepted (1982, 24 p.)

Parliamentary Assembly of the Council of Europe (thirty-fifth ordinary session)

Opinion No. 117 (1983)[1] *on some provisions of the European Social Charter which have not been accepted*

The Assembly,

1. Having regard to Part IV of the European Social Charter, and in particular to Articles 22 and 28;

---

1. Text adopted by the Standing Committee, acting on behalf of the Assembly, on 23 November 1983. See Doc. 5144, report of the Committee on Social and Health Questions.

2. Noting that the Committee of Ministers has, for the second time, asked states bound by the Charter to submit a report on certain non-accepted provisions in that instrument;

3. Having examined the second report of the Committee of Independent Experts on certain non-accepted provisions of the Charter, which analyses the reports submitted by contracting states as requested by the Committee of Ministers, and having taken into consideration the second report on the same subject submitted by the Governmental Committee of the European Social Charter;

4. Observing that the reports requested fro the Contracting Parties by the Committee of Ministers concerned the following provisions of the Charter: Article 2, paragraph 4 (working conditions for workers in dangerous or unhealthy occupations); Article 7, paragraph 4 (working hours of persons under 16 years of age); Article 8, paragraph 4 (regulation of night work and prohibition of dangerous, unhealthy or arduous work for women workers); Article 19, paragraph 8 (security against expulsion);

5. Considering that this procedure has enabled a number of states to review their legislation or practice regarding some of the above matters covered in their reports, and hence to consider the possibility of accepting further provisions of the European Social Charter;

6. Concluding that the procedure established under Article 22 of the Charter has thereby fully proved its worth.

7. Recommends that the Committee of Ministers:

    i. ask the governments of states whose legislation or practice already meets the requirements of any of the provisions of the Charter referred to in paragraph 4 above to accept such provision or provisions formally;

    ii. ask the governments of states whose legislation or practice appears relatively close to meeting the standard of protection required by the Charter to adopt measures enabling them to accept the aforementioned provisions;

    iii. ask the governments of states whose legislation or practice is still far short of the level of social protection required by the Charter under the aforementioned provisions to consider gradually approximating their standards to the requirements for the acceptance of those provisions;

8. Requests the Committee of Ministers to continue applying Article 22 of the Social Charter regularly, and to associate the

Assembly with the selection of the provisions on which national reports are to be submitted;

9. Hereby asks the Committee of Ministers to invite the following governments of member states: Belgium, Greece, Liechtenstein, Luxembourg, Malta, Portugal, Switzerland and Turkey, which have not ratified the Social Charter, to do everything possible with a view to ratifying the Charter.

Committee of Ministers

Resolution ChS (84) 1 on certain non-accepted provisions of the European Social Charter
(Adopted by the Committee of Ministers on 25 January 1984 at the 366th meeting of the Ministers' Deputies)

The Committee of Ministers,

Referring to the European Social Charter and particularly to the provisions of Part IV thereof;

Having regard to Article 29 of the Charter;

Acting in the context of the examination of the reports submitted under Article 22 – reports on non-accepted provisions – concerning the following articles:

- Article 2, paragraph 4,
- Article 7, paragraph 4,
- Article 8, paragraph 4,
- Article 19, paragraph 8;

Having taken note of the second report containing the conclusions of the Governmental Committee of the European Social Charter on certain provisions of the Charter which have not been accepted, to which is appended the second report of the Committee of Independent Experts concerning these same provisions, and Assembly Opinion No. 117 (1983), prepared from the information submitted by the Governments of Austria, Cyprus, Denmark, France, the Federal Republic of Germany, Iceland, Norway, Sweden and the United Kingdom,

Resolves to transmit the three aforesaid documents to the governments of these states, calling their attention to the passages concerning them and in particular to paragraphs 7.i, ii and iii of Opinion No. 117.

3. Third exercise

Third report on certain provisions of the Charter which have not been accepted (1989, 44 p., ISBN: 92-871-1744-6)

Parliamentary Assembly of the Council of Europe (forty-third ordinary session)

Opinion No. 160 (1991)[1] on some provisions of the Social Charter of the Council of Europe which have not been accepted

1. The Council of Europe's Social Charter is a catalogue of social rights which states that ratify the Charter may accept on an "à la carte" basis so they do not necessarily have to subscribe to all nineteen articles at once. The ultimate objective is nevertheless to achieve full acceptance of all the social rights embodied in the Charter; with this in mind, the Contracting Parties are requested, in principle at regular intervals, to submit reports on the articles or paragraphs they have not accepted (procedure under Article 22).

2. The Assembly is therefore pleased to note that, in accordance with Article 22, the Committee of Ministers has, for the third time,[2] invited the states party to the Charter to submit reports on certain provisions they have not accepted, namely:

    i.   reasonable daily and weekly working hours (Article 2, paragraph 1);

    ii. the right of young workers and apprentices to a fair wage or other appropriate allowances (Article 7, paragraph 5);

    iii. inclusion of the time spent by young persons in vocational training as part of the normal working day (Article 7, paragraph 6);

    iv. minimum of three weeks' annual holiday with pay for employed persons under 18 years of age (Article 7, paragraph 7).

3. The Assembly has examined the situations in the countries concerned (Austria, Cyprus, Denmark, Sweden, United Kingdom, Iceland and Ireland) in the light of the 3rd Report of the Committee of Independent Experts and the report on the same subject presented by the Governmental Committee.

4. It confirms its conviction regarding the usefulness of this critical examination in identifying and eliminating the real or imaginary obstacles to acceptance of the provisions concerned, thereby

---

1. Assembly debate on 24 September 1991 (17th Sitting) (see Doc. 6476, report of the Social, Health and Family Affairs Committee, Rapporteur: Mr Beix). Text adopted by the Assembly on 24 September 1991 (17th sitting).
2. The first two procedures under Article 22 date back to 1982 and 1983.

achieving a situation in which all the Contracting Parties share the same social values and together constitute a single European social area.

5. However, it also points out the current limitations to this procedure: the excessive lapse of time since the procedure was last implemented, the small number of additional aricles or paragraphs that have been accepted since the Charter came into force, the fact that it is limited to those Contracting Parties already bound by the Charter.

6. Accordingly, and subject to the renewal of the Social Charter foreseen for Turin in October 1991, the Assembly recommends that the Committee of Ministers:

    i.   implement this procedure on a regular basis, preferably every two years, linking the reports submitted by virtue of Article 22 to those on accepted provisions, submitted under Article 21, so that both reports can be examined together;

    ii. give priority, when the procedure under Article 22 is next implemented, to the questions of prior notice of termination of employment (Article 4, paragraph 4) and the treatment of migrant workers in respect of remuneration, working conditions, trade union rights and accommodation (Article 19, paragraph 4);

    iii. implement a procedure on the same grounds and for the same purpose as the procedure under Article 22, along lines yet to be define, with a view to determining the current situation of social rights in Council of Europe member states which have not ratified the Charter, and the reasons and obstacles behind their failure to do so;

    iv. invite the states concerned, in the light of the conclusions reached by the supervisory organs of the Charter, to bring their legislation and practice into line with the provisions of the Charter mentioned in paragraph 2 above, with a view to their acceptance in the near future;

    v.   urge the states concerned to pay particular attention to the status and protection of employed persons under 18 years of age; employment is the principal means of socially integrating young people and priority must be given to facilitating their search for jobs; but measures taken with this in mind must not result in their becoming cheap labour, underpaid and rejected as soon as they are adults. Conditions of work, including pay, for this category of workers must be fair; in particular, all young people throughout Europe must be given at least three weeks' annual leave with pay, considering that most adult workers nowadays have four or five weeks' annual leave.

Committee of Ministers

> *Resolution ChS (92) 1 on certain non-accepted provisions of the European Social Charter*
> *(Adopted by the Committee of Ministers on 13 January 1992 at the 469th meeting of the Ministers' Deputies)*

The Committee of Ministers,

Referring to the European Social Charter and particularly to the provisions of Part IV thereof;

Having regard to Article 29 of the Charter;

Acting in the context of the examination of the reports submitted under Article 22 – reports on provisions which are not accepted – concerning the following articles:

- Article 2, paragraph 1,
- Article 7, paragraph 5,
- Article 7, paragraph 6,
- Article 7, paragraph 7;

Having taken note of the 3rd report containing the conclusions of the Governmental Committee of the European Social Charter on certain provisions which have not been accepted, to which is appended the 3rd report of the Committee of Independent Experts of the European Social Charter concerning these same provisions, and Assembly Opinion No. 160 (1991), prepared from the information submitted by the Governments of Austria, Cyprus, Denmark, Iceland, Ireland, Sweden and the United Kingdom,

Resolves to transmit the three aforesaid documents to the governments of these states.

4. Fourth exercise

Fourth report on certain provisions of the Charter which have not been accepted (1995, 40 p., ISBN: 92-871-2912-6)

Committee of Ministers

> *Resolution ChS (95) 3 on certain non-accepted provisions of the European Social Charter*
> *(Adopted by the Committee of Ministers on 14 December 1995 at the 552nd meeting of the Ministers' Deputies)*

The Committee of Ministers,

Referring to the European Social Charter and particularly to the provisions of Part IV thereof;

Having regard to Article 29 of the Charter;

Acting in the context of the examination of the reports submitted under Article 22 – reports on non-accepted provisions – concerning the following articles:

- Article 7, paragraph 9,
- Article 19, paragraph 4;

Having taken note of the fourth report containing the conclusions of the Governmental Committee of the European Social Charter on certain provisions which have not been accepted, to which is appended the fourth report of the Committee of Independent Experts of the European Social Charter concerning these same provisions, prepared from the information submitted by the Governments of Austria, Cyprus, Denmark, Finland, Iceland, Ireland, Malta and Norway,

Decided to transmit the aforesaid documents to the governments of these states.

5. Fifth exercise

Fifth report on certain provisions of the Charter which have not been accepted (1997, 34 p., ISBN: 92-871-3423-5)

Committee of Ministers[1]

6. Sixth exercise

Sixth report on certain provisions of the Charter which have not been accepted (1998, 66 p., ISBN: 92-871-3732-3)

Committee of Ministers

> *Resolution ChS (99) 1 on certain non-accepted provisions of the European Social Charter*
> *(Adopted by the Committee of Ministers on 21 January 1999*
> *at the 657th meeting of the Ministers' Deputies)*

The Committee of Ministers,

Referring to the European Social Charter and particularly to the provisions of Part IV thereof;

Having regard to Article 29 of the Charter;

---

1. The Committee of Ministers adopted a single Resolution for the 5th and 6th procedures on non-accepted provisions (Article 22): see point 6 below.

Acting in the context of the examination of the reports submitted under Article 22 – reports on non-accepted provision – concerning the following articles:

- Article 4 para. 4,
- Articles 5 and 6;

Having taken note of the fifth and sixth reports of the Governmental Committee of the European Social Charter on certain provisions which have not been accepted, to which are appended the fifth and sixth reports of the Committee of Independent Experts concerning these same provisions prepared from the information submitted by the Governments of Austria, Cyprus, Denmark, Finland, Germany, Greece, Luxembourg and Turkey,

Decided to transmit the aforesaid documents to the Governments of these States.

7. Seventh exercise

Seventh report on certain non-accepted provisions of the Charter (2000, 65 p.) ISBN: 92-871-4391-9

Resolution ResChS(2001)1 of the Committee of Ministers on certain non-accepted provisions of the European Social Charter
(Adopted by the Committee of Ministers on 31 January 2001 at the 738th meeting of the Ministers' Deputies)

The Committee of Ministers,

Referring to the European Social Charter and particularly to the provisions of Part IV thereof;

Having regard to Article 29 of the Charter;

Acting in the context of the examination of the reports submitted under Article 22 - reports on certain non-accepted provisions - concerning the following articles:

- Articles 5 and 6
- Article 13;

Having taken note of the seventh report of the Governmental Committee of the European Social Charter on certain provisions which have not been accepted, to which is appended the seventh report of the European Committee of Social Rights concerning these same provisions prepared from the information submitted by the Governments of Austria, Cyprus, Greece, Poland, Slovakia and Turkey, and also concerning Luxembourg,

Decided to transmit the aforesaid documents to the Governments of these States.

8. Eighth exercise

eighth exercise on certain non-accepted provisions of the Charter (2001, 18 p.)

[Exercise under examination]

X. Collective complaints

A. Procedure

Decision of the Committee of Ministers adopted during the 541st meeting of the Ministers' Deputies on 22 June 1995.

The Deputies

1. adopted the text of the Protocol of the European Social Charter providing for a system of collective complaints as it appears in Appendix 18 to the current volume of Decisions see page 41 and the following of the current Collection.

2. decide to open this Protocol to the signature of member States setting the date for the 9 November 1995 (97th Session of the Committee of Ministers) to this effect;

3. authorised the publication of the explanatory report to the said Protocol, as it appears in Appendix 19 to the present volume of Decision;

4. adopted the procedure for selecting international non-governmental organisations other than employers' and workers' organisations as it appears in Appendix 20 to the present volume of Decisions.

Appendix 20

Procedure for selecting international Non-Governmental organisations other than employers' and workers' organisations

This list is drawn up by the Governmental Committee using the following procedure:

- INGOs which hold consultative status with the Council of Europe and consider themselves particularly competent in any matters governed by the Charter are invited to express their wish to be included on a special list of INGOs entitled to submit complaints;

- each application must be supported by detailed and accurate documentation aiming to show in particular that the INGO has access to authoritative sources of information and is able to carry the necessary verifications, to obtain appropriate legal opinions, etc. in order to draw up complaint files that meet basic requirements of reliability;

- all applications are transmitted to the Governmental Committee, accompanied by an opinion of the Secretary general which reflects the degree of interest and participation shown by the INGO in its normal dealings with the Council of Europe;

- an application is considered accepted by the Governmental Committee unless it is rejected in a ballot by a simple majority of votes cast;
- inclusion on the special list is valid for a period of four years, after which it lapses unless the organisation applies for renewal in the six-month period preceding the expiry date. The procedure described above applies to renewal applications.

B. List of non-governmental organisations entitled to submit collective complaints

The organisations are registered on the list – in English alphabetical order – for a duration of 4 years as from the date of entry into force of the Protocol (1st July 1998), with the exception of NGOs for which it is indicated that the duration of 4 years begins on 1st January 1999, or on 1st January 2000, or on 1st January 2001, or on 1st January 2002.

- Conference of European Churches (CEC)
- Council of European Professional Informatics Societies (1 January 2001)
- Education International (EI) (1 January 1999)
- Eurolink Age
- European Action of the Disabled (1 January 2000)
- European Antipoverty Network
- European Association for Palliative Care
- European Association for Psychotherapy (EPA) (1 January 2001)
- European Association of Railwaymen
- European Centre of the International Council of Women (ECICW)
- European Council of Police Trade Unions
- European Council of WIZO Federations (ECWF) (1 January 2000)
- European Disability Forum (EDF) (1 January 2001)
- European Federation of Employees in Public Services
- European Federation of National Organisations Working with the Homeless
- European Federation of the Elderly (1 January 1999)
- European Forum for Child Welfare
- European Movement
- European Non-Governmental Sports Organisation (1 January 1999)
- European Ombudsman Institute
- European Organisation of Military Associations
- European Regional Council of the World Federation for Mental Health
- European Union Migrant's Forum (1 January 2001)
- European Union of Rechtspfleger (1 January 1999)
- European Women's Lobby

- Eurotalent
- International Association Autism-Europe (IAAE)
- International Association of the Third-Age Universities
- International Catholic Society for Girls
- International Centre for the Legal Protection of Human Rights (INTERIGHTS)
- International Commission of Jurists (ICJ)
- International Confederation of Catholic Charities (1 January 2000)
- International Council of Environmental Law (ICEL) (1 January 2000)
- International Council of Nurses (ICN)
- International Council on Social Welfare (ICSW)
- International Federation of Educative Communities
- International Federation of Human Rights Leagues
- International Federation of Musicians
- International Federation of Settlements and Neighbourhood Centres
- International Federation for Hydrocephalus and Spina Bifida
- International Federation for Parent Education (IFPE) (1 January 1999)
- International Human Rights Organization for the Right to Feed Oneself (1 January 2001)
- International Humanist and Ethical Union (IHEU)
- International Movement ATD - Fourth World
- International Planned Parenthood Federation – European Network
- International Road Safety
- International Scientific Conference of Minorities for Europe of Tomorrow
- Marangopoulos Foundation for Human Rights (MFHR) (1 January 2000)
- Public Services International (PSI)
- Quaker Council for European Affairs
- Standing Committee of the Hospitals of the European Union
- World Confederation of Teachers

C. List of registered collective complaints

Complaint No. 1/1998

International Commission of Jurists v. Portugal

The complaint, relating to Article 7 para. 1 of the Charter (prohibition to work for children under fifteen years), was registered on 12 October 1998. It alleges that the situation in practice in Portugal is in violation of this provision.

The European Committee of Social Rights (ECSR) transmitted its report containing its decision on the merits of the complaint to the Committee of Ministers on 10 September 1999. The Committee of Ministers adopted Resolution ChS(99)4 on 15 December 1999.

Complaint No. 2/1999

European Federation of Employees in Public Services v. France

The complaint, relating to Articles 5 (the right to organise) and 6 (the right to bargain collectively) of the Charter, was registered on 13 August 1999. It alleges that the armed forces are denied these rights.

The ECSR declared the complaint admissible on 10 February 2000.

The ECSR transmitted the report containing its decision on the merits of the complaint to the Committee of Ministers on 12 December 2000. The Committee of Ministers adopted Resolution ChS(2001)2 on 7 February 2001.

Complaint No. 3/1999

European Federation of Employees in Public Services v. Greece

The complaint, relating to Articles 5 (the right to organise) and 6 (the right to bargain collectively) of the Charter, was registered on 13 August 1999. It alleges that the armed forces are denied these rights.

The ECSR declared the complaint inadmissible on 13 October 1999.

Complaint No. 4/1999

European Federation of Employees in Public Services v. Italy

The complaint, relating to Articles 5 (the right to organise) and 6 (the right to bargain collectively) of the Charter, was registered on 13 August 1999. It alleges that the armed forces are denied these rights.

The ECSR declared the complaint admissible on 10 February 2000.

The ECSR transmitted the report containing its decision on the merits of the complaint to the Committee of Ministers on 12 December 2000. The Committee of Ministers adopted Resolution ChS(2001)3 on 7 February 2001.

Complaint No. 5/1999

European Federation of Employees in Public Services v. Portugal

The complaint, relating to Articles 5 (the right to organise) and 6 (the right to bargain collectively) of the Charter, was registered on 13 August 1999. It alleges that the armed forces are denied these rights.

The ECSR declared the complaint admissible on 10 February 2000.

The ECSR transmitted the report containing its decision on the merits of the complaint to the Committee of Ministers on 12 December 2000. The Committee of Ministers adopted Resolution ChS(2001)4 on 7 February 2001.

Complaint No. 6/1999

Syndicat national des professions du tourisme v. France

The complaint, relating to Articles 1 (para. 2) (prohibition against all forms of discrimination in access to employment), 10 (the right to vocational training) and E (non-discrimination) of the revised Charter, was registered on 30 August 1999. It alleges discrimination in access to work and vocational training for guide-interpreters and national lecturers.

The ECSR declared the complaint admissible on 10 February 2000.

The ECSR transmitted the report containing its decision on the merits of the complaint to the Committee of Ministers on 13 October 2000. The Committee of Ministers adopted Recommendation R ChS(2001)1 on 30 January 2001.

Complaint No. 7/2000

International Federation of Human Rights Leagues v. Greece

The complaint, relating to Article 1 (para. 2) (prohibition of forced labour) of the Charter, was registered on 7 February 2000. It alleges that a number of legislative provisions and regulations do not respect the prohibition of forced labour.

The ECSR declared the complaint admissible on 28 June 2000.

The ECSR transmitted the report containing its decision on the merits of the complaint to the Committee of Ministers on 12 December 2000. The Committee of Ministers adopted Resolution ChS(2001)6 on 5 April 2001.

Complaint No. 8/2000

Quaker Council for European Affairs v. Greece

The complaint, relating to Article 1 (para. 2) (prohibition of forced labour) of the Charter, was registered on 10 March 2000. It alleges that the application in practice of the act authorising alternative forms of military service for conscientious objectors does not respect the prohibition of forced labour.

The ECSR declared the complaint admissible on 28 June 2000.

The ECSR declared the complaint admissible on 28 June 2000. It transmitted the report containing its decision on the merits of the complaint to the Committee of Ministers on 27 April 2001.

Complaint No. 9/2000

Confédération Française de l'Encadrement – CGC v. France

The complaint, relating to Articles 2 (the right to just conditions of work), 4 (the right to a fair remuneration), 6 (the right to bargain collectively including the right to strike) and 27 (the right of workers with family responsibilities to equal opportunities and equal treatment) of the revised Charter, was registered on 20 June 2000. It alleges that the provisions relating to the working hours of white-collar workers contained in the second Act on the Reduction of Working Hours (Act No. 2000-37 of 19 January 2000 – "Loi Aubry n° 2") violates these provisions.

The ESCR declared the complaint admissible on 6 November 2000. A public hearing was held on 11 June 2001.

Complaint No. 10/2000

Tehy ry and STTK ry v. Finland

The complaint, relating to Article 2 para. 4 (the right to additional paid holidays or reduced working hours for workers engaged in dangerous or unhealthy occupations) of the Charter, was registered on 23 October 2000. It alleges that the fact that hospital personnel who are subjected to the hazards of radiation during the course of their work are no longer entitled to special radiation related leave, violates this provision of the Charter.

The ECSR declared the complaint admissible on 12 February 2001.

Complaint No. 11/2001

European Council of Police Trade Unions v. Portugal

The complaint, relating to Articles 5 (right to organise) and 6 (right to collective bargaining) of the Charter, was registered on 18 July 2001. It alleges that members of *Polícia de Segurança Pública* are not guaranteed these rights.

Sales agents for publications of the Council of Europe
Agents de vente des publications du Conseil de l'Europe

AUSTRALIA/AUSTRALIE
Hunter Publications, 58A, Gipps Street
AUS-3066 COLLINGWOOD, Victoria
Tel.: (61) 3 9417 5361
Fax: (61) 3 9419 7154
E-mail: Sales@hunter-pubs.com.au
http://www.hunter-pubs.com.au

AUSTRIA/AUTRICHE
Gerold und Co., Weihburggasse 26
A-1010 WIEN
Tel.: (43) 1 533 5014
Fax: (43) 1 533 5014 18
E-mail: buch@gerold.telecom.at
http://www.gerold.at

BELGIUM/BELGIQUE
La Librairie européenne SA
50, avenue A. Jonnart
B-1200 BRUXELLES 20
Tel.: (32) 2 734 0281
Fax: (32) 2 735 0860
E-mail: info@libeurop.be
http://www.libeurop.be

Jean de Lannoy
202, avenue du Roi
B-1190 BRUXELLES
Tel.: (32) 2 538 4308
Fax: (32) 2 538 0841
E-mail: jean.de.lannoy@euronet.be
http://www.jean-de-lannoy.be

CANADA
Renouf Publishing Company Limited
5369 Chemin Canotek Road
CDN-OTTAWA, Ontario, K1J 9J3
Tel.: (1) 613 745 2665
Fax: (1) 613 745 7660
E-mail: order.dept@renoufbooks.com
http://www.renoufbooks.com

CZECH REPUBLIC/
RÉPUBLIQUE TCHÈQUE
Suweco Cz Dovoz Tisku Praha
Ceskomoravska 21
CZ-18021 PRAHA 9
Tel : (420) 2 660 35 364
Fax : (420) 2 683 30 42
E-mail : import@suweco.cz

DENMARK/DANEMARK
Swets Blackwell A/S
Jagtvej 169 B, 2 Sal
DK-2100 KOBENHAVN O
Tel.: (45) 39 15 79 15
Fax: (45) 39 15 79 10
E-mail: info@dk.swetsblackwell.com

FINLAND/FINLANDE
Akateeminen Kirjakauppa
Keskuskatu 1, PO Box 218
FIN-00381 HELSINKI
Tel.: (358) 9 121 41
Fax: (358) 9 121 4450
E-mail: akatilaus@stockmann.fi
http://www.akatilaus.akateeminen.com

FRANCE
La Documentation française
(Diffusion/Vente France entière)
124 rue H. Barbusse
F-93308 Aubervilliers Cedex
Tel.: (33) 01 40 15 70 00
Fax: (33) 01 40 15 68 00
E-mail: commandes.vel@ladocfrancaise.gouv.fr
http://www.ladocfrancaise.gouv.fr

Librairie Kléber (Vente Strasbourg)
Palais de l'Europe
F-67075 STRASBOURG Cedex
Fax: (33) 03 88 52 91 21
E-mail: librairie.kleber@coe.int

GERMANY/ALLEMAGNE
UNO Verlag
Am Hofgarten 10
D-53113 BONN
Tel.: (49) 2 28 94 90 20
Fax: (49) 2 28 94 90 222
E-mail: bestellung@uno-verlag.de
http://www.uno-verlag.de

GREECE/GRÈCE
Librairie Kauffmann
Mavrokordatou 9
GR-ATHINAI 106 78
Tel.: (30) 1 38 29 283
Fax: (30) 1 38 33 967
E-mail: ord@otenet.gr

HUNGARY/HONGRIE
Euro Info Service
Hungexpo Europa Kozpont ter 1
H-1101 BUDAPEST
Tel.: (361) 264 8270
Fax: (361) 264 8271
E-mail: euroinfo@euroinfo.hu
http://www.euroinfo.hu

ITALY/ITALIE
Libreria Commissionaria Sansoni
Via Duca di Calabria 1/1, CP 552
I-50125 FIRENZE
Tel.: (39) 556 4831
Fax: (39) 556 41257
E-mail: licosa@licosa.com
http://www.licosa.com

NETHERLANDS/PAYS-BAS
De Lindeboom Internationale Publikaties
PO Box 202, MA de Ruyterstraat 20 A
NL-7480 AE HAAKSBERGEN
Tel.: (31) 53 574 0004
Fax: (31) 53 572 9296
E-mail: lindeboo@worldonline.nl
http://home-1-worldonline.nl/~lindeboo/

NORWAY/NORVÈGE
Akademika, A/S Universitetsbokhandel
PO Box 84, Blindern
N-0314 OSLO
Tel.: (47) 22 85 30 30
Fax: (47) 23 12 24 20

POLAND/POLOGNE
Głowna Księgarnia Naukowa
im. B. Prusa
Krakowskie Przedmiescie 7
PL-00-068 WARSZAWA
Tel.: (48) 29 22 66
Fax: (48) 22 26 64 49
E-mail: inter@internews.com.pl
http://www.internews.com.pl

PORTUGAL
Livraria Portugal
Rua do Carmo, 70
P-1200 LISBOA
Tel.: (351) 13 47 49 82
Fax: (351) 13 47 02 64
E-mail: liv.portugal@mail.telepac.pt

SPAIN/ESPAGNE
Mundi-Prensa Libros SA
Castelló 37
E-28001 MADRID
Tel.: (34) 914 36 37 00
Fax: (34) 915 75 39 98
E-mail: libreria@mundiprensa.es
http://www.mundiprensa.com

SWITZERLAND/SUISSE
BERSY
Route de Monteiller
CH-1965 SAVIESE
Tel.: (41) 27 395 53 33
Fax: (41) 27 395 53 34
E-mail: jprausis@netplus.ch

Adeco – Van Diermen
Chemin du Lacuez 41
CH-1807 BLONAY
Tel.: (41) 21 943 26 73
Fax: (41) 21 943 36 06
E-mail: mvandier@worldcom.ch

UNITED KINGDOM/ROYAUME-UNI
TSO (formerly HMSO)
51 Nine Elms Lane
GB-LONDON SW8 5DR
Tel.: (44) 207 873 8372
Fax: (44) 207 873 8200
E-mail: customer.services@theso.co.uk
http://www.the-stationery-office.co.uk
http://www.itsofficial.net

UNITED STATES and CANADA/
ÉTATS-UNIS et CANADA
Manhattan Publishing Company
468 Albany Post Road, PO Box 850
CROTON-ON-HUDSON,
NY 10520, USA
Tel.: (1) 914 271 5194
Fax: (1) 914 271 5856
E-mail: Info@manhattanpublishing.com
http://www.manhattanpublishing.com

Council of Europe Publishing/Editions du Conseil de l'Europe
F-67075 Strasbourg Cedex
Tel.: (33) 03 88 41 25 81 – Fax: (33) 03 88 41 39 10
E-mail: publishing@coe.int – Website: http://book.coe.int